Reading with the Faithful

Journal of Theological Interpretation Supplements
MURRAY RAE
University of Otago, New Zealand
Editor-in-Chief

1. Thomas Holsinger-Friesen, *Irenaeus and Genesis: A Study of Competition in Early Christian Hermeneutics*
2. Douglas S. Earl, *Reading Joshua as Christian Scripture*
3. Joshua N. Moon, *Jeremiah's New Covenant: An Augustinian Reading*
4. Csilla Saysell, *"According to the Law": Reading Ezra 9–10 as Christian Scripture*
5. Joshua Marshall Strahan, *The Limits of a Text: Luke 23:34a as a Case Study in Theological Interpretation*
6. Seth B. Tarrer, *Reading with the Faithful: Interpretation of True and False Prophecy in the Book of Jeremiah from Ancient Times to Modern*

Reading with the Faithful

*Interpretation of True and False Prophecy
in the Book of Jeremiah
from Ancient Times to Modern*

SETH B. TARRER

Winona Lake, Indiana
EISENBRAUNS
2013

Copyright © 2013 Eisenbrauns
All rights reserved.

Printed in the United States of America

www.eisenbrauns.com

Library of Congress Cataloging-in-Publication Data

Tarrer, Seth B.
  Reading with the faithful : interpretation of true and false prophecy in the
    book of Jeremiah from ancient to modern times / by Seth B. Tarrer.
       p. cm. — (Journal of theological interpretation supplements ; 6)
    Includes bibliographical references (p.   ) and index.
    ISBN 978-1-57506-705-6 (pbk. : alk. paper)
    1. Bible. O.T. Jeremiah—Criticism, interpretation, etc.—History.
  2. Prophecy—Biblical teaching. I. Title.
    BS1525.52.T37   2013
    224′.20609—dc23
                                                    2012036621

The paper used in this publication meets the minimum requirements of the American National Standard for Information Sciences—Permanence of Paper for Printed Library Materials, ANSI Z39.48-1984.♾™

This is dedicated to Mary.

*All measure, and all language, I should pass,
Should I tell what a miracle she was.*

– John Donne (*The Relic*, 32-33, 1633)

Table of Contents

    Acknowledgments ix
    Abbreviations x

1. INTRODUCTION 1
2. THE EARLY CHURCH 5

    Introduction 5
    St. Jerome (c. 345-420) 6
    Theodoret of Cyrus (c. 393-c. 460) 18
    Summary 34

3. MEDIEVAL BIBLICAL INTERPRETATION OF TRUE AND FALSE
   PROPHECY 36

    Introduction 36
    Glossa Ordinaria 37
    St. Thomas Aquinas (c. 1225–1274) 40
    Summary 47

4. JOHN CALVIN AMIDST THE REFORMERS 48

    John Calvin (1509-1564) 48
    Summary 66

5. THE PROPHETS AND WHICH LAW? THE ENLIGHTENMENT ERA 69

    Introduction 69
    Thomas Hobbes (1588-1679) 70
    Benedict de Spinoza (1632-1677) 73
    Campegius Vitringa (1659-1722) 83
    Antoine Augustin Calmet (1672-1757) 88
    Thomas Newton (1704-1782) 90
    Summary 93

6. THE SEARCH FOR COHERENCE IN THE NINETEENTH CENTURY 94

    Introduction 94
    Conservative, or "Confessional" Readings 95
    Georg Frederick Seiler (1753-1807) 95
    Ernst Wilhelm Hengstenberg (1802-1869) 98
    Karl Friedrich Keil (1807-1888) 101
    Hans Conrad von Orelli (1846-1912) 105
    Mediating and Historical-Critical positions 107
    George Adam Smith (1856-1942) 107
    Georg Heinrich August Ewald (1803-1875) 110
    Bernhard Duhm (1847-1928) 115
    Abraham Kuenen (1828-1891) 121
    Summary 128

7. TRUE AND FALSE PROPHECY AND THE RISE OF OLD TESTAMENT
   THEOLOGIES IN THE TWENTIETH CENTURY (1910-1986) 130
   Introduction 130
   Gerhard von Rad (1901-1971) 131
   James A. Sanders 141
   Brevard S. Childs (1923-2007) 149
   Summary 156

8. A WAY FORWARD: SINCE 1986 158
   Introduction 158
   James E. Brenneman 159
   Armin Lange 163
   R. W. L. Moberly 168
   Summary 172

9. GENERAL CONCLUSIONS 175
   Bibliography 180
   Index: Author and Subject 202
   Index: Scripture Citations and Ancient Sources 205

Acknowledgments

This book is a slightly revised vesion of my PhD thesis, 'The Law and the Prophets: A Christian History of Interpretation of True and False Prophecy in the Book of Jeremiah,' submitted to the University of St. Andrews in 2009. It entails a sampling of the Christian interpretive tradition's various readings of the prophet Jeremiah, looking particularly at the way in which exegetes through the centuries approached prophetic conflict.

Without the help, encouragement, and support from a crowd of witnesses, this book would not have taken shape. Thanks are in order first to my supervisor, Dr. Mark Elliott, who has made his knowledge and expertise available not only to me, but also to the local church in St. Andrews. Thanks are also due to Dr. Steven Holmes and Prof. Christopher Seitz for their guidance in the early stages of this project. I am grateful for such brilliant and faithful friends and colleagues along the way: Patrick Egan, Daniel Driver, Mariam Kamell, Drew Lewis, Christopher Hays, Dave Lincicum, Meg Ramey, and Jake Andrews, just to name a few. Prof. Stephen Chapman has fed me on more than one occasion during my visits to Duke; his suggestions have been insightful and his encouragement timely. Also, Prof. Walter Moberly has kindly interacted with me around the themes of this book, even treating me to a magnificent steak dinner at SBL in 2009. I would also like to thank Dr. Gerald Bray, without whose support and direction I perhaps would have never considered such an undertaking. Dr. Mark Gignilliat has graciously allowed me to pilfer from his library.

I am especially grateful to Prof. Murray Rae, series editor for the *Journal of Theological Interpretation Supplement Series,* not only for accepting this monograph for publication, but for his guidance throughout. And, the recommendations of my external examinaers, Dr. Stephen Chapman and Dr. Nathan MacDonald, along with the two readers at Eisenbrauns, provided many helpful ways in which to improve the thesis for publication. I have labored to include most of them. And, Jim Eisenbraun's assistance and help warrant my gratefulness as well. I would also like to thank my church, Altadena Valley Presbyterian Church for their support these past several years. While all of these have had a greater hand in shaping my thoughts than they know, I alone bear full responsibility for any and all shortcomings within this work.

To my parents, Ray and Merry Tarrer, who have supported me unwaveringly from the beginning, thank you. Jim and Laura Pickens deserve heartfelt thanks as well. To my children, Sam, Owen, JP, and Caroline, thank you for giving me a quiet place to write. Finally, my wife Mary has shown me nothing but unconditional love, grace, and patience. That I may spend my life returning the favor.

(Holy Cross Day)

Abbreviations

ACCS	T. C. Oden (ed.) *Ancient Christian Commentary on Scripture, Old Testament XII: Jeremiah, Lamentations* (Downers Grove: InterVarsity Press, 2009)
ANF	A. Roberts and J. Donaldson (eds.), *Ante-Nicene Fathers* (Buffalo: Christian Literature, 10 vols., 1885-1896. Reprint: Peabody: Hendrickson, 1994)
BETL	BIBLIOTHECA EPHEMERIDUM THEOLOGICARUM LOVANISENSIUM
BHS	K. Elliger and W. Rudolph (eds.) *Biblia Hebraica Stuttgartensia* (Stuttgart: Deutsche Bibelgesellschaft, 4th ed. 1990)
BZAW	Beiheft zur Zeitschrift für die Alttestementliche Wissenschaft
CBQ	*Catholic Biblical Quaterly*
CCSL	Corpus Christianorum: Series latina. Turnhout, 1953—
CD	Karl Barth, *Church Dogmatics*, 4 vols. (Edinburgh: T&T Clark, 1956-1975)
CO	*Ioannis Calvini opera quae supersunt omnia*, ed. Wilhelm Baum, Edward Cunitz, and Edward Reus. 59 vols. bound in 31. *Corpus Reformatorum*, vols. 29-87 (Brunsvigae: Schwetschke [Bruhn], 1863-1900)
CTS	*Calvin's Commentaries*. 45 vols. Edinburgh: Calvin Translation Society, 1844-1856. Reprinted in 22 vols. (Grand Rapids: Baker Books, 1981)
De Veritate	*Quaestiones de veritate* Sancti Thomae de Aquino opera omnia iussu Leonis XIII P.M. edita, Tom. XXII (Rome: Romae ad Sanctae Sabinae, 1970—1976)
GO	*Glossa Ordinaria: Prophetia Jeremiae*, PL 114, ed. J.-P. Migne (Paris: 1879)
In Hieremiam	Jerome, *In Hieremiam*, ed. Sigofredus Reiter, CCSL, 74 (Brepol: Turnhout, 1960).
In Jeremiam	St Thomas Aquinas, *In Jeremiam prophetam expositio* (Opera Omnia, vol. 14; Parma: 1863)
Inst.	John Calvin, *Institutes of the Christian Religion*. Ed. John T. McNeill, trans. Ford Lewis Battles. 2 vols. Library of Christian Classics. (Philadelphia: Westminster Press, 1960)
JBL	*Journal of Biblical Literature*
JSOT	*Journal for the Study of the Old Testament*
JSOTSup	Journal for the Study of the Old Testament: Supplement Series
JTISup	Journal of Theological Interpretation: Supplement Series
LXX	Septuagint
MT	Masoretic Text

NPNF	P. Schaff, et al., (eds.), *A Select Library of the Nicene and Post-Nicene Fathers of the Christian Church* (Buffalo: Christian Literature, 2 series, 14 vols. each, 1887-1894, Reprint: Peabody: Hendrickson, 1994
OTL	The Old Testament Library
PG	Patrologia graeca [= Patrologiae cursus completus: Series graeca]. Edited by J.-P. Migne. 162 vols. (Paris, 1857-1886)
PL	Patrologia latina [= Patrologiae cursus completus: Series latina]. Edited by J.-P. Migne. 217 vols. (Paris, 1844-1864)
SC	Sources chrétiennes. (Paris: Cerf, 1943-)
StPatr	Studia patristica
ST	Thomas Aquinas, *Summa Theologiae*. 5 vols. (Ottawa: Studii Generalis, 1949)
TLZ	*Theologische Literaturzeitung*
TTP	Benedict de Spinoza, *Theological-Political Treatise,* trans. Samuel Shirley; 2nd ed. (Indianapolis: Hackett Publishing Co., 2001)
Typus	Campegius Vitringa. *Typus Dotrinae Propheticae, in Quo de Prophetis et Prophetiis Agitur, Hujusque Scientiae Praecepta Tradantur.* Leeuwarden, 1716.
VT	*Vetus Testamentum*
ZAW	*Zeitschrift für die alttestamentliche Wissenschaft*

1. INTRODUCTION

> If, therefore, someone is a prophet, he no doubt prophesies, but if someone prophesies he is not necessarily a prophet.

Origen, writing sometime in the mid third-century on the Gospel of John, has charted a course for the subsequent history of interpretation of true and false prophecy.[1] While our study will be concerned primarily with various readings of the Old Testament's construal of the problem, namely that of the book of Jeremiah, the ambiguity inherent in the above statement is glaring nonetheless. Consequently, Origen's answer to whether Caiaphas and Balaam 'prophesied' is an attenuated 'yes.' Authentic prophecy required the Holy Spirit's inspiration; anything less was not to be designated divine.

The issue of who spoke for God and who didn't was critical, especially at and around the church's inception (1 Cor 12:4-31). Throughout the course of the Christian church, countless voices have claimed the moniker 'prophet.' Interpreters from the early church through to the present have drawn on the Biblical prophets in order to affirm or combat contemporaneous 'prophets.' Whether it was Eusebius' fight with the Montanists or the racial bigotry opposed to Dr. Martin Luther King's call for equality, texts from scripture have been employed both to oppose a 'prophetic' voice and to lend it strength. Examples abound throughout church history of individuals, like Rupert of Deutz (c. 1075-1129/30), who self-identified with the prophets of the OT, and sought to ground their authenticity as such with appeals to similar, subjectively verifiable call or commissioning experiences.[2]

This is not the kind of prophecy in view here. For an excellent treatment of extra-biblical, post-canonical 'prophetic' movements, see Hvidt's *Christian Prophecy*.[3] The prophets taken up here are limited to those designated such in the Old Testament of the Christian Scriptures. While the historical work continues as to the personae, cultures, and contexts of the lives of the Hebrew prophets, not to mention those from the surrounding nations, our study will be limited to those within the pages of the Old Testament and the use made of them by the Christian interpretive tradition. As such, interpreters from throughout the tradition that treat them in this manner will figure prominently.

---

1. Origen, *Commentary on the Gospel According to John*, trans. Ronald E. Heine, (Washington D.C.: Catholic University of America Press, 1986), 314.
2. Abigail Ann Young, "Mission and Message: Two Prophetic Voices in the Twelfth Century." Pages 19-30. In *Essays in Medieval Philosophy and Theology in Memory of Walter H. Principe, OSBI*, eds. J.R. Ginther and C.N. Still, (London: Ashgate, 2005), 19-22.
3. Niels Christian Hvidt, *Christian Prophecy: The Post-Biblical Tradition* (Oxford: OUP,

The present study is a history of interpretation of sorts. In that sense it does not fit neatly into the category of *Wirkungsgeschichte*.[4] Moving through successive periods of the Christian church's history, we will select representative interpretations of Jeremiah, Ezekiel, and theological works dealing explicitly with the question of true and false prophecy in an effort to present a "sampling"[5] of material from the span of the church's existence. As evidenced by the list of "false prophets" uncovered at Qumran,[6] along with the indelible interpretive debt owed by Christian interpreters like Jerome and Calvin to Jewish exegetical methods, Jewish interpretation's vast legacy quickly exceeds the scope of this project. From the sixteenth-century onward, the focus on the Protestant church is, again, due to economy.

Pre-modern biblical interpretation is presently enjoying a more widespread availability than in previous times, evidenced by the recent proliferation of historical exegetical commentaries.[7] This could in part be due to the growing consciousness that the number and nature of the discoveries to be made in the history of interpretation far outpace those concerning the texts themselves. In much the same way, this study seeks to identify readings throughout the tradition that constitute an accurate cross-section of a given time period's approach to false prophecy in Jeremiah. That said, the task of this study is more than merely descriptive. For it seeks to function as a hermeneutical guide for the pre-

---

4. This study is primarily concerned with the manner in which the biblical text has been historically interpreted rather than tracing the generative effects of its reception in subsequent reading communities' cultural expressions such as art or music. See Brevard S. Childs' helpful discussion of Luz's *Wirkungsgeschichte* program in his *The Church's Guide for Reading Paul* (Grand Rapids: Eerdman's, 2008), 29, and Gadamer's discussion of *Wirkungsgeschichte* in *Truth and Method* 2nd, rev. ed. (New York: Crossroad, 1989), 299-300. Cf. the helpful article by Rachel Nicholls, "Is Wirkungsgeschichte (or Reception History) a Kind of Intellectual Parkour (or Freerunning)?" Conference Paper, Society for the Study of the New Testament.   Online [URL: http://www.bbibcomm.net/news/nicholls.pdf]. Last accessed: 25 May 2009.
5. For a similar approach, see the introduction of Judith Kovacs and Christopher Rowland, *Revelation* Blackwell Bible Commentaries, (Oxford: Blackwell Publishers, 2004), xii.
6. Magen Broshi and Ada Yardene, "4Q List of False Prophets Ar (Plate XI)," in *Qumran Cave 4; XIV: Parabiblical Texts, Part 2*, ed. Magen Broshi, Esther Eshel, Joseph Fitzmeyer, Erik Larson, Carol Newsom, Lawrence Schiffman, Mark Smith, Michael Stone, John Strugnell, and Ada Yardeni, Discoveries in the Judaean Desert XIX (Oxford: Clarendon Press, 1995), 77-79.
7. Cf. IVP's *Ancient Christian Commentary on Scripture (*ed. Thomas Oden); the most recent of this series is Dean O. Wenthe, *Jeremiah, Lamentations,* ed. Thomas C. Oden, ACCS, OT XII (Downers Grove: InterVarsity Press, 2009), however, treatments of our relevant passages deal almost exclusively with Jerome; and the forthcoming *Reformation Commentary on Scripture* (eds. T. George and S. Manetsch); Blackwell's *Blackwell Bible Commentaries* (eds. J. Sawyer, C. Rowland, and J. Kovacs); and Eerdman's *The Church's Bible*. (ed. R. L. Wilken).

sent interpretive problem of interpreting true and false prophecy in the Old Testament/Hebrew Bible by displaying ways various interpreters have broached the subject in the past. In this way it may prove useful to the current impasse concerning the notion of false prophecy in the Old Testament/Hebrew Bible.

In the last decade and a half of scholarship three dominant approaches to true and false prophecy have emerged as can be seen by a look at the most recent major monographs devoted to the subject. James Brenneman's *Canons in Conflict* represents the sociologically sensitive canon-criticicism of James Sanders and more recently Walter Brueggeman.[8] Armin Lange's *Vom prophetischen Wort zum prophetischen Tradition* represents a diachronic, redaction-critical reconstruction of the various stages of the text's transmission.[9] Walter Moberly's recent *Prophecy and Discernment* treats the subject with an eye towards the appropriation of the biblical message and criteria for the present believing community of faith.[10]

Lange's work alone treats the history of interpretation surrounding the question in any sustained manner. However, his review only reaches back to the middle of the nineteenth-century. This study seeks to fill in, with admittedly broad strokes, the virtual oversight of pre-modern readings of false prophecy. However, it seeks to do so without effectively caging them off from the modern discussion like exotic zoo animals. The conclusions will argue that the problem of true and false prophecy was, at times, successfully addressed in the pre-modern era. This study is not intended to be a rehabilitation of pre-modern exegesis. Seeing continuity, or a family resemblance, in the Christian church's interpretation of true and false prophecy in relation to the law's role amongst exilic and post-exilic prophets, we will observe those ways in which a historically informed reading might offer an interpretive guide for subsequent interpretations of true and false prophecy. It will seek to do this by looking for answers to such questions as 'What was at work historically, politically, and personally in various interpreters' attempts to delineate criteria within and throughout the prophetic books?' Also, 'With the dawn of modernity's pluralism coupled with the effects of historical-critical reconstructions of the Hebrew canon, is it reasonable

---

8. James E. Brenneman, *Canons in Conflict: Negotiating Texts in True and False Prophecy* (New York: Oxford University Press, 1997).
9. Armin Lange, Vom prophetischen Wort zur prophetischen Tradition: Studien zur Traditions und Redaktionsgeschichte innerprophetischer Konflikte in der Hebräischen Bibel, FAT 34 (Tübingen: Mohr Siebeck, 2002).
10. R.W.L. Moberly, *Prophecy and Discernment* (Cambridge: Cambridge University Press, 2006). As this taxonomy of monographs shows, in light of Old Testament/Hebrew Bible studies' continuing specialization, relying solely on commentaries' contributions—as with Jerome or Calvin (but not Aquinas)—would leave the portrayal incomplete. A recent work by Anthony Chinedu Osuji, *Where Is the Truth?: Narrative Exegesis and the Question of True and False Prophecy in Jer 26-29 (MT)* BETL CCXIV (Leuven: Uitgeverij Peeters, 2010), should also be included within this third trajectory. We will return to it in chapter 8.

to posit that the need for criteria fell away as the interpretive environment of the nineteenth and twentieth-centuries was increasingly marked by a lack of urgency and an increased sense of tolerance?'

Chapter two will first treat the commentaries of St Jerome and Theodoret of Cyrus on Jeremiah. Then, moving into the medieval period we will look at the Glossa Ordinaria on Jeremiah along with St Thomas Aquinas' commentary on Jeremiah, selections of his *Summa Theologica*, and *De Veritate*. Chapter three will be mainly occupied with John Calvin's commentary on Jeremiah. A largely ignored work, this study will utilize Calvin's Jeremiah commentary to explore his notion of prophecy's relation to the law in order to argue a more nuanced understanding of what constituted prophecy. Bullinger and Oecolampadius will also be brought into dialogue with Calvin at points. Chapter four covers the works of, among others, Thomas Hobbes, Benedict de Spinoza, Campegius Vitringa, Augustin Calmet, and Thomas Newton. The pivotal nineteenth—century is under review in chapter five. Examining the contributions of Seiler, Hengstenberg, Keil, and Orelli on the conservative side and Ewald, G.A. Smith, Kuenen, and Duhm among others on the historical-critical side, we will demonstrate the lines along which subsequent modern interpretations of the problem have fallen. Tracing these various trajectories into the twentieth—century via the readings of von Rad, James Sanders, and Childs primarily, chapter five demonstrates the crystallization of scholarship's approach to the question (broadly) into one of the three approaches represented by these figures. Chapter six will address the figures Brenneman, Lange, and Moberly in concert with other recent readings. In an effort to allow the history to unfold, detailed syntheses following each figure, era, and chapter will be kept to a minimum, reserving some final syntheses for the conclusions.

Building on the previous test cases, the conclusions will recap by showing that the early church and pre-modern tradition evidenced a recurring appeal to some form of association between Jer 28 and the deuteronomic prophetic warnings in Dt 13 and 18. Much critical scholarship in the eighteenth through the twentieth-centuries did not wholly resist an association between the prophets and the law, rather it often highlighted the existence of conflict between the two. Scholarship in this era widely recognized the criteria at work in Deuteronomy were most likely late, put into place by a post-exilic editor(s) to placate a fearful, recently exiled, populace in the face of numerous empty prophetic threats. Seeing that the criteria furthered in many prophetic books like Ezekiel (13) and Jeremiah (23-29) were different "in kind" from Deut 13 and 18, the result was the prioritization of the law and the prophets. This resulted in the subordination of one to the other. Against this, as we shall demonstrate, there are many places in the tradition where interpretations are offered which are true to the (seemingly incoherent) voice of Scripture as evidenced by innovative exegesis and genuine concern to deal with the texts as Christian Scripture.

2. THE EARLY CHURCH

Introduction

In a study such as this where, or with whom, does one begin? As we have seen above, the question of true and false prophecy was an urgent one. Was the church hearing the word of God or man? A pertinent question at any time, in an age of creedal formation and one replete with councils and anathemas, the distinction between true and false takes bore much weight. While the church struggled (as it does now) to hear the true amidst the false, exegetes in service to the church sought instruction from the Scriptures. Far more than an academic exercise, these interpreters looked to the prophetic tradition, a ready corpus for such a question, in order to glean mechanisms or criteria by which the prophets of old delineated good from bad. And, in the process, they developed ways of reading the Old Testament prophets and law that have survived — albeit modified or distorted, at times beyond recognition — to the present. These ways of reading stand as markers, not only showing where we've been, exegetically speaking. They also act as backdrops, of sorts, against which we should always sharpen and/or critique our own readings.

Our study begins with St. Jerome for several reasons. Along with Theodoret of Cyrus, Jerome's commentary on Jeremiah is one of the very few sustained commentaries from the early (first-fifth centuries CE) church's catanea (collections) of Old Testament exegetical works.[1] Among early exegetes treating Jeremiah, Jerome's interpretation would go on to exert the most pressure on subsequent western tradition of interpretation. As we will see in the following chapter, much of the *Glossa Ordinaria*'s comments on Jeremiah, indeed on many of the prophets, are essentially Jerome's comments condensed. Of the western fathers, Jerome's exegetical output in the prophets is unrivaled. Up through the sixteenth century, Jerome's exegesis of the prophets continued to make its presence known among interpreters like Luther and Calvin. Particularly impactful was his attention to the Hebrew text of the Old Testament, a regnant feature of Protestant Old Testament exegesis.

---

1. Of the four surviving works devoted to Jeremiah from the patristic era, Jerome and Thedoret of Cyrus treat the subject of true and false prophecy. Origen (collections of homilies, *Homilae in Ieremiam*, SC 232, 238, 1976 1977) and Pseudo-Chrysostom (a few fragments, PG 64:740-1037), in Charles Kannengiesser, *Handbook of Patristic Exegesis: The Bible in Ancient Christianity,* 2 vols., (Leiden: Brill, 2004), I:313-15, 324.

St. Jerome (c. 345–420)

Numerous authors have treated the significance of Jerome's contributions to Christian scholarship. Biographers such as Cavallera, Kelly, Nautin, Rebenich, and, more recently, Williams, have examined the life and contributions of the renowned doctor ecclesia.[2] This study's treatment of Jerome will be limited to a brief biographical overview outlining the provenance of selected pieces. This will be followed by addressing Jerome's methods of interpretation concerning the question of true and false prophecy primarily utilizing his incomplete commentary on Jeremiah, while not ignoring the remainder of his commentaries on the prophets, elements of his translations, and his correspondence.

Jerome's first effort at commentary writing comes from the desert in the year 375.[3] An allegorical reading of Obadiah, this first piece was lost. However, in the prologue to his *Comm. on Obadiah* written nearly 30 years later, Jerome addresses his earlier attempt at interpretation:

> I had allegorically interpreted the prophet Obadiah, of whose history I was ignorant. The mind burned with mystical knowledge, and, because I had been reading apart from the faithful, I was ignorant, having been diverted from grace; I knew the literature of the world and, on account of it, I supposed that I should be able to stamp a book myself. I was a fool...[4]

While this "rather unfortunate first display"[5] at commentary writing has been lost to us, one can detect, from comments in a later commentary on Obadiah

---

2. Ferdinand Cavallera, *Saint Jérôme, sa vie et son oeuvre* (Louvain: "Spicilegium Sacrum Lovaniense" Bureaux, 1922); J. N. D. Kelly, *Jerome: His Life, Writings, and Controversies* (New York: Harper & Row, 1975); Pierre Nautin's "Hieronymus," in *Theologische Realenzyclopädie* (Berlin: Walter de Gruyter, 1986), 304-315; "Études de chronologie hiéronymienne (393-397)," *Revue des études augustiniennes* 18 (1972): 209-218; "Études de chronologie hiéronymienne (393-397) (suite)," *Revue des études augustiniennes* 19 (1973): 69-96; "Études de chronologie hiéronymienne (393-397) (suite)," *Revue des études augustiniennes* 19 (1973): 213-239; and "Études de chronologie hiéronymienne (393-397) (suite et fin)," *Revue des études augustiniennes* 20 (1974): 251-284; Stefan Rebenich, *Jerome* (London: Routledge, 2002); and Megan H. Williams, *The Monk and the Book: Jerome and the Making of Christian Scholarship*, (Chicago: University of Chicago Press, 2006).
3. Concerning an alternate date situated in an argument for an early birth date for Jerome, cf. Alan D. Booth, "The Date of Jerome's Birth," *Pheonix* 33 (1979): 346-353, 349ff. Those in favor of 375 include Cavallera, *Jerôme*, 2.17, 154; Williams, *Monk*, 288; and Nautin, "Études," 272.
4. *Commentarii in prophetas minores*, CCSL 76-76A, Marcus Adriaen et al., eds., (Turnhout: Brepols, 1969), 349 (all subsequent commentary references will be to the CCSL editions unless otherwise noted).
5. Pierre Jay, "Jerome (CA. 347-419/420)," in *Handbook of Patristic Exegesis: The Bible in Ancient Christianity, Vol 2*, ed. Charles Kannengiesser, (Leiden: Brill, 2004), 1094-1133.

written from his hermitage in Bethlehem to Pammachius in 396, two overarching concerns emerging. First, Jerome is at pains to ground his interpretation in the historical or literal sense of the passages at hand. Also, and perhaps more germane to our present task, Jerome acknowledges that proper biblical interpretation is in some sense a ruled reading in his comments concerning reading apart from the faithful. These concerns will come to bear in the following discussion.

After a brief stay in Constantinople and two years in Rome, Jerome arrived in Bethlehem in 385.[6] It was here that Jerome would, among other things, establish a monastery, participate in numerous controversies, produce commentaries on select New Testament books[7], and write two minor works on the Psalms, *Commentarioli in Psalmos* and *Tractatus in Psalmos*, drawing heavily upon Origen's commentary on the Psalms for the former.[8] Along with these 'minor' contributions, Jerome would begin his translation *iuxta Hebreaos* (according to the Hebrew) of much of the Old Testament.[9]

Before we address his interpretive approach to his commentaries on the prophets, a brief look at Jerome's concept of *Hebraica veritas* is in order. Although he is commonly referred to as *Vir Trilinguis* (man of three languages),[10] Jerome's linguistic aptitude has long been a subject of debate and the precise extent to which he had mastery of Hebrew remains unknown. An advanced ability in Latin would have been ensured through his classical education in Rome. And, without a proficiency in Greek, Jerome would not have been able to work with the LXX, the various *recentiores* of his day, or Origen's *Hexapla* with any

---

6. The dates for works hereafter are attested to by Williams, Nautin, Jay, and Adam Kamesar, *Jerome, Greek scholarship, and the Hebrew Bible: A study of the Quaestiones hebraicae in Genesim* (Oxford: Clarendon Press, 1993).
7. Titus, Ephesians, Galatians, and Philemon, in 386.
8. Both written in 387; cf. René Kieffer, "Jerome: His Exegesis and Hermeneutics," in *Hebrew Bible / Old Testament. The History of Its Interpretation. I: From the Beginning to the Middle Ages (Until 1300)*, ed. Magne Sæbø, (Göttingen: Vandenhoeck & Ruprecht, 1996), 663-681. Perhaps the most telling description of Jerome's estimation of Origen comes from letter 33, written to his Roman matron Paula in 385. In it Jerome catalogues Origen's works, impressed by a life characterized by "productivity, single-minded engagement with the Bible, and sheer hard work"; in Mark Vessey, "Jerome's Origen: The Making of a Christian Literary Persona," Studia Patristica 28 (1993): 139.
9. Psalms, Prophets, Samuel, and Kings, and Job (389-392), Ezra and Nehemiah (394), Chronicles (396), Esther, Tobit, and Judith (404-5). Kamesar, *Jerome*, 58, interprets *iuxta Hebreaos* "according to the Hebrew."
10. See Dennis Brown, *Vir Trilinguis: A study in the Biblical Exegesis of Saint Jerome* (Kampen: Kok Pharos Pub. House, 1992) and Stefan Rebenich, "Jerome: The "Vir Trilinguis" and the Hebraica Veritas," *VC* 47 (1993): 50-77. Brown, 86, notes that Jerome's knowledge of Aramaic and Syriac, while attested to by Jerome himself, was most likely "superficial."

efficiency.[11] Regarding Jerome's knowledge of Hebrew, he "more than likely... at least knew some Hebrew."[12]

The phrase *Hebraica veritas* does not appear in Jerome's writings prior to 386.[13] However, in 383/4 Jerome partially adumbrates this concept in letter 20.[14] Kamesar notes that already in his Roman correspondence, Jerome's replies to exegetical questions are often based on the Hebrew. In the letter mentioned above Jerome makes the claim that "truth should be expressed from the Hebrew books."[15] Not only was the knowledge of Hebrew integral for a right interpretation of the Old Testament, but the fact that many writers of the New Testament, such as Paul and Matthew, knew Hebrew extended the relevance of the *Hebraica veritas* to the entire Christian canon. Hebrew, for Jerome, was the "language of creation"[16]; it was the "mother of all languages"[17]; unquestionably man's original language.[18]

Williams has recently argued that Jerome's authority as translator and interpreter rested on his recourse to the Hebrew truth.[19] Scholarship has traditionally considered the *Hebraica veritas* primarily in relation to Jerome's translations. But, as the extent of his reliance on Jewish interpretive traditions continues to

---

11. Cf. Brown, *Vir Trinlinguis*, 55ff.
12. Rebenich, *Jerome*, 56. Brown, *Vir Trilinguis*, 80, says that Jerome's knowledge of Hebrew would have surpassed that of Philo and Origen. However, Brown's evidence is almost exclusively internal, and is therefore subject to the challenge that Jerome, given his agenda with the Hebraica veritas, was projecting himself as a specific literary persona. Williams, *Monk,* 27ff., presents Jerome's Hebrew training more modestly. Cf. the strong case made by Michael Graves, *Jerome's Hebrew Philology: A Study Based on his Commentary on Jeremiah* Supplements to Vigiliae Christianae 90, (Leiden: Brill, 2007), for Jerome's developed ability in Hebrew.
13. Pierre Jay, *L'exégèse de saint Jérôme: D'après son "Commentaire sur Isaïe,"* (Paris: Études augustiniennes, 1985), 89, holds the first occurrence of the phrase is in *Comm. in Eccl.* 8:13, generally dated c. 388. Kamesar, *Jerome*, 42n6, posits the possibility that it was first attested to in *Quaestiones Hebraicae in Genesim*, some 3-4 years later (c. 391/2).
14. Kamesar, *Jerome,* 42f.
15. ex Hebraeis codicibus veritas exprimenda est, Ep. 20.2, cited in Kamesar, *Jerome*, 42.
16. Benjamin Kedar-Kopfstein, "Jewish Traditions in the Writings of Jerome," in *The Aramaic Bible: Targums in their Historical Context* (ed. David J. A. Clines *et al.*; Sheffield: Sheffield Academic Press, 1994), 423.
17. *Hebraicam omnium linguarum esse matricem. Comm.* on *Sophoniam* 3:18, CCSL 76A, 708; cf. Eva Schulz-Flügel, "The Latin Old Testament Tradition," in *Hebrew Bible / Old Testament* I/1 (1996): 661f.
18. Jerome, "Letter XVIII," in *Jerome: Letters and Select Works,* ed. Phillip Schaff and Henry Wace, Nicene and Post-Nicene Fathers, Second Series, vol. 6 (Peabody, Mass.: Hendrickosn, 2004), 22.
19. Williams, *Monk,* 89f.

emerge, this restricted view is being challenged.[20] In his use of the Hebrew Jerome saw himself drinking from the *fons veritatis*, "the fountainhead of truth," as opposed to Greek interpreters who drew from *rivuli opinionum*, "rivulets of opinion."[21] This fons was not limited to Hebrew texts, but "extend[ed] far beyond the texts of the Bible to include a whole range of Jewish materials—and not only Jewish materials, but a great deal of the biblical philology of Origen and his successors as well."[22] With Kamesar, Williams says that the *Hebraica veritas* may best be understood as the philological system underlying Jerome's *iuxta historiam* efforts and the whole of his Old Testament exegesis;[23] a system not only interested in texts, but with a tradition of exegesis. An example of this can be seen in Jerome's ordering of the 12 minor prophets in his *iuxta Hebraeos* following the Jewish canon, rather than the Church's Greek tradition.[24] In his *Comm. in Zachariam*, seeking to explain the historical reference of the fasts of the house of Judah (Zech 8:18-19), Jerome writes, "We are compelled therefore to return to the Hebrews, and to seek the knowledge of truth from the wellspring [*fonte*] rather than from the rivulets [*rivulis*]."[25]

Alongside his translations, Jerome would produce commentaries on all of the prophets.[26] Jerome's commentaries mark a redirection of sorts for biblical

---

20. For example see S. Krauss, "The Jews in the Works of the Church Fathers," *JQR* 6 (1894): 225-261; Jay Braverman, *Jerome's commentary on Daniel: A Study of Comparative Jewish and Christian Interpretations of the Hebrew Bible* (Washington: Catholic Biblical Association of America, 1978); Robert Hayward, "Jewish Traditions in Jerome's Commentary on Jeremiah and the Targum of Jeremiah," *Proceedings of the Irish Biblical Association* 9 (1985): 100-120; and Kedar-Kopfstein, "Jewish Traditions," 420-430; M. Rahmer, *Die hebräischen Traditionen in den Werken des Hieronymus 1-2* (Berlin: 1902); and F. Stummer, "Spuren jüdischer und christlicher Einflüsse auf die Übersetzung der Grossen Propheten durch Hieronymus," *JAOS* 8 (1928): 35-48.
21. In the preface to his *Comm. in Eccl.* Jerome writes, "I have occasionally referred also to the versions of Aquila, Symmachus, and Theodotion, but so as not to alarm the zealous student by too many novelties, nor yet to let my commentary follow the side streams of opinion, turning aside, against my conscientious conviction, from the fountainhead of truth." Cf. Kamesar, *Jerome*, 42, n. 6; cf. *Ep.*, 20.1-2., in Williams, *Monk*, 60, n.94.
22. Williams, *Monk,* 89.
23. Kamesar, *Jerome*, 80-81, refers to this as a "rabbinic-recentiores philology"; Williams, *Monk*, 89.
24. Cf. Jerome's *Comm. in Ioelem, prol.* 1, and *Comm. in Michaeam, prol.* 1 (CCSL 76:159f. and 421, respectively). Cf. Brown, "Vir Trilinguis," 35, and Kieffer, 669.
25. *Comm. in Zach.* CCSL 76A: 820; cited in Williams, *Monk*, 92, and Kamesar, *Jerome*, 178.
26. Seven volumes of Jerome's manuscripts are catalogued in Bernard Lambert, *Bibliotheca Hieronymiana Manuscripta: La Tradition Manuscrite des œuvres de Saint Jérôme* (The Hague: Martinus Nijhoff, 1969), of which Tome 2 treats his commentaries. Critical editions of his commentaries can be found in his *Opera, Patrologia Latina*, edited by J.-P. Migne, pp. 22-30. Parisiis, 1844-64, and the CCSL vol. 72-80 (commentary on prophets are found in vol. 73 and 73A (Isaiah); 74 (Jeremiah); 75 (Ezekiel); 75A(Daniel); 76

studies that has survived, in varying degrees, up to the present state of biblical scholarship. While many commentaries of his day were shaped by a particular hermeneutical approach to the Old Testament, Jerome's commentaries display elements of Christian and Jewish interpretive approaches.[27] At times heavily dependent on Origen and his tutor, Didymus, Jerome was comfortable, albeit reserved, to render an allegorical or spiritual interpretation of the passage at hand, often excusing it on the grounds that "obscure matters should be discussed more extensively."[28] Referring to previous Christian commentators renown for allegorical readings as *nostri*, 'ours,' Jerome located himself within a trajectory of Christian tradition that could be characterized by an allowance for allegorical or spiritual interpretation.[29]

It was with the historical or literal, however, that Jerome sought to ground his interpretations. In *Comm. in Sophoniam* he writes, "We must, therefore, in accordance with our usual custom, first explain the historical sense, and only after that discuss higher things."[30] The secondary spiritual interpretation, however, is not necessarily required. He qualifies his "usual custom" nearly a decade later in *Comm. in Zachariam*, writing, "Where a prophecy is quite obvious and the correct sequence of history is reported figuratively, a tropological explanation is superfluous."[31] Similarly in *Comm. in Malachiam* he writes, "It is the rule of scripture: where an evident prophecy concerning the future is carefully constructed, one must not diminish by uncertain allegory that which has been written."[32] The relationship, therefore, between the literal or historical and the

---

and 76A (Minor Prophets)). His comments on the prophets were written over a span of nearly 30 years. The following ordering is based upon Cavallera, *Saint Jérôme*, 2:52-53, Kieffer, "Jerome," 669, and Williams, *Monk*, 111ff. His first commentary on Obadiah notwithstanding, the dates of Jerome's commentaries are: Nahum, Micah, Zephaniah, Haggai, and Habakkuk in 393; in 397 he wrote on Jonah and his second commentary on Obadiah; he completes the 12 minor prophets in 406 with Zechariah, Malachi, Hosea, Joel, and Amos; Daniel was completed in 407; in 408 he began Isaiah, finishing in 410; Ezekiel, started in 410, was interrupted by, among other things, the sack of Rome, illness, and attacks in Palestine, to be completed in 414; Jeremiah was most likely begun soon after, sometime in 414, only to be left incomplete at Jerome's death (419/420).

27. Childs, *Struggle*, 91; and Louis N. Hartmann, "St. Jerome as an Exegete," in *A Monument to St Jerome* (ed. Francis Xavier Murphy; New York: Sheed and Ward, 1952), 47ff.

28. obscura latius disserenda sunt; Jer 22:13-17; cited in Graves, 176.

29. Considered primarily to be a tool of philosophical exegesis, allegory's place in Christian commentary writing was a comparatively new development. On this see Williams, *Monk*, 108.

30. *Comm. in Sophoniam* 1:2-3, CCSL 76A:658, (italics mine).

31. *Comm. in Zachariam* 11:4f., CCSL 76A:850; cited in Kelly, *Jerome*, 293.

32. Regula scripturarum est: Vbi manifestissima prophetia de futuris texitur, per incerta allegoriae non extenuare quae scripta sunt. *Comm. in Malachiam* 1:11-13, CCSL 76A:911.

spiritual or allegorical, was complex. His insistence upon the primacy of the literal sense of the Old Testament drew fire from some who saw his interpretive approach as too dependent upon Jewish exegesis. Rufinus of Aquileia, a lifelong acquaintance turned bitter antagonist, accuses Jerome of just this in his *Apology*, disparaging Jerome's Jewish tutor, Baranina, with the name "Barrabas."[33]

Against such claims, Jerome maintains that proper interpretation begins with the literal or historical but must necessarily move to the spiritual. The Jews, Jerome claims, do not do this. In his *Comm. in Osee* he writes, "The salvation of Israel and their return to God ... are not to be taken carnally [*carnaliter*], as the Jews think, but spiritually, as is most truly acknowledged."[34] Described as "carnal," the literal sense, derived most accurately from the Hebrew, plays an integral, yet penultimate, role in proper interpretation. In the prologue to *Comm. in Esiam* he writes, "After the truth of history, should the entirety be interpreted spiritually."[35] Authentic interpretation was dependant upon both the literal or historical sense, heretofore associated negatively with Jewish exegesis, and the spiritual or allegorical sense. Jerome, in his *Comm. in Zachariam* writes, "I have united the history of the Hebrews with the tropology of our own, so that I might build upon rock and not upon sand, and thus lay a stable foundation."[36]

This unification, however, was not reconciled through the interpreter's recourse to a single text. For Jerome the Hebrew text most clearly rendered the data from which to extract historical referents. But, since the LXX was the church's regnant text in his day, Jerome was compelled to address the numerous textual difficulties it posed to the *Hebraica veritas*.[37] His method of doing so was not to jettison the LXX. Rather, he regulary consulted it seeking an allegorical or spiritual interpretation. At one point in his comments on Hosea he writes, "The Hebrew and the Septuagint translation disagree greatly with each other. Therefore we will attempt to give an historical interpretation of the Hebrew, and an anagogical interpretation of the Septuagint."[38]

---

33. *Apology* 2.15 in Rufinus, *Opera* (CCSL 20; Turnhout: Brepols, 1961), 95; cited (erroneously) as 2.12 in Williams, *Monk*, 81n43.
34. *Comm. in Osee* 14:5-9, CCSL 76:157.
35. Vnde post historiae ueritatem, spiritaliter accipienda sunt onmia. *Comm. in Esiam* prol., CCSL 73:3; cf. "Having set down the foundations of the historical, let us cross over from these to the spiritual." Historiae iecimus fundamenta, ut ex his ad spiritalia transeamus. *Comm. in Zachariah* 14:16, CCSL 76A:894. Cf. Jay, "Jerome," 1105.
36. *Comm. in Zachariam* prol., CCSL 76A:748; cf. Williams, *Monk*, 117.
37. For a thorough discussion cf. Schulz-Flügel, "The Latin Old Testament Tradition," 642-662, Kamesar, *Jerome, passim*, and Brown, *Vir Trilinguis*, 55-62.
38 *Comm. in Osee* 11:3-4, CCSL 76:122; trans. Williams, *Monk*, 120. Similarly he writes, Haec iuxta Hebraicum diximus, transeamus ad LXX interpretes, et quid nobis iuxta anagogen uideatur in singulis, breuitas disseramus. *Comm. in Amos* 4:4-6, CCSL 76:261.

Jerome understood the literal sense as not only preceding the spiritual in an *ordo interpretamenti*, but also constraining it. In his *Comm. in Abacuc* of 393 he writes,

> The historical sense is narrow, and it cannot leave its course. The tropological sense is free, and yet it is circumscribed by no less than two laws. It must be loyal to the meaning and to the context of the words, and that things strongly opposed to each other must not be improperly joined together.[39]

Williams notes that this focus of Jerome's exegesis proved to be decisive in both legitimating and distinguishing his interpretive efforts in comparison with his predecessors.[40]

Although there is no date given internally, Jerome's *In Hieremiam* was most likely begun in 414, some time after he completed *In Hiezecheliem* earlier in the year.[41] The last of the four great prophets upon which he commented, *In Hieremiam* was written in the wake of and amidst much controversy and personal hardship. An elderly man having survived bouts of serious illness,[42] Jerome had been integral in the witch-hunt of the Origenist controversy that began in 393 and he had witnessed the sacking of Rome by Alaric in 410, all the while carrying on voluminous correspondence with figures such as Augustine and the bishops of Jerusalem, Carthage, and Rome. Our study, then, will examine what may be considered some of Jerome's more sober, mature exegesis and interpretation.

Jerome dedicated *In Hieremiam*, along with a work on Matthew, to Eusebius of Cremona. An abbot from Italy who spent some time with Jerome in Bethlehem, supported his work, and traveled abroad to raise funds to finance a lodging for Bethlehem pilgrims, Eusebius is reported to have preferred the literal sense.[43] Whether or not due to Eusebius' individual taste, Jerome's *In Hieremiam* is marked by his most strict adherence to a literal reading to date. Written in six books, we will be working from *Liber Quintus,* which covers Jer 24-29 (LXX 24:1-14; 32:1-3 – 36). The prologue to book five informs Eusebius (i.e., the reader) that book five is to be understood in tandem with book two as the latter's antithesis. Whereas book two exemplified the "proper agreeableness of faith," book five's objective is to "demonstrate the faithlessness of heretics."[44]

---

39. *Comm. in Abacuc* 1:6-11, CCSL 76A:589.
40. Williams, *Monk*, 118.
41. Jerome, *In Hieremiam,* ed. Sigofredus Reiter, CCSL, 74 (Brepol: Turnhout, 1960).
42. He was ill for an unknown period of time in 406 and again in 409; cf. Williams, *Monk*, 267ff.
43. Kelly, *Jerome*, 316.
44. Quintus commentariorum in Hieremiam liber a duobus, frater Eusebi, calathis habebit exordium, quorum alter rectae fidei dulcedinem, alter hereticorum perfidiae amaritudinemde monstrabit. CCSL 74:232. Whether these 'heretics' are the biblical characters Hananiah or Shemaiah, or those Jerome is in conflict with, is unknown at this point in his interpretation.

Truthfulness, rather than the word of God, is seen as determinative in the confrontations of the subsequent chapters.[45]

Turning to chapter 28 of his commentary, several common points emerge around which to center our discussion of Jerome's interpretation of true and false prophets. These include Jerome's *Hebraica veritas* in contact with the LXX; a recognition of the Hebrew's narratival construal as a tool for reading the Old Testament as literature; a comparison of Hananiah and Jonah; the question of the prophetic laws of Deut 18 in relation to Jer 28; and the application of the meaning of this text to current doctrinal disputes.

Jerome's interaction with the LXX is apparent immediately. Translating directly from a Hebrew text, Jerome's interaction with the LXX *In Hieremiam* is mainly limited to divergences from the Hebrew.[46] The majority of Jerome's comments concern the LXX's unwarranted liberty in designating Hananiah *pseudoprophetam* rather than *prophetam*.[47] Granting that the translators did so "in order to make unmistakable sense,"[48] Jerome nevertheless chides the LXX, asserting, "as I have said earlier, one must certainly not address what appears to be prophet as false-prophet."[49] Valuing the narrative quality of the Hebrew, he takes issue with the LXX for giving away the ending, spoiling an otherwise suspenseful prophetic drama. Jerome himself is free to address Hananiah as such;[50] however, regarding the veracity of Hananiah's textual status as prophet, it is the diligent interpreter's task to ask, "rather, which [prophet] accords to the Hebrew truth?"[51]

At 28:15 Jerome highlights the LXX's inconsistency in its failure to designate the prophet Hananiah, 'pseudo-' or otherwise. It is interesting to watch Jerome struggle to read the story as if the reader did not already know which prophet would be deemed false. Up until this point in the narrative, in the Hebrew Jeremiah has addressed Hananiah as 'prophet' and here as well the Hebrew

---

45. tamen ueritas claudi et ligari potest. CCSL 74:232.
46. Jerome's commentary is based upon a single lemma, translated directly from Hebrew. For a detailed analysis cf. Williams, *Monk*, 119n62.
47. Cf. the helpful discussion in Graves, 113-114, where he exhibits Jerome's Hebrew knowledge as having surpassed a mere dependance upon his Greek sources Aquila and Symmachus.
48. ut manifestiorem facerent intellegentiam. CCSL 74:269.
49. ne scicilet, ut prius dixi, 'pseudoprophetam' appellare uiderentur 'prophetam'. CCSL 74:273.
50. Optat 'fieri', quod pseudopropheta mentitur. "[Jeremiah] desires that which the false-prophet speaks falsely about 'to happen'." CCSL 74:270; and 'Ac ne uideretur pseudo-prophetae conprobare uaticinium.' CCSL 74:270. The title 'false prophet' is also reserved for those who argue from the proprio sensu, the 'particular sense,' as opposed to working from the Hebrew; Testis est mihi Dominus, me omnia quae secundum Hebraicum dissero, non de proprio sensu loqui, quod arguitur in pseudoprophetis, sed Hebraeorum qui expositionem. *Comm. in Naum.* CCSL 76A:541-2.
51. sed quid ad Hebraicam ueritatem? CCSL 74:273.

text gives Hananiah the designation 'prophet.' Jerome appears to think that the LXX decided prudent silence was the best option.[52] Jerome asks, "in what way, namely, was [Jeremiah] able to call [him] 'prophet,' whom he denied to be sent by the LORD?"[53] He answers, "However, the truth and order of history are not kept, in the same way I have asserted above, according to that which was, but rather according to that which was believed at that time."[54] And again, discussing the LXX's failure to designate Hananiah as 'prophet' in vv10-12a, Jerome, developing an *ordo historae*, writes,

> They [LXX] certainly do not seem to call someone who is not a prophet 'prophet'; as it were, the few in Holy Scripture called 'prophet' are titled 'prophet' on account of the belief of the time - where events are recorded - and not on account of the truth of the matters contained therein.[55]

He credits this phenomenon to a particular view of history. Jerome sees the biblical account as construing events as they have been recorded rather than their reality. He draws an analogy between Hananiah and Joseph, the father of Jesus, by way of explanation. In the gospels, while Joseph is designated the father and this title is attested to in several narratives, the implication is that the events recorded do not necessarily correlate with the reality of the divine patronage of Jesus. In the case of the title 'prophet' for Hananiah, in Jerome's opinion the tradition (Jeremiah included) assumed Hananiah to be a prophet until either he was disproved by the incompletion of his prediction, or the word of the LORD disclosed otherwise.

At other points throughout this chapter, Jerome notes divergences between the Hebrew and the often-shorter LXX. Jerome's translation of v4 *iuxta Hebraeos*, "I will bring back to this place Jeconiah, son of Jehoiakim, king of Judah, and all the Jewish exiles, who have been led to Babylon," has been rendered "Jeconiah and the Jewish exiles"[56] by the LXX. Rather than harsh rebuke, Jerome surprisingly credits the LXX as "briefly setting forth the sense of the Hebrew truth rather than the words."[57] Elsewhere, commenting on the year in which Hananiah died, Jerome notes the LXX merely records that he died in

---

52. 'audi, Anania, non misit te dominus,' 'prophetam' tacuerit. CCSL 74:274.
53. quomodo enim 'prophetam' poterat appellare, quem missum a domino denegabat? CCSL 74:274.
54. Sed historiae ueritas et ordo seruatur, sicut supra diximus, non iuxta id, quod erat, sed iuxta id, quod illo tempore putabatur. CCSL 76:274.
55. ne scilicet prophetam uiderentur dicere, qui propheta non erat, quasi non multa in scripturas sanctis dicantur iuxta opinionem illius temporis, quo gesta referuntur, et non iuxta quod rei ueritas continebat. CCSL 74:272.
56. LXX 35:4: kai\ Iexoni/an kai\ th\n apoiki/an Iouda.
57. breuiter Hebraicae ueritatis sensum magis quam uerba ponentes. CCSL 74:270.

the "seventh month," not "in the fifth year, in the seventh month" which the Hebrew attests.[58]

Jerome reads 28:5-6 as Jeremiah desiring that which Hananiah falsely prophesies to transpire.[59] The evidence for Jerome is Jeremiah's "amen."[60] Claiming that Jeremiah preferred Hananiah's prophecy to his own, Jerome draws an analogy here to Jonah. "Likewise another prophet has testified, saying, 'If only I was not a man having the Spirit, then I might utter falsehood!'"[61] Like Jonah, Jeremiah is constrained to deliver a message that was surely ill-received by both the prophet and his hearers. However, whereas Jeremiah was sure of his message and bold in the face of his opponents, Jonah was discouraged or afflicted, "having been deceived and practically charged by the LORD to be a prophet of falsehood."[62] In Jeremiah, as in Jonah, the true prophet is he who, having been commissioned by the LORD with an unappealing message, delivers it.

After comparing Jonah, Jerome next draws parallels from the prophetic warnings of Dt 18. Jerome shows caution concerning Jeremiah's apparent authority as prophet in his comments on verses 7-9. While he would have been justified in accusing Hananiah of speaking falsely and deceiving the people, Jerome notes Jeremiah abstains from such indictments because, "if he had said [this], the false prophet would have been able to fling the same back at Jeremiah; therefore [Jeremiah] does not cause offense, rather, as it were, speaks to a prophet."[63] Instead, addressing him cordially, Jeremiah recounts how the prophets of old prophesied "against many lands and kings without fear, instead delivering a message to them of great battles and adversity and the scarcity of all things."[64] That the truth to be revealed will vindicate the true prophet is seen in

---

58. Quodque sequitur: 'quia aduersum dominum locutus es. Et mortuus est Ananias propheta in anno illo, mense septimo', in LXX non habetur, pro quo tantum posuerunt: 'et mortuus est mense septimo'. CCSL 74: 274.
59. Optat 'fieri', quod pseudopropheta mentitur — hoc enim significant 'amen'. CCSL 74:270.
60. Interestingly, here Jerome inserts a passing comment concerning Jesus' use of this term from Jn 1:51: *quo uerbo ['amen'] saepe dominus abutitur in euangelio: amen, amen dico uobus*. CCSL 74:270. His use of this example seems to militate against his assertion that this term, for Jeremiah, should be used to denote assent on behalf of the prophet.
61. Unde et alius propheta testatur dicens: utinam non essem uir habens spiritum et mendacium potius loquerer! CCSL 74:270.
62. quare mentitus sit, et arguitur a domino utilius prophetae esse mendacium. CCSL 74:270. Several years earlier in his *In Ionam*, Jerome rhetorically asked what was the difference between "the city of God" and the "victims of the will of God?"; between a prophet and a false-prophet? Jerome goes on to note, without answering, the mere asking of such questions constituted a misdeed on the part of the prophet.
63. Quod si dixisset, poterat et pseudopropheta in Hieremiam eadem retorquere; ergo non facit iniuriam et quasi ad 'prophetam' loquitur. CCSL 74:271.
64. contra terrae multas et regna non parua, sed magna bellum illis et aduersa et rerum omnium penuriam nuntiantes. CCSL 74:271.

the words Jerome puts in Jeremiah's mouth by way of the summarizing paraphrase immediately following: "And whichever was not deceitful flattery, was proven by the end of the event."[65] Jerome understands this criterion to have been set forth by Moses:

> Therefore [Jeremiah] speaks about another example concerning himself and Hananiah, in so far as when the end of the event prophesied arrives, then the truth of the prophets will be revealed. Likewise, the Lord has also spoken this through Moses, that the prophet may be revealed at the end of the prediction. Even this being paid attention to might rebuke the liar, not menacingly nor aggressively, but with the confidence of truth and defer to the future, in order that those who hear might wait for the end of the event.[66]

Jerome understands the prophetic warnings of Dt 18:15ff. to convey the sense that the interim between prophetic utterance and the predictions' (in)completion is itself to be understood as standing against the prophet who speaks falsely. The burden of proof rests heavily on the prophet whose message deviates from those before him.

Hananiah has prophesied that the temple vessels, Jeconiah, and the exiles will return from a deflated Babylon within in two years. He has also broken the wooden yoke Jeremiah fashioned in chapter 27. Jerome sees Jeremiah's reaction as adhering to the prophetic principle outlined above (i.e., Dt 18) of waiting. Praising Jeremiah's prudence and humility, Jerome says Jeremiah has restrained "in order to tacitly demonstrate by the Holy Scriptures that prophets by no means have spoken by their own choice, rather by the will of the Lord, especially regarding the future, whose sole acquaintance is God."[67] Jerome notes that Jeremiah retreats defeated and he places the lament of Ps 37:15 (38:14) in Jeremiah's mouth. Perhaps Jerome understands the biblical report of Hananiah's response in 28:10-12 along with Jeremiah's subsequent silent departure to be demonstrating Hananiah's impatience over against Jeremiah's adherence to Dt 18's prophetic mandates.

Jerome's comments concerning Jeremiah's conviction of Hananiah as false and his ensuing death provide an opportunity to engage with his contemporaries on several polemical fronts. It appears Origen and his followers are the targets of two attacks in chapter 28, both occurring near the end of the pericope. At 28:12b-14 Jerome takes up the discussion of the interpretation of the yoke which bound Jeremiah, lambasting those who minimize or ignore the historical nature of the symbol in an effort to make sense of it spiritually: "The allegorical interpreter raves and here addresses wooden yokes and chains as ethereal and as hav-

---

65. Utrorumque sentential non adulatione mendacii, sed rerum exitu conprobata est. CCSL 74:271.
66. Hoc idem et dominus locutus est per Mosen, quod prophets uaticinii fine monstretur. CCSL 74:271. The editor here references Dt 18:22.
67. ut tacite sancta scripturea demonstret nequaquam prophetas suo tantum arbitrio loqui, sed et domini uoluntate, maxime de futuris, quorum solius dei notitia est. CCSL 74:272.

ing bodies of air."[68] Decrying not only those who viewed the body as the prison of the soul—along with this doctrine's open-endedness regarding the relationship of the divine and the human in Christ—Jerome took issue exegetically with those who would too readily spiritually interpret people, places, or objects possessing actual, historical referents.[69]

The second instance where those identified with Origen, and perhaps Origen himself, come under fire concerns the penalty levied against Hananiah. Jerome has been in conflict with the Origenists for nearly two decades at this point in his writing. An important element of Origenist doctrine concerned the soul's imprisonment in the physical body, an altogether undesirable condition. Jerome, however, is going to use this very belief to combat the same teaching in regards to the death of Hananiah. Dt 18:20 states that a prophet claiming to speak in the name of the LORD, yet has not been sent by him, is to die. What punishment is it, asks Jerome, "If, when I die, I am freed the body's prisons...in what way does death now inflict penalty to the false prophet by way of suffering?"[70]

Jerome's treatment of the prophets, particularly Jeremiah and the question of false prophets, may be described by an attentiveness to the literal/historical, an emphatic insistence on the narratival quality of the story, and a genuine concern to deal faithfully with the prophetic corpus in its received final form. Concerning the question of true and false prophets, Jerome, arguably, sets the pace for ensuing scholarship. The false prophet has not stood in the LORD'S council. In his comments at Jer 23:18, Jerome notes that the Hebrew, Aquila, and Symmachus, while often divergent, at least agree on this much over against the LXX and those of his own 'orthodox Christianity' who follow it.[71] And, Jerome places a premium on the Hebrew construal of the prophetic conflict in Jer 28 as a means to recover the reality of those events. Seeing direct intertextual linkages between the prophetic text and the prophet laws in Deuteronomy, Jerome understands the wait-and-see principle of Dt 18 at work both in the canonical book of Jeremiah and the prophet himself. And as a church Father concerned with a

---

68. Delirat et in hoc loco allergoricus interpres furcas et catenas ligneas aetheria appellans et aeria corpora. CCSL 74:273. Commenting on 27:9-11, Jerome similarly says "The allegorical interpreter raves in this place and exhorts one to place Jerusalem in the heavenly sense"; Delirat et in hoc loco allegoricus interpres et hortatur in cailisti positos Hierusalem, CCSL 74:265; cf. 24:1-10, CCSL 74:236.

69. "He raves here, whomever understands [the king and queen mother of Jer 13:18-19] to be Christ the king and either powerful angels or the apostles, in order to assume a body of humility and to sit in the dust and let go — either king or mighty — of his head's crown and courageous glory"; Delirat in hoc loco, qui regem Christum et potentes angelos uel apostolos intellegit, ut assumant corpus humilitatis et in puluere sedeant et amittant — uel rex uel potentes — de capite suo coronam et gloriam fortitudinis. CCSL 74:132.

70. Si, quando morimur, de carceribus corporum liberamur . . . quomodo nunc pseudoprophetae pro supplicio mors inrogatur? CCSL 74:274.

71. Graves, 177-178.

Christian apologetic, his use of New Testament allusions comes as no surprise. Jerome moves easily into Christological concerns when treating the penalty of the false prophet and then immediately returns to reject those who would overly spiritualize the importance of the number seven at Jer 28:17.

Theodoret of Cyrus (c. 393–c. 460)

One of the only completely preserved commentaries on Jeremiah preserved from antiquity, Theodoret of Cyrus' interpretation affords us an example of the so-called 'Antiochene' approach to exegesis. While tempting, our study seeks to resist the tendency to draft an ancient (particularly Antiochene) interpreter into service for or against a particular exegetical or theological agenda (be it Harnack's Marcion or Bultmann's Theodore of Tarsus).[72] That said, one sees among later pre-modern interpreters, like Calvin, similar interpretive priorities, as it were. Reading Theodoret on Jeremiah, one is struck less with an urgency to apply the text to a particular situation and more with the desire to deal with the text as it stands, as literature. Literature that points backward to an actual historical reality or realities, persons, figures and events that have been incorporated into an inspired text to educate, instruct, and, hopefully, lead the reader into the way of the Lord. In the hands of Theodoret, the text is not averse to a figural meaning, but never at the expense of the literal.

In order to develop Theodoret's approach to true and false prophecy as seen in his Commentary on Jeremiah,[73] a brief introduction situating him in the history of the Patristic era of biblical interpretation is in order. It is fitting that our focus on the so-called 'Antiochene' school of interpretation and exegesis be sharpened before proceeding to Theodoret's commentary on Jeremiah.[74] By Theodoret's own admission we are told of his instruction in the Scriptures with the works of available Fathers.[75] It is entirely reasonable to include the exegeti-

---

72. Cf. the recent book, John Behr, *The Case Against Diodore and Theodore: Texts and Their Contexts*, Oxford Early Christian Texts, (Oxford: OUP, 2011).
73. We will use Theodoret de Cyr, *Interpretatio in Ieremiam* (PG 81; Paris: 1864), 496-805. References to PG volume and column numbers are given in Arabic numerals separated by a colon. For example, PG 81:733-4 refers to vol. lxxxi, cols. 733-4.
74. The last century of patristic scholarship has done much to demolish any sharp delineation between 'Antiochene' and 'Alexandrine' hermeneutics or exegetical methodology. The terms themselves, however, still retain heuristic value. It is in this sense this study will employ them, firmly cognizant that no wholly identifiable, monolithic 'Antiochene' or 'Alexandrian' schools would have been readily recognizable per se. Cf. the recent work John Behr, *The Case Against Diodore and Theodore* (Oxford: Oxford University Press, 2011).
75. Jean-Noël Guinot, "Theodoret of Cyrus," in *Handbook of Patristic Exegesis: The Bible in Ancient Christianity, Vol 2*, ed. Charles Kannengiesser, (Leiden: Brill, 2004), 885f.

cal writings of both Diodore of Tarsus and Theodore of Mopsuestia, two pillars of the Antiochene school, among those at his disposal.[76] Both Theodoret's Letter 16[77]—a response to Irenaeus—and his *Ecclesiastical History*[78] approvingly refer to Diodore and Theodore as "teachers."[79] Along with alerting posterity to those from whom he drew, references to Theodore and Mopsuestia may also be understood as an effort by Theodoret to venerate his own interpretive endeavors. Kurt Smolak, later followed by Guinot, writes, "If he calls the great Antiochene exegetes Theodore of Mopsuestia and Diodore of Tarsus his teachers, then this ... is merely an avowal towards 'orthodox' Antiochene tradition."[80] Siquans, like Guinot's "inheritance common to the provision of all the exegetes",[81] offers the caveat that Theodoret is to be considered an interpreter "for whom an extensive exegetical-tradition was already present."[82] However, as scholarship has shown, this was a tradition with which he was critically engaged.[83]

---

76. Paul B. Clayton, *The Christology of Theodoret of Cyrus*, Oxford Early Christian Studies (Oxford: Oxford University Press, 2007), 9f. Frances M. Young, *From Nicaea to Chalcedon*, (Philadelphia: Fortress Press, 1983), 366-367, notes that, as the child of wealthy parents in the culturally forward city of Antioch, "it would be surprising if Theodoret had not followed the classical *paideia* — and for all his silence, it is quite plain that he did."
77. Jean-Noël Guinot, "L'importance de la dette de Théodoret de Cyr à l'égard de l'exégèse de Théodore de Mopsueste," *Orpheus* 5 (1984): 68-109.
78. PG 82:1256 D; 1277 AB., in John J. O'Keefe, "Rejecting One's Masters: Theodoret of Cyrus, Antiochene Exegesis, and the Patristic Mainstream" (personal correspondence; previously delivered at the Syriac Antiochian Exegesis and Biblical Theology for the 3rd Millennium, Mt St Mary's Seminar, Emmitsburg, MD, June 25, 2004), 10.
79. In *Eranistes* (ed. G. H. Ettlinger (Oxford: Oxford University Press, 1975), 95, 5-12), Theodoret notes that the dedicatee, because of Apollinarian sympathies, would not be able to appreciate "the interpretations of Diodore and Theodore, the victorious combatants of piety." While not directly linking these two fathers' works to Theodoret's tutelage, the above examples serve to situate Theodoret in a tradition in which these figures loom large.
80. "Wenn er einmal die grossen antiochenischen Exegeten Theodor von Mopsuestia und Diodor von Tarsus als seine Lehrer bezeichnet, so ist dies . . . bloss ein Bekenntnis zur 'orthodoxen' antiochenischen Tradition." Kurt Smolak, "Theodoret von Cyrus," in *Alte Kirche II*, Pages 239-250 (ed. Martin Greschat; Gestalten der Kirchengeschichte; Stuttgart: Verlag W. Kohlhammer, 1984), 240.
81. Jean-Noël Guinot, *L'exégèse de Théodoret de Cyr* Théologie historique 100 (Paris: Beauchesne, 1995), 72, writes, "Car l'exégèse patristique présente des lieux communs et des constantes d'interprétation dont l'origine est souvent difficile à cerner: cela constitue en fait un patrimoine commun à la disposition de tous les exégètes."
82. "...dem bereits eine umfangreiche Exegesetradition vorlag." Siquans, 32.
83. "Von dieser [Exegesetradition] beeinflußt, aber auch in kritischer Auseinandersetzung mit ihr, erarbeitete er sein Werk." Agnethe Siquans, *Der Deuteronomiumkommentar des Theodoret von Kyros*, Österreichische Biblische Studien 19 (Frankfurt/Main: Peter Lang, 2002), 32.

Like Jerome, Theodoret has often been accused of contributing nothing more than 'compiled' commentaries, lacking originality and spark.[84] Treating Theodoret's works based on his position as heir to a rich heritage rather than viewing him as a mere epigone of Diodore and Theodore, Guinot forcefully challenged the consensus that Theodoret plagiarized the school of Antioch, compiling his predecessor's works of merit.[85] A major contribution, Guinot argues, is Theodoret's synthesizing of seemingly polarized hermeneutical focal points that, before and during his life, were at times violently at odds. Furthering the notion of Theodoret's inventiveness, Siquans also sees Theodoret's exegetical contribution as synthetic in nature: "It receives its originality...through its openness for other [interpretive] currents."[86] To this end O'Keefe references Theodoret's exegesis as an "exegetical mean."[87]

In the preface to his *Interpretatio in Psalmos*,[88] Theodoret navigates between a strict historical reconstruction and unfettered allegory. In the oft-quoted introduction he complains of commentaries that either "take refuge in allegory with considerable relish," or render the text as "historical narratives...with the result that the commentary represents a case rather for Jews than the household of the faith."[89] While, in typical commentary-writing fashion, Theodoret names no names, reading Diodore or Theodore for those who would confine the text historically is no great stretch.[90] Guilty, in Theodoret's estimation, of an overly

---

84. H. B. Swete, "Theodorus of Mopsuestia," in *A Dictionary of Christian Biography, Literature, Sects and Doctrines, vol. 4* (ed. William Smith *et al.*; London: J. Murray, 1887), in Godfrey W. Ashby, "The hermeneutic approach of Theodoret of Cyrrhus to the Old Testament," in *Studia Patristica 15* (ed. Elizabeth A. Livingston; Berlin: Akademie Verlag, 1984), 131-135, 134, writes, "Theodoret is little else than a judicious compiler from Chrysostom and Theodore." Ashby also cites E. Venables, "Theodoretus," in *Dictionary of Christian Biography: Literature, Sects, and Doctrines, vol. 4*, ed. W. Smith and H. Wace, (London: J. Murray, 1887), where Venables asserts that Theodoret is "if not distinguished by originality, yet remarkable for terseness, good sense and appreciation of his subject." G. Bardy, "Commentaires patristiques de la Bible," in *Dictionnare de la Bible: Supplément; 2*, ed. L. Pirot *et al.* (Paris: 1928), 102, called Theodoret, "un commentateur sans originalité." Similarly Quasten, "Theodoret of Cyrus," 539, writes, "Theodoret does not pretend to originality."
85. Guinot, *L'exégèse*, 306ff.
86 "Seine Originalität erhält er jedoch durch die Öffnung für andere Strömungen." Siquans, 32.
87. O'Keefe, "Rejecting One's Masters," 12.
88. Theodoret of Cyrus, *Interpretatio in Psalmos* (PG 80; Paris: 1864). ET: *Commentary on the Psalms* trans. Robert C. Hill (Washington, D.C.: Catholic University of America Press, 2001).
89. PG 80:860; Hill 2001, I:40-41.
90. Hill 2001, I:41n10, points out that the editor, Shulze, intimates Apollinarius of Laodicea and Theodore, respectively, as representative of the above approaches. Hill notes that Origen could also have been in Theodoret's purview as exemplary of an unwarranted allegorical approach. Comparing interpretations on the Psalms of Diodore, Theodore, and

restrictive *historia*, "the commentaries of his predecessors did not have enough Christian content; they were, in his view, too Jewish."[91] While delimiting that trait which sets an Antiochene apart from an Alexandrian exegete to, say, strict historicism bears (limited) warrant, this means of delineation has been shown to be inadequate. Readers familiar with the debate are aware that differences between Antiochene and Alexandrian exegesis are often cast in terms of typology versus allegory. O'Keefe cautions, however, "both sides used both typology and allegory when it suited their purposes."[92]

Observing the aforementioned Fathers', along with their contemporaries', efforts in commentary writing, correspondences, and polemics, the reader becomes aware of the fact that the task of distinguishing between Antiochene and Alexandrian schools is a relatively recent one.[93] A comprehensive summation of the problem is outside the scope of this study. It is fitting, however, to focus on select points in the history of Christian interpretation in order to more fully appreciate the innovative quality of Theodoret's Old Testament exegesis, particularly in the prophets.[94] To begin with, the hermeneutical term *theōria* has long been at the center of discussions concerning these two schools. Traditionally thought to have been employed synonymously by both Antiochene and Alexandrian interpreters, this position was challenged as early as the late nineteenth century by Heinrich Kihn.[95] Kihn argued that the *theōria* of the Antiochenes was not analogous to the Alexandrians' allegory.[96] Alberto Vaccari would further this when, in 1920, he sketched four characterizing tenets of a distinctly Antiochene appropriation of the term.[97] Vaccari saw a strong ontological link between the occurrence of the event described by a biblical author and the second future to

---

Theodoret, O'Keefe (2004) understands Theodoret's prefatory remarks to be directed towards his predecessors.

91. O'Keefe, "Rejecting One's Masters," 13.

92. John J. O'Keefe, "'A Letter that Killeth': Toward a Reassessment of Antiochene Exegesis, or Diodore, Theodore, and Theodoret on the Psalms," *JECS* 8 (2000): 94n24. Cf. David Dawson, *Allegorical Readers and Cultural Revision in Ancient Alexandria* (Berkley: University of California, 1992); also Frances M. Young, *Biblical Exegesis and the Formation of Christian Culture* (Cambridge: Cambridge University Press, 1997), 152-160.

93. Theologically, the distinction made itself notoriously evident in the Christological battles of the fourth and fifth centuries. The question of the interdependency of methodology and theology is fodder for another study.

94. For a thorough synopsis of recent scholarship focused on figural, or 'spiritual' elements within Patristic exegesis cf. Bradley Nassif, "The 'Spiritual Exegesis' of Scripture: The School of Antioch Revisited," *ATR* 75 (1993): 437-470.

95. Heinrich Kihn, "Über 'Theōria' und 'Allegoria' nach den verlorenen hermeneutischen Schriften der Antiochener," *TQ* 20 (1889): 531-582.

96. Kihn, "Über 'Theōria'," in Childs, *Struggle*, 130.

97. Alberto Vaccari, "La 'teōria' nella scuola exegetica de antiochus," *Bib* 1 (1920): 3-36. For the points outlined cf. Childs, "Theodoret of Cyrus," 130-131.

which it pointed. Childs writes of Vaccari, "Both the present and future events together were described as direct objects of *theōria*, but in different ways. The present functioned as the less significant vehicle through which the prophet knowingly described a greater future event in human history through the use of hyperbolic language."[98]

Post-World War II interest in an Antiochene approach to interpretation hastened Kihn's and Vaccari's attempts at dismantling the erroneous, however widely accepted, conflation of *theōria* with allegory. In Germany, although primarily outside of confessional theology, this renewed interest in typology found a somewhat substantial (however short-lived) foothold.[99] Gerhard von Rad, whose interest in typology had prompted a generative essay entitled "Typological Interpretation of the Old Testament,"[100] would eventually distance himself from the term, replacing it with terms like *Vergegenwärtigung* and "kerygmatic."[101] Yet works from Bultmann,[102] Eichrodt[103] and Kraus[104] emerged which explored the use and appropriateness of typology in Old Testament interpretation. Similarly, Goppelt's monograph *Typos* sought to delineate 'positively' between typology and allegory on the grounds of allegory's illegitimacy.[105]

In France, Daniélou sought to demarcate clearly between typology and allegory, championing typology as inherent to early Christian interpretation while seeing allegory as having slipped into Alexandrian exegesis from philosophy and the schools of rhetoric, a distinction de Lubac resisted.[106] Daniélou held "the heart of the difference to be that allegory is concerned with words, typology

---

98. Childs, *Struggle*, 131.
99. Brevard S. Childs, "Allegory and Typology Within Biblical Interpretation" (paper presented at St Mary's College, University of St Andrews, 2000), esp. 4ff.
100. Gerhard von Rad, "Typologische Auslegung des Alten Testaments," *EvT* 12 (1952): 17-33, first translated into English in "Typological Interpretation of the Old Testament," *Int* 15 (1961): 174-192; reprinted in *Essays on Old Testament Hermeneutics* (ed. Claus Westermann; Richmond, Va.: John Knox Press, 1966), 17-39.
101. Childs, "Allegory," 4.
102. Rudolf Karl Bultmann, "Ursprung und Sinn der Typologie als hermeneutischer Methode," *TLZ* 75 (1950): 205-212.
103. Walther Eichrodt, "Ist die typologische Exegese sachgemäße Exegese?," *TLZ* 11 (1956): 641-654.
104. Hans Joachim Kraus, *Die Biblische Theologie. Ihre Geschichte und Problematik* (Neukirchen-Vluyn: Neukirchener Verlag, 1970).
105. Leonhard Goppelt, *Typos. Die typologische Deutung des Alten Testaments im Neuen* (Darmstadt: Wissenschaftliche Buchgesellschaft, 1969); ET: *Typos, The Typological Interpretation of the Old Testament in the New* (Grand Rapids, Mich: Eerdmans, 1982).
106. Jean Daniélou, *Sacramentum futuri; Études sur les origines de la typologie biblique. Études de théologie historique* (Paris: Beauchesne, 1950); and *From Shadows to Reality: Studies in the Biblical Typology of the Fathers* (London: Burns and Oates, 1960); cf. Henri de Lubac, *Histoire et Esprit. L'Intelligence de L'Écriture d'après d'Origène* (Paris: Aubier, 1950), 92f. and 119; cited in Childs, Struggle, 67.

with events; allegory elides history, typology is rooted in history."[107] Against this, de Lubac, along with Young and Louth, resisted delineating too minutely between allegory and typology, arguing that the early church's use of these figural interpretive tools was not so easily schematized.

While affecting German hermeneutics relatively little, Daniélou's work had a notable impact on the English conversation. With Lampe and Woollcombe's Daniélou-influenced *Essays on Typology*, it became standard fare to reject allegory as unhistorical. Typology, however, was allowed since it "seeks to discover and make explicit the real correspondences in historical events which have been brought about by the recurring rhythms of the divine activity."[108] James Barr vociferously attacked attempts at the rehabilitation of typology such as these.[109] Combating what he deemed a "modern event-oriented Biblical Theology,"[110] Barr saw no distinction between typology and allegory; there was no difference between the two beyond the external application of systems brought to bear upon the texts. "It would seem that the essential differences are not between methods statable separately from the resultant system (as seems to happen when we try to distinguish typology and allegory as methods), but between different kinds of resultant systems."[111] For Barr, any attempt to bridge the gap between Old and New with a modern approach, such as typology, was doomed since the New Testament's use of the Old, while resembling typology, was an entirely different method of exegesis.[112] Works from Whitman,[113] Louth,[114] Young,[115] Torjesen,[116]

---

107. Cited in Andrew Louth, *Discerning the Mystery: An Essay on the Nature of Theology* (Oxford: Clarendon Press; Oxford University Press, 1983), 118.
108. G. W. H. Lampe and K. J. Woollcombe, *Essays on Typology* (SBT 22; London: SCM Press Ltd, 1957), 29.
109. James Barr, "Typology and Allegory," in *Old and New in Interpretation: A Study of the Two Testaments.* (London: SCM Press Ltd, 1966).
110. In Brevard S. Childs, *Biblical Theology of the Old and New Testaments: Theological Reflection on the Christian Bible* (Minneapolis: Fortress Press, 1992), 14.
111. Barr, "Typology," 108.
112. Cf. Childs, *BTONT*, 13-14. Barr likens the modern rehabilitation of typology to the construction of a "bridge which reaches neither side of the river", failing to pass muster with the historical-critical requirements of the day and insufficiently relating itself to the interpretive life of the early church (Barr, *idem*, 132). Childs' critique that Barr's approach fails to treat the shared ontological and soteriological unity attested to in both the Old and New Testament seems well founded.
113. Jon Whitman, *Allegory: The Dynamics of an Ancient and Medieval Technique*, (Oxford: Clarendon Press, 1987).
114. Louth, *Mystery*.
115. Esp. *Exegesis*, and "Alexandrian and Antiochene Exegesis," in *A History of Biblical Interpretation: Volume I: The Ancient Period*, ed. Alan J. Hauser *et al.* (Grand Rapids: Eerdman's, 2003).
116. Karen Jo Torjesen, *Hermeneutical Procedure and Theological Method in Origen's Exegesis*, PTS 28 (Berlin: De Gruyter, 1986).

and recently Dawson[117] have renewed interest in figural interpretation, particularly concerning allegory and typology as axiomatic tools of traditional Christian interpretation. The concerns, however, remain the same. First, in what way could modern biblical interpreters talk of an Antiochene versus an Alexandrian school? Second, how did these 'schools' relate *theōria* to typology, allegory, and the *sensus plenior*?[118]

Regressing for a moment, a development came about in the midst of the lull in the figurative hermeneutics discussion of the early 1970's concerning the Antiochene method of exegesis. In 1974 Schäublin argued the rhetorical and grammatical schools were the dominant influences on early (until 500) Christian biblical interpretation.[119] Young has recently developed the same.[120] Utilizing grammatical and historical analysis, rhetorical schools trained readers to seek out moral principles and ethical models from literature. Schäublin and Young have shown that the primary components of rhetorical training are present in the Antiochene commentators. The standard comment opens with a hypothesis, a setting forth of the subject matter of the work at hand, including textual details, text-critical notes, and etymology. This is known as the *methodikon*. Intertextuality and contextual background would also be explored in an effort to examine a text's logic. Along with a text's harmony, its *akolouthia* (coherence), *skopos* (intent), and *telos* (end) all share weight in the preliminary explication of its meaning. All of this constituted the "'first level" of exegesis, the *historia*.[121] While the Antiochenes' interpretation of texts did rest on *ta pragmata*, "the facts", Young asserts, "It is quite misleading to think they had developed a historical consciousness which their contemporaries did not have."[122] Rather it is the freight afforded the relationship of those historical occurrences that has traditionally set the schools apart. Whereas words themselves often served as tokens in the hands of Alexandrian interpreters' allegorical readings of Scripture,

---

117. John David Dawson, *Christian Figural Reading and the Fashioning of Identity*, (Berkeley: University of California Press, 2002).
118. Childs, *Struggle*,131.
119. Christoph Schäublin, *Untersuchungen zu Methode und Herkunft der antiochenischen Exegese* (Köln: P. Hanstein, 1974).
120. Young, *Exegesis*, in which she credits Schäublin with "anticipating my own argument that the Antiochenes were principally formed by exegetical practice in the schools" (170n33); and most recently Young, "Alexandrian and Antiochene Exegesis."
121. Guinot, "Theodoret of Cyrus," 902. O'Keefe, "Rejecting One's Masters," 8, defines *historia* as "a process by which the narrative and chronological sequence of the text was analyzed and commented on."
122. Young, *Exegesis*, 172. Handily cataloging the numerous technical terms inherent to this discussion Young writes, "the terms [*historia, theōria*, and *allegoria*] are not about 'senses' of the text so much as activities of the exegete. The exegete attends to the wording and the 'story', the *methodikon* and the *historikon*; the exegete may then probe the narrative and by 'insight' (*theōria*) and 'elevation' (*anagōgē*) perceive the moral and spiritual import built into the text's wording and content" (175).

the Antiochenes were seen to have valued the unity and subject matter of the narrative itself. Out of the schools hypothesis Young speculates that the Antiochenes rejected the term *allegoria* "because it had been misappropriated by a particular tradition of exegesis which had a different background, and which shattered the narrative coherence of particular texts, and the Bible as a whole."[123]

An ambiguous term that often serves the agenda of whomever wields it, *theōria*, as mentioned above, has been at the center of the discussion over the past 125 years. Froelich has shown that the Antiochenes sought a higher sense of scripture, a sense they called *theōria*.[124] While Froelich eventually conflates an Alexandrian allegory with the *theōria* of the Antiochenes, his distinction that the Antiochenes' *theōria* remained subject to the *historia* is, if an oversimplification, nonetheless accurate.[125] In the same vein Hidal has shown that the *sensus litteralis* generates what *theōria* an Antiochene would accept: "to say something else than is intended in the text (or its *theōria*), that is an allegory."[126]

When moving from the "first level" of an Antiochene's exegesis to the "second," or from matters of *historia* to a higher reading by way of *theōria*, the use of figurative interpretation featured prominently.[127] Antiochenes, especially Theodoret, selectively employed modal terms such as *tropological, anagogical*, and *mystikos*. According to Guinot *tropikōs* (i.e., *sensus moralis*) played the largest role in Theodoret's figural interpretations.[128] When Theodoret identified a text's sense as *tropikos*, then it is to be understood that the meaning rendered was not another, separate meaning, but rather an extension of the word or concept being treated. Childs, relying on Guinot, says this is best understood as a

---

123. Young, *Exegesis*, 182.
124. Karlfried Froehlich, *Biblical Interpretation in the Early Church* (Philadelphia: Fortress Press, 1984), 20.
125. Froelich, discussing the historical content of Psalms as commented upon by Diodore, notes "Their [Psalms'] conceptual content may indeed be lifted up into higher anagogy but such *theōria* must be left to those endowed with a 'fuller charisma.'" (22). Young appears to agree with Froelich's notion of *theōria*'s dependance upon the interpreter's exegetical stance or positioning toward a text.
126. Sten Hidal, "Exegesis of the Old Testament in the Antiochene School with its Prevalent Literal and Historical Method," in *Hebrew Bible / Old Testament* I/1, 548; cf. G. Bardy, "Interprétation. Chez les pères IV," in *Dictionnare de la Bible: Supplément; 4* (ed. L. Pirot *et al.*; Paris: 1949), 569-591, 580, where Hidal translates him having said, "[*Theōria*] takes its starting point in the *sensus litteralis* and never leaves it." Young (*Exegesis*, 177) makes this point when she notes that allegory was allowed only when the text itself sign-posted this particular figure of speech.
127. In his preface to his commentary on Song of Songs, Theodoret likens moving from the literal to the figural as going "beyond the veil of the letter to reach the spirit and interior" or gazing, "as in a mirror, to contemplate the Lord's glory with unveiled faces." PG 81:32D-33A, in Guinot, "Theodoret of Cyrus," 903.
128. Guinot, "Theodoret of Cyrus," 898ff.

"metaphorical sense."[129] The *tropological* sense for Theodoret has several possible meanings, some which "would well merit the name allegory."[130] Therefore, Guinot maintains, for Theodoret "it becomes artificial to attempt to oppose the literal exegesis of the Antiochenes to the allegorical exegesis of the Alexandrians."[131]

Along with a metaphorical sense or mode of interpretation, typology was used by the Antiochenes, particularly Theodoret. Traditionally the discussion has turned on the presupposed historicity of both events being typified. Wallace-Hadrill's comments epitomize recent literature on the subject:

> In short, [for Antiochene exegesis] typology based upon historical fact is permitted, allegory is not . . . Historical reality can only be typified by that which is also historical reality, and to depart from this principle is to drift into the realm of 'nocturnal dreams.'[132]

Guinot too sees the expediency of an Antiochene interpretation in the value placed on matters historical. He says that a "typological explanation offers the advantage ... of preserving the reality and historical dimension of the scriptural text."[133]

An example of typology's usefulness to a Christian interpreter dealing with prophecy and its value for the church can be found in Theodoret's famous comment on Isa 60:1, "Arise, shine, [LXX = Jerusalem] for your light has come, and the glory of the Lord has risen upon you."[134] Building on the notion of double fulfillment, a natural by-product of typology, Theodoret reads the promise of

---

129. Childs, *Struggle*, 137; cf. Guinot, "Theodoret of Cyrus," 904f.
130. Guinot, "Theodoret of Cyrus," 904.
131. Ibid., 905. It seems likely, however, that Guinot would agree with Young's remark that an Antiochene interpretation did not reject allegory per se; what they objected to was "the type of allegory that destroyed the textual coherence," Young, *Exegesis*, 176.
132. D. S. Wallace-Hadrill, *Christian Antioch: A Study of Early Christian Thought in the East* (Cambridge: Cambridge University Press, 1982), 36.
133. Guinot, "Theodoret of Cyrus," 905f. Guinot sees at least two criteria or rules governing Theodoret's use of typology concerning the relationship of type to antitype. (1) There must be "sufficiently broad similarity"; (2) the type's relation to the antitype must contain a difference of nature or degree (906).
134. Theodoret of Cyrus, *Commentaire sur Isaïe; Tome III (Sections 14-20)*, ed. Jean-Noël Guinot, Sources Chrétiennes, 315 (Paris: Les Éditions du Cerf, 1984), 238-240 = SC 315:238-240. Cf. the helpful introductory essay by Mark Elliott, *Isaiah 40—66*, ed. Thomas C. Oden, Ancient Christian Commentary on Scripture, Old Testament XI (Downers Grove: InterVarsity Press, 2007), xvii—xxx; Robert C. Hill, *Reading the Old Testament in Antioch* (Bible in Ancient Christianity 5; Leiden: Brill, 2005), 163, sees this section of Theodoret's comment as an explicit enumeration of his prophetic hermeneutic. Reversing Antioch's rules and moving "from situating Old Testament books, events and characters within a broadly Christological οικονομία, like Theodore, to finding reference to Jesus in individual verses in the manner of Cyril, Theodoret was accepting a notion of biblical truth which to that point had not been current in Antioch."

Jerusalem's reconstruction and restoration as only an element of this passage's interpretation. Theodoret understands the prediction to have three subjects in view simultaneously. First, this prediction outlines a "sketch" of the rebuilding of the city under Darius and Cyrus.[135] Next, the prophecy, in its secondary fulfillment, understands the picture coming into sharper focus, being filled in with color to reveal the Christian church.[136] Finally, the future existence of the heavenly city is revealed as the original, full picture painted by the prophet.[137] These gradually enlarging—in—scope fulfillments designate not two (or three) separate fulfillments, rather "successive fulfillments of the same prophetic announcement."[138] Elsewhere Guinot says that this mode of multiple fulfillments in its relation to typology highlights the importance of the literal in that without the proper recognition of the type the antitype could not be located since the former "authorizes" the existence of the latter.[139]

This view of the Antiochene's historical sobriety has done much to engender this school to those who would in some way seek to rehabilitate a Diodore of Tarsus, Theodore of Mopsuestia, or Theodoret in service of historical approaches to biblical interpretation.[140] One among many, Horbury sees the Antiochenes' historically delimited interpretation of prophecy and psalms as "an anticipation, despite big differences, of much in modern historical exegesis, and as an attempt to integrate historical commentary with a theological understanding of the Old Testament."[141] Hidal also notes the significance of Bultmann writing on Theodore of Mopsuestia. While he suggests that the tools of interpretation employed by the Antiochenes did not "necessarily" adumbrate a critical approach to the text, Hidal does view their historical acumen as "something which they have in common with modern scholarship."[142] And, Simonetti notes Theodore's literal-

---

135. ὠ μὲν εν σκιογραφια. SC 315:238.
136. ω εν εικόνι δὲ εκ πλειόνων γεγραμμένη ξρωμάτων καὶ τῆ αληθείᾳ ακριβεστέρου δεικνυσι τοῦ τύπου, τὴν τῆ αγίᾳ εκκλησίᾳ λαμπρότ́τα. SC 315:238.
137. προδηλοι δέ ὁμῶ καὶ αυτό τό τη εικόνο αρξέτυπον, τουτο δέ εστιν ο μέλλων βίο καὶ η εν ουρανοὶ πολιτεία. SC 315:239.
138. Guinot, "Theodoret of Cyrus," 906f.
139. Ibid., 907.
140. For examples of this see Rowan A. Greer, *Theodore of Mopsuestia: Exegete and Theologian* (London: Faith Press, 1961), 111, in his attempt to extract an "almost plenary" doctrine of inspiration, linking Theodore to the modern critical endeavor by way of progressive revelation. Or, Godfrey W. Ashby, *Theodoret of Cyrrhus as Exegete of the Old Testament* (Grahamstown: Rhodes University, 1972), as he cites Theodoret as a forerunner of the 'New Hermeneutic.'
141. William Horbury, "Old Testament Interpretation in the Writings of the Church Fathers," in *Mikra*. ed. Martin Jan Mulder (Philadelphia: Fortress Press, 1988), 770.
142. Hidal, "Exegesis," 568.

ism finding expression in investigations into the history of Israel.[143] It would appear, then, that in some fashion the conscious historical enquiry prevalent in much of the exegesis of those associated with an Antiochene school has been and is currently being understood as begging association with the regnant historical-critical method.

While relatively widespread, this position increasingly gains detractors. Childs asserts, "the conflict between these two schools of interpretation has often been misconstrued as if the Antiochenes rejected allegory out of hand and adumbrated the modern historical-critical approach of the nineteenth century."[144] Citing Daniélou's clear delineation between typology and allegory in the 1950's, Childs journals the ready acceptance of typology since it was perceived to have sought the retention of the centrality of biblical history, the key component of the critical enterprise.[145] Outlining lines of consensus concerning the last 50 years of patristic exegetical research, Childs asserts Antiochenes were not "precursors of the modern historical approach.[146] He rightly locates the difference between the two endeavors in their respective views of history: "Rather the controversy turned on how one properly understood Scripture's context."[147] Young also saw history as the key difference at work. She pointedly addresses the issue of history when she writes:

> No Antiochene could have imagined the kind of critical stance of the Biblical Theology movement, explicitly locating revelation not in the text of scripture but in the historicity of events behind the text, events to which we only have access by reconstructing them from the texts, treating the texts as documents providing historical data. This is anachronistic, and obscures the proper background of the Antiochene's protest.[148]

With Childs, Young, and O'Keefe we are right to resist attempts to conflate the agenda of one with the other. Looking for "circumstantial" evidence fails to take into account the social context operative for Diodore or Theodore's exegesis. O'Keefe's calls for the exploration of a ruled reading and the recovery of the text as a form of witness to the divine economy are well sounded.

As we move into his comments on Jeremiah, it will become evident that for Theodoret, the grounding of theological readings so prevalent in the historicist interpretations of his immediate predecessors would not suffice to serve the needs of the Christian church. With Theodoret we are attempting to show merely that his interpretive methods derived from outside a single exegetical trajecto-

---

143. Manlio Simonetti, *Biblical Interpretation in the Early Church: An Historical Introduction to Patristic Exegesis,* ed. Anders Bergquist and Markus Bockmuehl, trans. John A. Hughes, (Edinburgh: T & T Clark, 1994), 71.
144. Childs, *Struggle,* 132.
145. Ibid., 65.
146. Childs, "Allegory," 6f.
147. Ibid., 7.
148. Young, *Exegesis,* 167.

ry. Guinot helpfully notes that with Theodoret "the method is the same, but the orientation is different."[149] Theodoret, the Antiochene interpreter with one of the greater of shelf lifes among his peers, can be seen to have synthesized (rather than united) the exegetical approaches of the two schools.[150] Rather than neatly adhering to what has, at times, been caricatured as the historicism of the old Antiochenes, Theodoret sought to underscore the Old Testament's messianic content through the use of figural interpretation, namely typology.

This study has selected three entry points into the interpretation of true and false prophecy in Theodoret's Jeremiah commentary. First, the subjective elements of the prophets come into play. The commission of the prophet and the prophet's communion with the Lord are seen to be vital components in the true prophet's execution of his duties. Related to these are a prophet's esteem for and access to the words of God. Second, Theodoret's dependence upon Deuteronomy's prophetic laws, together with an *ex vaticinu* verification of fulfillment, figures heavily into his understanding of the truth or falsehood of a prophet. Third, figural reading plays a large role in Theodoret's understanding of false prophecy. Theodoret's most original contribution to the question of true and false prophecy comes as he interprets Moses as the definitive type of Christ and unfolds the implications this typological reading has on the problem of false prophets.

As attested to in Theodoret's relative ambivalence towards the authorship of Psalms,[151] the influence of the Holy Spirit plays no mean role validating words purportedly from God. Theodoret, discussing the prophet's foretelling the Israelites' responsibility for the troubles to befall them (Jer 5:12), sees Jeremiah accusing the false prophets of causing the very things they promised would pass by. Understanding the phrase "all wind" as the futility and falsity of what the false prophets spoke, Theodoret then gives the underlying reason for the false prophets' lies: "they had no share in the divine Spirit."[152] Nine chapters later, commenting on the people's expeditious repentance and its subsequent rejection by the Lord, Theodoret discusses Jeremiah's reaction and the Lord's reply. At Jeremiah's instigation, the Lord responds to Jeremiah concerning those prophets who would continue to prophesy peace and abundance. Theodoret says the Lord tells Jeremiah that the false prophets predict lies, "not serving the divine words or

---

149. Guinot, "Theodoret of Cyrus," 909f.
150. Smolak, "Theodoret von Cyrus," 248, writes, "This moderate connection of the interpretation methods allowed him, like Ambrosius in the west, to similarly become one of the best exegetes of the Patristic epoch, without whose Bible explanation one did not want to do after 553, so that in the so-called Byzantine catenae Theodoret was widely used."
151. PG 80:861; Hill 2001, I:42.
152. 81:539; Theodoret of Cyrus, *Commentary on the Prophet Jeremiah* (trans. Robert C. Hill; *Commentary on the Prophets*, vol. 1; Brookline, Mass: Holy Cross Orthodox Press, 2006), 45 = Hill 2006, I:45.

acting as instruments of grace."[153] Continuing, Theodoret identifies what it is they do serve: demons and their own ideas. With Jerome Theodoret sees false prophets as willfully malicious in their deception.

Viewing a true prophet's stance toward and possession of the word of the Lord as paramount, Theodoret condemns false prophets in Jer 23 for "adulterating and corrupting the divine word."[154] Reading the LORD's condition in 23:22 ("If they had been part of my substance and heard my words, they would have instructed my people and turned them aside from their evil way and from their evil exploits"), Theodoret implies the lack of direct communication with the LORD on the part of the false. He also sees an organic link between the law's prescriptions and the true prophet's mandatory response in the face of rebellion. We shall return to this below. Finally, at 23:28-29, Theodoret notes Jeremiah figuratively contrasting the word of God mediated by the true prophet with that of the false as grain to straw, respectively. Theodoret holds that Jeremiah explains the difference between true and false prophets thus: "some of them, like thieves, steal some prophetic words and spoil them by distortion, while others concoct false prophecy, and others recount dreams they have not had."[155]

At Jer 17:15-16, Theodoret discusses those Jeremiah has prophesied against. The promised punishment has not come, prompting the people to exclaim, "Where is the word of the Lord? Let it come." Theodoret paraphrases Jeremiah, "they find fault with the delay in retribution, and think the prophecy false, since you postpone retribution."[156] Calling their distrust of his prophecy "insensible," Theodoret sees in Jeremiah patience and genuine concern for the very people he has been prophesying against. Still in the voice of Jeremiah Theodoret writes, "for my part, though seeing this insensibility of theirs, I did not want them to fall victim to troubles."[157]

In Jer 23 we see Theodoret's insistence on history's role as the final arbiter of a prophet's message. Here we find both positive and negative aspects of the fulfillment of prophecies of doom. Because of the lies of the false prophets, at 23:19-20 Jeremiah predicts the rage of God, a "shaking from the Lord," that will not be satiated until "[God] puts into effect the endeavors of his heart." Theodoret's comments deal first with the LORD. Of v19 he writes, "By this [Jeremiah] indicates successive disasters, and the fact they are sent by God; he it is who inflicts the punishments."[158] Theodoret then simply asserts, "what he prophesied

---

153. PG 81:592; Hill 2006, I:75. In Jer 36 Theodoret begins his comment noting that a true prophet is "inspired by divine grace," PG 81:683; Hill 2006, I:126.
154. PG 81:629; Hill 2006, I:96.
155. PG 81:632; Hill 2006, I:98. Cf. PG 81:631; Hill 2006, I:97.
156. PG 81:607; Hill 2006, I:84.
157. PG 81:607; Hill 2006, I:84.
158. PG 81:631; Hill 2006, I:97.

will come to pass."¹⁵⁹ The term τά πράγματα, "that which is done or happens," is used by Theodoret to explain the 'fulfillment' of a prophecy. When in the future the people look back remembering the wrath of the Lord and its subsequent relinquishment, they will recall Jeremiah's promises, both of punishment and restoration.¹⁶⁰

At chapter 28, in a relatively brief section on the narrative of Jeremiah and Hananiah,¹⁶¹ Theodoret treats the response of Jeremiah to Hananiah's promise of peace and abundance. Theodoret says that in response to Hananiah's initial oracle (vv2-4), Jeremiah wishes to convey his desire that he too hopes for all that Hananiah has foretold. Qualifying Jeremiah's response of "Amen, may it be as you have said," Theodoret says, "he did not actually allow the prophecy to be endorsed with his approval."¹⁶² Going on to contrast Hananiah's message with the prophecies of doom of previous prophets (vv7-9), Theodoret distills Jeremiah's qualifying remarks: "The outcome in events, he is saying, will demonstrate the truth of the prophecy; so we shall see if for one thing we are given over to the Babylonians according to my prophecy."¹⁶³ Again, relying on the subjective authority possessed by true prophets, Jeremiah is seen to be the privileged recipient of divine communication in Theodoret's straightforward view of prophetic inspiration. After having his wooden yoke broken off his neck and prophesying a yoke of iron in its stead, the word of the LORD comes again to Jeremiah.¹⁶⁴ Here Jeremiah learns, as if heretofore unknown, a piece of information to which he alone is privy.¹⁶⁵ Moralizing Hananiah's death, Theodoret notes the biblical

---

159. "What he prophesied will come to pass...whenever they see the fulfillment [τά πράγματα], they will recall the promises." PG 81:631; Hill 2006, I:97.
160. Commenting on 30:24, Theodoret again charges the people with unbelief, interpreting "You will know this in the last days," with "since you do not believe the words, you will learn from experience of the events themselves," PG 81:659; Hill 2006, I:113.
161. Theodoret's relatively sparse treatment of true and false prophecy in chapter 28 is explained by his lengthier discussion of false prophets in chapter 23. In the endnotes of the English translation Hill explains this brevity saying Theodoret is "picking the eyes out" of the chapters, treating only those passages of note (218n1). Hill goes on to mention that Theodoret captures well the pathos between the opposing prophets, mentioning Theodoret's sensitivity to Jeremiah's desire that Hananiah's prophecy be correct. However, in titling Hananiah 'false prophet' (ψσευδοπροφήτή; PG 81:647; Hill 2006, I:106), it appears Theodoret is constrained to identify Hananiah with those spoken of earlier in chapter 23 and the like.
162. PG 81:647-648; Hill 2006, I:106.
163. PG 81:648; Hill 2006, I:106.
164. Theodoret interprets the iron yoke as "a form of punishment that would be heavier on account of disobedience." PG 81:648; Hill 2006, I:107.
165. Theodoret mentions that Jeremiah was "disappointed" to learn that Hananiah spoke falsely, lending authenticity to Jeremiah's voiced 'amen' of v6.

author recounting both the patience of God and the false prophet's death due to his persistent wickedness.[166]

Theodoret's predecessors utilized figurative interpretation under certain circumstances, as we have seen. The *historia* grounded and governed interpretation and only when the text itself indicated figurative language was the interpreter free to follow. Among the figurative tools most readily accessible to Theodoret was typology. Typology allowed the reader to discern patterns and then apply those patterns to other events in scripture without forfeiting the historically moored events therein, particularly when applied to prophetic texts.[167] In seeking to trace Theodoret's treatment of true and false prophecy in his interpretation, typology and its 'results' have yet to be examined.

General Christological typologies can be found scattered throughout the commentary. For example, at Jer 23:5-6, commenting upon the Lord's granting his people a "righteous branch" whose name will be Jozadak (Κύριό Ἰωσεδέκ = "the Lord is our righteousness"), Theodoret rejects Diodore's (and the Jews') interpretation of this prophecy. He refutes those who "shamelessly" apply the title Jozadak to Zerubbabel, calling them "stupid."[168] Zerubbabel cannot be the

---

166. Hill calls this an "unusually moral elaboration on the text" (218n3). However, as Schäublin, *Untersuchungen*, and Young, *Exegesis*, have shown, the rhetorical-grammatical school's emphasis on the moral explication of texts would serve to explain this and similar readings throughout the commentary. Concluding his comments on 23:39-40, Theodoret treats the Lord's threat of captivity and the subsequent promise of return. As the Israelites were exhorted to keep the words of the prophets as they accurately attested to the word of God, Theodoret exhorts his readers to follow the words of both the Old and New Testaments and, worshipping the one who spoke through both, to keep the Lord's "life-giving" laws (PG 81:633; Hill 2006, I:98-99). Again, at the end of the tome dealing with chapters 27-29, Theodoret entreats the reader, in light of the examples just enumerated, to "dread falsehood, trust in the truth . . . and follow the divine sayings" so that they might take part in blessing of the "Jerusalem on high" (PG 81:652-653; Hill 2006, I:110). Elsewhere Theodoret urges his readers to be patient amidst suffering (on Jer 45; PG 81:708; Hill 2006, I:140-141) and to fear the judgement of the Lord while relying on his lovingkindness, looking forward to divine mercy's ultimate manisfestation, the Lord Jesus Christ (PG 81:759; Hill 2006, I:168).

167. In Derek Krueger, "Typological Figuration in Theodoret of Cyrrhus's *Religious History* and the Art of Postbiblical Narrative," *JECS* 5 (1997): 393-419, Krueger sees typology as a means by which the church fathers also connected figures (saints) in the life of the church back to the scriptures. For example, Theodoret's *Religious History*, in which the lives of 4th and 5th century monks are recounted, alludes to biblical figures as types that found their successive antitypes in the ascetic hermits of Syria. He writes, "typology that connects the monks to the Bible is identical to the typology that connects the Old and New Testaments . . . a mode of reading the Bible becomes a mode of reading the saints" (409).

168. It is not entirely unreasonable to read Theodoret indicting not only Jewish interpreters, but whomever would fall prey to a purely 'carnal' reading, be it Theodore or Diodore as well.

fulfillment of such a promise since the name neither characterizes the man nor is it ever applied to the historical person. Since Zerubbabel failed to fulfill the promise, where does the value of an interpretation of Jozadak lay? Theodoret answers:

> Since, however, [Zerubbabel] was a type of Christ the Lord and brought back the captives from Babylon to Judah, just as the Lord transferred those enslaved by the devil to truth, anyone applying this to him in the manner of a type would do nothing beyond reason.[169]

It is Jesus Christ, Theodoret simply maintains, who is proclaimed by the prophets as "righteous king" and "Lord of righteousness."[170]

When finding Christ-types in Jeremiah, doctrinal points often accompany them. Combatting Arian subordinationists, Theodoret, commenting on Jer 10:11, reminds the reader "it belongs to God to create, not be created by someone else. So, if the Son is created, he is not God; but if he is creator and maker of all things, he is truly God."[171] All of this has been spoken of in the prophets. Creation language in the prophets is, for Theodoret, descriptive of Jesus Christ's being ὁμοούσιος with the Father. Commenting on Baruch's public reading before Jehoiakim in Jer 36, Theodoret again inserts a brief Christological remark concerning the hypostatic union constructing an incarnational analogy to explain his view of Scriptural inspiration. "Whereas the writing matter was consumed by fire, the divine Law remained intact; likewise also the Word, when the body that was assumed suffered, remained immune to suffering."[172]

While typological references to Jesus Christ are in short supply throughout the Jeremiah commentary, Theodoret's reading of Jer 6:16 warrants a closer look as it directly applies to his understanding of true and false prophecy. Up to this point Theodoret has been lambasting the prophets who foretell peace (vv11-15). Supposedly treating the wounds of the people, when called to account for their deception, these false prophets will be shown for what they are: liars who have applied promises of peace to wounds that required drastic remedies.[173] Theodoret sees in v16, "Stand at the crossroads, and look, and ask for the ancient paths, where the good way lies; and walk in it, and find rest for your souls. But they said, 'We will not walk in it,'" a harsh invective leveled against the Jewish nation's present hardening and the foreshadowing of the calling of the nations. Building upon the term ἡ ὁδός, "the way," Theodoret plots Jeremiah along a prophetic trajectory originating in Moses and finding its ultimate destination in Jesus.

---

169. PG 81:628; Hill 2006, I:96.
170. PG 81:628; Hill 2006, I:96.
171. PG 81:567-568; Hill 2006, I:61.
172. PG 81:684; Hill 2006, I:127.
173. PG 81:545; Hill 2006, I:48.

While the holy prophets are many ways, our Lord himself is the truly good way - in fact, listen to his words, "I am the way, the truth and the life." But each of the prophetic ways leads to this way, Moses the lawgiver hinting at this in his words, "The Lord our God will raise up for you from among your brethren a prophet like me" and so on. David, king and prophet, and also Isaiah, Micah, Ezekiel and each of the prophets give a glimpse of this way.[174]

For Theodoret, the message of the prophets finds its inception with Moses. Citing Dt 18:15, Theodoret understands the ways put forth by Israel's prophets to be variations on a theme, as it were, of Moses' original score. Inherent in the formation of the prophetic office was the promise of one whose way to which all other prophetic ways would lead.[175] At Jesus' declaration of himself as "the way" in Jn 14:6, Theodoret links these texts, and in some sense the testaments, with this term, using prophecy as a bridge between Law and apocolyptic. He says that just as there is usually one major thoroughfare leading to the largest of cities, so too has there always been one way to God. Failing to grasp this from the prophets, the Jews resisted, saying, "We will not go" (6:16), and "We will not listen" (6:17). Befitting a discussion concerning Jesus as the way, Theodoret closes this chapter's comment with the responsiveness of the nations. Given the rejection of the prophets' attestations to the true way, Theodoret understands Paul and Barnabas' mission to the Gentiles as fulfilling the prophecy laid out in Jer 6:18-19.[176]

Summary

By way of summary, we may note three characteristics of Jerome's treatment of true and false prophecy: an attentiveness to the literal/historical sense of the text; an insistence on the narratival quality of the story; and a focus on the text's final form. As will be seen to varying degrees later, the subjective element of the prophet's derived authority also plays a minor role: the false prophet has *not* stood in the council of the Lord, something the LXX fails to note. He highly values the Hebrew construal of the conflict in Jer 28 as a means to recover the realia of those events. Concerning his view of the Law's informing or exerting pressure on Jeremiah, Jerome sees their relationship in a rather straightforward manner. He understands the wait-and-see principle of Dt 18 as bearing on both the prophet and the book of Jeremiah. And, wary of allegorical or overly figural readings, Jerome openly criticizes those who would see things in the text that, to an historical eye, are not there.

---

174. PG 81:545; Hill 2006, I:49.
175. "[E]ach of the prophetic ways leads to this way"; cf. PG 81:545; Hill 2006, I:49.
176. PG 81:547-548; Hill 2006, I:49-50. Citing Acts 13:46-47 (Isa 49:6), Theodoret sees Paul's custom of first entering the local synagogue before preaching the gospel to the Gentiles as the fulfillment of the promised exclusion of the Jewish nation on account of their failure to see, follow, and attest to the 'way'.

Theodoret understands the way of Moses as the Law. This connection is made most clearly at 23:22 where he writes of the false prophets' failure to attest to the true way: "I clearly forbade in the Law the forms of wickedness; so if they had followed my words, they would have criticized the people's transgressions and led them to the straight and narrow."[177] Once this association is crystallized, Theodoret's discussions of Moses and the Law take on new significance. Theodoret's mention of Moses in the first paragraph of comment now serves to situate the prophet Jeremiah in an interpretive prophetic context dependent upon and derivative of Moses.[178]

When interpreting prophetic texts concerned with prophetic veracity, Theodoret determines a prophets' authority (i.e. truth) using four key criteria: their call; their divine inspiration; the necessity of waiting on the occurrence of foretold events in accordance with the prophetic laws of Dt 18; and the degree to which their message resonates with others within the lineage of prophets who find their headwaters in Moses and their consummation in Christ. We will note at this point in our study, Theodoret clearly sees Jeremiah establishing a criterion based on Dt 18 in his response to Hananiah at 28:5-9. Also, we see as early as Theodoret a limited preoccupation with Jeremiah's psychology, evinced by discussions concerning his emotional responses to Hananiah and the false prophets. Hermeneutically, there is little resistance in either Theodoret or Jeremiah to associate prophecy with eschatological projection, seeing references to the ingathering of all peoples in Moses and Jeremiah as readily as in the words of the New Testament.

---

177. PG 81:631-632; Hill 2006, I:97.
178. At 1:6 Theodoret says that Jeremiah imitates Moses' piety in protesting the office of prophet on grounds of immaturity; PG 81:500; Hill 2006, I:23. Continuing chapter one's comment, Theodoret again holds up the situation surrounding the call of Moses as prototypical of Jeremiah's. He compares the Lord's promise to accompany Moses in the face of Pharaoh to the Lord's response to be with and deliver Jeremiah (1:8).

3. Medieval Biblical Interpretation of True and False Prophecy

Introduction

Study of the Bible dominated the life and thought of the Christian Church through the medieval period. From the Venerable Bede (c. 673–735) through the humanism of Erasmus at the dawn of the Reformation, exegesis and interpretation were perpetuated both in monastic life and in the various schools. A hallmark of this period's biblical interpretation was a focus on the spiritual sense, that is, the hidden or deeper meaning contained within the human words of Scripture. Following Jerome, Bede refers to the 'outer rind' of scripture, its human words, and the inner 'pith,' the divine message hidden within.[1] Schematizing this approach to interpreting scriptures, Bede, following Augustine and Cassian, speaks of a fourfold way (*quadriformi ratione*) of deriving meaning from the text: "The word of the heavenly oracle can be received in either an historical, or allegorical, a tropological (that is, moral), or even an anagogical sense."[2] While this method was widely applied to the narratives of the Old Testament and to the Song of Solomon, interpretation of the prophets continued to rely on Jerome via the *Glossa Ordinaria*.[3]

Naturally, prophecy received its fair share of attention elsewhere. The prophetic theology of monastic mysticism, a rebound of sorts from the church's withdrawal away from prophecy in light of Montanism's debacle centuries before, flourished. St. Benedict is recorded as having the gift of prophecy, once even 'seeing' a drowning monk and sending for his rescue. St. Dominic, who would later exert considerable influence on Thomas Aquinas, characterized the

---

1. Bede's commentary on 1 Samuel, *In Primam Partem Samuhelis Libri IIII*, ed. D. Hurst CCSL 119A (Turnholt: Brepols, 1969), 237. Jerome's *Epistle* 53 to Paulinus, in which, writing of Old Testament figures, he says of them, "These references convey one meaning upon the surface, but another below it," *NPNF*, 6: 101; Bonaventure employed similar language. Cf. Bernard P. Robinson, "The Venerable Bede as Exegete," *DRev*, 112 (388): 201-26.
2. "verba cailestis oraculi vel historico intellectu vel allegorico vel tropologico, id est morali, vel certe anagogico solent accipi," in Bede, *De Tabernaculo et Vasis eius ac Vestibus Sacerdotum*, CCSL 119A: 24-5.
3. In Bede's sole comment on the prophets, a letter to Bishop Acca, (PL 94:202-10), Bede's apocalypticism (ingredient to medieval mysticism) can be seen in his reading of Is 24:22 as foretelling both the coming final judgment of the world and the individual's personal judgment at death; cf., George H. Brown, *A Companion to Bede* (Woodbridge: Boydell Press, 2009), 55.

inception of the Dominican order with the terms "mysticism and prophecy."[4] Rupert von Deutz (c.1075-1129), a Benedictine abbot, claimed a prophetic 'call' and commission early in life—comparable to that of the canonical prophets—in which he was enabled to 'see' enlightened truths of Holy Scripture.[5] Hildegard of Bingen (1098-1179), again a Benedictine abbess of the twelfth century, claimed not only to have received divine insight as to the interpretation of Scripture, but also the prophetic charism whereby she might utter apocalyptic prophecies.[6] I mention these facets of prophecy at the outset of this chapter by way of drawing into relief the scarcity of focused attention of biblical appropriations of true and false prophecy in scriptural commentaries.[7] Turning to the main streams of Jeremian exegesis, we will first observe the primacy of the *Glossa Ordinaria* and then look at the use of Jeremiah by the most formidable theological voice of the period, Aquinas.

Glossa Ordinaria

Often reaching the modern interpreter in abbreviated quotes and anonymous fragments, the *Glossa Ordinaria* (GO) has served to facilitate the survival of much of the biblical exegesis prior to the eleventh and twelfth-centuries.[8] Gib-

---

4. Cited in Hvidt, *Christian Prophecy*, 95.
5. Young, "Mission and Message," 19-22; Hivdt, 95f.
6. For an extensive litany of women situated within the mystic/prophetic stream of the late medieval period, see Hvidt, *Christian Prophecy,* 99-100.
7. I direct the reader toward Hvidt and Young, as well as numerous others, who have excellently chronicled this side of medieval spirituality. Cf. also Bernard McGinn, "Trumpets of the Mysteries of God': Prophetesses in Late Medieval Christianity," pages 125-42 in *Propheten und Prophezeiungen/Prophets and Prophecies*, edited by T. Schabert and M. Riedl (Würzburg: Königshausen und Neumann, 2005); and Richard Woods, *Mysticism and Prophecy: The Dominican Tradition*, (London: Darton, Longman and Todd, 1998).
8. The classic English treatment of the GO as representative of medieval biblical exegesis finds its font in Beryl Smalley, *The Study of the Bible in the Middle Ages* ([3d ed. (rev.)]; Oxford: Basil Blackwell, 1983), 46-66. Margaret Gibson and Karlfried Froehlich have contributed much to the study of the *GO* in recent years; Margaret T. Gibson, "The Twelfth—Century Glossed Bible," in *Studia Patristica 23,* 232-244 (ed. Elizabeth A. Livingston; Leuven: Peeters Press, 1989), "The Glossed Bible," in *Biblia Latina Cum Glossa Ordinaria: Facsimile Reprint of the Editio Princeps Adolph Rusch of Strassburg 1480/81,* VII-XI (Turnhout, 1992), "The Place of the *Glossa ordinaria* in Medieval Exegesis," in *Ad Litteram: Authoritative Texts and Their Medieval Readers,* 5-27 (ed. Mark D. Jordan *et al.*; Notre Dame Conference in Medieval Studies 3; Notre Dame, Ind: University of Notre Dame Press, 1992). Karlfried Froehlich, "The Printed Gloss," in *Biblia Latina Cum Glossa Ordinaria,* XII-XXVI (Turnhout, 1992). See also the helpful works of Gillian R. Evans, *The Language and Logic of the Bible: The Earlier Middle Ages* (Cambridge: Cambridge University Press, 1984), E. Ann Matter, "The Church Fathers

son has gone so far as to designate it as the *Wendepunkt* between the old exegesis of the fathers and the new exegesis of the schools.[9] Restricting our queries to its comments at Jer 23-29, we find the GO to be echoing—transmitting—much of the 'noteworthy' exegesis of the patristic era by way of the Carolingians.[10] In particular, Jerome emerges as the dominant voice revived and worked over[11] in the GO's treatment of the book of Jeremiah.[12] Briefly surveying the GO's comments on our passage, it is our intent to focus on those interpretations of Jerome that the GO included in an effort to demonstrate western exegesis' dependence upon an increasingly self-restrictive strain.

Perpetuated amongst the monastic and cathedral schools, the GO's interpretive choices were directed expositionally towards the life of the church as well as the blossoming scholastic conversations of the mid—Medieval period. In consolidating much of that noteworthy exegesis of previous generations, the GO served as a textbook for beginners pointing 'backwards.'[13] Noting that the GO was not intended to be read as a "normal" text — answerable to questions concerning authorship, date, etc. — Froehlich writes of the GO, "Rather it is the expression of a living tradition and, in this sense, no more than a textual tool."[14]

The GO's editorial history and numerous revisions demonstrate its vital role in both comprising and nourishing a living tradition of interpretation.[15] In 1617, the counter-reformers of the French abbey at Douai, led by Leander and Galemart, published a revision of the Parisian GO of 1590.[16] In the preface of this edition, which included a number of new interpretations of Jerome's prologues,

---

and the *Glossa Ordinaria*," in *The Reception of the Church Fathers in the West, Vol. 1,* 83-111 (ed. I. Backus; New York: Brill, 1997), and most recently Jenny Swanson, "The *Glossa Ordinaria*," in *The Medieval Theologians,* 156-167 (ed. G.R. Evans; Oxford: Blackwell Publishers Ltd, 2001).

9. Gibson, "The Place of the *Glossa ordinaria* in Medieval Exegesis," 5.

10. The text of the GO consulted is *Glossa Ordinaria: Prophetia Jeremiae*, PL 114, ed. J.-P. Migne (Paris: 1879). For the GO's refinement of patristic Jeremian commentary see Gibson, "The Glossed Bible," VII-IX. Matter, 88, notes that the far less fully glossed Deuteronomy draws primarily on the works of Augustine and Gregory/Paterius.

11. Matter, 101, concludes, "In the case of Jeremiah, it seems that the *Glossa Ordinaria* is quoting Hrabanus quoting Jerome." On the rewriting and expansion of Jerome at the hands of Rabanus and its subsequent assimilation by the GO, cf. Gibson, "The Twelfth—Century Glossed Bible," 237ff.

12. A. Andrée, Gilbertus Universalis: Glossa Ordinaria in Lamentationes Ieremie Prophete. Prothemata et Liber I. A Critical Edition with an Introduction and a Translation (Studia Latina Stockholmiensia; Stockholm: 2005), 7-8, who notes, "Without the commentary work of St Jerome, the Gloss would surely have been radically different" (8, n3).

13. Evans, *Language*, 47.

14. Froehlich, "The Printed Gloss," XXVI.

15. Cf. Froehlich's thorough survey in "The Printed Gloss," 1992.

16. On them: H. Hurter, *Nomenclator Literarius Recentis Theologiae Catholicae*, Tom. I (Innsbruck: 1892), 329ff., in Freohlich, "The Printed Gloss," XXIV, n107.

the editors cite the needs of contemporary apologetics and the numerous errors of the Parisian editions' apparatus as grounds for their revision. The goal for this revision was that it "may rightly be called a thesaurus for theologians and preachers."[17] The gloss was the voice by which the mouth of the church's commentators had spoken. And that they still demanded an audience is conveyed in the words of the Douai preface: "Many generations... thought of this collection of scriptural interpretations so highly that they called it the 'normal tongue' (*glossa ordinaria*), the very language (*lingua*) of Scripture, as it were. But when we read the sacred words without it, we think we hear a language which we do not know."[18]

With such practical intentionality in mind, it follows that the GO be insistent that any discussion concerning false prophets in Jer 23-29 finds a contemporary analog. Perhaps with the prevelant mystic prophetic theology gaining increasing ground among the monasteries and schools, an analog is readily evident at Jer 23:14 [13] as those "heretics in the *ecclesia*" that "speak by demons."[19] Among select elements of false prophecy treated by Jerome and subsequently picked up on by the GO we find falsehood's cloaking itself in a guise of truth;[20] Scripture's tendency to designate false prophets as *Nebi'im*;[21] the development of a wait-and-see criterion of truth;[22] and it should be observed that over half of Jerome's treatment of the 17 verses of chapter 28 in his commentary has been distilled to form the bulk of the GO's comments on Jer 28.[23] In the course of receiving Jerome's comments in précis, the editors of the GO appear to have brusquely selected those comments that would most succinctly portray and transmit the salient components of the Latin doctor's exegesis.

In highlighting the conspicuous overlap between the GO and Jerome, one might venture that the subject matter of those comments of Jerome, et al., which

---

17. Froehlich, "The Printed Gloss," XXV. The Douai edition was reprinted in Antwerp in 1634, and remained the standard for over 2 centuries until the publication of the much-critiqued Migne editions from Paris began in 1852. On the (numerous) faults of the Migne, cf. Froehlich, "The Printed Gloss," XXV-XXVI. Andrée, *Gilbertus Universalis*, 7ff., argues that theologians of all calibers availed themselves to the GO as the standard reference tool. See Joshua Moon, *Jeremiah's New Covenant: An Augustinian Reading*. JTI Supplement 2, (Winona Lake: Eisenbrauns, 2011), 35n18.
18. Froehlich, "The Printed Gloss," XXVI.
19. GO on Jer 23:13 [cited as 23:14]: ...sic haeretici in Ecclesia...loquuntur in daemonibus. PL 114, Col. 0038D; Jerome, CCSL 74:220 (at 23:13).
20. Jer 23:20: Semper enim mendacium imitatur veritatem, aliter enim non potest decipere. PL 114, Col. 0039B; cf. Jerome, CCSL 74:273.
21. Jer 27:14: Notandum [/observandum] in Scripturis sanctis pseudoprophetas vocari [/appellat] prophetas... PL 114, Col. 0042C; Jerome CCSL 74:266.
22. Jer 27:18: occurrant, et quae praedicunt opere completa demonstrent, et tunc veritate vaticinium probabitur. PL 114; Jerome, CCSL 74:271.
23. Of the 17 verses of Jer 28 commented upon by Jerome, vv. 2, 5, 8, 9, 11, and 12 are not treated by the GO.

were omitted or drastically altered were coming to be viewed as nonessential or superfluous. For example, the GO does not bracket the prophetic laws of Deuteronomy 13 or 18 together with its discussion of false prophets.[24] The closest the GO comes is at Jer 27:18, where we read that only upon the actual occurrence of the prophesied event or outcome, "will the prophecy then be approved of by the truth."[25] This does not appear, however, to be the case in subsequent interpretations of the prophets prior to the Enlightenment. Below we will see Aquinas relying on Deuteronomy—if only slightly more prepensely than Jerome—in order to shed light on this question. Suffice it to say that for periods of interpretation there have always been select readings of texts that have found purchase more readily than others. For those involved in the collaboration of the GO, the presence of the explicit intertextual couplings sought by an Aquinas or to a greater extent, Calvin, did not determine the success or failure of an interpretation of Jeremiah. As evidenced by the applicative nature of the above remarks at Jer 23:14 and the historical reconstruction of the development of the GO,[26] the biblical GO was didactic. It could not wholly reproduce the tradition. Rather, by handing on select commentary, the GO served both to shape and to locate current interpretation by exposing the exegesis of the day to the tradition's time—honored readings of Scripture.

St. Thomas Aquinas (*c.* 1225-1274)

Baglow, following Torrell, has noted a unique, singular development in Thomas' approach to biblical prophecy.[27] Whereas much biblical prophecy had primarily been understood to be dealing exclusively with the foreknowledge of events to come, Thomas, in the vein of his teacher Albert the Great, would seek to develop another, less-rigid take on prophecy, grounding his understanding of it on revealed knowledge.[28] Noting that prophecy necessarily deals with matters

---

24. To be fair, Jerome does not cite Deut 13 or 18 in his running comment at Jer 28:7-9 either, but he does refer to Moses; Hoc idem et dominus locutus est per Mose, CCSL 74:271.
25. Occurrant, et quae praedicunt opere completa demonstrent, et tunc veritate vaticinium probabitur. PL 114, Col. 0042D; cf. Jerome, CCSL 74:268-269.
26. Cf. Smalley, 1952, 51f.
27. Christopher T. Baglow, "Modus et forma": A New Approach to the Exegesis of Saint Thomas Aquinas with an Application to the Lectura super Epistolam ad Ephesios (Rome: Pontificio Istituto biblico, 2002), esp. 29-36. J.-P. Torrell, "Le traité de la prophétie de s. Thomas d' Aquin et la théologie de la révélation," in La doctrine de la révélation divine de saint Thomas d' Aquin. Actes du Symposium sur la pensée de saint Thomas d' Aquin tenu à Rolduc, les 4 et 5 Novembre 1989, ed. Leo Elders, (Città del Vaticano: Libreria Editrice Vaticana, 1990), 173f.
28. Baglow notes Thomas' version of Cassiodorus' original formulation of the long-held predictive definition of prophecy, which Peter Lombard would subsequently champion into the medieval period: "a divine inspiration or revelation which proclaims the outcome

of salvation,[29] Thomas understands the content of prophecy to contain such matters or events, "whether they are past, or future, or even eternal."[30] Synave and Benoit, in their comprehensive study of Thomas on prophecy, *Prophecy and Inspiration*, explain the etymological reason for this.[31] Thomas follows Isidore of Seville in understanding the first part of the term prophet, *pro—*, either preferentially, that is, with "instead of," "in the place of," or "in exchange of;" or temporally, the idea being "before" with regard to time.[32] For Thomas prophets were primarily interpreters of God. The implications for such a shift in the understanding of prophecy, and, by extension, the role of biblical prophets, have the capacity to be far-reaching. In his discussion on the prophet's *habilitas*[33] Thomas suggests, "[a] prophets ability is sharpened by the prophetic light, even if he does not have the liberty to decide when he exercises that ability."[34] Baglow extrapolates the impact of such an effect of the prophetic *habilitas*: "It is clear that prophecy understood as the seeing of future events has receded into the background—Thomas is referring primarily to judgment."[35] The prophet's reception of divine light—enabled by the presence of the prophetic *habilitas*—along with the prophet's knowledge of what presently is as opposed to what may come to pass, allows the prophet to excavate the true meaning of his surrounding events. This 'insight' then enables the prophet to convey an accurate message that would, if heeded, at best minimize, at worst prepare the people for, impending divine judgment.[36] Thomas looks to the prophet Jeremiah's authority as proof that prophetic certitude entails clear knowledge that God is the revealing

---

of events with unspeakable truth," Thomas Aquinas, *Summa Theologiae* 5 vols. (Ottawa: Studii Generalis, 1949), II-II. 171.3. Cf. Cassiodorus, *Exposition on Psalms*, Prol., CCSL 97:7.

29. Thomas cites Augustine (*De Genesi ad litteram*, II:9) and the GO in defense of this in his *Quaestiones de veritate* Sancti Thomae de Aquino opera omnia iussu Leonis XIII P.M. edita, Tom. XXII (Rome: Romae ad Sanctae Sabinae, 1970—1976), 12.2; ET: *Truth*, trans. Robert W. Mulligan, James V. McGlynn, and Robert W. Schmidt, Library of Living Catholic Thought, 3 vols. (Chicago: Regnery, 1952-54).

30. *De Veritate*, 12.2.

[31] Paul Synave and Pierre Benoit, Prophecy and inspiration: A Commentary on the Summa Theologica II-II, questions 171-178 (New York: Desclee Co, 1961), 16f. Cf. Van den Oudenrijn, De Prophetiae chraismate in populo isrealitico (Rome: 1926), 4f.

[32] Synave and Benoit, 16.

33. *ST* II-II. 171.2.; *De Ver.*, 12.7. Cf. Christoph Berchtold, *Manifestatio Veritatis: zum Offenbarungsbegriff bei Thomas von Aquin* (Dogma und Geschichte; Bd. 1; Münster: Lit, 2000), 93-95.

34. Baglow, *"Modus et forma,"* 34.

35. Ibid., 34.

36. Cf. Per Erik Persson, *Sacra Doctrina: Reason and Revelation in Aquinas*, trans. Ross Mackenzie, (Oxford: Blackwell, 1970), esp. 20ff.

agent at work in the prophet.[37] True prophets, Thomas concedes, may at times be uncertain of his message's divine origin; personal lack of surety was part of the job. However, a true prophet was able to intellectually delineate what was revealed and what were his own thoughts. In the case of Jonah, for example, we see a true prophet internally conflicted on account of his mission to deliver a message he considered futile. This ambiguity was inherent in the mechanisms of prophetic inspiration.[38]

Synave and Benoit note that for Thomas, the prophets' morality does not *to a degree,* constitute the prophets' authenticity. Thomas writes,

> Some of the sins by which charity is lost hinder the use of prophecy, and some do not... Sins of the flesh draw the mind entirely away from things spiritual... but sins of the spirit do not to the same extent interfere with the mind's spirituality. Therefore, it happens that one who is subject to sins of the spirit, but not to those of the flesh, or even to the endless cares of life... can be a prophet. And, therefore, Rabbi Moses says that the entanglement in the pleasure and cares of this world is a sign that one is a false prophet.[39]

In light of Jer 23:14 and 29:23, Thomas saw Jeremiah's indictment of the wickedness of his prophetic opponents as evidence of their falsehood.

Stump, and more recently Healy, date Thomas' commentary on Jeremiah, *In Jeremiam prophetam expositio,*[40] along with his work on Lamentations, *Post. super Threnos,* to roughly the same period as his commentary on Isaiah, circa 1251.[41] This is between the dates held by Tugwell[42] and Weisheipl.[43] This places the commentary near the outset of Thomas' exegetical career. The object of little scrutiny, Thomas' commentary on Jeremiah remains largely ignored. Stump explains that this is due to its lack of sophisticated philosophical and theological content. This critique has been leveled on a larger scale towards the majority of Thomas' exegetical works, the exceptions being Job, Ephesians, and Romans.[44]

---

37. *ST* 171 *a.* 5 *c*, in Benoit and Synave, 23-24. The second and third proofs include our present faith and Abraham's obedience.
38. *De Veritate,* 12.10.
39. *De Veritate,* 12.a5; cited in Synave and Benoit, 29.
40. St Thomas Aquinas, *In Jeremiam prophetam expositio* (Opera Omnia, vol. 14; Parma: 1863).
41. Eleonore Stump, "Biblical Commentary and Philosophy," in *The Cambridge Companion to Aquinas,* ed. Norman Kretzmann and Eleonore Stump (Cambridge: Cambridge University Press, 1993), 253; Nicholas M. Healy, "Introduction," in *Aquinas on Scripture: An Introduction to his Biblical Commentaries,* ed. Thomas G. Weinandy, Daniel A. Keating, and John Yocum (London: T & T Clark International, 2005), 10-11.
42. Simon Tugwell, *Albert and Thomas: Selected Writings* (New York: Paulist Press, 1988), 211.
43. James A. Weisheipl, *Friar Thomas D'Aquino* (Washington, D.C.: Catholic University of America Press, 1983), dates the commentary to the period in which Aquinas studied under Albert at Cologne.
44. For a thorough objection to this strain of critique see Baglow, 53-88.

As briefly exhibited in the section on the GO above, Jerome's comments on the book of Jeremiah have witnessed the greatest shelf-life among those writing commentary in service of the western Christian church over the course of its first millennia. Jerome's commentary exists as that exegetical work on Jeremiah still finding a hearing well into the high medieval period.[45] Thomas' commentary is, as expected, at many points heavily reliant upon Jerome's. Thomas does not deviate from Jerome's historical findings. In fact, at places we find him following Jerome explicitly, much in the fashion of the GO. At Jer 25:25-26, Thomas discusses at some length the cryptogram שֵׁשַׁךְ (*Sheshach*) employed for בָּבֶל (*Babel*/*Babylon*). Thomas is here summarizing Jerome's laborious excurses on the use of this and other linguistic novelties in the education of children in the Hebrew language.[46] In his comments on Jer 28:10-11, Thomas, like Jerome, places the psalmist's humble utterances in the mouth of the prophet Jeremiah (Ps 38:15 [37:14], "I am like one who does not hear, and in whose mouth is no retort").[47] So, in both instances we see Thomas relying on Jerome's historical and intertextual work, albeit without explicitly notifying the reader of this dependence. Of the ten references to the GO in Thomas' *In Jeremiam*, three refer to it as the conduit of Jerome's exegesis.[48]

Thomas' discussions concerning Jeremiah's interplay with Deuteronomy stand at the forefront of the places where his exegesis is markedly more developed and divergent than Jerome's.[49] Thomas sees the law (as yet a non-technical term in Thomas' Old Testament exegesis) providing a framework for the book and message of the prophet. In chapters 23-29, Thomas first addresses Deut 13

---

45. Largely a conduit for Jerome's interpretation, the commentary of Rabanus Maurus, *Expositionis supers Jeremiam prophetam, libri viginti*, PL 111, ed., J-P. Migne. (Paris, n.d), deserves mention as well. Rabanus' comments on Jer 23-29, and particularly 28, follow closely those of Jerome.
46. Aquinas, *In Jeremiam*, cap. 25, 1.3; Jerome, *In Heremiam*, CCSL 74:245f. However, Thomas makes no mention of Jerome's interpretation of *why* this linguistic tool was employed. Jerome saw Jeremiah coding his language so as not to offend the Babylonians who were presently occupying Judah; Graves, 179.
47. Aquinas, *In Jeremiam*, cap. 28, 1.4; Jerome, *In Heremiam*, CCSL 74:272. Jerome interestingly does not refer explicitly to Ps 38 [37] or a psalmist. However, he understands Jeremiah to be borrowing the words of another prophet.
48. Once in Thomas' comment at Jer 18:7ff. (cap. 18, 1.2) and twice in his comment on Jer 31 (cap. 31, 1.12).
49. Thomas references the book of Deuteronomy no less than fifty times in *In Jeremiam*, six of which occur within chapters 23-29, two concern Deut 13 and two 18. Clearly Thomas saw the prophet's reliance on the law as integral to a responsible reading of Jeremiah. Thomas is not flexing many metaphysical or philosophical 'muscles' here in this rather straightforward interpretation of Jeremiah, an observation that would at first blush lend substance to Stump's thinly veiled critique of *In Jeremiam* (253). However, Thomas' use and vision of the role Deuteronomy played in the formation of the prophetic witness of Jeremiah must not be dismissed as simplistic.

at his discussion on Jer 23:15-16.[50] Concerning Jeremiah's opening prohibition for the people not to follow those prophets "who prophesy to you; they are deluding you," Thomas employs Deut 13. Thomas sees Jeremiah maintaining that the prophets whom the people have been obeying and listening to have been shown to be false.[51] These prophets' messages of peace are such that Thomas allows the prophetic laws of Deut 13, which prohibit following any gods esteemed by such prophets, to bolster Jeremiah's indictment against the false prophets in view. Their message of peace constitutes idolatry. Therefore, Thomas sees Deut 13:3, "you must not heed the words of those prophets or those who divine by dreams," as logically informing and lending weight to Jer 23:16, "Do not listen to the words of the prophets who prophesy to you."

The point in his commentary at which Thomas most readily utilizes the restrictive laws of Deut 13 and 18 is at his reading of Jeremiah's initial response to Hananiah at Jer 28:5-9. Upon hearing Hananiah's prophecy of glad tidings for the inhabitants of Jerusalem, Thomas sees two points of note in Jeremiah's response. First, Thomas, like Jerome before him, understands Jeremiah to be desirous of the peace Hananiah foresees, yet constrained by his prophetic insight (*habitus*) in knowing otherwise. Thomas places the words of Micah 2:11 (Vg.) in the mouth of Jeremiah, denoting his awareness that Jeremiah's "Amen, may the Lord do so," is to be understood conditionally.[52] To the degree that he was alerting the reader to the fact that Jeremiah's view of the Lord's will (*voluntatem divinae*) was not wholly static—namely, that Jeremiah was not merely privy to a 'script' of upcoming events—Thomas' interpretation of prophecy is innovative. I believe this is firmly linked to his use of Deut 13 and 18 in his interpretation of Jeremiah's reply to Hananiah. Both are brought to bear on Jer 23:5-9 as constitutive of criteria. Thomas sees Jeremiah being required to employ reason and his

---

50. Our treatment of Jer 23-29, and particularly chapters 27-29, finds warrant in Thomas' own exposition. Thomas' bracketing of our pericope can be seen first at chapter 27. Thomas understands Jer 27 as having drawn the lie of the false prophets into sharp relief when contrasted with the truth as illustrated in 28: Hic praemisso claro titulo, excludit falsas consolationes prophetarum: et primo in generali; secundo descendendo ad quosdam speciales prophetas, *cap. 28*, (*In Jeremiam*, cap. 27, 1.1). Then, in the first *lectio* of chapter 28, Thomas intends 28 and 29 to be read together: Hic descendit specialiter ad quosdam falsos prophetas: et primo ad quemdam qui praedicebat relictis in Jerusalem; secundo ad quosdam qui prophetabant captivis in Babylonia, cap. 29, (*In Jeremiam*, cap. 28, 1.1). Chapter 28 deals with false prophets that had remained in Jerusalem and 29 with those in captivity in Babylon.

51. Primo ponitur prohibitio ad populum, ne tales pseudoprophetas audiant, eis obediendo et credendo: nolite audire. Aquinas, *In Jeremiam*, cap. 23, 1.6.

52. Nec obstat quod sciebat dominum contrarium velle, quia haec optatio sub conditione intelligenda est, scilicet si Deus vellet, et quia in hoc suam voluntatem divinae conformat quod vult quod Deus esse vult. Aquinas, *In Jeremiam*, cap. 28, 1.2. In *De Veritate* (12.I.) locating the gift of prophecy, and implicitly the prophet's response, as originating solely in the will of the Lord, he writes, "prophecy depends on the divine will alone."

intellect in discerning the false prophet and Deuteronomy provides Jeremiah the authoritative source for doing so. After seemingly agreeing with Hananiah's prophecy Thomas sees Jeremiah qualifying his remark: "Lest [Jeremiah] appear to consent to falsehood, he proposes a sign of proof: *But listen now* [Jer 28:6]. And Deut 18 is the sign selected: *If a prophet speaks in the name of the Lord, but it does not come about, the Lord has not spoken it.*"[53] While Deut 18's prophetic laws would come to be understood more as protection for the people rather than criteria to measure the validity of a true prophet, Thomas employs it unhesitatingly in the service of the latter. Deut 18 proves the truth of Jeremiah for Thomas. Earlier, at 23:19, Thomas says as much when commenting on the "storm of the Lord" that will "burst upon the head of the wicked." Citing Isa 55:11's promise that no word from the Lord returns unanswered, Thomas sees Jeremiah drawing upon a rich prophetic lineage marked by a message of judgment that has and will at all times come about. The "wicked" of 23:19 are the very people to whom the false prophets have been catering, offering messages of hope and peace. Thomas understands Jeremiah here to be indicting those prophets on the grounds of a wait-and-see criterion as found in Deut 18:22. The mere *delivery* of any message other than judgment—its failure to occur notwithstanding—proved the falsity of such an oracle, rendering the deliverer guilty of lying. In light of this, Thomas succinctly writes, "It is thus clear that they are not good prophets."[54]

Interestingly, in a brief comment on Uriah, son of Shemaiah, at Jer 26:20, Thomas links the message delivered by the prophet with a historically 'standardized' prophetic message. Thomas writes, "Here the repression of the fury of the people towards Jeremiah is presented, by means of the words of the ancients."[55] Believing 1 Cor 14:33, "God is a God not of disorder but of peace," to be witness to the reasonableness of Jeremiah's prophecy as it comports to Uriah's own message of judgment, Thomas appears again to be interjecting Jeremiah's message into a prophetic trajectory characterized by at least a stiff message of warning.[56] That those prophets delivering such messages met with various outcomes—Micah of Moresheth (Jer 26:18-20) invoked a tempered repentance from Hezekiah and presumably lived while Uriah (Jer 26:20-23) was hunted down in Egypt, returned to Jerusalem, and slaughtered—little concerns Thomas at this point in his comment. What does figure prominently in his interpretation is Jeremiah's deliverance (and by default, authenticity) on account of his accordance with the classical prophetic tack.

---

53. Secundo ne videatur falsitati consentire, proponit veritatis signum: verumtamen audi. Et sumitur hoc signum Deut. 18: 'quod in nomine domini propheta ille praedixerit, et non evenerit, hoc dominus non est locutus.' Aquinas, *In Jeremiam*, cap. 28, 1.2.
54. unde constat eos non esse bonos prophetas, Aquinas, *In Jeremiam*, cap. 23, 1.6.
55. Hic ponitur repressio furoris populi contra Jeremiam, per verba seniorum, Aquinas, *In Jeremiam,* cap. 26, 1.5.
56. Aquinas, *In Jeremiam*, cap. 26, 1.5.

Returning to our survey of Thomas' comments on Jer 28:5-9 and the intertextual affinity he sees at work there with the book of Deuteronomy, Deut 13's negative regulations come into play directly on the heels of the preceding discussion of Deut 18. Immediately after showing that those prophesied events that did *not* occur, were not, in fact, of the Lord, Thomas turns his attention to the false prophets' (i.e., Hananiah's) self-damning reversed dialectic. Claiming to know with certainty that within two years the temple vessels, Jeconiah, and all those exiled with him would return, Hananiah leaves himself open to Deut 13's critique. According to Thomas, Jeremiah is cognizant of the poor logic of the false prophets and this informs his reply at 28:5-9. Thomas notes that prophets such as Hananiah, who were promising peace and restoration, were effectively arguing in reverse. Thomas writes, "However, [false prophets] appear to argue from the contrary sense: and that appears to be un-salutary, because it would be the destruction of that which has preceded (*antecedentis*)."[57] The false prophets are opposing Jeremiah's message of judgment with prophecies of peace that had heretofore yet to materialize. Thomas claims this is their undoing: "One finds the opposite in Deut 13... And it should be said that this argument [Deut 13] is effective to reveal the falsehood of them [false prophets]; and that he himself [Jeremiah] had intended this."[58] While Deut 18 evinced the truth of the prophet, Deut 13 exposed false prophets as counterfeit. Thomas concludes with the exhibition of the fulfillment of Jeremiah's prediction of Hananiah's death at 28:16. Referencing 1 Thess 5:3, "When they say, 'There is peace and security,' then sudden destruction will come upon them," Thomas ends his discussion by pointing the reader to the fact that scripture records both that Jeremiah predicted Hananiah's demise and that he, in fact, died. Thomas reads chapter 28 as if Deuteronomy's laws concerning prophets were known to Jeremiah. In Thomas' estimation, a prophet in sixth century Judah was bound by and compelled to function within those parameters laid out in the law.

In his discussion on prophecy's cessation, Thomas identifies two criteria with which the church at present may distinguish true and false revelations, noting that the charism of prophecy did not cease with John or the close of the Apostolic Age.[59] Both are linked to the Church. The first dictates that when a prophet's message deals with the public life of the institutional Church, they are not to be heeded unless they convincingly perform miraculous signs or produce "incontrovertible scriptural proofs."[60] The second concerns a message concern-

---

57. Sed ipse videtur a contrario sensu arguere: et videtur quod non valeat, quia est destructio antecedentis. Aquinas, *In Jeremiam,* cap. 28, 1.2.
58. et propterea contrarium habetur Deut. 13...Et dicendum, quod argumentum efficax est ad ostendendum ejus falsitatem; et hoc ipse intendit. Aquinas, *In Jeremiam,* cap. 28, 1. 2.
59. *ST*, 174, *a.* 6; cited in Synave and Benoit, 46-47.
60. A positive case cited by Synave and Benoit is the recognition of the Sacred Heart of St Margaret Mary, 47.

ing the behavior of individuals or groups. Simply, if it is at variance with any doctrine of the Church, it is to be ignored; conversely, if it is in broad agreement, adherence to it is left to the discretion of its intended hearers. For Thomas, the Church becomes the final arbiter, since its posterity is proof that its laws are approved by God and not to be ignored in favor of innovators.[61]

Summary

Long before critics unanimously heralded Jeremiah's dependence upon a deuteronomistic redactor shaping the book of Jeremiah, Jerome, Theodoret, the GO, and Thomas freely borrowed from and clearly saw a direct linkage between the two. That their leaning on Deuteronomy was at times too influential upon their interpretation of Jeremiah—the book and the prophet—is not under consideration. The (inter-) dependence of these books has been shown to be sure and yet immensely complex. All the facets of this relationship have yet to be identified, let alone exhaustively defined. Nostalgic glances back to a simpler period of exegesis are unproductive and often little rewarding. We are not suggesting such here. However, in the case of the interpreters we have treated thus far we are not prepared to declare our findings bankrupt or inconsequential.

The Christian tradition has, in all times and places, struggled to appropriate their writings as scripture. In his preface to *The Struggle to Understand Isaiah as Christian Scripture*, Brevard Childs asks, "Has the church been able to learn…from its misuse of Scripture?"[62] The question could also be inverted: Has the church learned from its *proper* use of Scripture? The findings of the eighteenth and nineteenth-centuries' historical-critical examination of the prophets were being prepared for throughout the span of the Christian church's interpretive history. The historical acumen of Jerome; the ambitious figuration of Theodoret of Cyrus; the GO's distillation of vast stretches of the church's exegetical past into useful running commentary; and Thomas' innovative advancements in the church's explication of scripture's prophetic content have been shown to be ingredient to the church's reading of false prophets in the OT. With a backdrop now in place we turn in our study to Calvin's reading of Jer 23-29 amidst select reformers. In the following chapter we will focus both on Calvin's congruity with those preceding him and points at which he departed from readings that had become entrenched and stale.

---

61. Ibid.
62. Childs, *Struggle*, x.

4. JOHN CALVIN AMIDST THE REFORMERS[1]

John Calvin (1509-1564)

On 15 April 1560, Calvin began the lectures on the book of Jeremiah that would be published in the form of a commentary.[2] Lecturing three times per alternating week, Calvin worked his way through the entire book of Jeremiah in just over two years.[3] The last of his commentaries on OT prophets, save the first twenty chapters of Ezekiel, *Jeremiah and Lamentations* was dedicated to Prince Freder-

---

1. An earlier edition of this chapter appeared as "John Calvin and the Prophetic Curriculum in Jeremiah," *Churchman* 123 (2009): 29-52.
2. See Peter Wilcox, "The Lectures of John Calvin and the Nature of his Audience, 1555-1564," *ARG* 87 (1996): 139f., and Wilcox, "Calvin as Commentator on the Prophets," in *Calvin and the Bible,* ed. Donald K. McKim, (Cambridge: Cambridge University Press, 2006), 111. For a useful chronology, see Erik A. de Boer, *John Calvin On The Visions Of Ezekiel: Historical and Hermeneutical Studies of John Calvin's sermons inédits, especially on Ezek. 36-48* Kerkhistorische Bijdragen, vol. 21, (Leiden: Brill, 2004), 3.
3. Colladon (*CO* XXI:93) reports that Calvin concluded Jeremiah on 9 September 1562. Taking two weeks off, Calvin began Lamentations on September 21 (cf. Wilcox, *Calvin and the Bible,* 111n22 concerning exact dating), only requiring a few months to finish it (Lamentations' lectures ended on Jan 19, 1563). On 20 January 1563, Calvin started his lectures on Ezekiel. He anticipated, due to his declining health, that this exposition would see completion at the hands of "a more competent commentator" (Wilcox, *Calvin and the Bible,* 111). He died before they were completed. Richard Stauffer, *Creator et rector mundi. Dieu, la creation et la providence dans l'œuvre homilétique de Calvin* (Lille: Atelier de reproduction des theses, 1978), reports Calvin as having preached twenty-five sermons on Jeremiah in 1549, beginning on Friday, 14 June through Friday, 16 August. A critical edition of these can be found in Rudulphe Peter, ed., *Sermons sur les Livres de Jérémie et des Lamentations,* Supplementa Calviniana; Sermons inédits, vol. VI (Neukirchen—Vluyn: Neukirchener Verlag des Erziehungsvereins, 1971). ET: John Calvin, *Sermons on Jeremiah,* trans. Blair Reynolds, Texts and Studies in Religion 46, (Lewiston: E. Mellen Press, 1990). The sermons run virtually verse-by-verse from Jer 14:19 to 18:23. Calvin himself put no pen to paper in the creation of his commentary on Jeremiah. As has been amply demonstrated, all of his commentaries on the Old Testament prophets except Isaiah were products of the collaboration of detailed transcripts of a corpus of secretary—scribes who attended his lectures at the Academy (the title page to the first edition of *Lectures on Jeremiah and Lamentations* reads, "*Ioannis Budaei et Caroli Jonvilaeo labore et industria exerptae*"), *CO* XXXVII: 13-14, and XL:23-24; cf. T. H. L. Parker, *Calvin's Old Testament Commentaries,* (Edinburgh: T&T Clark, 1986; reprint, Louisville: Westminster John Knox Press, 1993.), 26-28; David L. Puckett, *John Calvin's exegesis of the Old Testament,* (Louisville: Westminster John Knox Press, 1995), 147-51; and Wilcox, in *Calvin and the Bible,* 108-110.

ick III, Lord Palatine of the Rhine, on 23 July 1563.[4] Two points concerning the dedicatory letter are of note. First, a great deal of the dedication is taken up with a discussion and defense of an evangelical understanding of the nature of Christ and the sacrament of the Holy Supper.[5] Were the dedicatory letter written in the wake of the ecumenical Colloquy of Poissy (1561), the inclusion of the salient points concerning the body of Christ and the Holy Supper would not be unexpected. Second, toward the end of the letter Calvin makes mention of Frederick III's deception by François Bauduin.[6] Calvin relates the circumstances wherein Bauduin came into Frederick III's good graces. Under Frederick III, Bauduin was granted patronage and a professorship at the University of Heidelberg only to abandon it in 1561 when he left for France. There, siding with the enemy, he offered his services to Cardinal Charles van Lotharingen.[7] Up until this point, Bauduin is reported to have displayed a fickle allegiance to both Protestantism, namely Calvinism, and Catholicism. It is said that he moved between the two no less than seven times. Beza refers to him as the Changeling.

The dedicatory letter, like the commentary itself, displays Calvin's urgency to contend for what he deems worthy causes of truth. In light of the following commentary on Jeremiah, Calvin's dedication assumes a prophetic tone as he both encourages the faithful Frederick, urging him to persevere, and decries those unprincipled men who bark against true Religion and its defenders. The major players of the religio-political landscape of 1563 Reformation Europe appear to be ready-made examples of prophetic confrontation similar to those found in the book of Jeremiah. Noting Bauduin's clandestine consorts with the Cardinal, Calvin perhaps has in view those false prophets with whom Jeremiah—and by transference, Calvin—will concern himself in the subsequent commentary. Perhaps Bauduin and the Cardinal's secret treachery may assist in shedding light on Calvin's interpretation at Jer 23:30-32. Against Oecolampadius and others Calvin writes,

---

4. Wulfert de Greef, *The Writings of John Calvin: An Introductory Guide*, trans. Lyle D. Bierma, (Grand Rapids: Baker Books, 1993), 109.
5. Here too Calvin laments the fact that the pejorative moniker "Calvinism" has been applied to Prince Frederick III in an effort to brand the prince.
6. See the brief synopsis of this episode in Bernard Cottret, *Calvin: A Biography*, trans. M. Wallace McDonald, (Grand Rapids: Eerdmans, 2000), 248-50; cf. also de Greef, 207-208; a more complete treatment can be found in Mario Turchetti, *Concordia o tolleranza? F. Bauduin e i "Moyenneurs"* (Milan: F. Angeli, 1984) and "Religious Concord and Political Tolerance in Sixteenth— and Seventeenth-—Century France," *SCJ* 22 (1991): 17.
7. De Greef (207) notes that at this point his relationship with Calvin "came to a definite end." For a synopsis of Calvin, Beza, and Bauduin's correspondence, see Cornelis Augustijn, Christoph Burger, and Frans P. van Stam, "Calvin in the Light of the Early Letters," in *Calvinus Praeceptor Ecclesiae,* ed. Herman J. Selderhuis, DROZ 388 (Geneva: Librairie Droz S.A, 2004), 155-56.

Many explain this verse as though God condemned the false prophets, who borrowed something from the true prophets...I rather think that their secret arts are here pointed out, that they secretly and designedly conspired among themselves, and then that they spread abroad their own figments according to their usual manner.[8]

Beginning in the early twentieth–century, a proliferation of works emerged seeking to categorically outline Calvin's principles of interpretation. In fact, a cottage industry was birthed in which Calvin's exegetical methods have been re-tooled, re-arranged, or re-named.[9] The stomping grounds for such discussions have historically been Calvin's letter to Simon Grynaeus, which was attached to the first edition of Calvin's commentary on Romans.[10] Next is his *Latin Preface to Chrysostom*.[11] While the *Preface* has received less attention, it does reinforce what has been found elsewhere concerning Calvin's exegesis, as Thompson has recently shown.[12] The secondary literature has primarily revolved around two emphases: the extent to which Calvin can be seen to be doing something markedly different from his predecessors, particularly the schoolmen, and the bearing Calvin's theological presuppositions (hermeneutics) have had upon his exegesis, focusing particularly upon his commentaries.

Another fairly common entry point into Calvin's exegetical method has been to seek incongruity between what Calvin says and what he does; or, between his doctrine of Scripture as it is systematically worked out and his exegetical method. While the observation of inherent tensions can yield interesting results, ultimately the questions governing the modern critical enterprise overshadow and obstruct those operational in the time of the piece in question. In response to such programs it need be noted that genre and referentiality played a

---

8. John Calvin, *Commentaries on the Book of the Prophet Jeremiah and the Lamentations,* trans. John Owen, 5 vols. (Grand Rapids: Baker, 1979), 3:201.
9. For an exhaustive bibliography see the notes to the recent work of R. Ward Holder, *John Calvin and the Grounding of Interpretation: Calvin's First Commentaries* (Leiden: Brill, 2006), 29-35, and Peter Opitz, "The Exegetical and Hermeneutical Work of John Oecolampadius, Huldrych Zwingli and John Calvin," in *Hebrew Bible/Old Testament; Volume II; From the Renaissance to the Enlightenment,* ed. Magne Sæbø, (Göttingen: Vandenhoeck & Ruprecht, 2008), esp. 428-29, 438-39.
10. On the nature of Calvin's relationship with Grynaeus see Augustijn, Burger, and van Stam, "Calvin in the Light of the Early Letters," 145-47.
11. The translated text of the *Preface* can be found in Ian P. Hazlett, "Calvin's Latin Preface to His Proposed French Edition of Chrysostom's Homilies," in *Humanism and Reform: The Church in Europe, England, and Scotland,* ed. James Kirk, (Oxford: Blackwell, 1991).
12. See John L. Thompson, "Calvin as a Biblical Interpreter," 63f., where he points out three additional interpretive insights found in the *Preface*: (1) Calvin's critical interaction with the fathers; (2) Calvin's dedication to serve the uneducated laity; and (3) Calvin's commitment to the 'literal/historical' sense of the text as evidenced by his choice of Chrysostom to emulate.

far less vital role than the prevalent late twentieth-century reconstructions of Calvin's exegetical model have usually led one to believe.

References to the Jeremiah commentary regarding Calvin's supposed principles of interpretation are sparse throughout the secondary literature. This is surprising considering his lectures filled over two tomes.[13] Our main concern in this study is not methodological in the first place.[14] That is to say, we will not proof-text Calvin's Jeremiah commentary for fodder that supports or refutes claims made regarding Calvin's exegetical method. However, we will be observing Calvin as he deals contextually with the question of false prophets. More directly, we will examine in detail Calvin's construal of true and false prophets in relation to the Law. This includes the assumption that the prophets referenced and intended to evoke pre-existent, known commands that had been and were ever before the people. This for Calvin is the well from which true prophecy draws.

For Calvin, God's contractual obligations as contained in the final four books of the Pentateuch are in view whenever he mentions the "law/Law" in his commentaries. Based on the re-arrangement of Exodus through Deuteronomy by subject matter grouped according to the ten headings of the Decalogue in his penultimate commentary proper, the *Mosaic Harmony*,[15] all the material contained therein constituted those covenantal duties God demanded of his people.[16] Calvin refers to this corpus as "the Law": "Moses in this passage [Deut 31:9] calls by the name of "the Law," not the Ten Commandments engraved on the two tables, but the interpretation of it contained in the four books."[17] As to when

---

13. *Ioannis Calvini opera quae supersunt omnia*, ed. Wilhelm Baum, Edward Cunitz, and Edward Reus. 59 vols., *Corpus reformatorum* 29-87 (Brunsvigae: Schwetschke [Bruhn], 1863-1900). His commentary on Jeremiah can be found at *Praelectioines in librum prophetiarum Ieremiae et Lamentationes, Ioannis Budaei et Caroli Ionuillaei labore et industria exceptae, CO* 37:469-39:646.
14. Zachman has demonstrated that such a study can be done, and rewardingly so, utilizing Jeremiah; cf., *Calvin as Teacher*, 109ff.
15. Mosis Libri v, cum Iohannis Caluini Commentariis. Genesis seorsum: reliqui quatuor in formam harmoniae digesti (Geneva: Henr. Stephanus, 1563). The French appeared the following year. Cf. DeGreef, 105f. We will use the English Commentaries on the Four Last Books of Moses, Arranged in the Form of a Harmony, trans. Charles W. Bingham, Calvin Theological Society, 4 vols. (Grand Rapids: Eerdmans, 1950) = CTS volume: page.
16. Parker, *Old Testament Commentaries*, 122. Parker's chapter on the Law in his *Old Testament Commentaries* remains a standard, extensively engaging with Calvin's *Harmony*. For a helpful bibliography of recent works on Calvin's Harmony, see Raymond A. Blacketer, "Calvin as Commentator on the Mosaic Harmony and Joshua," in *Calvin and the Bible*, ed. Donald K. McKim, (Cambridge: Cambridge University Press, 2006), 30n1.
17. *Mo. Harm.* on Deut. 31:9, CTS 2:231. Calvin understands the prophet/psalmist David to employ 'law' in the same way: "[U]nder the term law, he not only means the rule of living righteously, or the Ten Commandments, but he also comprehends the covenant by

it was given, Calvin sees a two-tiered transmission. First, he believes the law was initially given in the incubatory form of the Decalogue very soon after the Israelites' exodus from Egypt. "In order the better to remove all ambiguity, we must briefly calculate the time. In the third month from their exodus the people reached Mount Sinai. On what day the Law was given is nowhere stated, unless we may probably conjecture that it was promulgated about the end of that month."[18] Then, thirty0nine years after God had spoken from Mt Sinai, Moses (Dt 31:9) entrusted the Levites with the duty of expounding and teaching people according to the book of the law.[19]

Relying primarily upon the Jeremiah commentary for the remainder of our study, the prophets' self-understanding of and role in interpreting the law is evident throughout. In an effort to demonstrate this, we must first determine what law Calvin held to be normative for the prophet Jeremiah. Calvin understood Jeremiah to be using the term 'law' generally, that is, it was intended to encompass the covenant obligations demanded of the people by God.[20] Elsewhere he writes, "There were indeed in the law these two distinct things — doctrine, or a rule of life; and threatenings, which were added as stimulants to rouse the sloth of men, or rather to subdue their perverseness."[21] This was the authoritative law of Moses given to Israel's fathers. Calvin writes, "[Jeremiah] doubtless claims here authority for the law on the ground of time."[22] According to Jeremiah, through it the very authority of Moses, the archetypal prophet, was brought to bear on the people.[23] In God's demand that Jeremiah publically call the people

---

which God had distinguished that people from the rest of the world, and the whole doctrine of Moses, the parts of which he afterwards enumerates under the terms testimonies, statutes, and other names." *Comm. on Psalms* 19:7-9, CTS 1:318.

18. *Mo. Harm.* on Ex. 25:25; CTS 2:145.

19. "The circumstances took place thirty-nine years after God had spoken on Mount Sinai…the Book of the Law was given in trust, as it were, to the Levites, that the people might learn from them what was right." *Mo. Harm.* on Deut. 31:9, CTS 2:231.

20. "The word Law is general; and one of those which is special and often occurs in Scripture, is the statute." *Comm. on Jer.* 10:3, CTS 2:13. The term "covenant" is also used, but often in the context of threats: "He indeed mentioned before the words of the covenant for the commands of God; but now, on finding that he had to do with refractory men, who were not capable of receiving any doctrine, he comes to threatenings." *Comm on Jer.* 11:6-8, CTS 2:84; cf. *Comm. on Jer.* 34:18-19.

21. *Comm. on Jer.* 11:6-8, CTS 2:84.

22. *Comm. on Jer.* 17:22, CTS 2:382.

23. Calvin sees Jeremiah effectively saying, "I have taught nothing at variance with Moses; there has been nothing additional in my doctrine: but as I cannot convince you of this, I now give over speaking to you; Moses himself speaks, hear him." *Comm. on Jer.* 11:1-5, CTS 2:72-73. "Here the Prophet borrows his words from Moses, in order to secure authority to his prophecy; for the Jews were ashamed to reject Moses, as they believed that the Law came from God." *Comm. on Jer.* 24:9; CTS 3:235-36.

to return to the obedience of the law, even the textual form of Jeremiah's transmission of the law's precepts aligns with Moses'.[24]

The law given to the fathers was understood by Jeremiah as the "way."[25] The crime for which the prophets demanded repentance, then, was a deviation from this way.[26] Calvin ties this to the antiquity of the law, noting that the law's long-standing presence among the people should have had the opposite effect, namely shoring up their faith in God's law.[27] The people's exposure throughout Israel's history to the paths of ages rendered them all the more guilty, "for they had not only been taught, but had also been led as it were by the hand, so that the way of the law ought to have been well known by them."[28] Moses, in the law, had set before the people the "way of life" and the "way of death."[29] However, in the mouth of Jeremiah, the choice between life and death was no longer that of avoiding correction. Rather, it was whether the people would submit their neck to the yoke of bondage willingly, or rebelliously defend themselves.[30] For Calvin the law was foundationally normative due to its divine origin: "[T]herefore this principle ought to be maintained, that there is no right way but what God himself has pointed out. Had any one else come and boasted antiquity, the Prophet would have laughed to scorn such boasting."[31]

Throughout the book of Jeremiah Calvin notes those passages wherein some precept or particular duty is commanded of the people. Calvin sees Jeremiah, when referencing some facet of the law, as speaking, "according to what was commonly thought."[32] The prophet's references to such cultic practices as first-fruit offerings,[33] gleaning laws,[34] the prohibition of the construction of high places[35] or the offering of sacrifices to God near graves,[36] the observance of the Sabbath,[37] and the release of servants at the end of seven years[38] serve as grist

---

24. *Comm. on Jer.* 11:1-5, CTS 2:72-73.
25. "We hence see that, by the ways of his people, we are not to understand those glosses which the Jews had devised, but the law itself, which God had delivered to them." *Comm. on Jer.* 12:16, CTS 2:157.
26. *Comm. on Jer.* 18:14-15, CTS 2:411-412.
27. *Comm. on Jer.* 18:14-15, CTS 2:411-412.
28. *Comm. on Jer.* 18:14-15, CTS 2:411-412.
29. *Comm. on Jer.* 21:8-9, CTS 3:63.
30. *Comm. on Jer.* 21:8-9, CTS 3:62.
31. *Comm. on Jer.* 18:14-15, CTS 2:412. This leads to the question of whether a prophet can actually *add* to what is contained in the law, or rather if the law is to be understood as ever fresh. We will discuss this in more detail below.
32. *Comm. on Jer.* 5:4-5, CTS 1:265.
33. *Comm. on Jer.* 2:3, CTS 1:72-73.
34. *Comm. on Jer.* 6:9, CTS 1:325.
35. *Comm. on Jer.* 7:31, CTS 1:410-411.
36. *Comm. on Jer.* 7:32, CTS 1:415.
37. *Comm. on Jer.* 17:19-21, 22, CTS 2:377.
38. *Comm. on Jer.* 34:8-17, CTS 4:281-282.

for Calvin as he portrayed Jeremiah as an executor of this law. At other times, the law was used to frame the people's culpability more poignantly by drawing their sorry state into relief with the righteousness of the law. At Jer 7:21-24, Calvin asserts the Jews of Jeremiah's day, attentive merely to the rote, mechanical practice of animal sacrifice, had incurred God's anger due to their lack of faith. True, God had given the law and it did demand slaughter, but God had not commanded sacrifices for their own sake. His intent was and had always been, "to remind the Jews of their sin, and also to show to them the way of reconciliation."[39] In this way Calvin explains Jeremiah's puzzling statement at 7:22, "...I did not speak to your fathers or command them concerning burnt offerings and sacrifices." Calvin understood the law as a mirror in which the Israelites beheld their deserved judgment. Thus he credits Jeremiah with grasping the spiritual nature of the law, capping off this comment by noting that, once his, Calvin's, views on the law are taken into account, then the reader is able to "understand the meaning of the Prophet."[40]

Calvin has identified Jeremiah's prophetic task to be restorative, calling the people "back to the pure doctrine of the law, which the greater part were then treading under their feet."[41] When those initially entrusted with the keeping of the law—the priests[42]—were found derelict in their duty, "God raised up prophets in their place."[43] If those appointed by God would not fulfill their duty, God would make prophets of herdsmen.[44] The prophets were then called upon to tend the people with the rod of the law, interpreting and applying it in an accommodating manner[45] to their lives and times in obedience to the Divine will. They

---

39. *Comm. on Jer.* 7:21-24, CTS 1:393. Calvin says the same in his *Comm. on Ps* 50:8, CTS 2:267.
40. *Comm. on Jer.* 7:21-24, CTS 1:393.
41. *Comm. on Jer.* 1:1-3, CTS 1:31. In the context of the confrontation with Hananiah, Calvin writes, "Now Jeremiah had been furnished with a twofold message, to expose the vices of the people, to show that the Jews were unworthy to inherit the land, as they were covenant-breakers and despisers of God and of his Law; and then, as they had been so often refractory and perverse, he had another message, that they would not be suffered to escape unpunished, as they had in so many ways, and for so long a time continued to provoke God's wrath." *Comm. on Jer.* 28:5-6, CTS 3:391.
42. "As then [the priests] were the guardians of the Law and of knowledge, as they were messengers from God himself to the people, how was it that their stupidity was so monstrous, that they did not distinguish between truth and falsehood, but were led astray, together with the most ignorant, by what the false prophets delivered!" *Comm. on Jer.* 27:16, CTS 3:376.
43. *Comm. on Jer.* 32:32, CTS 4:194.
44. "As then they had neglected their office, it was necessary to choose other prophets... even of herdsmen, as in the case of Amos." *Comm. on Jer.* 29:24-27, CTS 3:454-55.
45. "And we know that the Spirit has not spoken in the Law and the Prophets with rigorous exactness, but in a style suited to the common capacities of men." *Comm. on Jer.* 10:12-13, CTS 1:35.

were God's "substitutes."[46] Bullinger, however, sees the prophetic office as springing up immediately upon Moses' transmission of the law to the people. There is no mention of the priests' abdication of their duties. He writes, "After that [Moses' reception and writing of the law], immediately followed the prophets, who, interpreting the law of Moses, did apply it to the time, places, and men of their age."[47]

Throughout his commentary Calvin, like Bullinger, stresses this explicative function of the prophetic office.[48] Jer 26:4-6 is an example of Calvin's coupling of the law with the prophets, distilling Jeremiah's message to the people. "If God's law was sufficient," asks Calvin, "why were the prophets to be heard?"[49] Noting what appear to be mutually exclusive means of direction and punishment, the law and prophets, Calvin attempts to fuse the two together. "The law alone was to be attended to, and also the prophets, for they were its interpreters."[50] Since the unalterable law was perfect from its inception, what exactly were the prophets to do? Calvin answers, "To make more manifest the law, and to apply it to the circumstances of the people."[51] What was not permissible was the invention or avocation of new or deviant doctrines. The law dictated what the prophets could and could not authoritatively preach.[52]

For Calvin, the law and prophets belong to one another. Calvin writes, "the Jews had been plainly taught by the Law and by the Prophets, God had contin-

---

46. *Mo. Harm.* on Deut. 18:21, CTS 1:448.
47. Henry Bullinger, *The Decades of Henry Bullinger* 5 vols. in 4 (Cambridge: Cambridge University Press, 1849—1852), 1:72. Bullinger goes on to register the product and value of the prophets' work: "and [they] left to us, that follow, their sermons as plain expositions of God's law."
48. *Comm. on Jer.* 3:13; 9:13-15; 24:9; 36:9-10; and 50:41. Perhaps nowhere else in Calvin's commentaries does he more clearly outline his understanding of the prophetic task than in the argument leading into his commentary on *Hosea*. "But with regard to the Prophets, this is true of them all, as we have sometimes said, that they are interpreters of the law. And this is the sum of the law, that God designs to rule by his own authority the people whom he has adopted. But the law has two parts,—a promise of salvation and eternal life, and a rule for a godly and holy living. To these is added a third part,—that men, not responding to their call, are to be restored to the fear of God by threatening and reproofs. The Prophets do further teach what the law has commanded respecting the true and pure worship of God, respecting love; in short, they instruct the people in a holy and godly life, and then offer to them the favor of the Lord. And as there is no hope of reconciliation with God except through a Mediator, they ever set forth the Messiah, whom the Lord had long before promised." *Comm. on Minor Prophets.* Hosea. Argument, CTS 1:36.
49. *Comm. on Jer.* 26:4-6, CTS 3: 314.
50. *Comm. on Jer.* 26:4-6, CTS 3:314.
51. *Comm. on Jer.* 26:4-6, CTS 3:314.
52. *Mo. Harm.* on Num. 12:6, CTS 4:47, where Calvin notes true prophets' assurance in themselves and their prophecies, based on their acknowledgment of their heavenly appointment as "God's lawful interpreters."

ued morning and evening to repeat the same things to them."[53] To reject one was to reject the other: "[E]very one who rejected the prophets must surely ascribe no authority to the Law,"[54] because "these two things well agree together."[55] In fact, God's commissioning of prophets who continually exhorted the people to repentance unto salvation condemns the people's rejection of the law all the more. "Even if prophets had not been sent, one after the other, the Law ought to have been sufficient."[56]

Before turning to Jeremiah's treatment of false prophets in Jeremiah, a look at Calvin's discussion of them in the *Harmony* is in order.[57] Then, returning to Jer 23-29, a more complete composite of Calvin's handling of the question will take shape. Explaining the signs of Moses and the magicians of Pharaoh's court at Ex 7:10, Calvin references Matt 24:24, noting that Jesus and the scriptures teach that false prophets shall be empowered by God to signs, while Satan takes the credit.[58] Referencing Deut 13:3, Calvin writes, "God elsewhere testifies that when He permits false prophets to deceive, it is to prove men's hearts."[59] Preferring a simple explanation for the magicians' turning the water to blood at Ex 7:22 over Augustine's subtle philosophizing,[60] Calvin believes that the deeds wrought by Pharaoh's sorcerers were most likely to be understood as illusions. Addressing the staff-turned-snake earlier, Calvin, like Bullinger, understands Moses and Aaron's signs to be real.[61] But, those of the magicians were illusory. Why else, Calvin asks, would Moses refer to them as "enchantments?"[62] Here we gain another insight into Calvin's understanding of the question. Relying on Paul (2 Thess 2:11), Calvin believes that the signs of the prophets along with the supposed actions of the false prophets were actually God's just vengeance enacted upon a people who, like Pharaoh, refused to believe the truth. While the

---

53. *Comm. on Jer.* 6:18-19, CTS 1:343; cf. *Comm. on Jer.* 19:14-15.
54. *Comm. on Jer.* 26:4-6, CTS 3:314. Cf. *Comm. on Jer.* 9:13-15; 19:14-15; and 22:9.
55. *Comm. on Jer.* 26:4-6, CTS 3:314.
56. *Comm. on Jer.* 44:20-23, CTS 4:552.
57. In his *Harmony* (CTS 1:438-49) Calvin treats Deut 18:21-22 immediately after commenting on Deut 13:1-3, seeing the two as comprising the prescriptive portion of the Law's teaching on true and false prophecy.
58. *Mo. Harm.* on Ex. 7:10, CTS 1:146.
59. *Mo. Harm.* on Ex. 7:12, CTS 1:149.
60. *Mo. Harm.* on Ex. 7:22, CTS 1:155-56.
61. *Mo. Harm.* on Ex. 7:8-13, CTS 145-46; Bullinger, *Decades*, 5:261-62. In a sermon on the sacraments, Bullinger uses Moses' rod and the turning of the Nile into blood, along with Jesus' miracle in Cana to argue for a Zwinglian view of the Lord's Supper. The Nile was really blood, not blood mixed with water; the snake was wholly snake, not part snake and part stick. Therefore, these signs "do nothing agree with the sacramental signs; but are so far from being like them, that they are altogether unlike them." On top of that, Bullinger quips, "Who knoweth what form also of words the Lord used, when he changed water into wine?"
62. *Mo. Harm.* on Ex. 7:22, CTS 1:155-56.

faithful observed the identical deeds of the magicians and their faith was no doubt shaken, Calvin is sure God "opened [His people's] eyes, so that they should regard with contempt the tricks and deceptions of the magicians."[63]

At his comments on Deut 13, Calvin expands his discussion of the testing nature of the false prophets' retributive role in the hands of the just God. On the surface, Deut 13's message is straight-forward: "God espoused His ancient people to Himself, and bade them close their ears against impostors, who are, as it were, the seducers of Satan tempting them to violate that sacred and special bond of marriage whereby God would be united with His people."[64] However, he warns it is not as simple as it appears, since there were those who accurately predicted future events, an ability belonging solely to God (Isa 45:27), and yet led the people astray.[65] Calvin concedes, then, that Deut 13 appears to cast doubt on the final discernment of a prophet's legitimacy based on their accurate predictions. True, unfulfilled prophecy is a sure sign of a prophet's falsity. Deut 18 is clear concerning this false-hood criterion. However, Calvin sees Deut 18 as problematic in its apparent utilization of such a litmus test in distinguishing between true and false. In response he writes, "Thus I resolve the difficulty, God's claiming to Himself the glory of foretelling events does not prevent Him from occasionally conferring even on the ministers of Satan the power of prophecy respecting some particular point."[66] Accurately predicted and fulfilled prophecies come from God alone. Calvin writes, "The principle, therefore, is established, that those speak in God's name who predict what really comes to pass; for they could not declare the truth respecting things unknown to man unless God Himself should dictate it to them."[67] As for those false prophets who predicted truly, Calvin is happy to consign them to the role of God's agents of judgment. These imposters are "the ministers of God's vengeance."[68] This naturally means the business of discernment is further muddled rather than simplified. Any attempt to read these passages in the hopes of finding an easy answer, some ready-made *criteria*, is misguided. In light of the propensity of humanity to be so easily misled, Calvin asks if it was fair for God to test as he did. Not surprisingly, he answers yes, since "all the good are sure to overcome."[69] Moses does not demand unmitigated credit and acceptance be automatically granted those prophets whose prophecies are fulfilled. Rather Calvin believes the litmus

---

63. *Mo. Harm.* on Ex. 7:22, CTS 1:155-56.
64. *Mo. Harm.* on Deut. 13:1, CTS 1:440.
65. *Mo. Harm.* on Deut. 13:1, CTS 1:441.
66. *Mo. Harm.* on Deut. 13:1, CTS 1:441.
67. *Mo. Harm.* on Deut. 13:1, CTS 1:442.
68. *Mo. Harm.* on Deut. 13:1, CTS 1:443. Elsewhere Calvin alludes to either Ezek 14:9 (so thinks the editor) or Jer 20:7 noting that false prophets are deceived by God so that "by them he may inflict just vengeance on the reprobate, who eagerly go in search of their destructive deceit." *Mo. Harm.* on Deut. 13:2, CTS 1:446.
69. *Mo. Harm.* on Deut. 13:2, CTS 1:446.

test of fulfillment is the touchstone from which further criteria can be applied. And, in the people's vigilant observance of those prophets who appear to be true, there is the admonition for them to trust God as he further affirms or exposes the prophet in question.[70] For Calvin the issue turned on the mind of God, "for we must take into consideration His intention."[71] God desired to test his people by means of 'true' false prophets in an effort to shore up their faith (Deut 13) and at the same time meant to protect them from those who would lead them astray by abusing his name, promising to expose those prophets that did (Deut 18).

Having alluded to Balaam throughout his exposition of Deut 13 and 18, we now turn briefly to Calvin's comments on non-Israelite prophets to shed light on the question of *true* false prophets. Those true false prophets, such as Caiaphas or Balaam, are considered imposters, yet are "still endowed at the same time with a particular gift of prophecy."[72] This prophetic gift can originate from no other place than God.[73] In a discussion concerning Balaam where he contrasts those outside of Israel with authentic prophets, Calvin writes, "In a word, they were the organs of the Holy Spirit."[74] While directed by the Holy Spirit, divine inspiration rendered Balaam no less culpable in Calvin's eyes: "Balaam was worse than any hireling crier, wishing as he did to frustrate the eternal decrees of God, and yet we know that his tongue was directed by the divine inspiration of the Spirit so as to be the proclaimer of that grace which he had been hired to quench."[75]

The office of prophet was not restricted to the Israelites alone. God had appointed prophets for the heathen nations as well and they operated in several capacities. First, their very existence, much like the created order, rendered the nations excuse-less. "God willed, indeed, that [prophets] should exist even among heathen nations, so that some sparks of light should shine amidst their darkness, and thus the excuse of ignorance should be taken away."[76] This phe-

---

70. *Mo. Harm.* on Deut. 18:21, CTS 1:449. Cf. Calvin's similar warning: "…for when the event corresponds with the prophecy, there is no doubt but that he who predicted what comes to pass must have been sent by God. But we must bear in mind what is said in Deut 13:1, where God reminds the people that even when the event answers to the prophecy, the prophets are not to be thoughtlessly and indiscriminately believed." *Comm. on Jer.* 28:7-9, CTS 3:396.
71. *Mo. Harm.* on Deut. 13:1, CTS 1:442.
72. *Mo. Harm.* on Deut. 13:1, CTS 1:442.
73. Referencing Isa. 44:7 Calvin writes, "We see that God ascribes to himself alone this peculiarity, that he foreknows future events and testifies respecting them." *Comm. on Jer.* 28:7-9, CTS 3:397.
74. *Mo. Harm.* on Num. 22:8, CTS 4:185; cf. Num. 23:4, CTS 4:203.
75. *Mo. Harm.* on Deut. 13:1, CTS 1:441.
76. *Mo. Harm.* on Num. 22:8, CTS 4:185. In the Psalms Calvin similarly writes, "[T]he Gentiles, to whom God has spoken only by the dumb creatures, have no excuse for their ignorance." *Comm. on Ps.* 19:7-9, CTS 1:317-18.

nomena, Calvin notes, was particularly the case prior to the promulgation of the law, since by the bourgeoning emergence of Israelite prophets God was increasingly distinguishing his people from neighboring countries. Second, Gentile prophets — even 'true' false prophets — shared, albeit unknowingly, in the proliferation of God's grace. Extolling the mysterious purposes of God, Calvin says,

> It is wonderful that God should have determined to have anything in common with the pollutions of Balaam... But, however hateful to God the impiety of Balaam was, this did not prevent Him from making use of him in this particular act. He well knows how to apply corrupt instruments to His use, so by the mouth of this false prophet, He promulgated the covenant, which He had made with Abraham, to foreign and heathen nations.[77]

Turning to Jer 23-29, paying particularly close attention to the Hananiah narrative of chapter 28, we may now collate his interpretation here with what we have observed from his comments at Deut 13, 18, and Balaam. Calvin understands Jeremiah's remarks at 23:9, 10, 22, and 28 against false prophets in light of the prophets' assuming the mantle of interpreters of the law in the face of the priests' abdication of their duty. The false prophets spoken of "ought to have been the expounders of the law."[78] However, deluded and rebellious, "they were dumb!"[79] Not only does Calvin see Jeremiah indicting the false prophets on their silence regarding the law; when they do, they are guilty of misinterpreting it. Explaining the "wheat and the chaff" of 23:28, Calvin writes, "And by this comparison [Jeremiah] shows how foolishly and absurdly many detract from the authority of the Law on this pretense, that there are many who falsely interpret it."[80] Reading Jeremiah to be at great pains to convince the people that the wrath of God could be stayed only by repentance and adherence to the law, Calvin underlines the centrality of the law for Jeremiah's prophetic existence. "Were God then to descend a hundred times from heaven, he would bring nothing but this message, that he has spoken what is necessary to be known, and that his Law is the most perfect wisdom."[81] By both muzzling and corrupting or altering the message of the law, the false prophets stood guilty of leading the people astray.

Having pointed out the particular emphasis Calvin sees Jeremiah placing on the role of the law informing a true prophet's words, the testing nature of prophetic opposition as far as the people are concerned, and the reality that God occasionally conscripted false prophets to deliver true messages, a few points specific concerning the narrative of chapter 28 are in order. First, Calvin saw false prophets' title of prophet as purely expedient. At Jer 26:7-8 Calvin writes,

---

77. *Mo. Harm.* on Num. 23:4, CTS 4:203.
78. *Comm. on Jer.* 23:9, CTS 3:153
79. *Comm. on Jer.* 23:10, CTS 3:157.
80. *Comm. on Jer.* 23:28, CTS 3:197.
81. *Comm. on Jer.* 26:4-6, CTS 3:313.

"[Jeremiah] then allowed them an honorable title, but esteemed it as nothing."[82] The title held no intrinsic merit; false prophets were called prophets merely "with regard to the people."[83] Hananiah, while labeled prophet in the Hebrew, "had no proof of his own call...and, as it were, avowedly obtruded himself that he might contend with the Prophet."[84] Calvin is not only sure that Hananiah knew himself to be parading as a true prophet driven by a "satanic impulse,"[85] he wonders at his insensitivity. "Hananiah ought to have been touched and moved when he heard Jeremiah speaking."[86] As to how the faithful saw Hananiah, they considered him an "awful spectacle of blindness and of madness."[87] In one fell swoop it seems Calvin answers the question of Jer 28 before he engages the remainder of the story by crediting the obedient present with discernment. "It was easy for [the obedient] to distinguish between Jeremiah and Hananiah; for they saw that the former announced the commands of God, while the latter sought nothing else but the favor and plaudits of men."[88] As for Jeremiah, Calvin says that whenever the prophet called Hananiah by the name prophet, he attached his own name and title to the statement. This had the double effect of reminding those present of his valid title and of warning "us in due time, lest novelty should frighten us when any boasts of the title of a prophet."[89]

An additional element of importance is the prophetic sign. Hebrew commentators in and prior to Calvin's day clearly demarcated between prophetic signs that were akin to props or expressions, such as those utilized by Isaiah (20:2) or Jeremiah (28:10), and signs of a miraculous or magical nature.[90] Due to their questionable signatory value, Calvin raises the possible objection that, signs being what they are, might not they "be as well dangerous deceptions as confirmations of the truth"? He writes, "I reply, that such license has never been accorded to the devil, as that the light of God should not in the end shine forth from the midst of the darkness."[91] So we see Calvin tethering the nature of the sign to God's perseverance of his people amidst tests he himself inflicts upon them by way of false prophets.

We come, then, to the contentious sign of Jeremiah's yoke. Fashioned in chapter 27, the yoke served a dual purpose. It was a useful sign to the teachable,

---

82. *Comm. on Jer.* 26:7-8, CTS 3:318.
83. *Comm. on Jer.* 26:7-8, CTS 3:318.
84. *Comm. on Jer.* 28:1-2, CTS 3:388.
85. *Comm. on Jer.* 28:1-2, CTS 3:385.
86. *Comm. on Jer.* 28:1-2, CTS 3:388; cf. "Ought not Hananiah then to have trembled when any other had alleged God's name?" CTS 3:386.
87. *Comm. on Jer.* 28:1-2, CTS 3:386.
88. *Comm. on Jer.* 28:1-2, CTS 3:386.
89. *Comm. on Jer.* 28:10-11, CTS 3:402.
90. *Mo. Harm.* on Deut. 13:1, CTS 1:443. The editor believes Calvin consulted Sebastian Munster (CTS 1:443n1).
91. *Mo. Harm.* on Deut. 13:1, CTS 1:443.

like a sacrament that established the credit of Jeremiah's message.[92] Bullinger also notes the prophets' paradigmatic use of common objects in making visible the correlative prophecy.[93] Signs were also a signifier of coming judgment to those hardened in obstinacy.[94] With the grievous act of desecrating Jeremiah's symbol, and therefore his message, aside, Calvin notes the selfish nature of Hananiah at 28:10-11. By breaking the yoke he "attracted the attention of men."[95] Then, succumbing further to his delusion, Hananiah fashioned a new yoke, thereby "imitating the true prophets of God."[96] Central for Calvin is the proposition that no prophetic sign is complete without an accompanying doctrine. Hananiah's doctrine was plausible, therefore Calvin says it found much purchase in the Temple.[97] That the accompanying message substantiates the sign was more forcibly shown in Jeremiah's recast yoke of iron. Calvin notes that when Jeremiah added his explanation of the iron—cast yoke, one of two responses was the result. Either the people believed his prophecy, or the hardened obstinate rendered themselves further inexcusable.[98] Bullinger also saw the sign linked with its accompanying words. Comparing these signs of the prophets to the rhetorician's practice of *chriæ activæ*, or the oratorical use of both word and deed, Bullinger acknowledged an "affinity" between the prophetic sign and the signatory value of the sacraments of baptism and the Lord's supper, "for they are given unto us from above and are taken from natural things... they renew things past, and shadow out things to come."[99] They differ from present sacraments in that, unlike the prophets' signs, sacraments of the church have prescribed ceremonies laid out in the New Testament coupled with them.

Calvin understands the test by which the people discern God's prophet and the true prophet's very definition to be one and the same. "For when the event corresponds with the prophecy, there is no doubt but that he who predicted what comes to pass must have been sent by God."[100] So, we see that for Calvin the fulfillment of a prophecy is grounds upon which the people may stake confidence. For Bullinger the accurate prediction of things to come, such as Isaiah's naming Cyrus, also bolstered his doctrine of inspiration. Fulfilled predictions proved (at least) "that the doctrine and writings of the prophets are the very word of God."[101] However, as noted earlier, fulfilled prophecy does not preclude

---

92. *Comm. on Jer.* 28:10-11, CTS 3:401.
93. Bullinger, *Decades*, 5:232.
94. *Comm. on Jer.* 27:1-5, CTS 3:352. Calvin notes the yoke was useless as long as no word accompanied it. In the same way, Calvin condemns the lack of sound doctrine accompanying the Papists' plethora of symbols as deplorable.
95. *Comm. on Jer.* 28:10-11, CTS 3:401.
96. *Comm. on Jer.* 28:10-11, CTS 3:401.
97. *Comm. on Jer.* 28:10-11, CTS 3:403.
98. *Comm. on Jer.* 28:14, CTS 3:405.
99. Bullinger, *Decades*, 5:233.
100. *Comm. on Jer.* 28:7-9, CTS 3:396.
101. Bullinger, *Decades*, 1:51.

ill intent. Calvin writes, "But we cannot hence conclude, that all those who apparently predict this or that, are sent by God... for one particular prophecy would not be sufficient to prove the truth of all that is taught and preached."[102] Fulfilled prophecy holds limited discriminatory value for Jeremiah; it does not secure a prophet's veracity. In fact, for Calvin, Jeremiah is less intent on proving his own authenticity than Hananiah's falsehood: "[Jeremiah's] design was not to prove that all were true prophets who predicted something that was true...he took up another point, —that all who predicted this or that, which was afterward found to be vain, were thus convicted of falsehood."[103] Calvin sees in Jeremiah a confidence that, after the predicted two years, peace would not reign, as Hananiah projected.[104] In this way, Calvin sees Jeremiah employing a form of the prophetic warning at Deut 18.[105]

Calvin is insistent that Jeremiah's primary object in the Hananiah episode was to prove his opponent false. How then does Calvin understand Jeremiah to discern a true prophet?

> As to the ancient people, they could not...be deceived, for the prophets were only interpreters of the Law. With regard to future things, this or that was never predicted by the prophets, unless connected with doctrine, which was as it were the seasoning, and gave a relish to the prophecies; for when they promised what was cheering, it was founded on the eternal covenant of God; and when they threatened the people, they pointed out their sins, so that it was necessary for God to execute his vengeance when their wickedness was incurable.[106]

As we saw with Jeremiah's yoke, Calvin is quick to point out the futility of a doctrine-less sign. The basal doctrine Calvin understands to be operative for the prophet is the covenant, the Law of Moses. Only to the degree that a prophet's message of peace accorded with the law's promises of glad tidings was that prophet of peace said to be sent from God. The same can be seen in Bullinger's treatment of Ezek 13's "flattering preachers" who offered peace where there is none.[107] Likewise, when the law was transgressed, the guilty were to be called to account. Jeremiah's contention with Hananiah, then, has to do with his message: falsely predicted peace. As Calvin goes on to show in Jer 37:1-2, those who rejected Jeremiah, rejected the law: "for if [the Israelites] had examined the doctrine of Jeremiah, they would have found that it had certain marks by which they could have easily seen that it was altogether consistent with the law."[108] There-

---

102. *Comm. on Jer.* 28:7-9, CTS 3:398.
103. *Comm. on Jer.* 28:7-9, CTS 3:398-99.
104. *Comm. on Jer.* 28:7-9, CTS 3:399.
105. "And the same thing Moses had in view, as I have already explained." *Comm. on Jer.* 28:7-9, CTS 3:399.
106. *Comm. on Jer.* 27:15, CTS 3:373.
107. *Decades*, 3:119.
108. *Comm. on Jer.* 37:1-2, CTS 4:363.

fore, Hananiah's open defiance towards Jeremiah constituted deviance from a true prophet's duty: proper interpretation of the law.

Bullinger, after laying out a who's-who of Old Testament prophets, notes the singularity of all prophets' messages. Their most notable characteristic, he says, is their acknowledgement that God has spoken to the world first through the Fathers, and then to Moses, and that this communication was written down for those to come. The prophets,

> all, with one consent, acknowledge that God spoke to the world by Moses, who (God so appointed it) left to the church in the world a breviary of true divinity, and a most absolute sum of the word of God contained in writing. All these priests, divines, and prophets, in all that they did, had an especial eye to the doctrine of Moses. They did also refer all men, in cases of faith and religion, to the book of Moses. The law of Moses...they did diligently beat into the minds of all men.[109]

In the prophets are contained both Moses' doctrine and the traditions of the fathers, normative and binding for all who follow. To highlight the prophets' historical unanimity Bullinger writes, "Neither did they teach any other thing than that which the fathers had received of God, and which Moses had received of God and the fathers."[110] Bullinger sees in this perpetual transmission of the prophets' message a honing taking place. In this way the law is ever fresh, applicable to the present situation.

Calvin writes of those prophets throughout Israel's history, "[T]he Jews had been plainly taught by the Law and by the Prophets, God had continued morning and evening to repeat the same things to them."[111] For Calvin, the law constitutes *what* the Israelites were taught; the prophets were, in a sense, supplemental.[112] He refers to the prophets' messages of warning and repentance as "reproofs" which were appended to the law's lessons.[113] Calvin sees a common thread, or similarity, running through the messages of Israel and Judah's prior prophets, originating in Moses, the prototypical prophet. That Calvin understood Moses in this way is evident from numerous places throughout both the Harmo-

---

109. *Decades*, 1:49.
110. *Decades*, 1:50.
111. *Comm. on Jer.* 6:18-19, CTS 1:343.
112. De Boer has brought to light Calvin's final address to the *congrégations* in 1564 on Isaiah 1:1-3, in which he maintains the prophets "taught the people even more than is retained in their books." Then, following Calvin's own flow of argument, de Boer highlights the prophets' foretelling of future events. Calvin himself insists that the value of the prediction of future events lay in their application: "the visions alone would be quite poor and sterile, but the main thing was to make them known. There is no doubt that it was only as a supplement that the prophets have revealed the things to come. The main thing was that they would instruct the people in the fear of God" (Ms.fr. 40b.f. 159b; cited in de Boer, *Visions of Ezekiel*, 6).
113. *Comm. on Jer.* 16:10-13, CTS 2:313-18.

ny and the Jeremiah commentary. His statements from the final paragraph of his Harmony (on Deut 34:10) clearly show that Calvin considered Moses the font from which all prophecy (and law) sprung. "[F]or although prophets were from time to time raised up, still it was fitting that the superiority should remain with Moses, lest they should decline in the smallest degree from the rule of the Law. It must be concluded, therefore, that Moses was here placed in a position of supremacy, so as to be superior to all the prophets."[114] Calvin notes two "signs of his excellency": his familiar intimacy with God, and his miraculous signs. These two facets of Moses' prophetic office find analogs in the subsequent prophets' dual roles of interpreter of the Law in the absence of regular, direct divine communication, and exhibitors of signs, whether descriptive, predictive, or miraculous. When a prophet spoke the law to the people, it was actually Moses doing the reprimanding. This is evident in Calvin's discussion of the spiritual nature of the sign of circumcision at Jer 9:25-26. "When, therefore, the Jews presented only the sign, they were justly derided by Moses and the prophets."[115]

Calvin believes Jeremiah sees himself furthering this universal message. Concerning the people's wickedness on account of which impending judgment from the North loomed, Calvin writes, "what other prophets had denounced Jeremiah now confirms more strongly."[116] While vengeance made up the bulk of Jeremiah's message, thereby linking him with past prophets, Jeremiah's commission—the extension of a pardon—was one of mercy as well.[117] In both the harsh words of punishment and the hope of reprieve, Jeremiah's message toes the historical line of God's prophets. "The Prophet, then, does not here simply teach, but reminds the Jews of what they had before heard from Isaiah, and also from Micah, and from all the other prophets."[118] Calvin sees Jeremiah particularly indebted to the prophet Isaiah's message. "As then Isaiah reproached the people with tardiness in learning the law, so Jeremiah shows now that they were not to think it strange that God commanded his law to be proclaimed to them, because it had been hitherto despised by them."[119] Calvin further shows Jeremiah's dependency upon Isaiah by highlighting Jeremiah's prophecy against the Babylonians at the hand of the Medes. Calvin comments that it echoes Isaiah's

---

114. *Mo. Har.* on Deut. 34:10, CTS 4:408-409.
115. *Comm. on Jer.* 9:25-26, CTS 1:508.
116. *Comm. on Jer.* 1:13-14, CTS 1:54.
117. *Comm. on Jer.* 2:1-2, CTS 1:69-70.
118. *Comm. on Jer.* 2:25, CTS 1:121.
119. *Comm. on Jer.* 11:6-8, CTS 1:80. For Calvin, Isaiah (55:9) exemplifies Jeremiah's contrast between the council of God and the vain imaginations of the Israelites at Jer. 29:11; Jeremiah proof-texts Isaiah (58:9) when he promises the discovery of the Lord rewards those who earnestly seek Him (29:13); and Isaiah (22:12,13) is quoted as representative of those prophets who, like Jeremiah, "continually threatened" the people in their insensible immoderation (*Comm. on Jer.* 25:10, CTS 3:255).

(13:17), though the latter had been dead for some time.[120] No mention is made of Hananiah or any other false prophet aping the message of Isaiah.

Briefly, discernment on the part of the people is not without mention in Calvin's treatment of false prophets. Calvin is sure God always leads his people to the truth, allowing them to discern finally, if not immediately, God's messenger. In Jer 26, regardless of the means, Jeremiah was saved and a contingent was preserved that listened to and heeded (in some degree) Jeremiah's message. Calvin has more to say about those who were "willfully blind," who did not inquire into a prophet's message. These, Calvin said, "willfully put on nooses and also wished to be deceived."[121] They are unmoved even by "an event so memorable" as Hananiah's foretold and realized death sentence.[122] Alongside these, a third group can be identified. Pleading ignorance in the face of such an ambiguous choice, Calvin describes these as undecided. It was for these, Calvin says, that God ratified Hananiah's death sentence. "[I]t was God's purpose to have regard to the ignorance of many who would have otherwise stumbled, or made their ignorance a pretext, for they could not determine which of the two had been sent by God, Hananiah or Jeremiah."[123] The connection of signs and faith is also seen in Oecolampadius' commentary on Jeremiah.[124] In Wolfgang Capito's preface, Capito notes concerning the nature of prophetic signs, that, in the case of Jeremiah's prediction of Hananiah's death, the sign (*splendido signo*) lacks the power ultimately to sway those present. He writes, "This blessed sign is ratified, the prophet is of the Lord: nevertheless, they [the people], not believing, hold back: all the same it is the truth, faith is the gift of God."[125] Given the Reformation's formulaic *sola fide*, it is little wonder the people's inability to discern true from false is linked to their lack of faith.

---

120. "And the same thing is expressed also by Isaiah; and you ought to compare this prophecy with that of Isaiah for the two Prophets wholly agree, though Isaiah was dead when Jeremiah uttered this prophecy and wrote it." *Comm. on Jer.* 50:42, CTS 5:186.
121. *Comm. on Jer.* 27:15, CTS 3:372.
122. *Comm. on Jer.* 28:16, CTS 3:410.
123. *Comm. on Jer.* 28:16, CTS 3:410.
124. Johann Oecolampadius, *In Jeremiam prophetam commentariorum*, ed. Jean Crespin, (Geneva: E Typographie Crispiniana, 1558). Oecolampadius' lectures on Jeremiah and Lamentations were given in 1527.[124] Capito goes on to ask whether a prediction's fulfillment necessarily denotes a prophet's veracity: Si propheta pacem praedixerit, & euenerit res prophetae, notum erit quod Dominus in veritate illum miserit?, iib. Here, as throughout many of the Reformer's treatments of the prophets, the transference of analogous elements between the *Sitz em Leben* of the prophets and that of the sixteenth—century preachers and their hearers is ever apparent.
125. Hoc splendido signo comprobatus est esse Propheta Domini, nec tamen credere ei sustinuerunt: tam verum est, fidem esse donum Dei. Oecolampadius, *In Jeremiam*, iib.

Summary

This chapter has modestly sought to explore Calvin's interpretive approach to the question of true and false prophecies in the book of Jeremiah. Second, it has tried to situate Calvin amidst the Christian interpretive tradition as it grapples with Jeremiah's construal of false prophets. Calvin understood his own exegesis as growing in the tradition's shade: "The common consent of almost all interpreters also influences me, from which I wish not to depart, except necessity compels me, or the thing itself makes it evident that they were mistaken."[126] Assessing Calvin's reading of the question, embryonic signs of a shift in the interpretation of prophets start to take shape. Looking ahead to the nineteenth century, Old Testament prophets' foretelling ability—until then one of their hallmark characteristics—is all but dismissed. However, with Calvin this trait was still alive and well; indeed formative and requisite. Organs of the Holy Spirit, Old Testament prophets were granted a "special gift to predict future and hidden events."[127]

Before Calvin, Thomas understood the prophets' intellect to be inspired with the charism of prophecy, enabling authentic knowledge of future events. This resulted in a true prophet's ability to judge or interpret those future representations presented him. Calvin's understanding of the prophet's office casts the prophet more in the role of pupil. Perhaps the most programmatic treatment of prophetic knowledge per se in his commentary, Calvin's comments at Jer. 32:16-18 afford us a closer look at its limits.[128] Noting what he considers a confused response from Jeremiah in the face of the vision ("Houses, and fields, and vineyards shall yet be bought in this land"), Calvin seeks to hold together prophetic knowledge and ignorance.[129] Calvin maintains Jeremiah was perplexed at the nature of the vision of restitution and ignorant to the reason lying behind it. He then extrapolates a general prophetic principle: "It hence appears that God's counsel was not always made known in everything to the Prophets, but as far as it was expedient."[130] There remained a level of ambiguity for Calvin concerning the degree of the prophets' knowledge concerning future events. The prophets knew as much of the future as God deemed fit, no more. "Such was the height or the depth of this mystery, that [Jeremiah] was constrained to confess that it was a work of God which surpassed all his thoughts."[131] What could be deduced was the reason the vision was given: "that the Jews might know their calamity would

---

126. *Comm. on Jer.* 26:20-23, CTS 3:345.
127. *Comm. on Jer.* 27:15, CTS 3:372.
128. *Comm. on Jer.* 32:16-18, CTS 4:167-74.
129. Cf. Parker, *Old Testament Commentaries*, 206-207.
130. *Comm. on Jer.* 32:16-18, CTS 4:168.
131. *Comm. on Jer.* 32:16-18, CTS 4:168.

not be perpetual."[132] Calvin also stresses the prophet's restrained comportment. God's prophets were not "seized with ecstasies" or "carried away." Rather, they soberly received what the Lord "discovered to them," their prophetic 'curriculum.'[133] This curriculum, unsurprisingly, was not neoteric. Granted, the Israelites had been furnished with prophets, "through whom God published new oracles which were added to the law."[134] The important thing Calvin wishes to highlight, however, is the delimited nature of new prophecy. A prophecy such as Jeremiah's vision of restitution in Jer. 32 may be unheard of in its particularities, but never so new that it did not "flow from the law and hark back to it."[135] With this we return to Calvin's insistence that a prophet's primary function was the interpretation of the Law. "As for doctrine, they were only interpreters of the law and added nothing to it except predictions of things to come. Apart from these, they brought nothing forth but a pure exposition of the law."[136]

Tying doctrine to prediction in the face of the rise of the prominence of the role of the law, Calvin sees the decline of prophecy being defined by foretelling and prediction. Prior to the publication of the law, Calvin understands the dominant feature of the prophetic office to be its predictive element.[137] Much in the role of preachers, the prophets were responsible for the application of these predictions to the surrounding circumstances. After the law's promulgation, "they were its interpreters."[138] Prediction did not fall to the wayside. True prophets, if inspired to do so, were able to foretell future events. Once they had the law, however, Calvin understands the majority of prophets to be working from the same source. This explains Calvin's insistence that a prophetic sign to be heeded must be accompanied by doctrine. Conversely, those prophets, like Balaam, who may have predicted "this or that," did so "without any admixture of doctrine."[139]

In the history of interpretation, Calvin's readings of the prophets provide a view of an expositor seeking to do justice to a doctrine of God's providence realized through his prophets. Calvin's humanist predilection for a textual appraisal of biblical prophecy could perhaps serve to explain, at least in part, his insistence to shift the epicenter of the interpretation of prophecy away from discussions of ecstasy and fanaticism. Particularly innovative is Calvin's relocation of the center of interpretation of prophecy to a written tradition, the Book of the

---

132. *Comm. on Jer*. 32:16-18, CTS 4:167. Throughout the commentary, Calvin points out Jeremiah's "special care" for his own, chosen people, following prophecies of ruin with those of restoration (esp. Comm. on Jer. 25:34, CTS 3:298).
133. *Comm. on Jer*. 32:16-18, CTS 4:168.
134. John Calvin, *Institutes of the Christian Religion,* ed. John T. McNeill, trans. Ford Lewis Battles. 2 vols. Library of Christian Classics (Philadelphia: Westminster Press, 1960), 4.8.6.
135. *Inst.*, 4.8.6.
136. *Inst.*, 4.8.6.
137. *Mo. Harm.* on Num. 22:8, CTS 4:185.
138. *Mo. Harm.* on Num. 22:8, CTS 4:185.
139. *Mo. Harm.* on Num. 22:8, CTS 4:185.

Law. At times, in this surprisingly nuanced reading of the question, one is not sure if Calvin's prophets are looking forward via their predictions, or backward via their texts.

5. THE PROPHETS AND WHICH LAW? THE ENLIGHTENMENT ERA

Introduction

In an aptly titled essay, "Growing Tension between Church Doctrines and Critical Exegesis of the Old Testament," Nellen highlights the widening gap between the functional exegesis of the Old Testament within Protestant Orthodoxy and rationalist approaches akin to preceding Humanist and Renaissance tendencies.[1] It is here, in the century following the Reformation's bold attempts to redraw the lines of biblical interpretation, that several 'givens' of the preceding era began to give way to an emerging historical-critical method of textual study.[2] The Bible came more and more to be examined outside of traditional ecclesiastical settings. One example of the relocation of the interpretive setting is Hugo Grotius.[3] Throughout this period, Scripture's textual, philological, and historical findings were questioned and in many cases drastically redrafted with ever-increasing rational acumen. Simultaneously developing fields of science, philology, and history were brought to bear on biblical interpretation often with devastating effect to long-held Christian beliefs. As will be seen clearly in Spinoza, among those tenets to be superseded was the hallmark dogma of divine inspiration. Once dispensed with, Grotius could deny the inspiration of such historical books as Ezra or Luke on historical grounds while allowing the words of the prophets, Jesus Christ, or any others whom the *text expressly claimed to be inspired* to

---

1. H. J. M. Nellen, "Growing Tension between Church Doctrines and Critical Exegesis of the Old Testament," in *Hebrew Bible/Old Testament*, II.
2. Jon D. Levenson, *The Hebrew Bible, the Old Testament, and Historical Criticism* (Louisville, KY: Westminster/John Knox Press, 1993), 90.
3. Grotius' position may be characterized as the traditional view, possessing several recognizable characteristics. Interpreting Old Testament prophecy out of a messianic context, Grotius' notion of prophetic inspiration is one-dimensional. God has spoken to a few, the prophets, and in doing so, revealed to them alone the future. This revelation has come from without; the prophet does not arrive at it through the course of reason alone. Discernment on the ground entailed two criteria that we will meet, in some form, throughout the remainder of our study: the working of signs and the promotion of YHWH worship. So, as we move from Hobbes into Spinoza, a growing separation from these principles will emerge. Hugo Grotius, *De Veritate Religionis Christianae* (1st; Opera Omnia, vol.3; 1622), pp. 1-98; edited and reprinted as *The Truth of the Christian Religion* (trans. John Clarke; London: William Baynes, 1829).

stand as divine.⁴ But inspiration was not the only traditional pillar under fire. The perspicuity of the Bible, the notion of a straightforward transmission of one incorruptible and uncorrupted source, and theology's stranglehold on philosophy were now fair game as well. In this period we will also see the proliferation of criteria for true prophets that are derived from scriptural texts as well as external ideologies or systems.

The task of fully enumerating the repercussions that advancements in the fields of science, geography, and philosophy have had on biblical interpretation lies outside the scope of our study. What is of interest to our study is the way in which the subject of true and false prophecy affords the reader a view into the ways that the emerging critical approach to scripture was to affect the reading and appropriation of Christian Scripture. It was around discussions of prophets and prophecy that the locus of a particular spokesperson's authority was to be located. Among the myriad of writers addressing questions of the Bible's veracity, historicity, and continued utility, selections from a few deserve mention. After briefly looking at Hobbes' *Leviathan*, we will examine in greater detail Spinoza's contribution to the question of true and false prophecy in his *Tractatus Theologico-Politicus*. Then, we will sample readings of the question from some of the better-known (if not always the most well-received!) theologians and exegetes of the Netherlands (Campegius Vintringa), France (Augustin Calmet), and England (Thomas Newton). It is to these we now turn.⁵

Thomas Hobbes (1588-1679)

Published in 1651, Hobbes' *Leviathan* quickly joined the ranks of heterodox literature. As could be too readily seen the aftermath of the Thirty Years War, the politicization of religion—and religions' texts—left a bitter taste in the mouth of those desirous of peace. Believing religion should lead to peace, not war, the *Leviathan* sought to free the "political order from the subservience to religion."⁶ This could be done, as would become increasingly apparent, by associating religious documents with "a vanquished political order."⁷ Hobbes' *Leviathan* would enjoy a reception by such thinkers as Leibniz and Spinoza later in

---

4. Nellen, 814f.; cf. H. J. de Jonge, "Hugo Grotius: exégète du Nouveau Testament," in *The World of Hugo Grotius (1583-1645)*, 97-115 (Amsterdam: Maarssen, 1984), 112f; cf. M. H. de Lang, "Excurs IV, Hugo Grotius," in *De opkomst van de historische en literaire kritiek in de synoptische beschouwing van de Evangeliën van Calvijn (1555) tot Griesbach (1774)*, 125-135 (Leiden: 1993).
5. The secondary literature is vast, as are the works under consideration. It is this study's intention to restrict the focus to those relevant to prophecy and discernment while addressing, where needed, peripheral discussions that may arise out of the subject matter.
6. Levenson, *The Hebrew Bible*, 95.
7. Levenson, The Hebrew Bible, 95.

the seventeenth-century, playing an integral role in the formation of their own critiques on the standing religious order as they employed similar tactics.[8]

Chapters 32 and 36 of *Leviathan* contain the bulk of Hobbes' exegesis of prophets and prophecy. Martinich's negative assessment notwithstanding,[9] we will focus our attention on the first of these two. And, while not engaging Jeremiah explicitly, Hobbes' treatment of Deuteronomy is germane to our task. For Hobbes, the designation of 'prophet' is not a highly exclusive one. One is reminded of the early church and the ease with which it might be applied to a person claiming to speak for God. It includes all priests, any who worship God, women who foretell the future, any spokesman, and even less-than-desirable characters, such as Caiaphas.[10] In short, anyone to whom God has communicated immediately.[11] These people are designated privileged, or 'extraordinary.' As to *how* God spoke to these prophets, it was through dreams and visions, since God lacked a corporeal presence and any ascriptions of him as such were anthropomorphisms.

> [T]he prophets extraordinary in the Old Testament took notice of the word of God no otherwise, than from their dreams, or visions; that is to say, from the imaginations which they had in their sleep, or in an e[c]tasy: which imaginations in every true prophet were supernatural; but in false prophets were either natural or feigned.[12]

Given the ambiguous nature of dreams and the fact that even those who have dreams or visions sometimes believe themselves to be awake, Hobbes exhibits reservation about a person's ability to be certain that God has immediately communicated to them. However he does grant, as we saw with Origen, that God has indeed communicated, but it is only a surety to those privy to the conversation.[13]

In order to prove an immediate revelation not false *prima facie*, the prophecy must be accompanied by a sign, (i.e., a miracle). In chapter 32 two prophetic narratives receive attention: 1 K 22 (Micaiah and Ahab) and then 1 K 13 (the

---

8. Conal Condren, *Thomas Hobbes,* Twayne's English Authors Series (New York: Twayne Publishers, 2000), 157f.
9. According to Aloysius Martinich, "Hobbes' treatment of prophets is by and large deflating." *Hobbes; A Biography* (Cambridge: Cambridge University Press, 1999), 240.
10. We will be using Thomas Hobbes, *Leviathan,* ed. J.C.A. Gaskin (Oxford: Oxford University Press, 1998), 36.11.
11. The other way in which God has spoken is *mediate* revelation, that is, through the "natural word of God." *Leviathan* 32.1; on the two types of revelation see Martinich, *Hobbes: A Life,* 238f.
12. *Leviathan* 36.11.
13. Cf. Martinich, *Hobbes: A Life,* 239, where he quotes Hobbes, "How God speaks to a man immediately may be understood by those well enough to whom he has spoken." *Leviathan,* 32.5.

man of God from Judah and the old prophet from Bethel).[14] In an effort to establish that there are in fact true prophets by means of these scriptural passages, most Hobbesian scholars agree that in doing so, he effectively "undermines faith in the ability to know who they are."[15] Hobbes puts the problem this way:

> If one prophet deceive another, what certainty is there of knowing the will of God, by other way than that of reason? To which I answer out of the Holy Scripture, that there be two marks, by which together, not asunder, a true prophet is to be known. One is the doing of miracles; the other is the not teaching any other religion than that which is already established. Asunder (I say) neither of these is sufficient.[16]

For Hobbes, these dual criteria are what Deut 13:1-5 is teaching. Moving seamlessly between biblical times and his own, Hobbes warns that prophets preaching dissension from God in Deuteronomy are equivalent to those who would urge, "revolt from your king."[17] And, as Deut 13 showed that the presence of a sign accompanied by an errant doctrine (revolt) evinced falsehood, Deut 18 shows the reverse. "[I]f a man that teacheth not false doctrine, should pretend to be a prophet without showing any miracle, he is never the more to be regarded for his pretence, as is evident by Deut 18:21-22."[18]

Hobbes' formulation of criteria has eluded any easy identification of true prophets. Even the results of a wait-and-see litmus test — after the fact proof — are insufficient since it is too late once the prophet is or is not vindicated. Marti-

---

14. Cooke examines why Hobbes chose these passages and not the more traditional Jeremianic texts, coming to the conclusion that these more fully stress the role of reason in matters concerning the divine will and its apprehension, Paul D. Cooke, *Hobbes and Christianity: Reassessing the Bible in Leviathan* (Lanham, MD: Rowman & Littlefield, 1996), 138f. That true prophets, not merely false, may engage in a "willful lie" acting as both a deceiver and the deceived, for Hobbes means the act of "human beings seeking to know the will of God by some other means than reason—by some direct revelation from the Almighty—is very precarious." (139).
15. See especially H. G. Reventlow, "Thomas Hobbes: the Philosophical Presuppositions of his Biblical Criticism," in his *The Authority of the Bible and the Rise of the Modern World* (trans. John Bowden; London: SCM Press Ltd, 1984), 194-222, esp. 216-218; cf. also Cooke, *Hobbes and Christianity*, 133-154; and the seminal work of Aloysius P. Martinich, *The Two Gods of Leviathan: Thomas Hobbes on Religion and Politics* (Cambridge: Cambridge University Press, 1992), 228; *Hobbes*, 240f; John Whipple, "Hobbes on Miracles," *PPQ* 89 (2008): 117-142, esp. 130f.; Edwin Curley, "Calvin and Hobbes, or, Hobbes as an Orthodox Christian," *JHP* 34 (1996): 257-271, esp. 262; Franck Lessay, "Hobbes' Covenant Theology and its Political Implications," in *The Cambridge Companion to Hobbes' Leviathan*, 243-270 (ed. Patricia Springborg; Cambridge: Cambridge University Press, 2007), 258-260, and A.P. Martinich, "The Bible and Protestantism," in *The Cambridge Companion to Hobbes' Leviathan*, 375-391.
16. *Leviathan*, 32.7.
17. Ibid.
18. Ibid.

nich's observations on this are insightful and, we believe, get at the issue as far as Hobbes apprehended it. "The problem is epistemological, not ontological."[19] All other considerations aside, it is only after the fact that the prophets of the Old Testament are accepted and have been subsequently canonized.[20]

In summary, Hobbes anticipates the complaints of those who would question whether or not there was any point in discerning true from false. The means by which both those in the Old Testament and those in the New and at the current time distinguished between the two was similar. Using "natural reason," the Old Testament observer was to

> apply to all prophecy those rules which God hath given...to discern the true from false. Of which rules, in the Old Testament, one was, conformable doctrine to that which Moses the sovereign prophet had taught them; and the other the miraculous power of foretelling what God would bring to pass.[21]

With the coming of Christ and the New Testament's teaching, Hobbes reduces the number of criteria. Doctrine, not signs or miracles, remains as the measure of truth. Specifically, the teaching that "Jesus is the Christ."[22] 1 Jn 4:2-3 framed the issue of testing the spirits. Since there were those who could produce signs while not affirming Christ's preeminence, confession alone sufficed for Hobbes. This allowed Hobbes to organically connect his discussion of true prophets to his overall thesis in *Leviathan*. "Every man therefore ought to consider who is the sovereign prophet...who it is that is God's vicegerent on earth...and to observe for a rule, that doctrine, which in the name of God, he hath commanded to be taught."[23] Reason, Hobbes teaches, over and against an appeal to divine revelation, is the safer way to apprehend and discern truth.

Benedict de Spinoza (1632-1677)

Because Spinoza's pivotal position in the history of ideas has long been recognized, we turn now to his treatment of true and false prophecy.[24] This study will limit our coverage of the *TTP* to hermeneutical developments in the area of

---

19. Martinich, *Hobbes; A Biography*, 240.
20. Hobbes writes, "the Israelites were commanded not to account any man for a true prophet but him whose prophecies were answered by the events. And hence peradventure it is that the Jews esteemed the writings of those whom they slew when they prophesied for prophetic afterwards; that is to say, for the word of God." *de Cive* 16.12, cited in Martinich, *Hobbes; A Biography*, 240.
21. *Leviathan*, 36.20.
22. Ibid.
23. Ibid.
24. On the geo-political historical context out of which Spinoza wrote see Richard Popkin's brief yet insightful essay "Spinoza and La Peyrère," in *Spinoza: New Perspectives*, ed. R. W. Shahan et al.; (Norman, OK: University of Oklahoma Press, 1978), 177—198.

prophecy, specifically the question of discernment. Modern Old Testament scholarship on true and false prophecy can trace many of its tributaries back to Spinoza's innovative handling of the question of discernment and the message of the prophets. Of the many works treating Spinoza's contributions to biblical studies in the last half-century, a recent monograph stands out as helpful in reassessing Spinoza's role in the proliferation of the 'critical' study of Scripture, Travis Frampton's *Spinoza and the Rise of Historical Criticism of the Bible*.[25] Seeking to answer the age-old question of "whether or not Spinoza was the father of historical criticism," Frampton sees much of what Spinoza would inaugurate in the field of historical-criticism to find its inception in the Protestant—particularly Calvinist—penchant for literal, historical interpretation of the Old Testament.[26] The Reformers' radical practices of questioning of religious tradition and authority, as well as attacking traditional exegesis on historical grounds, were carried to their "ultimate conclusions" by the seventeenth-century "latecomer."[27] With Strauss and Levenson, Frampton concludes that the Reformation principles of *sola scriptura* and the freedom of the conscience, along with the 'new science', helped shape Spinoza's historical consciousness.[28] Granting the Reformers' existential conviction of Scripture's veracity along with their rejection of unbridled spiritual interpretations, it is natural that a seventeenth-century reader of Scripture would take the logical next step and question the facts of the Bible itself.[29]

---

25. Travis L. Frampton, *Spinoza and the Rise of Historical Criticism of the Bible* (New York: T & T Clark, 2006). For an immensely helpful single-volume bibliography of Spinoza-related scholarship in English see Wayne I. Boucher, *Spinoza in English: A Bibliography from the Seventeenth Century to the Present* (2nd ed.; Bristol: Thoemmes, 1999). For a recent (2008) list of general works see the bibliographies in Steven Nadler, "The Bible Hermeneutics of Baruch de Spinoza," in *HB/OT II*, 827; and Frampton, 5n.5. Other works include Seymour Feldman, "Maimonides — A Guide for Posterity," in *The Cambridge Companion to Maimonides*, 324-360 (ed. Kenneth Seeskin; Cambridge: Cambridge University Press, 2005). Cf. Mark S. Gignilliat, *A Brief History of Old Testament Criticism: From Benedict Spinoza to Brevard Childs*, (Grand Rapids: Zondervan, 2012); Michael C. Legaspi, *The Death of Scripture and the Rise of Biblical Studies*, Oxford Studies in Historical Theology (Oxford: Oxford University Press, 2010), 23-24; John Sandys-Wunsch, "Spinoza — The First Biblical Theologian," *ZAW* 93 (1981): 327-341; Hans-Joachim Kraus, *Geschichte der historisch-kritischen Erforschung des Alten Testaments* (2nd ed.; Neukirchen-Vluyn: Neukirchener Verlag, 1969), 61-65; James S. Preus, "A Hidden Opponent in Spinoza's Tractatus," *HTR* 88 (1995): 361-388; idem "Anthropomorphism and Spinoza's Innovations," *Religion* 25 (1995): 1-8; Roy A. Harrisville and Walter Sundberg, *The Bible in Modern Culture: Baruch Spinoza to Brevard Childs* (2nd ed. Grand Rapids, Mich: Eerdmans, 2002).
26. Frampton, *Spinoza*, 24.
27. Ibid., 40.
28. Ibid., 236
29. In his discussion of Calvin's rationalism, Frampton notes that the Genevan's proofs, particularly in the area of prophecy/fulfillment, were of a different order than Descartes

Spinoza's work on biblical interpretation came in a period characterized by "hermeneutical uncertainties"[30] of the preceding century that often 'blurred the lines' between the biblical world and the reality of the reader.[31] In his volatile *Tractatus theologico-politicus*[32] Spinoza lays out "most of the important principles of an interpretation at once rationalistic and historical-critical."[33] His starting point was the conviction that the mechanics of responsible biblical interpretation are similar, if not identical, to those operative in the natural sciences. They are not *sui generis*. Like the study of plants or the human body, the biblical reader is to collect and evaluate data and then derive according principles.[34] In the arena of biblical interpretation it would run as follows:

> Our historical study should set forth the circumstances relevant to all the extant books of the prophets, giving the life, character and pursuits of the author of every book, detailing who he was, on what occasion and at what time and for whom and in what language he wrote.[35]

In an attempt to set aright the relationship between state and church, Spinoza begins his *TTP* by noting the above problem and pointing out how improper use (i.e., interpretation) of Scripture has contributed to the malaise. In short, taking their cue from the clergy, the people worship the Bible as the Word of God. "I have to say...instead of God's Word, they are beginning to worship likenesses and images, that is, paper and ink."[36] The corrective, Spinoza goes on to unfold in the remainder of the *TTP*, is a thorough naturalizing of the biblical account. Levenson notes how the return to the sources that rallied the Reformers has, in Spinoza' rationalism, come full circle.[37] The very principle that granted absolute authority to Scripture (*sola Scriptura*), freeing the masses from the rule of the Roman Catholic church, would come to be the same grounds on which

---

or Leibniz. Frampton essentially says that Calvin saw straightforward prophecy and fulfillment as proof of the prophecy at the time of the utterance, invoking Zachman's contra-Frei/Lindbeck position as support; Zachman, "Gathering Meaning from the Context: Calvin's Exegetical Method," *JR* 82 (2002): 1-26. Seeking to loose Calvin from some of his pre-critical moorings, Frampton overlooks a crucial hermeneutical dictum for Calvin by failing to adequately note the determinative nature of Scripture's *res* for Calvin.
30. Zachman, "Gathering," 2.
31. Cf. Frei, *Eclipse*, esp. 17-37.
32. This study will use the 2001 English Shirley translation of the Gebhart edition, Benedictus de Spinoza, *Theological-Political Treatise*, trans. Samuel Shirley; 2nd ed. (Indianapolis: Hackett Publishing Co, 2001), hereafter *TTP* chapter, *S*, page.
33. Frei, *Eclipse*, 42.
34. Steven Nadler, "The Bible Hermeneutics of Baruch de Spinoza," 831.
35. *TTP*, VII; *S*, 90.
36. *TTP*, XII; *S*, 145f., in Steven Nadler, *Spinoza: A Life* (Cambridge: Cambridge University Press, 1999), 272. Nearly a century earlier Bailou, in the Pyrrhinic Catholic tradition, accused Protestants of being each his own 'Pope,' each with their 'own' bible.
37. Levenson, *Hebrew Bible*, 92f.

Spinoza would argue that no preference or special reverence be rendered the Scriptures. It was literature, just like any other book, and to be examined as such, without any superficial claims of eternality or absolute reference.

What was the character of the material contained in Scripture? For Spinoza, Scripture was not, as understood by the Scholastics and Reformers, a source of natural knowledge, but rather a "book of imagination, speaking to...emotions and moral intuitions."[38] The Bible rouses humanity *to* God. Misunderstandings and distortions came about when readers appealed to the Bible in defense of what it did not offer: proofs. Appeals to Scripture on these grounds, Spinoza maintains, have allowed the tyrannical religious authorities (Dutch Calvinists, in particular) to play on the fears of the people, resulting in a state religion that is void of all true worship of God. What it *does* offer, however, is an ethical injunction to piety and obedience. Love for God and fellow man make up the twin columns of support for Spinoza's "true universal religion,"[39] that ecumenical set of beliefs shared by Jews, Muslims, and Christians.

A key principle, though by no means exclusive to Spinoza, is the differentiation between Scripture's meaning and those truths that are historically and philosophically discoverable. The responsible interpreter is after meaning: "The point at issue is merely the meaning of the texts, not their truth."[40] Meaning for Spinoza is linked to a passage's historical context: the author's intent and the linguistic nature of the text. Frei has noted the careful nuance Spinoza displays in his treatment of meaning.[41] After examining a passage's sense, the universal truth inherent in it must be uncovered. This universal truth is "without question identical with what we know in any case to be religious truth."[42] What about passages in which reason and the text's literal sense appear to conflict? Spinoza warns against resorting to a figural solution in the case of texts whose literal readings contradict reason. Since the occurrence of a miracle, for example, would have no historical referent, yet the language was not metaphorical, the reader must accept that the point being made was peripheral to religious truth.

Historical knowledge or truth is outside Scripture's purview. "To understand Scripture and the mind of the prophets is by no means the same thing as to understand the mind of God, that is, to understand truth itself."[43] Because Scripture is replete with examples of *un*truths, the faculty of reason cannot externally govern the interpretation of Scripture. Since the material contained within Scripture is different in kind from that in scientific or philosophical texts, its interpretive parameters must fit. Here we see the moral message of love of God and neighbor functioning as the governing principle. Apart from a text's literal

---

38. Feldman, *Introduction* to *TTP*, xxi.
39. Ibid., xxxiii-xxxv.
40. *TTP*, VII; *S*, 88.
41. Frei, *Eclipse*, 43-45.
42. Ibid., 45.
43. *TTP*, XII; *S*, 149.

meaning and the truthfulness of the historical account portrayed, the religious meaning of a passage always comports with what is and has always been known of God's truth as naturally discoverable outside of Scripture.

The first two chapters of Spinoza's *TTP* constitute a sustained critique of notions of divine revelation (i.e., *prophecy*) the likes of those employed by Maimonides and later Calvinists. The concept of divine anthropomorphism in the Scriptures presented an imposing problem for the Jewish philosopher in the late twelfth and early thirteenth-centuries. In order for the text to say anything at all about God, it must be interpreted allegorically since God had no attributes. Anthropomorphic descriptions of God are to be interpreted as "the result[s] of divine condescension, as expressed in the Rabbinic axiom, 'The Torah speaks in the language of men.'"[44] Endowed with both excellent imaginations and superior learning, the prophets employed anthropomorphic language about God the reader was expected to recognize and look beneath. For descriptions of God as such were crude and unworthily applied.[45]

For Calvin accommodation was for anthropomorphism what Aaron was for Moses: an interpreter. Many Christian writers of Spinoza's age accepted Calvin's literalistic view of God-talk. Granting divine authorship, any self-representations of God in Scripture must be accurate, albeit 'lisped' to us so that we may grasp them. Blyenbergh, a correspondent with Spinoza, who argued that such anthropomorphisms must be allowed to represent God's attributes, took up this view.[46] Philosophical and theological discourse must not be mixed; nor should theology be reduced to philosophy. Spinoza's own position concerning Scripture's God-talk is complex and will be filled out throughout our examination of prophets and prophecy in the *TTP*. However, it is worth noting that, for Spinoza, "when Scripture speaks in the language of men...it is speaking *the only language it can*."[47]

As mentioned earlier, in order to show the Bible's *un*inspired character, Spinoza begins by discussing and clarifying just what is going on in biblical revelation, namely prophecy. To do this he begins by discussing the prophets themselves. Devotion of our study to the *TTP* is justified since the question of false prophets and prophecy appears throughout. However, Spinoza's treatment of what prophecy is, a prophet's certainty, and the extent to which his treatment of these issues deviates from much of what we have seen further confirm that our time with him is not wasted.

In chapter one prophecy is tersely defined in what appears to be Aquinian terms: "Prophecy, or revelation, is the sure knowledge of some matter revealed

---

44. James S. Preus. "Anthropomorphism," 3.
45. Cf. Moses Maimonides, *The Guide of the Perplexed* (trans. Shlomo Pines; Chicago: University of Chicago, 1963), II:32-48.
46. Preus, "Anthropomorphism," 3, for correspondence citations.
47. Ibid., 4.

by God to man."[48] But, far from understanding this knowledge to have been revealed *supra*naturally, Spinoza notes the apparent converse: all natural knowledge may be called prophecy. Prophetic knowledge and natural knowledge, in so far as they both proceed from God and are apprehended by the light of reason, have much in common. However, prophetic knowledge, as set forth in Scripture, was limited to a few and must therefore "exclude natural knowledge."[49] In a supplementary note (3), Spinoza warns against regarding the prophets as having surpassed human nature. They were, however, endowed with "extraordinary virtue, exceeding the normal."[50] Prophets received their knowledge through words, images, or some confluence of both, whether real or imaginary. Places in Scripture at which a prophet heard or saw a vision are to be understood as imagined. For example, Samuel imagined a voice that apparently sounded like Eli and inferred it was God. Likewise Abimelech heard God in a dream, at a time when "the imagination is not naturally apt to depict what is most existent."[51] The only instance of an audible divine voice was at Sinai, where God promised to meet and commune with Moses (Ex 25:22). Spinoza makes much of the fact that the only occurrence of God's voice being heard was in conjunction with the giving of the law. This allows Spinoza to associate the mind of God with the law.

Using Num 12:6-7, Spinoza bolsters his claim that the only means of communication God employs with post-Mosaic prophets are images and words. Spinoza cites the verses, interspersing his own annotations throughout.

> 'If there be a prophet among you, I the Lord will make myself known unto him in a vision (*that is, through figures and symbols, for in the case of Moses' prophecy God declared that there was vision without symbols*) and I will speak unto him in a dream (*that is, not in actual words and a real voice*). But not thus (*will I reveal myself*) to Moses. With him will I speak mouth to mouth, by seeing and not by dark speeches, and the similitude of the Lord shall he behold' *that is to say, beholding me as a friend might do, and not in terror shall he speak with me.*[52]

God's revelation was apprehended or received with the aid of the imagination by means of words and/or images. This required a more "lively imaginative faculty," not superior learning (Calvin, Blyenbergh) or external illumination (Aquinas). At first glance, Spinoza's subsequent discussion of the Holy Spirit's role in prophecy appears to strain this position. Aware of this, Spinoza catalogs several possibilities explaining those places in Scripture where prophets are said to to speak according to the Spirit of God. Its meanings are as diverse as a "very fierce, dry, deadly wind," "high courage," "virtue or power above the normal,"

---

48. *TTP*, I; *S*, 9.
49. *TTP*, I; *S*, 9.
50. *TTP* I; *S*, 19; *S*, 231-232.
51. *TTP*, I; *S*, 11.
52. *TTP*, I; *S*, 13; italics indicating Spinoza's words mine.

"man's mind," or "the mind, disposition, emotion, strength and breath of God."[53] He distills these possibilities further, tethering the mind of the prophets to the mind of God and the Law in an innovative manner:

> [T]he prophets were endowed with an extraordinary virtue exceeding the normal and...they devoted themselves to piety with especial constancy. Furthermore, they perceived the mind and thought of God...and it was for this reason that the Law, since it displays the mind of God, is called the Spirit or the mind of God. Therefore the imaginative faculty of the prophets, insofar as it was the instrument for the revelation of God's decrees, could equally well be called the mind of God, and the prophets could be said to have possessed the mind of God.[54]

Early in chapter one Spinoza claims Jews commonly attribute those events or occurrences for which they lack a discernible cause to the hand of God. This is done, he quips, out of a questionable devotion and piety towards God, to "serve religion."[55] Later, Spinoza returns to this in order to illustrate a final way in which prophets may have been said to possess the 'Spirit of God.' Simply, when men (i.e., the prophets) possessed knowledge with no discoverable cause and which evoked wonder, the Jews of that time "referred it like all other portents to God."[56]

As we noted earlier, according to Levenson, Spinoza uses Scripture's self-witness against the dominant Dutch Calvinist authorities' appropriation of *sola scriptura*. The first causes behind prophecy are beyond what is naturally discoverable. Spinoza takes great care to alert the reader that he goes no farther in explaining prophecy than Scripture. "I deliberately resolved to examine Scripture afresh, conscientiously and freely, and to admit nothing as its teaching which I did not most clearly derive from it."[57]

Prophecy, then, was knowledge from God, apprehended by the imagination and favoring no superior intellect. Its ultimate cause is unknowable in the sense that the power of God in itself is unknowable.[58] It was expressed in metaphorical, parabolic terms because the imagination was better suited for this form of language. Each prophecy was tailored to a particular imagination, setting, and upbringing.[59] And, of direct consequence to the question of true and false prophecy, Spinoza says that, due to the infrequency and fleeting nature of prophecy,

---

53. *TTP*, I; *S*, 17-18.
54. *TTP*, I; *S*, 19. Unlike many before him, Spinoza stresses the Law's signatory value. Rather than a source of doctrine from which the prophets drew, the law stood as an external sign to which the prophets could point as corroborative evidence. We will treat this further in the section on prophetic doctrine below.
55. *TTP*, I; *S*, 10.
56. *TTP*, I; *S*, 19.
57. *TTP*, Preface; *S*, 5.
58. *TTP*, I; *S*, 20.
59. *TTP*, II; *S*, 21.

the question of a prophet's "certainty" is paramount. This is because prophecy's mode of reception was imaginative not scientific, that is, it was not perceived through "assured rational principles."[60] How could a prophet, and those to whom they spoke, be certain a prophecy was from God? Twice Spinoza gives three certainties, or criteria, for verification:

> 1. That the things revealed were most vividly imagined...
> 2. The occurrence of a sign.
> 3. Lastly and most important, that the minds of the prophets were directed exclusively towards what was right and good.[61]

Although three criteria are operative for Spinoza, he recognizes the subjective nature of #1. "Therefore, our certainty regarding revelation can rest, and ought to rest, entirely on the other two, the sign and doctrine they taught."[62] It is to these two we now turn.

Spinoza begins chapter two by noting that the imagination, prophetic or otherwise, carries no certainty.[63] Reason must accompany prophecy. However, prophecy itself affords no proof; simply *because* revelation claims to be divine does not make it so. An observable sign must accompany true prophecy. "[T]he prophets always received some sign to assure them of the certainty of their prophetic imaginings."[64] This is why Moses in Deut 18:22 tells the people to acknowledge a prophet's veracity only after the thing predicted occurred. So, the sign served to assure both the people and the prophet. At this point Spinoza makes a distinction in the nature of the certainty afforded by a prophetic sign. Prophecy that was attested by a sign was not granted "mathematical certainty, but only a moral certainty."[65] This, for Spinoza, is the message of Deut 13. Even if the prophet in question produces signs and wonders to validate his prophecies, he must still be executed. Why? The prophet's intention was immoral: he was advocating the worship of false gods. The signs and wonders were tests introduced by God to test his people, Moses says. Spinoza also sees this principle at work in Ezekiel (14:9), Micaiah (1 K 22:23), and Christ (Mt 24:24). Spinoza sees in the case of Micaiah evidence of the truth that, while signs afford only a limited measure of certainty and remained "open to much doubt," God is still operative in the affairs of his prophets and people. He does not deceive his own. In order to deceive Ahab, only false prophets were used; "to the good prophet [God] revealed what was true and did not forbid him to proclaim the truth."[66] In his treatment of miracles (ch. 6), Spinoza makes the case that we cannot gain

---

60. *TTP*, I; *S*, 20.
61. *TTP*, II; *S*, 23; *TTP*, XV; *S*, 170-171.
62. *TTP*, XV; *S*, 170.
63. *TTP*, II; *S*, 21.
64. *TTP*, II; *S*, 22.
65. *TTP*, II; *S*, 22; Spinoza defines mathematical certainty as "the certainty that necessarily derives from the apprehension of what is apprehended or seen." *TTP*, II; *S*, 23.
66. *TTP*, II; *S*, 22.

any useful knowledge of God from miracles. He returns to Deut 13 to make the point. A sign (i.e., "miracle") can be performed by false prophets as well as true and "from miracles men may accept false gods quite as readily as the true God."[67] The only protection against being duped was true knowledge and love of God.

True signs, although at times not mentioned explicitly by the text, were always received by a prophet. Scripture, Spinoza adds, seems to take their presence for granted. An exception was granted to those prophets whose prophecies "revealed nothing beyond what was contained in the Law."[68] The presence and binding nature of the law was their assurance.

> Jeremiah's prophecy concerning the destruction of Jerusalem was supported by the prophecies of other prophets and by the threats of retribution contained in the Law, and so needed no sign; but Hananiah, who in the face of all the prophets prophesied the speedy restoration of the state, necessarily needed a sign, in the absence of which he ought to have doubted his prophecy until it might be confirmed by the event he had prophesied. See Jeremiah ch. 28 v. 9.[69]

The signs various prophets received were particularly suited to that prophet's disposition. "A sign that would validate his prophecy for one prophet might fail to convince another who held different beliefs."[70] So too did the prophets' revelation. A prophet's temperament, imagination, and previously held beliefs were determinative of the tenor of revelation received and the manner in which it was apprehended. Directly refuting Maimonides' Aristotelian teaching (that God does not communicate with the angry),[71] Spinoza surveys the Bible pointing out characters of less-than-sunny disposition with whom God communicated. Moses' fury burned against Pharaoh and he prophesied the death of the Egyptians' firstborns; an angry Ezekiel spoke with fury at the disobedient Jews; a gloomy Jeremiah foresaw utter devastation;[72] Micaiah's message for Ahab was a consistent barrage of judgement and coming evil. Likewise, a refined Isaiah's prose was in stark contrast to the rustic speech of Amos or Ezekiel as was the dialectical sophistication of Jeremiah's argument to that of Obadiah.

A prophet's previously held beliefs determine the nature of their revelation. For example, the prophet Samuel (1 Sam 15:29) denied God was capable of repentance while Jeremiah believed he was (18:8, 10). Joel taught God repented, but only from evil (2:13). While elements of a prophet's doctrine appear flexible, their thrust or meta-narrative aligned across the spectrum. In other words the

---

67. *TTP*, VI; *S*, 77.
68. *TTP*, II; *S*, 23.
69. *TTP* II; *S*, 23.
70. Ibid.
71. Maimonides, *A Guide of the Perplexed*, II. 36.
72. His gloominess, Spinoza says, is the reason why Josiah opted to consult with Huldah (2 Chr 34), since she was "more fitted from her feminine character to receive a revelation of God's mercy." *TTP*, II; *S*, 24.

"substance and purpose" of a prophet's revelation never varies.[73] As shown above, the prophets were free to differ on matters of "philosophic speculation."[74] The reader should not expect too much of them on matters of detail. Of lasting import are those teachings that address one's charity and moral conduct. This, for Spinoza, is as true for Micaiah as for Jesus.[75]

The prophets', and derivatively Scriptures', divinity and authority reside in the degree to which a prophet's message "teaches moral doctrine."[76] Of the three criteria listed above, "the chief characteristic which established the certainty of the prophets was that their minds were directed to what was right and good."[77] Scripture is true *because* it instructs the reader in virtue. And, as Scripture's authority is dependent upon the prophets', it follows that the prophets' message is a moral one. In fact, the prophets did not base their authority on any other grounds. Those places at which a prophet appears to argue according to principles of reason or on grounds of natural knowledge are not to be understood as revelatory. The presence of a logical dialectic as seen throughout Paul's epistles, is proof that such apologetic was not revelatory or supernatural in nature. In the case of Moses and the prophets to follow, "the more use the prophets make of logical reasoning, the more closely does their revelatory knowledge approach to natural knowledge."[78]

Spinoza understood the prophets' use of and admonitions according to the Law binding only to the degree that they adhered to the universal law of virtue. The ceremonial law (sabbath laws, food, circumcision) was instituted to "strengthen and preserve the Jewish state" only.[79] If Isaiah teaches us anything, Spinoza maintains, it is that the ceremonial law fails to lead one into the way of "true life."[80] As noted above, Spinoza's relegation of the law to sign is a notable divergence from previous interpreters. This can be explained by Spinoza's understanding of the different benefits derived from obeying the ceremonial and universal laws. When a prophet exhorted the people to an observance of the ceremonial law, they could expect "nothing but material benefits,"[81] such as national security, wealth, and success; rewards of a 'lower' order. When Jeremiah or Isaiah urged the fair treatment of the outcast, the care of widows or orphans, or the freeing of the bound, they were calling the people to the obedience of the

---

73. *TTP*, II; *S*, 33.
74. *TTP*, II; *S*, 32.
75. *TTP*, II; *S*, 33.
76. *TTP*, VII; *S*, 88. Balaam was to be understood as a prophet since he "possessed that which especially afforded prophets certainty of truth of their prophecy, namely, a mind bent on that which is good and right." *TTP*, III; *S*, 42.
77. Ibid.
78. *TTP*, XI; *S*, 140.
79. *TTP*, V; *S*, 59.
80. *TTP*, V; *S*, 59.
81. *TTP*, V; *S*, 60.

universal law. The rewards for obedience of this order include mental and physical health, blessedness, and "the glory of the Lord even after death."[82] Israel's pre-70 CE existence as a recognizable political entity had been bound up in its adherence to the ceremonial law. With the abolition of temple worship at the destruction of Jerusalem, the ceremonial law was rendered dead. What did remain, however, were those elements of a universal law that both preceded and outlasted the ceremonial law of Moses. The universal law—the law to which the prophets *really* called the people—was there before the Mosaic law came on the scene and it will be there (indeed, is still present) until time immemorial. It is on these grounds that Spinoza denies the prophets drew on some form of the Pentateuchal law as a source of doctrine.

In conclusion, Spinoza himself neatly (though by no means exhaustively) summarizes his take on true and false prophets and prophecy:

> Hence it follows that a true prophet can be distinguished from a false prophet by his doctrine and his miracles taken together. For it is such a one that Moses declares to be a true prophet, and bids us trust without fear of deceit; while he condemns as false prophets deserving of death those who make false prophecies even in the name of the Lord, or those who preach false gods, even if they have wrought true miracles...Therefore we too must accept only this one reason for believing in Scripture—that is, in the prophets—namely, their teaching as confirmed by signs.[83]

As can be seen in varying degrees with both Hobbes and Spinoza, the authority of the books of the Bible, both its message and facts, were tied to the veracity of the prophets alongside other writers of Scripture. We witness in their works a loosening of the certainty that can be afforded to the basic questions of which prophet got it right and how can we know. We see here at the close of the seventeenth-century that the certainty of the truth of a prophet — even one implicitly considered true by means of canonical status — can and ought to be questioned by the faculties of reason, the hermeneutic of suspicion. While the criteria remain the same (sign and doctrine), what constitutes each has shifted and, as in the case of Spinoza, the moral message of Scripture has trumped the dogmatic, propositional certitude of the previous generation.

Campegius Vitringa (1659-1722)

Vitringa's exegesis was formative among Protestants, particularly the Reformed church. His output was impressive and much of his focus was on the prophetic. Interestingly, Vitringa wrote a sustained treatment of the office of the biblical prophet. A great deal of attention has been paid to the Frisian theologian's

---

82. *TTP*, V; *S*, 61.
83. *TTP*, XV; *S*, 170.

commentary on the book of Isaiah.[84] Also publishing a commentary on the book of Revelation,[85] Vitringa's interest in the nature of prophecy—as shown in his hesitant millenarianism—is evident in his systematic treatment of the prophetic office in his *Typus Doctrinae Propheticae*.[86] Vitringa's Old Testament exegesis was initially an attempt to curb what he saw as outbursts of *typomania* in Coccecian interpretation. Vitringa ultimately sided with Cocceius; perhaps it was more palatable to find Christ than to excoriate him from the Old Testament.[87]

After defining the terms prophet and prophecy in chapter one, Vitringa takes up the question "which modes may be received as divine revelation?"[88] A prophet's election being safely assumed, Vitringa says that a prophet's revelation may be either internal or external. Internal revelations are received by means of the imagination and may be identified as such by the following characteristics. They may be dreams or visions in which an angel or the Spirit of God communicates with the prophet, but there is no auditory message. Vitringa gives a lengthy argument for a dream's veracity: (1) There is clarity of revelation; (2) the image device presented to the imagination during sleep is beautiful as well as elegant, and its component parts adhere to one anther proportionately; (3) there is the distinct impression, while dreaming, that the revelation's origin is from above. There is also the question of whether what was dreamed would lead to the prophet's own glory or not. Other characteristics of true dream revelations include them being ethical; prophetic; including a promise; holy; important; pious; and divinely breathed-out.[89] Revelation may consist of an ecstatic vision, mystical and symbolic in nature. External revelations may be recognized and subsequently validated by either the apprehension of an "unadorned symbolic

---

84. Cf. Childs, *Struggle*, 244-250, which is a distillation of his brief essay "Hermeneutical Reflections on Campegius Vitringa, Eighteenth-Century Interpreter of Isaiah," in *In Search of True Wisdom*, 89-98 (ed. Edward Ball; Sheffield: Sheffield Academic Press, 1999); Gerald L. Bray, "Campegius Vitringa," in *Biblical Interpretation: Past and Present*, 238 (Downer's Grove: IVP, 1996).
85. Campegius Vitringa, *Anacrisis Apocalypsios Joannis Apostoli* (Franeker: ^{1}1705; Amsterdam: ^{2}1719; Wittenberg, ^{3}1721).
86. Campegius Vitringa, Typus doctrinae propheticae, in quo de prophetis et prophetiis agitur, hujusque scientiae praecepta tradantur (Franeker: ^{1}1708); we will be using the Typus as is usually found together with his Hypotyposis (Franeker: ^{1}1708; Leeuwarden ^{2}1716; ^{3}1722). We will be using the second edition of 1716.
87. Cf. the thorough essay by Ernestine van der Wall, "Between Grotius and Cocceius: The 'Theologica Prophetica' of Campegius Vitringa (1659-1722)," in *Hugo Grotius, Theologian, op. cit.*, 195-215, and the notes throughout for bibliography.
88. Quot modis Prophetae Divinam Revelationem exceperint? *Typus*, II, p. 8.
89. *Typus*, III.8

figure,"[90] a "lone voice,"[91] a voice accompanied by some sort of figure, or, rather vaguely, "another sign of the divine presence."[92]

The title of chapter three is "The criteria by which one may discern the true prophet from the false, the true prophecy from the spurious."[93] Before listing seven criteria, Vitringa has some interesting remarks concerning the need for discernment and the nature of the Bible's handling of the question of true or false prophecy. When an event prophesied comes about, the prophet who foretold it is heralded, and rightly so. Therefore, it is no surprise that there are those who, upon seeing the favorable reception of the true prophets, desire to emulate them. The other response is less desirable. There are those who respond to a prophet's success by slanderous talk, attempting to undermine their authority. Scripture calls these mockers, "false prophets, deceitful, and crafty."[94] Either response, however, is proof that many aspire to this gift.[95] Ahab's four hundred prophets in 1 K 22 are guilty of the latter response. Having convinced themselves and others that they are, like Micaiah, true prophets, they are motivated by fame and glory coupled with the perverse power of imagination.[96]

The search for working criteria, or "diagnostic signs"[97] is a worthwhile one, says Vitringa, for at least two reasons. First, the prophet himself needed to know his oracles' source, the Spirit of God or some malevolent intent.[98] Second, other people need to be able to distinguish between true and false so that at the critical time (*maximi momenti*) they "are able to avoid error or unbelief."[99] People present at a prophetic disputation could rightly ask of the prophets' messages, 'Is what is being revealed worthy of God?' "Does *revelationis materiam* lead towards (*duceret*) or away from (*abduceret*) God?"[100] The bystander must ask whether the prophecy's "principles conform (*conformis*) or not (*difformis*) with the revelation at the ancient time of the patriarchs, the law and the docrine of Moses, and the certain revelations of other prophets?"[101] This much is clear from Isaiah (6:1-2) and Ezekiel (1:1-2). If, at the time of the prophecy, a judgement concerning an oracle cannot be made based on the subject matter of the prophe-

---

90. nudis figuris Symbolicis, *Typus*, II.7., p. 13.
91. *Voce pura*, *Typus*, II.7., p. 13.
92. signis Divinae praesentiae aliis, *Typus*, II.7., p. 13.
93. De Criteriis, ex quibus veri Prophetae a falsis, verae prophetiae a spuriis, discernuntur. *Typus*, III, p. 15.
94. *Pseudoprophetai*, Prophetas falsos, mendaces, dolosos. Typus II.1., p. 15.
95. Vitringa notes the entourage of such prophets as Samuel, Elijah, and Elisha.
96. *Typus*, III.3., p. 16-17.
97. Signis diagnosticis, *Typus*, III.4., p. 17.
98. *Typus*, III.4., p. 17; III.6., p. 18.
99. sibi cavere ab errore aut incredulitate. *Typus*, III.4., p.17.
100. revelationis materiam... an duceret ad Deum; an abduceret a Deo? *Typus*, III.7., 18.
101. an revelationi Patriarchali antiqui temporis, Legi Doctrinaeque Mosaicae, & aliorum Prophetarum indubiis revelationibus conformis esset, an difformis? *Typus*, III.7., p. 18-19.

cy (*earum materia*), then credibility may be sought on the basis of its external form, that is, its "mode, attributes, and circumstances."[102]

In typical Baroque fashion, Vitringa gives seven arguments and criteria by which the *materia, forma, adjunctis,* and *effectis* of a prophet's revelation may be judged.[103] The first criterion is "the foremost criterion above all, deliberately commended by Moses himself."[104] It holds that any true prophecy will be "in consensus with *canone doctrine* and the prophecies of Moses and the Patriarchs... according to the Law and Testimony."[105] If this is not heeded, those who disobey forfeit eternal life. What exactly constitutes an infraction of this principle?

> If a prophet recommends a false cult and a fictitious divine will; if they overlook the faults of the people; if he speaks pleasantries to the sinner and the covenant-breaker (*foedifragis*); if he does not inculcate reverence and love for the God of Israel as the first of all the commandments; if, in fact, he would loosen the law of Moses in any way: he is to be considered a false prophet.[106]

He goes on to elaborate on this "loosening" of the Law. Guilty are those prophets who "protect the perverse customs of the people, and loosen the bridle on carnal lusts."[107] The damning title of false prophet is their reward.

Vitringa considers the second criterion of wait-and-see to be a given. "Fulfilled prophecy, is obviously that which distinguishes true from false."[108] No thorough discussion of criteria can omit the obvious. Only here does Vitringa cite Jer 28 (v9), rehearsing the fact that Jeremiah knew that only what happened could have ever been said to be true. While a false prophet may, say, be convinced of his or her prophecy's divine origin, this is a fail-proof means by which to prove an unfulfilled prophecy false.

The third criterion is dualistic in nature. First, the evident miracles that attend (some) true prophecies are obtained or performed only in response to a request. The true prophet will seek a sign of Divine power as a testimony of divine

---

102. modo, adjunctis, & circumstantiis. *Typus*, III.9., 20-21.
103. As evinced by the presence of the qualifying clause *inter alia*, Vitringa does not intend this taxonomy to be exhaustive, merely representative.
104. Hoc omnium erat primum criterium, ab ipso Mose presse commendatum. *Typus*, III.12., p. 23.
105. Consensus Prophetie cum Canone doctrine & prophetie Mosaicae ac Patriarchalis...Ad LEGEM et TESTIMONIUM. *Typus*, III.12., p. 23.
106. Quare si Propheta suaderet cultum falsorum & fictitiorum Numinum; si in vitiis Populi conniveret; si peccatoribus & foedifragis laeta nunciaret; si non inculcaret reverentiam & amorem Dei Israëlis ut primum omnium praeceptorum; si denique Legem Mosis solveret: habendus erat pro falso Propheta. *Typus*, III.12., p. 23-24.
107. corruptis Populi moribus patrocinatur, & cupiditati carnali fraena laxat. *Typus*, III.12., p. 24.
108. Implementum prophetia, quippe quod verum prophetam a falso discernit. *Typus*, III.13., p. 24.

favor and grace that will in turn reaffirm his office of prophet before the people. Second, relating to the prophet's stance before God, the prophet must exhibit a respect and reverence. For, "God does not hear sinners... neither does divine power serve wickedness, deceit, or fraudulence."[109]

Prophetic speech that contains a burden (*pondus*), strength (*vis*), and wisdom (*sapientia*) meets Vitringa's fourth criterion. Pointing to the textual transmission of prophetic speech, particularly Jer 23:28-29, he notes that this kind of speech has been preserved in the writings of the older prophets. Given to aide later readers in discernment, they are ignored to one's own peril.

Returning to the prophet's personal demeanor, the next criterion is that of "Purity of life and a weighty demeanor."[110] Jeremiah (23:14) and Micah (2:11) both attest this. For Vitringa, the adultery, lies, and all around 'Sodomy' of the prophets of Jerusalem at Jer 23:14 is literal. He says where a prophet is ruled by greed and his own indulgent and libidinous desires there is proof enough that God has not recommended him.

The sixth criterion demands that a prophet deliver firm announcements of God's judgments against the unrepentant and covenant-breakers. Ever in danger, these prophets were hated, ridiculed, and thrown before the rulers of their day, often to an unhappy fate. Vitringa effectively says, compare a prophet's reception with that of Elijah, Elisha, Jeremiah, Zechariah, or John the Baptist. The true prophet will be treated just as badly. Vitringa's application of this criterion is interesting. "That criterion is applicable for any true teacher of any time... The true teacher of the church and the faithful minister of God and Christ may not placate evil nor please all men."[111] While the negative reaction of those being upbraided was the focus of the criterion at work for the prophets of old, the present-day application addressed the intent, actions, and message of the speaker.

The final criterion is an extension of the first. There we saw a prophet's message must adhere to a prior message, or flow from a common source: the Mosaic Law and the Patriarchs. Here he points to a prophet's participation in the transmission of prophetic doctrine as proof of his or her authenticity. He explains it as "The consensus and testimony of other true prophets who are known and are esteemed as authoritative. That is to say, a prophet has bestowed a testimony to a prophet: which, if properly received, pertains to a particular place."[112]

---

109. Deus enim non audit peccatores...nec Divina potentia servit mendacio, errori, fraudi. *Typus*, III.14., p. 25.
110. puritas vitae & gravitas morum. *Typus*, III.16., p. 26.
111. imo est illud criterium Doctorum verorum omnis temporis...Veri Ecclesiae Doctores & fideles Dei ac Christi ministri non placent malis, non placent onmibus. *Typus*, III.17., pp. 27-28.
112. Consensus & testimonium aliorum Prophetarum verorum notae probataeque auctoritatis. Propheta enim Prophetae perhibebat testimonium: quo pertinet locus, recte acceptus. *Typus*, III.18., p. 28.

The focus is on a consensus or testimony handed down from prophet to prophet. This prophetic word, accurate and timely at its first utterance, remains pertinent down through 'generations' of prophets, granted its proper reception and handling. Few are the privileged upon which this gift is bestowed; many feign having received it. However, Vitringa's sixth criterion makes painfully clear the cost of such a lineage.

Antoine Augustin Calmet (1672-1757)

Author of a topically arranged dictionary of the Bible,[113] the French Catholic traditionalist Augustin Calmet's contributions to Old Testament interpretation, particularly the prophets, have had minimal lasting impact.[114] Recently, in Childs' call for the reassessment of OT/HB studies, he asked if scholarship's neglect of Calmet was "more a commentary on the present state of the biblical discipline than on Calmet himself?"[115] Childs cites several positive evaluations of Calmet's works from contemporaneous eighteenth and early nineteenth-century authors as proof that, as the temporal gulf widens ever farther between Calmet's day and our own, we should resist the compulsion on this end to ignore his exegsis.[116] While Calmet's contributions to our discussion are relatively brief, they represent the continuation of the traditionalist stream of interpretation

---

113. Augustin Calmet, Dictionanaire historique, critque, chronoligique, gèographie et littèral de la Bible (2 vols.; Paris: 1720). ET: Edward Robinson, ed., Calmet's Dictionary of the Holy Bible (Boston: Crocker and Brewster, 1832); hereafter Dictionary.
114. Cf. the dismissive remarks of both Diestel, *op. cit.,* 441-442; and J. H. Hayes, ed., *Dictionary of Biblical Interpretation,* (Nashville: Abingdon, 1999), 156.
115. *Struggle*, 255.
116. A fair critique in and of itself, but is it possible that Calmet did in fact deserve what reception he received? Arnold Ages, "Calmet and the Rabbis," *JQR* 55 (1965): 340-349, has helpfully distilled the public's varied reception of Calmet's *Commentaire*. Beginning with its initial publication in 1707, many praised Calmet's commentaries (Horne, Clarke, Darling). However, his detractors were also many, and among them were such names as Richard Simon, Voltaire, and Fourmont. In an open letter to Calmet, the French Orientalist Fourmont castigates Calmet for ignoring the contributions of the Rabbis in his commentary. And, when they did receive mention, they were grossly misrepresented. The only extant document from this exchange is Calmet's reply to Fourmont. Ages points out many of Calmet's prejudicial and borderline anti-Semitic comments to Fourmont, making the case that those who praised Calmet's work were effectively already on his side. Alongside these are numerous examples of Calmet's ignorance of Rabbinical learning compounded by his disdain for Rabbincal beliefs. According to Ages, the real tragedy of this episode in the history of interpretation is that Calmet's errant views on the Rabbis were "transmitted to generations of Christian divines which followed him" (Ages, 349). So, it is puzzling that Childs, in light of this letter to Fourmont, would compare Calmet's understanding of the difference between the literal and spiritual sense with none other than Rashi (*Struggle*, 257).

in the early eighteenth-century, and are thus important. Also, perhaps Calmet's several 'new' criteria evince an eagerness to take the entire witness of Scripture seriously.

God's regular means of communication with his true prophets included both the inspiration of their minds and the rousing of their wills to action.[117] Their main task, however, is revealed by Calmet's glossing of the term *nabi'*: "Sometimes it signifies to foretell what is to come; at other times to be inspired, to speak from God."[118] Scripture does not withhold the title 'prophet' from imposters, Calmet tells us, for they were often indistinguishable from their true counterparts.[119] Calmet's description of true prophets contains the rote characterizations of most interpreters before him. Prophets received and exhibited signs, or miracles. These signs, Calmet said, utilized objects ordinary people would recognize out of everyday life.[120] Ezekiel's refusal to mourn for the dead (29); Isaiah and his children; Jeremiah's yoke and 'marred girdle;' these were all actions which would be readily understood. As such, prophetic signs were to be distinguished from types,

> in that signs were occasional, and usually pointed to a time, but little distant, in the first place; though ultimately to a much more distant event, of whose accomplishment the accomplishment of the sign was a token, an earnest, and in some sense a proof; as it manifested a divine interposition on the subject to which the sign related.[121]

Elsewhere Calmet calls miracles — "an action, event, or effect, superior (or contrary) to the general and established laws of nature,"[122] — signs. These are wrought by the true and false alike. Miracles prove neither the "sanctity of those who perform them" nor the truth of the accompanying doctrine.[123] This is the message of Deut 13. The Lord tests his people. The proof of the miracles or signs displayed "is not always unquestionable."[124]

> To the mission of him who works miracles, must be joined the truth of the doctrine he advances, the holiness of his life, his good understanding, and his concurrence with those whose life, mission and doctrine have been already ascertained and approved...If these marks and characters be found in him who works miracles, we must allow such a one to be a messenger from God.[125]

---

117. "Prophet," *Dictionary*, 764.
118. Ibid.
119. Ibid.
120. "Eye," *Dictionary*, 423.
121. "Type," *Dictionary*, 899.
122. "Miracle," *Dictionary*, 675.
123. Ibid., 676.
124. Ibid.
125. "Miracle," *Dictionary*, 676.

Here signs are joined to a prophet's doctrine. Also, the prophet's intelligence and personal piety are requisite. Added to these, a prophet's "concurrence" with a received, accepted prophetic lineage is required. The presence of *all* of these criteria signifies the true prophet.

Elsewhere Calmet notes that Israel and Judah's prophet have been mistreated, harassed, and killed by king and people alike.[126] One criterion which has not been touched upon up to this point is the true prophet's appearance and lifestyle. The Jews, Calmet claim, refuse to consider Daniel among the prophets due in part to the fact that he "lived in the splendor of temporal dignities, and led a life different from other prophets."[127] How then, was the typical life of a prophet to be characterized?

> They generally lived retired, in some country retreat, or in a sort of community, where they and their disciples were employed in study, prayer and labor. Their habitations were plain and simple... Elijah was clothed with skins... Isaiah wore sack-clothe, that is a rough habit, of a dark brown color, which was the ordinary clothing of the prophets.[128]

True prophets, then, could be identified by their 'uniform.' That this was true is evident, Calmet says, in Zechariah's prediction (13:4) that the day is coming when those who deceptively donned the "hairy cloak in order to deceive" will no longer imitate the true prophets. Austerity and frugality are hallmarks of God's messengers as well. Nothing beyond bare necessities were enjoyed by God's prophets. Calmet cites here the examples of Elisha (2 K 4:10, 38, 40), Elijah (1 K 19:6), and Obadiah (1 K 18:4).[129] God's messengers where called to a harsh existence, but it did not require celibacy. While there were no women or wives in prophetic societies, Samuel's children and the wives of Hosea and Isaiah prove the point.[130] At times somewhat unnuanced, one can see in Calmet's criteria a general approach to the Old Testament prophets that remains close to the surface of the text. Affording the stories and descriptions of their ancient personas historicity, Calmet makes the interpretive leap to the present with relative ease and simplicity, a trait that can also be seen in today's more popular treatment of prophets and prophecy.

Thomas Newton (1704-1782)

In England, numerous studies devoted to the prophets appeared in the eighteenth-century. William Whiston (1667-1752) and Thomas Sherlock (1677-1761) argued for the truth of traditional Christian claims from OT prophecies that, they

---

126. "Prophet," *Dictionary*, 766.
127. Ibid., 765.
128. Ibid.
129. "Prophet," *Dictionary*, 765.
130. Ibid., 766.

believed, pointed to Christ as their literal, referential fulfillment.[131] Shortly after Sherlock, Thomas Newton would publish the first of two volumes entitled *Dissertation on the prophecies, which have been remarkably fulfilled, and are at this time fulfilling in the world*.[132] The number of volumes of this nature multiplied in this century in England, not to mention on the continent, as Vitringa and Calmet have shown. We will limit our attention to Newton's *Dissertation*.[133]

The work contained twenty-six treatises on the subject of prophecy. Ranging from Noah to Revelation, and paying special attention to Daniel and the Pope, Newton concludes with a grand declaration of divine communication and its self-evidence: "There must be a divine revelation, if there is any truth in prophecy."[134] He follows logic to its natural terminus, saying, "if the Scripture-prophecies are accomplished, the Scripture must be the word of God; and if the Scripture is the word of God, the Christian religion must be true."[135] While modest, Newton's accounts of a prophet's signs, doctrine, and lineage are worth noting here because they are representative of English scholarship of the period. Also of note is Newton's preference of a literal sense over a typological explanation.

Newton's discussions of false prophets are scattered throughout his treatment on false Christs and miracles. Scripture teaches that miracles—or signs—may be caused by evil spirits as well as by God. How then is one to ground their belief in a truth agreeable to reason? He answers, "the best answer is, that reason must judge in this case as in every other, and determine of the miracles by the doctrines which they are alleged to confirm ... For God can never set his hand and seal to a lie." [136]

Good spirits cannot be employed as confirmation of bad doctrine, nor evil spirits for good; "Satan would be divided against himself" (Lk 11:18). This teaching of Christ, Newton says, echoes that of Deut 13. The gospel doctrines of Christ are not only "agreeable to reason," but they have been amply vetted by miracles in history. This allows Newton to deny the authenticity of Apollonius

---

131. William Whiston, *The Accomplishment of Scripture Prophecies*, (London: B. Tooke, 1708); Thomas Sherlock, *Discourses on the Use and Interpretation of Prophecy* (London: J. Pemberton, [4]1744).

132. Thomas Newton, Dissertation on the prophecies, which have been remarkably fulfilled, and are at this time fulfilling in the world, (London: J. F. Dove, 1832), hereafter Diss.

133. See the works of William Whiston, Thomas Sherlock, and, from across the aisle, Anthony Collins *inter alia*. In light of the masterful treatments of the Deist debates of eighteenth-century England by both Frei (*Eclipse*, 66- 85) and Reventlow (*Authority*, 354-360; 366-369), this study will only be concerned with those contributions made to the study of true and false prophecy per se, since, as Reventlow himself said of Lechler, "it is impossible to add anything of substance to [them]" (*Authority*, 369).

134. *Diss*. Concl. 637.

135. Ibid.

136. *Diss*. XIX.II.6. 359.

and "other impostors." Their miraculous signs' origins properly adhered to the messages espoused by the agent: an evil spirit animated both sign and doctrine; certainly not desirable revelatory activity, but Newton credits it nonetheless for congruity.

Newton saw the prophets connected across all times. Prophetic texts, as well as their authors, the prophets,

> have yet a visible connexion and dependency, an entire harmony and agreement one with another. At the same time that there is such perfect harmony, there is also great variety; and the same things are foretold by different prophets in a different manner and with different circumstances; and the latter usually improve upon the former.[137]

In way of summary, Newton's discussion of Deut 18:15 is worth brief mention. The identity of the prophet in question has, by Newton's day, become the object of some speculation. Some think it Joshua, drawing evidence from the book of Sirach (46:1) and Joshua (1:17). Others think it to be Jeremiah, noting Jeremiah's regular application of Moses' words and their shared tenure (40 years) as prophets. A considerably larger number of interpreters believe that it refers to the subsequent succession of prophets. Opting for the "literal interpretation" of the prophet to be raised up, Newton grants each possibility a limited measure of credibility, if only for a short while.

> The propounders and favourers of these different opinions, I think, agree generally in this, that though Joshua, or Jeremiah, or a succession of prophets was primarily intended, yet the main end and ultimate scope of the prophecy was the Messiah: and indeed there appear some very good reasons for understanding it of him principally, if not of him solely, besides the preference of a literal to a typical interpretation.[138]

Merely interpreters of the law, the prophets between Moses and Christ stood in until the literal fulfillment, Jesus arrived. Newton cites several reasons why Christ best fits the description of a prophet like Moses. All other possible candidates can be written off in light of Deut 34:9-11. Newton holds that, as is common knowledge, the phrase, "There arose not a prophet since in Israel" (34:10) is most likely a post-exilic interpolation of Ezra. Granting its late date, Israel must not consider any one from among the succession of prophets, Joshua and Jeremiah included, to fit the bill. A further proof that the succession of prophets was not in view was the Lord's own response to Miriam and Aaron's grumbling in Num 12:6-8. Here the Lord delineates between his standard mode of communication to prophets and to Moses. The prophets receive visions and dreams; the Lord speaks directly to Moses, "mouth to mouth" (12:8). The positive markers for identification of the prophet to come, then, include face-to-face communication and frequent fantastic miracles.

---

137. *Diss. Concl.* 634.
138. *Diss.* VI.I., p. 78.

Summary

With Vitringa and Calmet, Newton sees the message of true prophets according neatly with what has gone before, displaying a family resemblance amongst them. With a flexible understanding of the contextually-proressive messages of Israel's prophets throughout history, Newton nearly speculates that were Isaiah to hear Jeremiah's words against Jerusalem's oppressors some 150 years later, Isaiah would have nodded approvingly. One gets the sense, however that Spinoza would have protested, noting that the commonality between the prophets lay not in their message, but in the morality 'underneath' their pronouncements, doom or salvation. Little is made in Newton or Calmet of the difference between the salvation offered by Isaiah and Jeremiah's booming judgments. The message of the prophets is flattened out. However, while the stark contrast between Isaiah and Jeremiah, for example, has not yet been drawn out by the work of source and redaction-criticism, it is likely Spinoza would have approved, seeing then a reason for the disparate voices within the prophetic corpus. Newton, and more traditional interpreters explained this dissonance by arguing that later prophets not only perpetrate those prophetic tenets that have been passed down, they remold or tailor them for their era's needs, all the while retaining their salient doctrines.

The traditional view of Grotius received a considerable expansion at the hands of Vitringa. With an eye for the aesthetic, Vitringa described prophetic revelation in terms of its apprehension in the mind of the prophet. And, as in Vitringa, criterion after criterion were piled upon one another in Calmet's formulations of the problem. With Sir Francis Bacon, he warned of those false prophets whose externals glittered. In addition to his asceticism, the true prophet could be recognized by his wardrobe. And, Newton's reluctant acceptance of a post-exilic interpolation at Deut 34:10 signals the coming shift in Old Testament scholarship's assessment of Deuteronomy's role in the message of the prophet and the formation of the book of Jeremiah. Meanwhile, Spinoza sees morality and the universal law as the ground upon which any true prophet stood. Stripping away the externals, both from the prophetic figure in history and the text before him, Spinoza and Hobbes sought the kernel or nucleus of prophecy and found it —they believed — in ideals not too far from their own. Here, at the end of the eighteenth century, the theological lines are being deeply drawn around the revelatory nature of prophecy. While never quite reaching the pitch of the battle raging for the Pentateuch (see Spinoza again!), questions surrounding who the prophets were and how one could know they spoke for God were as alive as ever. And, as we shall see, they were beginning to take on a more urgent tone.

6. THE SEARCH FOR COHERENCE IN THE NINETEENTH CENTURY

Introduction

For much of the century and a half following the Reformers' fascination with prophecy and the role and utility of prophets in the face of political and social upheaval, there was little in the way of substantive development in Old Testament scholarship dealing with the prophets. But, the pentateuchal protestations muttered first by Spinoza and Simon did not remain unheeded. By the end of the eighteenth-century, Old Testament scholarship, particularly in Germany, was experiencing an unprecedented, heretofore unknown freedom.[1] The nineteenth-century, bookended by the works of de Wette[2] and Wellhausen,[3] would prove to be a (if not the) pivotal epoch in the history of Old Testament scholarship's approach to the prophets.

Stated simply, the hitherto prevailing notion of the law pre-dating the prophets now came under review. When the once sacrosanct tenet of the law's priority was first breached, the lines were drawn deeply, and often what doctrine of inspiration and revelation one held determined which side of the issue one took up. Who the prophets were and what they actually did were among the questions raised time and again as nineteenth-century Old Testament scholarship warmed up to (or bristled at) the critical inquiry of the prophets. In the spirit of Romanticism, the view of prophet as poet became standard along with the notion that the oral utterances of the prophet were their original.[4] With Graf's hypothesis — the law was to be found in the post-exilic Priestly documents and as such was later than the prophets — the prophets came to be seen more and more as ethical moralists and religious innovators.[5] Alongside this, the "internal evi-

---

1. Cf. J. W. Rogerson, Old Testament Criticism in the Nineteenth Century: England and Germany (Philadelphia: Fortress Press, 1985), 27. See also H.-J. Kraus, Geschichte, 152-170; and R. J. Thompson, Moses and the Law in a Century of Criticism since Graf (Leiden: Brill, 1970), esp. 15-50.
2. Wilhelm Martin Leberecht de Wette, *Beiträge zur Einleitung in das Alte Testament*; 2 vols. (Halle: Schimmelpfennig, 1806/07).
3. Julius Wellhausen, *Prolegomena zur Geschichte Israels* (4. ausg; Berlin: Druck und verlag von G. Reimer, 1895).
4. Robert Lowth, *De sacra poësi Hebræorum prælectiones* 2 vols, (London: 1753), is credited with pioneering this, as he encouraged his readers to "as much as possible read Hebrew as the Hebrews would have read it," in Smend, *Astruc*, 23. For Michaelis and Herder's critique, cf. Smend, *Astruc*, 23-24.
5. Common to many recent treatments of the prophets is the qualification that many, including Wellhausen's staunchest adherents, misread Wellhausen's own placement of the

dence"[6] of the prophetic books was free to be examined on its own. Needless to say, both of these developments have generated countless treatments, too numerous to list, let alone meaningfully engage. Rather, it is the modest goal of this chapter to explore some of the ways in which this sea change in the interpretation of the prophets affected the understanding of the phenomenon of true and false prophecy. While no simplistic either/or categorization of various interpreters as "conservative" or "critical" is wholly sufficient, as a means of organizing the following material it is the scheme we have adopted. We turn first to the conservatives.

Conservative or "Confessional" Readings
Georg Frederick Seiler (1753-1807)

In 1770 Georg Frederick Seiler was appointed Ordinary Professor of Divinity at Erlangen, a position he held for three decades. A prolific writer and devoted churchman, Seiler was installed as Preacher to the University (1772) and later Minister of the principal Lutheran Church and Superintendent of the diocese (1778). Seven years before his death, Seiler published an eight volume *Biblische Hermeneutik*.[7] Here Seiler, like many of the figures we will treat in this century, displays concern for the proper training of students of theology.[8] In looking at Seiler we will be seeking themes in the interpretation of prophets and prophecy around which the following century of conservative interpretation will rally or refuse to yield.

Seiler alerts the reader to his confessional stance early in his introduction, pointing to what he understands as insidious malice towards Christianity inher-

---

prophets. Gene M. Tucker, "Prophecy and the Prophetic Literature," in *The Hebrew Bible and Its Modern Interpreters*, 325-368 (ed. Douglas A. Knight *et al.*; Chico, Calif: Scholars Press, 1985), 327, writes, "prophetic morality, even for Wellhausen, did not appear out of thin air... for Wellhausen the relationship between law and prophets was not so simple as it became for his successors." Cf. William McKane, "Prophet and Institution," *ZAW* 94 (1984): 251-266, for the reception of Wellhausen's understanding of Israelite prophecy's inception.

6. R. E. Clements, *One Hundred Years of Old Testament Interpretation* (Philadelphia: Westminster Press, 1976), 52; cf. Tucker, "Prophecy and the Prophetic Literature," 326-327.

7. G. F. Seiler, Biblische Hermeneutik; oder Grundsätze und Regeln zur Erläuterung der heiligen Schrift des A. und N. T. (Erlangen, 1800; 8 vol.) ET: with Jodocus Heringa, Biblical Hermeneutics, or, the Art of Scripture Interpretation, trans. William Wright, 8 vols., (F. Westley and A. H. Davis, 1835), xviii.

8. Seiler, Pt. I, Pref., 1-3.

ent in the critical school.⁹ However, much of what he has to say concerning the interpretation of the prophets has a decidedly modern sound to it.¹⁰ For example, those who would see in prophetic books such as Daniel or Ezekiel predictions for their present times are in error. "The common rule of interpretation, viz. that the predictions of the prophets are to be understood of the times near at hand, and should not be applied to remote objects."¹¹

In another place, Seiler outlines the way in which one is to approach the form of the prophetic writings. They are, for the most part, "to be treated of as the works of poets."¹² Seiler's designation of prophet as poet is an (albeit unintended, or at best, attenuated) acknowledgement of current literary advancements in prophetic form and literary-criticism. Seiler is quick, however, to qualify the degree to which the poetic is to dominate. This notion of prophet as poet is to be "applied in a much more confined and limited sense than has been done by many."¹³ It is not impossible to imagine the "many" whom Seiler has in mind.¹⁴

As for Seiler's view on true and false prophecy, his treatment compresses rather than expands upon the traditional view. There were various types, or kinds, of prophets. Deut 18, along with Ex 7:1, Num 12:6ff., and Deut 13:1, describe the paradigmatic prophet. This prophet's peculiarity lay in his announcement of future events, promises, and threats at the command of God.¹⁵ Another category was the learned prophets, or prophetic schools (2 Sam 10:5). Finally, there were false prophets, as described in Jer 2:21, "who only gave out, or falsely imagined, that God had called and inspired them to speak and an-

---

9. Seiler, I, Pref., 13. After noting the possibilities inherent in the linguistic and historical advancements resultant from the end of the eighteenth and early nineteenth-centuries, figures such as Michaelis and Eichhorn, Seiler warns, "May these expectations not be frustrated! and may the rash and licentious attempts at hazardous interpretations, and the subtlety of a (so called) higher criticism, which cuts into the very life blood of Christianity, not have the effect of introducing a skepticism in to the investigation of Scripture more dangerous than the dreams of Mystics and Allegorists—nay, than even ignorance itself!" Seiler, I, Pref., 18." I, Pref., 18

10. Ludwig Diestel, *Geschichte des Alten Testamentes in der christlichen Kirche* (Jena: Mauke, 1869), 624, identifies in Seiler's *Erläuterung* a normative *Vernunftprincipien* that governs all interpretation.

11. Seiler, Pt. II, §204, 278. Elsewhere (Pt. II, §194, 267), Seiler notes the significant difference between a prophecy's objective sense (that is, the truth of the divine promise) and its subjective sense (various notions entertained of these prophecies which were liable to human misunderstanding and error).

12. Seiler, Pt. II, §184, 254.

13. Ibid.

14. At §192, 261-263, Seiler lists seven distinctions between Israel's prophets and the poets of the other nations, noting that to study both in the same manner, as the alleged the critics (Lowth, et al.) did, was to contradict reason itself.

15. Seiler, Pt. II, §186, 255.

nounce future events."[16] Seiler's description of the origin of these false prophets' messages is ambiguous. Was their entire vocational call to the office of prophet erroneous? Were they malicious liars, intentionally misleading the people? Or, were they misled? This also says nothing of their predictive capability. Seiler does not go on to answer these questions per se. False prophets are to be identified primarily by what they lacked.

Unsurprisingly, Deut 18:20-22 comprises the "characteristic and sure criterion of a true prophet."[17] The definitive calling card was prediction fulfillment. However, unlike many before him, Seiler lists several qualifying preliminaries. Those events he foresaw and predicted had to be hidden from his contemporaries. Also, those events' contingencies could not be solely discoverable by his use of reason. And, one or two correct predictions would not suffice. The prophet needed a track record of accuracy. Once these were all established, the prophet was to be heralded as authentic.

Heringa, the Dutch editor of the English edition of Seiler's *Hermeneutics*, inserts a comment following Seiler's discussion of the differences between Israel's prophets and the nations' soothsayers and poets concerning the need for certain criteria on the ground. He too sees confirmed predictions to be completely satisfactory in this regard. The people had need of knowing whom they could and could not trust, not only in order to designate properly the true prophets, but in order to perceive through them what the Lord was saying to them to promote faith and obedience.

One also sees in Seiler, as in many of his stripe to precede him, a succession of prophets originating with Moses. However, in Seiler we see a different thread holding this woven succession together. For Calvin it was the Mosaic law; Spinoza understood it to be universal law. For Seiler, all true prophets, from Moses to Malachi were "animated by the *same spirit*."[18] The phenomenon of prophetic ecstasy that would, in many ways, be carried into the present discussion on prophecy, is here seen to have found a foothold, however minor, in a Romantic confessional reading of the question. The reason for this, Seiler writes, is Divine Providence. There is no hint of naturalistic origins by way of explanation. What we have instead is a divinely sanctioned occurrence "altogether out of the common order of things."[19] God, not the individual, is the source of true prophetic utterances. This delineation, among others, is one that will recur throughout the remainder of our study.

---

16. Seiler, Pt. II, §187, 255-256.
17. Seiler, Pt. II, §188, 256.
18. Seiler, Pt. II, §188, 257, italics included.
19. Seiler, Pt. II, §188, 257.

Ernst Wilhelm Hengstenberg (1802-1869)

The seemingly unlikely successor to de Wette's chair in Berlin was E. W. Hengstenberg, arguably the foremost Confessional orthodox Old Testament scholar of the nineteenth-century.[20] No treatment of nineteenth century Old Testament interpretation should omit such a formative influential voice. Hengstenberg held this chair in Berlin for 41 years (1828-1869) at the same time as other Confessional 'allies' holding appointments at Dorpat (Keil, 1833-1858), Halle (Tholuck, 1826-1877), Rostock (Delitzsch, 1846-1850), and Tübingen (Oehler, 1852-1872).[21] Unsurprisingly, Hengstenberg took issue with the shape criticism had taken in the works of de Wette, Vater, and Vatke. Central to Hengstenberg's critique of this brand of 'negative' criticism, almost exclusively pentateuchal, was the central conviction that the Pentateuch was sacred, and, as such, a repository of genuine doctrine.[22] Where the prophets were concerned, Hengstenberg believed the messianic idea pervaded all their writing, harnessing their individual values under one pervading strain.[23] Therefore, according to Hengstenberg, the reality of Old Testament prophecy is best apprehended by the examination of prophetic individuals, bearing in mind that the prophetic office was free (as opposed to fixed, like priests) and divinely sanctioned, not learned.[24] In clear oppo-

---

20. Rogerson, *Criticism*, 79. Standard secondary sources include Johannes Bachmann, *Ernst Wilhelm Hengstenberg. Sein Leben und Wirken.* 2 vols., (Gutersloh: 1876-80), (3rd ed. completed by T. Schmalenback, 1892); Max Lenz, *Geschichte der königlichen Friedrich-Wilhems Universität zu Berlin* 4 vols., (Halle: 1910-18), vol. 2, 1, 387ff.; Walter Elliger, *150 Jahre Theologische Fakultät Berlin. Eine Darstellung ihrer Geschichte von 1810 bis 1960 als Beitrag zu ihrem Jubiläum* (Berlin: 1960); Kraus, *Geschichte*, 222-226; cf. the helpful article by Mark Elliott, "Ernst Wilhelm Hengstenberg," *DMBI*, 517-520.
21. See Rogerson, *Criticism*, 89, for a representative list of the scholars who have displayed elements of a shared lineage tracing back to Hengstenberg.
22. Kraus, *Geschichte*, 223; Elliott, "Hengstenberg," 518.
23. Kraus, commenting on Hengstenberg's tendency to ignore the history of the Old Testament in service of the messianic, writes, "Die christologischen Perspektiven lassen alles geschichtliche Leben zusammenschrumpfen," *Geschichte*, 222. Elliott argues that Kraus' assessment is too heavy-handed; in fact Hengstenberg can be seen to be at the head of a tradition of supernaturalistic exegesis that valued the historical while simultaneously maintaining a high view of inspiration that would come to characterize the Old Princeton School, "Hengstenberg," 519-520.
24. Hengstenberg, in his treatment of the Prophet of Isaiah in his *Commentary on Ecclestiastes, With Other Treatises,* trans. D. W. Simon, (Philadelphia: Smith, English, & Co, 1860), 345-346. Unfortunately, Hengstenberg wrote no commentary on Jeremiah. As a result our study will rely upon primary works that treat the subject of true and false prophecy most thoroughly.

sition to Herder and Eichhorn, Hengstenberg viewed prophets as foretellers of an unknown future and harbingers of a coming savior, the messiah.[25]

In his commentary on Ezekiel Hengstenberg begins by temporally plotting the prophet Ezekiel's ministry in Babylon alongside Jeremiah's in Jerusalem.[26] A key feature of this reconstruction centers on the activity of false prophets. Jeremiah's letter to the exiles (29) in which he decries the false prophets Ahab, Zedekiah, and Shemaiah was sent just before Ezekiel's call to the office of prophet. Nine months prior Jeremiah's prophecy of Hananiah's death (28:17) had been fulfilled.[27] Just as God had called Jeremiah to combat the false notion of security espoused by the lying prophets in Judah, so too had Ezekiel been called to combat the same foes abroad.[28]

Jer 29 affords a substantive link between the two prophets, allowing Hengstenberg to comment on characteristics of false prophecy to which both attested. Commenting on 29:8c, Hengstenberg understands the dreams that Jeremiah warns against to be self-fabricated. He writes, "the false prophets prophesied to order; they flattered the then ruling humour of the people."[29] And, pointing to Graf's literal interpretation of v23's adultery, Hengstenberg argues that Jeremiah alludes to a spiritual, not physical or corporeal, adultery among the exiled prophets. Here again the connection between the contexts of Jeremiah and Ezekiel serves as a hermeneutical guide. The adultery is an "abridged comparison," one that Hengstenberg is not willing to push as far as Graf.[30] He ends this portion on false prophets with the summary statement: "It was high time for the Lord to raise up among the exiles a counterforce against such adulterous behavior. This was accomplished by the calling of Ezekiel."[31] For Hengstenberg the true prophet could also claim the moral high ground.

Hengstenberg believes the Lutheran gospel/law dichotomy proves helpful in delineating between true and false. He defines the false prophets' chief characteristic as the preaching of the "Gospel without law, a thing worse even than law without Gospel."[32] A similar note was sounded in his treatment of Ezek 1:4 when God's character was envisioned as a storm, cloud, and fire. These visions,

---

25. Rogerson, *Criticism*, 87, concerning the popularity of Hengstenberg's *Christologie des Alten Testamentes und Commentar über die Messianischen Weissagungen* (Berlin: 1829, (2nd) 1856-7), amongst his followers. Cf. Ronald E. Clements, "Messianic Prophecy or Messianic History," *HBT* 1 (1979): 88-89.
26. E. W. Hengstenberg, *The Prophet Ezekiel Elucidated*, trans. A. C. Murphy and J. G. Murphy, (Edinburgh: T. & T. Clark, 1869),.
27. Hengstenberg, *Ezekiel*, 4. This is done by denying Jer 27 takes place during the reign of Josiah's son, the elder Jehoiachim Rather, following 2 K 24:9, Hengstenberg posits instead Mattaniah, "he who revives again in [the name of] Zedekiah."
28. Ibid., 4-5.
29. Ibid., 4.
30. Ibid., 5.
31. Ibid., 5.
32. Hengstenberg, *Comm. on Ecc.*, 348.

Hengstenberg notes, were not the visions of an "impending future of prosperity."[33] Rather, they were accurate, and as such, true. The true prophet of Jeremiah and Ezekiel's day proclaims a coming judgement. The question of true or false revolves around this judgement.

> The contrast of the false prophets and the true is not that of deliverance and judgment, but that of deliverance without punishment and without repentance, and of the deliverance which after judgment falls to the lot of the penitent people—of a bare gospel, crying, Peace, peace, when there is no peace, and of the law and the gospel, each in its own time. A prophet who proclaimed only punishment, would be no less false than one who presents nothing but peace. Law and gospel, each in its entire fullness—this is, even to this very day, the token of the true servant of God.[34]

Rather than equating true prophecy with judgment and false with hope in a straight-forward manner, Hengstenberg says such univocal messages from *either* are suspect. While elsewhere he quips, "*prophecy* and *roughness*...go hand in hand among a sinful people," Hengstenberg is insistent that only the combined elements of judgment, repentance, and restoration constitute a true prophet's message.[35]

At Ezek 13 Hengstenberg points to "foxes," devious figures throughout Scripture represented in the same manner as Ezekiel's false prophets (SoS 2:15; Herod in Lk 13:31,32; corresponding to the wolves in Mt 7:15 and Acts 20:29). Here Hengstenberg moves away from historical matters and more towards a spiritual interpretation. The Day of the Lord is the moment of decision, of crisis; the hostile power is sin; the breached wall is spiritual in nature. The false prophets have "daubed this wall; they gave to the impious and ungodly movement of the people, that was condemned by the word of the true prophets."[36] These "false theologians" will be utterly disgraced at the fall of Jerusalem for they set "death before the pious...and life before the ungodly."[37]

Hengstenberg summarizes Ezek 13 and introduces 14 with the sobering reminder that true prophets will fare no better than the wicked and false prophets themselves. Highlighting his hermeneutic of law/gospel, Hengstenberg writes, "These shall perish along with the sinful people who are led astray by their responses. Only by punishment is a faithful people of God raised up, on whom His grace may unfold itself."[38] A historical linkage between the prophets Jeremiah and Ezekiel afforded Hengstenberg a viable entry point for observing the way in which both handled the notion of false prophets. Along with this there is apparent in his Ezekiel and Ecclesiastes commentaries and his *Christology*, a concern

---

33. Hengstenberg, *Comm. on Ezek.*, 9.
34. Ibid., 9.
35. Ibid., 110.
36. Ibid., 114.
37. Ibid., 117.
38. Ibid., 118.

to connect the theological substance of prophetic conflict with the New Testament up through his own time by virtue of a law/gospel hermeneutic.

Karl Friedrick Keil (1807-1888)

We now turn to one of Hengstenberg's students, Keil. After studying under Hengstenberg in Berlin, Keil spent 25 years in Dorpat (1833-1858) before taking up the chair of exegesis at Leipzig for the remainder of his life (1888). Keil was a Lutheran in the *Erweckungbewegung,* or revival movement, and staunch antagonist to the perceived threat of rationalism in Germany. Keil is most famous for his part in co-authoring a comprehensive exegetical commentary on the Old Testament with his Leipzig colleague Franz Delitzsch (1813-1890).[39] Delitzsch had studied under Hofman at Erlangen, but in later years, upon embracing Günther's speculative theology, moved away from Hofman's *Heilsgeschichte*.[40] Keil wrote the lion's share of the commentary series with Delitzsch authoring the books of Job through Isaiah.[41] Brothers in arms against the rising tide at the beginning of their overlapping Leipzig tenures (1867-1888), Delitzsch's revised and edited commentary on Isaiah (1889) bore witness to his growing acceptance of the historical—critical approach, particularly concerning the book's authorship. Two years after these commentaries began to appear in German they were translated into English in Edinburgh (1863 onwards in T. & T. Clark's *Foreign Theological Library*), evincing their lasting impact on conservative scholars of the mid nineteenth-century.[42]

Keil wrote commentaries on Genesis through Esther and Jeremiah through Malachi.[43] We will look at his work on both Deuteronomy[44] and Jeremiah.[45] Deut 13 affords three case studies in which we see the warning to cut off both the idolatrous tempter and the tempted. Deut 13:1-5 comprised the first case. False prophets and their attending miraculous signs were given, according to Deut 13, in order to test the people. This leads Keil to agree at length with Baumgartner that these signs were not intended as absolute certainty of proof.

---

39. See J. W Rogerson, "Keil, Carl Friedrich (1807-1888), and Franz Delitzsch (1813-1890)," in *Dictionary of Major Biblical Interpreters,* ed. Donald K. McKim, (Grand Rapids: IVP, 2007), 606.
40. Rogerson, *Criticism,* 104-120, esp. 114-116; and Rogerson, "Keil and Delitzsch," 607.
41. Ibid., 606.
42. Rogerson, "Keil and Delitzsch," 608. This commentary series remains a mainstay on many pastors' shelves to the present.
43. Ibid., 606.
44. K. F. Keil, *The Pentateuch* III (Grand Rapids: Eerdmans, 1971; orig. Ediburgh: T. & T. Clark, 1864).
45. K. F. Keil, *The Prophecies of Jeremiah* (Grand Rapids: Eerdmans, 1975; orig. Edinburgh: T. & T. Clark, 1874).

According to Keil, Luther, not Baumgartner, gets it right. Baumgartner's certainty, the "knowledge of Jehovah," is too vague to function as a useful criterion.[46] Rather, Keil sees Luther's "word of God, which had already been received, and confirmed by its own signs," in the form of the law, as the Israelites' only certainty.[47] Deut 18 adheres to this. Keil writes,

> The command to hearken to the prophets whom the Lord would send at a future time (Deut 18:18ff.) is not at variance with this: for even their announcements were to be judged according to the standard of the fixed word of God that had been already given; and so far as they proclaimed anything new, the fact that what they announced did not occur was to be the criterion that they had not spoken in the name of the Lord, but in that of other gods (Dt 18:21, 22).[48]

According to Keil, Dt 13 and 18 are two sides of the same coin. When a prophet prophesied in a familiar way he was to be held to the light of the already-revealed word of God, presumably the law. Not surprisingly, no mention is made of the law in a 'pre-canonical' or fluid form; Keil terms it "fixed." For Keil, familiar prophecies originated from a common source, the law, and were, in turn, held accountable to the same. When a novel prophetic note was sounded, Keil sees a wait-and-see criterion in effect. However, in neither case does Keil attribute any acquitting or accusing efficacy to prophets' signs. He emphatically states, "the signs and wonders of the prophet are not made the criteria of their divine mission."[49]

At Deut 18 Keil writes, "all the prophets of the Old Testament stood within the economy of the law."[50] False prophets could be identified by the non-occurrence of their predictions. This theme, noted above in Deut 13, is repeated here at the end of his treatment of ch. 18. And, he also repeats the injunction that signs and wonders were of no discernible value.[51] But, of more interest is what Keil does not mention. He notes that the prophetic lineage can be traced back to Moses and that the law integrally informs the message of all the prophets. But, one is left thinking that, for Keil, even a false prophet could sound true. That is, his message could in large part comport with the law. Therefore, at least in Deuteronomy, the necessity for a real-time criterion of discernment does not seem pressing. It is only after some time that the prophet's authenticity is revealed. One gets the sense reading Keil on Deuteronomy that the question of false prophecy and discernment takes place on a plane removed from the urgency of the historical prophetic moment. Moving into his commentary on Jeremiah, an increased sense of urgency can be detected. This could perhaps best be seen in

---

46. Keil, *Pentateuch*, III:363.
47. Ibid.
48. Ibid.
49. Keil, *Pentateuch*, III:363.
50. Ibid., III:396.
51. Ibid., III:397.

Keil's attention to the ways in which false prophecy in the book of Jeremiah is exposed.

In his comment at Jer 23:17, Keil refutes Graf and Hitzig's preferred reading of the unusual phrase יְהוָה דִּבֶּר with the LXX's λέγουσιν τοῖς ἀπωθουμένοις τὸν λόγον κυρίου.[52] On linguistic grounds Keil throughout appears eager to attack his opponents. Here he attempts to note the inconsistency that arises from such a reading. Opting for the *lectio difficilior*, Keil defends the Masoretic, arguing that the author, Jeremiah, has left a textual signpost to alert the attentive reader to telltale language of false prophets.[53] Since "thus says the Lord" is the usual introduction of the Lord's sayings, the LXX has emended it here, replacing דִּבֶּר with דָּבָר. Hitzig's own view, says Keil, is that this phrase is used exclusively to denote the word of the Lord "published by the prophets" as opposed to the Mosaic law.[54] Therefore, Hitzig's own reading prevents this formula from functioning in any other than the way the MT, according to Keil, uses it. The very next verse affords Keil another instance to take issue with his opponents. Scarcely a page goes by in which Keil does not attempt to refute the interpretations of the critics, most notably Graf.[55]

At Jer 23:29 Keil notes the way in which God's word was understood to be a hammer and a fire. In this we get a glimpse of the ontological distinction Keil is eager to draw between false and true prophecy.

> There is here no question of the mixing of God's word with man's word. The false prophets did not mingle the two, but gave out their man's word for God's. Nor, by laying stress on the indwelling power of the word of God, does Jeremiah merely give his hearers a characteristic by which they may distinguish genuine prophecy; he seeks besides to make them know that the word of the Lord which he proclaims will make an end of the lying prophets' work.[56]

At Jer 23:30-32, Keil lists three characteristics of false prophets: they camouflage their words with those of other prophets; they counterfeit God;[57] and they feign revelation by deceptive dreams.[58] Keil asserts that these three aspects of false prophecy are only visible against the backdrop of God's ultimate power at v29. Behind the scenes in all true prophecy is the generative power of God that will triumph in the end (thus the wait-and-see criterion of Deut 13 and 18).

The narrative of Jer 28 allows Keil to illustrate what he has previously said and to insert a few additional comments concerning the archetypical false

---

52. Keil, *Jeremiah*, I:359.
53. Ibid.
54. Ibid.
55. An antagonist, Graf, more so than any other, features prominently in Keil's treatment of Jer 23-29.
56. Keil, *Jeremiah*, I:364.
57. This against Graf's reading in which their prophesying is a "mere wagging of the tongue," Ibid., I:364.
58. Ibid., I:364.

prophet, Hananiah. First, Hananiah has aped Jeremiah's signature title for the LORD, יְהוָה צְבָאוֹת אֱלֹהֵי יִשְׂרָאֵל. in his introductory formula (28:2).[59] While not entirely helpful, Keil is toeing the conservative line, advocating a robust doctrine of divine prophetic inspiration that supersedes focusing on those elements of prophecy that may be deemed naturalistic (i.e., their historical or political circumstances, ideological axes to grind, etc...). Keil reads Jeremiah's "amen" of v6 as assent; Hananiah's prophecy is desirable. Keil goes on to explain Jeremiah's response by qualifying, "only threatening predictions have carried with them the presumption of their being true."[60] The reason for this Keil posits is that "these [threats] alone... have been in harmony with the predictions of all previous prophets."[61]

In conflict again at 28:8-9, this time with Ewald, among others, Keil dispenses with the findings of Hitzig accusing the latter essentially of arriving at the right conclusion the wrong way. The question revolves around the term רָעָה, "evil," of 28:8. Many manuscripts prefer the more frequent רָעָב, "famine," as in "sword, famine, and pestilence," found throughout Jeremiah, over the more general term "evil" found in the MT.[62] Hitzig rules out רָעָב due to its lack of difficulty, unacceptable grounds for doing so according to Keil. Ewald accepts it, seeing simple dittography as the explanation; a ב for an ה is not too far-fetched, and "famine" does fit the context. Keil opts for "evil," making his case not on textual—critical grounds, but rather based on the prophetic law of Deut 18:21f. What Ewald misses, Keil writes, is the general logic of Jer 28:5-9. For Keil, the thrust of the prophetic message is evil or wrath writ large. The prediction of "evil" in the sense of judgment was ingredient to true prophecy. Jeremiah is not weighing in on whether a famine will or will not occur; the *kind* of evil is beside the point. "[T]he truth expressed in v9 is based on the Mosaic law concerning prophecy... where the fulfillment of the prediction is given as the test of [the] true."[63] For Keil the issue turns on whether what is predicted occurs. Regardless of the formulae elsewhere, the prophet Jeremiah meant evil, strengthening his backhanded rebuke of Hananiah in vv8-9. Here we see Keil sounding a great deal like Ewald himself.[64] Hitzig's mistake almost sounds admissible compared with Ewald's obtuseness in failing to grasp Jeremiah's dialectic.

Keil makes the interesting point at v10 had Hananiah been a true prophet, he would have retired. But his insistence to the point of violently smashing Jer-

---

59. Ibid., I:405-406.
60. Ibid., I: 406.
61. Ibid., I:406.
62. Keil references 14:12; 21:9; 24:10; 27:8, 13; 29:17f., where sword, famine, and pestilence comprise the "three modes of visitation by God," *Jeremiah*, I:407.
63. Ibid., I:406.
64. See especially Rogerson, *Criticism*, 102-103, for instances of Ewald's excoriating comments of other scholars' work.

emiah's yoke is an example, Keil notes, of seeking validation.[65] In Jeremiah's final pronouncement of judgment, Keil notes the play on the term שׁלה, "send," in vv15-16, drawing to mind Jer 14:14 and 23:32, where the LORD says of the false prophets, "I did not send them." While the LORD did not "send" or commission Hananiah as prophet (v15), he is going to "send" him on one final, terminal envoy (v16).

Throughout Keil's commentaries on Deuteronomy and Jeremiah we see an insistence on divine exposure of the false prophet to a degree not seen before. As for principles of discernment at work 'on the ground,' a wait-and-see criterion is favored. While the law plays an indissoluble part in the infrastructure of the prophetic office, Keil makes little mention of an explicit constraint placed on the prophets or their message by the law. With this is a determination to defend the text as it stands. Repeatedly, when an argument revolves around the existence of textual variants, Keil advocates for what is given in the MT before him. Disparaging and, at times, dismissive of dissenting voices, Keil was no stranger to polemic. The attention to philological and etymological detail and the historical care that characterize his exegesis have done much to commend the author to generations of confessing conservatives as an exemplary interpreter in the service of orthodoxy.

Hans Conrad von Orelli (1846-1912)

We now turn to the little studied and oft-overlooked Swiss champion of Reformed Orthodoxy in the end of the nineteenth—century, Conrad von Orelli.[66] Studying at Laussane, Zurich, Erlangen, Tübingen, and Leipzig, Orelli was exposed to many of the most innovative Semitists and Old Testament scholars of his day. As such one can expect from his scholarship a complex of ideas and methodologies. Particularly interested in the developing *Religionsgeschichtliche* school, he held Zurich's chair of Old Testament and History of Religion from 1881 until his death in 1912.[67] A student of Delitzsch in 1866, Orelli credits Delitzsch with being at least partially responsible for bridging the gap between

---

65. Keil, *Jeremiah*, I:407.
66. Little has been written on Orelli. The biography of his life and works is Ernst Kappeler, *Conrad von Orelli: Sein Werden und Wirken aus dem Schriftlichen Nachlass dargestellt* (Zurich: 1916).
67. C. T. Begg, "Orelli, Conrad von (1846-1912)," in *Dictionary of Biblical Interpretation*, ed. John H. Hayes, (Nashville: Abingdon Press, 1999), 224. Interestingly, one year after taking up his chair at Zurich, Orelli would be invited to replace Wellhausen on Greifswald's faculty of theology; cf Kappeler, *Orelli*, 358; cited in Thompson, *Moses*, 43n.1.

conservatives and the Higher criticism of Wellhausen and others, a bipartisanship Orelli himself did not especially appreciate.[68]

Much of Orelli's work focused on the prophets of the Old Testament. We will focus on his *Die alttestamentliche Weissagung* (1882)[69] and *Der Propheten Jesaia und Jeremia* (1887).[70] Put simply, false prophets only proclaim that which serves either themselves or the crowds they pander to.[71] Where prediction is in order, false prophets trade on probability—true prophets actually receive knowledge of the future. The office of prophet is not characterized merely by the telling of the future, but also of the past. Orelli considers the historical authors' work prophetic in so far as it told of God's ways in history.[72] In quick order, Orelli constructs a rudimentary doctrine of inspiration in which a biblical writer at any time, once divinely illuminated, could see perfectly forward or backward in time to record God's activity there. Ezekiel, for example, sees not only the far distant coming kingdom of God, but also penetrates into the depths of his fellow man. A nascent Hofmanian *Heilsgeschichte* via Delitzsch is discernible when he writes,

> But of course, not only is the prophetic word always significant for the future, because it announces divine truth, and because it has the kingdom of God for its subject, having reference chiefly to its future completion, but the divine mission of its bearers is proved to the contemporary world most obviously by the fact that they are able even to lift the veil of the future.[73]

But, Orelli adds, this is nothing new. Deut 18:22 clearly sets the criterion for discernment on the back of a prophecy's fulfillment.[74] This criterion not only enabled the people to delineate between true and false, but, perhaps more importantly for Orelli, it was also canonically generative. "Undoubtedly the prophets, whose writings we still have, owed their high reputation in great part to the

---

68. Orelli writes that Delitzsch was "einer der ersten unter den Konservativen Theologen, der einer freiern Stellung zur Tradition über den Kanon innerhalb der Gläubigen Theologie die Anerkennung errungen hat."; "[he was] one of the first conservative theologians who achieved a free position for tradition beyond canon within the acceptance of the theology of the faithful." Kappeler, *Orelli*, 73, cited in Thompson, *Moses*, 60n.1. However, Begg does note the moderate nature of Orelli's conservatism, pointing out Orelli's dating of Isa 40-66 as exilic, most likely in line with Delitzsch and his notion of unity; cf. Childs, *Struggle*, 274-275, on Delitzsch and *"Jesaia's Doppelgänger"* that pervades exilic texts that bear the name Isaiah.
69. 1882; ET: H. C. von Orelli, *The Old Testament Prophecy of the Consummation of God's Kingdom*, trans. John Banks, Clark's Foreign Theological Library New Series; 22 (Edinburgh: T. & T. Clark, 1885).
70. 1887; ET: H. C. von Orelli, *The Prophecies of Jeremiah*, trans. John Banks, Clark's Foreign Theological Library New Series; 39 (Edinburgh: T. & T. Clark, 1889).
71. Orelli, *Prophecy*, 6, 329.
72. Orelli, *Prophecy*, 7.
73. Orelli, *Prophecy*, 7.
74. Orelli, *Prophecy*, 7.

fulfillment of their oracles in reference to the future, while later prophets laid great stress on the fulfillment of earlier predictions."[75]

Orelli sees another motif in the text that sets true prophetic speech apart from false. At Micah 2:11-13, Orelli (with Michaelis, Ewald, Hofman, and Kleinert, and "in opposition to most expositors") places these words of comfort and restoration in the mouths of false prophets, a tactic he says Micah employs for dramatic alternation without warning.[76] The false prophets have neglected the temporal force of Micah 4:6, "On that day…"[77] He writes, "In this indication of time lies the difference between a divine oracle and the otherwise similar talk of false prophets…What carnal hope expects prematurely comes only, according to God's word, at the end after purifying judgment."[78]

The nature of false prophecy serves Orelli in his attempt to salvage Zech 12-14's preexilic date. Zech 12's prophecy addresses the dual threat of idolatry and false prophecy, pre-exilic maladies which prophets the likes of Jeremiah address. Prophets operating after the Exile "no longer…rebuke these two sins [false prophecy and idolatry]."[79] At Zech 13:2, Orelli prefers the reading of the LXX, Targum, and Syriac, which have 'false prophets' for 'prophets' since true prophets would not be spoken of as pollutants.[80] That Jeremiah also spoke this way (23:13ff.; Lam 2:14; 4:13) is further proof of Zech 12-14 being pre-exilic in provenance. Almost as an aside and unmentioned up to this point, is Orelli's reference to 1 K 18:28. It appears he sees the "physical macerations" of the Ba'al prophets as an ecstatic manifestation of prophecy that accompanied false prophecy.[81]

Mediating and Historical-Critical positions
George Adam Smith (1856-1942)

The son of Scottish Free Church missionaries to India, Smith was to take up William Roberston Smith's vacated position at Aberdeen. A student of A.B. Davidson at New College, Edinburgh, Smith was trained in the historical-criticism his professor embraced during his studies at Göttingen.[82] In the sum-

---

75. Orelli, *Prophecy*, 7.
76. 1888; ET: *The Twelve Minor Prophets* (Edinburgh: Clark, 1888), 199.
77. Orelli, *Prophecy*, 305-306.
78. Orelli, *Prophecy*, 306.
79. Orelli, *Prophecy*, 345. A tendentious argument at best, Orelli even enlists the high frequency of Zechariah's name in his defense to explain the possibility of other authors or prophets so named.
80. Orelli, *Prophecy*, 353.
81. Orelli, *Prophecy*, 353.
82. W. D. Tucker Jr., "George Adam Smith (1856-1942)," in *Dictionary of Major Biblical Interpreters,* ed. Donald K. McKim, (Downers Grove: IVP Academic, 2007). See also

mer of 1878, during his second trip to Germany, Smith worked under Delitzsch and Harnack in Leipzig. Smith was a self-titled Evangelical with strong ecclesial ties he sought to maintain, rather than sever. In much the same way as his predecessor, Smith believed historically rigorous, critical exegesis of the biblical text affirmed, not destroyed, the church's derivative theology.[83] His appointment in itself, along with the fact that he labored from within the Christian community of faith to promote a critical reading of the Old Testament, suggest that his insistence on the positive contributions to be gained from criticism did not fall on completely deaf ears.

An entry point into Smith concerning our question comes first from his commentary on the Twelve Prophets. Befitting the son of foreign missionaries, Smith sees the final and most important phase in the development of Israel's religion in ethical and missional terms.

> It was in the peace and liberty of this day [eighth-century] that Israel rose a step in civilization; that prophecy, released from the defence, became the criticism of the national life; and that the people, no longer absorbed in their own borders, looked out, and for the first time realized the great world, of which they were only a part.[84]

For Smith, the notion of Israel's development or growth from a primitive, ritualistic religion to an embodiment of spiritual doctrine can help shed light on the nature of discernment in the case of Jeremiah. Although they shared much in common, there were two distinctive differences between true prophets, represented in Jeremiah, and false, Hananiah.[85] The first was moral. While their messages were "diametrically opposite,"[86] both prophets operated out of certain beliefs about their God. Their predictions were based on an interpretation of their history and a reasonable certainty of what was to come. For Hananiah, Yahweh of Israel could not, for any reason, forsake his people. He would surely protect them, all evidence to the contrary. With no mention of Isaiah, Smith holds that Jeremiah believed in a holy and just God who was bound to punish a people so negligent of his law. Corresponding to a traditional understanding of atonement as love fulfilling justice Smith sees in the dogmatic formulation of

---

Iain D. Campbell, *Fixing the Indemnity: The Life and Work of Sir George Adam Smith (1856-1942)* (Carlisle: Paternoster, 2004). On Smith's hermeneutic see Childs, *Struggle*, 284-287, and Christopher Seitz, *Prophecy and Hermeneutics: Toward a New Introduction to the Prophets* (Grand Rapids: Baker Academic, 2007), 222-229. Cf. Bernhard Maier's recent work, *William Robertson Smith: His Life, His Work, and His Times*, FAT 67 (Tübingen: Mohr Siebeck, 2009).

83. Tucker Jr., 221.

84. George Adam Smith, *The Book of the Twelve Prophets* I (New York: AC Armstrong and Son, 1896), 31-32; cited in Campbell, *Indemnity*, 116-117.

85. George Adam Smith, *Jeremiah: Being the Baird Lecture for 1922* 4th ed. (New York: Harper, 1929), 258.

86. Smith, *Jeremiah*, 258.

Hananiah the remnants of a former, "simplistic" tribal system of religion, one taken up with the worship of a "lower god."[87] This explains Jeremiah's charge that false prophets caused the people to forget the name (i.e., the "revealed Character and Nature") of God. And, in Jeremiah we can see a flexible, more responsive prophetic theology taking shape. Such a skewed view of God, Smith says of the false prophets, unsurprisingly manifested itself on the societal level. Promising peace, the false prophets condoned the wicked actions of the people; the very actions, according to Jeremiah, for which the wrath of God was coming.[88]

The second main difference Smith sees is intellectual. God's word, along with faith in the divine character, led the true prophet. Also, the will of God was "suggested to him by the sight of certain physical objects."[89] While false prophets' eyes were "blinded by their patriotism," the true prophet had the "right eyes for the events" to read the signs of the times.[90] Here the issue turned on what James Sanders in the next century will call a 'prophetic hermeneutic.' Smith writes, "the truth was with Jeremiah's word and not with that of his opponents, and...the causes of this were his profoundly deeper ethical conceptions of God working in concert with his unwarped understanding of the political and military movements of his time."[91]

Smith outlined several secondary, or peripheral, differences between true and false prophets. By attaching no contingencies to their predictions, false prophets turned truths into "fetishes."[92] As opposed to the traditional view in which prophets knew their traditions, true prophets for Smith "spoke to the time and freely acted according to the character and the needs of the present generation."[93] True prophets displayed a patience and confidence. Jeremiah's words at 28:5-9, therefore, are not to be read sarcastically. Rather, as a Romantic advocate of the "liberty of prophesying," Jeremiah can freely proclaim "The prophet with whom is a dream, Let him tell his dream" (23:28).[94] As far as the true

---

87. Ibid., 260.
88. Similarly in *The Book of Deuteronomy* (Cambridge: Cambridge University Press, 1918), 177, Smith writes of the false prophets' dreams: "These dreams of the false prophets appear to have been optimistic and unethical in contrast to the true prophet's word that convinced of sin and predicted disaster."
89. Smith, *Jeremiah*, 261, such as the almond branch, the boiling caldron, or the potter's wheel.
90. Ibid., 261-262.
91. Ibid., 262-263.
92. Ibid., 263.
93. Ibid.
94. Ibid., 264. Painting Jeremiah as quite the modern, Smith approvingly writes, "All these [acts of patience] are the marks of an honest, patient and reflective mind which weighs opinions opposite to its own." Eichhorn, conversely, sees in this verse the true prophet's being compelled to speak in the face of impostors: "Den einem wahren Propheten ist der Drang zu sprechen unwiderstehlich," "for true prophets, the urge to speak is

prophets' prophecies, Smith tells us that such a calling is an unwelcome one. Per Jer 23:21, the false prophet shows no reluctance to prophesy, while the true prophet is pulled, constrained against his will.[95] With Orelli, Smith reads Jeremiah's initial answer to Hananiah to imply that the "presumption was in favour of those who still preached doom."[96] However, libertine that he was, Jeremiah was open to a message of peace — time would tell.

Georg Heinrich August Ewald (1803-1875)

Heinrich Ewald is regarded by many as the "most important Old Testament scholar of the mid-nineteenth century."[97] A student in his hometown of Göttingen under Eichhorn and Tychsen, Ewald would spend the greater part of his academic life there, save a decade at Tübingen.[98] Opposed to both the 'negative' criticism of de Wette and the Hegelian Vatke, Ewald believed that the historical method made it possible to uncover the processes at work in God's revelatory action.[99] Therefore, traditional Christian belief had nothing to fear from the critical study of Scripture. This belief issued chiefly in Ewald's staunchly held position that much of the Pentateuch and historical books' 'historical' content contained true information. Ewald believed that his findings were the results of an "objective historical method," while the negative findings of de Wette or Vatke were clouded by their governing philosophical concerns.[100] Ewald's work on the Pentateuch appeared to share much with older, more traditional views of Mosaic authenticity.

---

irrepressible." J. G. Eichhorn, *Die hebräischen Propheten* (Göttingen: Vandenhoeck & Ruprecht, 1819), 100-101.
95. Smith, *Jeremiah*, 265.
96. Ibid., 265-266.
97. Stephen B. Chapman, "Ewald, Georg Heinrich August (1803-1875)," in *Dictionary of Major Biblical Interpreters,* ed. Donald K. McKim, (Downer's Grove: IVP Academic, 2007), 426; cf. John W. Rogerson, "Ewald, Georg Heinrich August," in *Dictionary of Biblical Interpretation,* ed. J. H. Hayes, (Nashville: Abingdon, 1999), 363-364.
98. Ewald was among the "Göttingen Seven," a band of professors that refused to accept King Ernst August's suspension of the Hanover constitution of 1833, resulting in their dismissal in 1837. Ewald's time in Tübingen (1837-1848) was productive. While there his multi-volume *Commentary on the Prophets* along with his *History of Israel* were published in German. Toward the end of his life, Ewald's political outspokenness cost him his job due to his refusal to swear allegiance to Hanover's new Prussian king (1867). And, in the year before his death, Ewald was sentenced to three-weeks in jail for libeling Bismarck. Cf. Chapman, "Ewald," 426; Rogerson, *Criticism*, 91-92.
99. Rogerson, "Ewald," 363.
100. Rogerson, *Criticism*, 93. Rogerson helpfully points to Ewald's own—"perhaps unconscious"—historical presuppositions that were grounded in the (Niebuhrian) belief that history was guided; that it had a beginning and an end. Cf. also Rogerson, *Criticism*, 140.

We are interested in Ewald's contribution to the study of the prophets in his *Die Propheten des Alten Bundes*.[101] It is perhaps not surprising that Ewald's most extensive treatment of the prophets came during his 'exile' to Tübingen. Our attention will be taken primarily with volume 3, Ewald's treatment of Nahum, Zephaniah, Habakkuk, Zechariah 12-14, and Jeremiah. That our study of Ewald's understanding of true and false prophecy be concerned with his treatment of Jeremiah is founded by Ewald himself. At the outset of his comments on the book of Jeremiah Ewald sees in Jeremiah, the last of the great prophets, the culmination of Israel's prophetic activity. "Jeremiah exhibits the prophetic character in even a purer and more perfect form than Isaiah, and thus accomplishes the highest things possible within the limits of Old Testament prophecy."[102] Ewald sees a maturation or development of prophecy from Jeremiah's predecessor. Isaiah's prophecy was characterized as "immediate" and "violent," demanding faith and intruding upon the listeners regardless of their receptivity.[103] This "immediacy" did not characterize the later (i.e., better) prophecies of Jeremiah. He writes, "Jeremiah represents in the whole of his long life the pure power of the word or of thought, and of the [prophetic] sign as simply the interpreter and initiator of the thought, without so much as even an involuntary compulsion."[104]

Along with the development of prophecy, Ewald also notes a growing reverence for sacred texts, a by-product of Josiah's deuteronomistic reforms. This "scholastic wisdom" was characterized by hypocrisy and "idolatry of the letter."[105] Nascent in Isaiah's time, by the seventh-century it had blossomed into a "kind of book-science with its pedantic pride and erroneous learned endeavors to interpret and apply the scriptures."[106] In Jeremiah's conflict with the false prophets we observe what transpired when "scholastic wisdom came into a conflict with genuine prophecy."[107] The lengthy quote below illustrates this conflict between true and false prophecy as it pertains to Jeremiah and his place within the historical development of Hebrew prophets.

---

101. *Die Propheten des Alten Bundes*, (186—68); ET: *Commentary on the Prophets of the Old Testament*, trans. J. Frederick Smith, 5 vols. (London: Williams and Norgate, 1875-81). Chapman, "Ewald," 427, comments, "In short, Ewald saw the prophets as models and warrants for his own political engagement within the church and civil state."
102. Ewald, *Prophets*, III:61-62.
103. Ibid., III:62.
104. Ibid., III:63.
105. Ibid., III:64.
106. Ibid., III:64.
107. Ibid., III:64.

Accordingly, there crop up in the utterances of this last great prophet the clearest conceptions of the nature of true prophecy, as if Hebrew prophecy only now, just as it becomes perfect, fully discovered its own character and boundaries; no earlier prophet separated so accurately as Jeremiah all lower form of prophecy from those that are genuine and more perfect, dreaming and enthusiasm from clear intuition and productive, effective action, words of human fancy and passion from pure divine words, 23:9-40, no earlier prophet so consciously and definitely limits true prophecy to the purely spiritual department of proving and testing men and things according to divine truth and of the consequent bold, fearless speech in the name of Yahweh, 6:27-30; 15:19; no one refutes the false prophets so thoroughly by exhibiting their own perversity, 27:18-22; 28:6-9, or when he is persecuted relies with such self-forgetfulness upon the simple consciousness that he could not have acted differently, 26:12-15; 11:19.[108]

Amidst Jeremiah's prophetic "perfection," Ewald sounds a more somber note. While Jeremiah represents the pinnacle of Hebrew 'prophetism,' Ewald saw his historical location as that of turning point.[109] According to Ewald, by the time of Jeremiah prophecy exceeded its efficacy. Raised on a steady diet of prophetic rebuke and admonishment and exalted, in fact, by the mere existence of prophecy, the people no longer heeded the voice of the true prophet. Jeremiah's prophetic growth came with a price: "When prophecy had so far advanced that it cast off the last traces of that antique violence which it still showed in the case of Isaiah...its previous power and activity were reduced."[110] In line with many of the central tenets of the regnant *Sturm und Drang* movement in Germany at the time, for Ewald the highest point of Hebrew prophecy was also the inception of its dissolution.

Ewald's treatment of Jeremiah is pertinent to our study on another level. His placement of Jer 26-29 provides an example of critical scholarship's attempts to locate and explain the implication of these chapters' position within the scope of the book as it now stands. In a section titled "Three Historical Supplements concerning True and False Prophetism,"[111] Ewald offers what he calls proof-from-life examples of the "general discourse against the false prophets"[112] of Jer 23:9ff. These chapters' present position both "presuppose[s] the prospect" of a seventy-year Babylonian exile, mentioned initially at 25, and "point[s] back to it with allusions" found only throughout these chapters, namely at 27:6,7, and 29:10.[113] Not only does the placement of these four chapters indicate unity and intentionality, so too does the similarity of their subject matter. In light of the inevitable and required fall of the temple and ultimately the kingdom, the people

---

108. Ibid., III:64-65.
109. Ibid., III:72.
110. Ibid., III:73.
111. Ibid., III:226-240.
112. Ibid., III:226.
113. Ibid.I, II:226.

were called to trust solely in the Lord and wait patiently for restoration. For Ewald, then, these chapters tacitly rule out a predictive quality functional in Jeremiah as they were most likely written after the destruction of Jerusalem. Ewald believes 26 most likely had its place in an earlier, larger edition of Jeremiah, and 27-29 were added by Baruch's somewhat "freer" pen after Jerusalem's fall while retaining a germ of the original Jeremiah.[114]

Ewald treats each section independently, looking first at 26, then 27 and 28 together, and finally at 29. Chapter 26, the original of the three units, is a compressed synopsis of Jeremiah's temple speech and subsequent activities noted earlier at Jer 7-10. Vv1-19 are nothing new, Ewald tells us, while the fate of Uriah, vv20-24, forms the counter piece. Although his message adhered with Jeremiah's, he met with an unhappy ending, forming a kind of foil for Jeremiah that lends an added air of credibility to the account. Elsewhere Ewald mentions that one mark which sets a true prophet apart is not so much what is said (i.e., their message), rather how one says it. In the case of Uriah, Ewald labels it the counter piece perhaps due to the fact that while Uriah's message sounded like the true prophets', his actions—fearfully running away to Egypt—belied a lack of faith. We will return to this below in Ewald's treatment of 27 and 28.

Chapter 27 and 28 constitute "the most important of this series of narratives" since they "exactly" confirm chapter 25's message.[115] The donning of a yoke signified Jeremiah's surety of Jerusalem's fate. Opposed by the false and "impudent" prophet Hananiah, Jeremiah's sign was ultimately proven victorious. Interestingly, Ewald here terms Hananiah *Irrprophet*, as opposed to the more ubiquitous *falsche* used throughout.[116] After Hananiah's initial declaration, Ewald interprets Jeremiah to say to Hananiah in vv5-9 that it is

> easier to flatter and to promise good things than to speak sternly and conscientiously after the manner of the ancient prophets, and that in former and better times a prophet of this noble type who promised happiness simply was nevertheless not deemed a genuine and divinely sent messenger until the result accredited him.[117]

Ewald's characterization of prior prophetic activity as "stern" and "conscientious" contrasts such prophecy with the welcoming, reassuring tone and intention of Hananiah. Jeremiah, as a prophet modeling his career after true prophets before him, spoke *in the same way*. What was being said here takes back seat to the manner in which the prophet speaks. Prior interpreters of the prophets tended

---

114. Ibid., III:227.
115. Ibid., III:229-230.
116. The translator touches briefly on this at Ewald, *Prophets*, III:234n*, perhaps intimating that the "somewhat more neutral" term *Irr* was used in order to soften Ewald's own indictment of Hananiah. However, the more accurate connotation of *Irr* as "errant" or "wayward," along with Ewald's own characterization of Hananiah as "traitorous" and "impudent," little supports such a 'softening' on Ewald's part.
117. Ewald, *Prophets*, III:234.

to relegate the tone and manner to the periphery, preferring to concentrate on a prophet's message. Here, in line with Eichhorn and Hitzig, the uncovering of the historical peculiarities and processes at work in the prophets themselves and the observance of the ways in which subsequent prophets did or did not comport to a mean, drew Ewald's attention. In his commentary on the anonymous prophet of Jer 50 and 51, Ewald notes that a true prophet—presumably never exiled but operating somewhere in Israel outside of Jerusalem—unaware of Jeremiah's later work in Egypt, was "laboring and speaking just as Jeremiah certainly would have labored and spoken."[118]

The person and actions of the prophet Hananiah are the subject of Ewald's closing remarks on Jer 28. What Hananiah does in the moment matters. When Jeremiah, at vv6-9, references the ancient prophets and their general mode of operation, Hananiah is left with no remaining recourse. Ewald, psychologizing the scene for us and perhaps landing a deft blow to aspects of the more critical readings of false prophets in his day, notes that Jeremiah's sound reasoning by means of precedent would surely have had a calming effect on those present. "But the false prophet would not acknowledge the force of this reference to the history of ancient times, and could find no other means of meeting its truth than the use of rude force."[119]

Chapter 29 is placed at the end of the illustrative units, Ewald tells us, in order to demonstrate Jeremiah's prophetic concern for effect of his message on those outside his direct influence, particularly the exiles in Bablylon.[120] Ewald said the prophet was concerned that his message be heard in the same way abroad as in Jerusalem. Naturally, whether or not a prophet's prediction occurred served as positive proof. Prediction for Ewald, however, does not entail perfect accuracy or some external sight granted supernaturally. Brief mention is made of Jeremiah's "prophetic eye."[121] In the context of Jeremiah's predictions of the fate of the nations at Jer 25, Ewald grants Jeremiah no more foretelling ability than any other prophet. Jeremiah's prophetic eye was trained not necessarily to see perfectly into the future, but rather to see the present in all its effective reality. "[Jeremiah] discerned far too clearly the courage and the strength of the young Nebuchadnezzar, [and] the moral degeneracy and effeminacy of the rest of the nations."[122] The future that Jeremiah saw "could not then be further described or more definitely indicated than as of such an exceedingly general character."[123] Beyond hazarding a guess as to the duration of an exile that harmonized with those of his contemporaries (i.e., Ezekiel's 40 year exile), "Jere-

---

118. Ibid., V:5.
119. Ibid., III:235.
120. Ibid., III:236.
121. Ibid., III:219.
122. Ibid.
123. Ibid.

miah was unable to prophesy regarding the future of the Chaldeans more than this."[124]

According to the example of Jeremiah, the last and greatest exemplar of prophecy in Israel's history, it is the figure and actions, the way a prophet carried himself, that signal a true prophet for Ewald. At the textual level, there is not much mention of the prophet's use or dependence upon the law or some variant of an extant tradition like Deuteronomy.[125] For Ewald, an explicative sense could also be detected in his interpretations of Dan 3.

> As we are here, therefore, no longer, as in ch 2, concerned with the mere revelation of secrets and the antithesis between the genuine and all the innumerable kinds of false prophets, but with the marvelously protecting and delivering power of the true God, a great example...is depicted...A man like this powerful king...must first come into personal contact with a perfectly clear instance of such profound sufferings for the sake of divine truth...in order to receive his first ideas of the wonderfully redeeming power of the true God.[126]

In his commentary at Dan 3, the self-revelation of God to the Babylonian king only comes as God's plan of salvation is enacted on behalf of Daniel's three friends. It is in the unfolding of the divine drama, here amidst suffering, that the question of false prophets leads the reader, as it did Nebuchadnezzar, upward toward the knowledge of the true God.

Bernhard Duhm (1847-1928)

A student of Ritschl, Ewald, and Wellhausen, Duhm finally accepted Graf's late date for the Priestly document, placing him firmly in the formative Wellhausen school. Wellhausen saw prophecy as the "breaking through of truth."[127] The unity into which earlier scholarship had bound the law and the prophets was dissolved. As Zimmerli notes, prophecy could now be examined independently.[128] Beginning with Moses, Israelite religion matured from a cultic to an ethical religion under the tutelage of the prophets. The zenith was reached during eighth-century prophetic activity, the result of which was the transition from cultic to ethical religion as evidenced in the (late) Decalogue of Ex 20. Rogerson

---

124. Ibid., III:220.
125. In the introduction to the first volume of his *Prophets*, Ewald writes, "...whoever gave satisfactory proof that he was a true prophet, had to be heard (Deut 18:15f.). Here prophecy attained its true influence freedom and spontaneity; for although several schools of prophets were founded, the law did not prevent any one of the people, without distinction of rank, age, or sex, from appearing as a prophet if he only showed his credentials." *Prophets*, I:24.
126. Ewald, *Prophets*, V:206-207.
127. Walter Zimmerli, *The Law and The Prophets* (Oxford: Basil Blackwell, 1965), 26.
128. Zimmerli, *Law and Prophets*, 27.

writes of Duhm's pivotal role in this shift, "Duhm's basic view was that for the religion of Israel to develop, there were needed individuals who were sensitive to the divine leading."[129]

Ewald's influence lingered in Duhm's history of religions approach. Smend notes Duhm's reliance on Ewald at those points where Duhm needed support emphasizing the psychological elements at work in the "formation of religious ideas and concepts" at the hands of the innovative ethicists, the prophets.[130] Like Herder, Duhm stressed the individuality and experiences of the prophets.[131] Governing his exegesis was the commitment to "discover in the biblical writings the works of living people."[132] Wellhausen would later accuse Duhm of attributing too much to the prophets.[133] Our study will briefly examine the second edition of *Israels Propheten*, then examine in more detail the commentary which has in many significant ways, set the pace for subsequent Jeremian studies.

First published in 1916, Duhm's *Israels Propheten* contains few programmatic statements concerning true and false prophecy. He does, however, briefly address the underlying character of prophecy itself at the outset of this popular re-working of the less influential 1875 *Theologie der Propheten*.[134] The authentic, or *rechte* ("true" or "proper") prophet, was both *Bußpredigter*, that is, a preacher of repentance, and *Seelsorger*, minister or pastor.[135] Thus far, standing in line with the majority of the tradition, the prophet's message inherently contained a moral streak, one that would have invariably demanded repentance. As the people's pastor, the prophet's job was to confront, not coddle, "naïve faith":

> [Prophecy] is not a timeless revelation of supernatural truths, its task is not to 'prophesy' events in the distant future so that naïve faith can build on the correspondence between prophecy and fulfillment.[136]

---

129. Rogerson, *Criticism*, 260.
130. Rudolf Smend, *From Astruc to Zimmerli: Old Testament Scholarship in Three Centuries*, trans. Margaret Kohl, (Tübingen: Mohr Siebeck, 2007), 109.
131. Zimmerli, *Law and Prophets*, 28.
132. Smend, *Astruc*, 109. In the *Einführung* of his *Israels Propheten*, Duhm writes, "So kann man die Propheten nur aus der Geschichte heraus kennen lernen, aus ihrer eigenen und der ihres Volkes und seiner Religion." "So one can get to know the prophets only from history, from their own and that of their people and its religion." Bernhard Duhm, *Israels Propheten* 2nd ed. (Tübingen: Mohr Siebeck, 1922), 3; cf. Seitz, *Prophecy and Hermeneutics*, 80-81.
133. Smend, *Astruc*, 108-109.
134. Bernhard Duhm, *Die Theologie der Propheten* (Bonn: Adolph Marcus, 1875).
135. Duhm, Israels Propheten, 395.
136. "Sie [Prophetie] ist nicht eine zeitlose Offenbarung überirdischer Wahrheiten, hat auch nicht die Aufgabe, Ereignisse einer fernen Zukunft zu "prophezeien", damit der naive Glaube sich an der lückenlosen Übereinstimmung von Weissagung und Erfüllung erbauen kann." Ibid., 4.

The promise of peace, for Jeremiah, was naïve, as were those who, having heard the message of the prophets of old, believed such. Duhm saw two supports for Jeremiah's position against those prophets who cried peace. First, there was "seiner Übereinstimmung mit den 'Propheten von uran.'"[137] That Jeremiah was in accord with previous prophets drew into sharp relief Hananiah's divergence. Duhm briefly surfaces at this point to make an historical observation concerning the existence of prophetic traditions that may have been available to Jeremiah of which later readers (or editors) of the book were unaware. He writes of Jeremiah's "agreement with the prophets of old," "von denen er vielleicht mehr kannte als wir."[138] Duhm here entertains the notion that traditions outside the scope of the prophetic corpus not only existed, but also were likely drawn upon for precedent. Second, Duhm highlights the content of Jeremiah's message: "...alle früheren Propheten weissagten von Unglück."[139] This message of misfortune or doom (*Unglück*, later to be termed *Unheils-prophetie*) struck a chord that called for repentance; promises of peace did not. He also mentions in passing the personal inner-workings of Jeremiah's prophetic self-identity. Continuing, Duhm cautions the reader against assuming that in light of the 'proofs' sketched above, Jeremiah was in some way insecure or uncertain (*ungewiss*) of his own *inspiration*. His pronouncement of death on Hananiah "proves the opposite," since its *Nichteintreffen*—its non-occurrence—would have incurably proven Jeremiah false on this and, presumably, other matters prophetic.[140]

Duhm's commentary on Jeremiah in Marti's *Kurzer Hand-Commentar zum Alten Testament*,[141] along with his work on Isaiah, was considered "nothing short of epoch-making."[142] Carl H. Cornill, a fellow Jeremiah commentator and contemporary of Duhm, called it "the most brilliant thing that Duhm has done up to now."[143] Duhm's own estimation of his handling of this book was reserved: "...I was afraid of this book, more than any of the other Old Testament Scriptures.."[144] In light of this, it is with no small measure of trepidation that we now turn to this text.

Much of the initial comment at Jer 28 is taken up with the LXX's shorter and, according to Duhm, more authentic, text. Among other standard exegetical

---

137. Ibid., 275.
138. Duhm, Israels Propheten, 275.
139. Duhm, Israels Propheten, 275.
140. "Daraus folgt aber nicht, daß er seiner eigenen Inspiration ungewiß war; die Ansage des Todes an Hananja beweist das Gegenteil, da ihr Nichteintreffen ihn selber unheilbar getroffen hätte." Duhm, *Israels Propheten*, 275.
141. Bernhard Duhm, *Das Buch Jeremia* (Kurzer Hand-Commentar zum Alten Testament 11; Tübingen: Mohr Siebeck, 1901).
142. Professor Bewer's memorial minute, "Duhm, Bernhard, 1847-1928," *JBL* 48 (1929): iii.
143. Carl H. Cornill, *ThR* (1903): 284; cited in Smend, *Astruc*, 113n.30.
144. "...ich habe mich vor diesem Buch immer mehr gefürchtet als vor irgend einer anderen alttestamentlichen Schrift," Duhm, *Jeremiah*, vii; cited in Smend, *Astruc*, 113.

points, Duhm notes the LXX/MT difference concerning Hananiah's prediction of the exiled people and vessels in the exact formulation of two years in days. Duhm notes that Hananiah's prediction of exactitude ("two years in days") is "probably less an estimation of the time, which is necessary for the overthrowing of the Babylonians and the return of the vessels, than the desire" of the occurrence.[145] Duhm says that this bold prediction carries risk and is effectively a bet "to engender an impression of security and to compel their belief."[146] No negative judgment is rendered against Hananiah at this point. In fact, Duhm points the reader to the preceding chapter, reminding us that since discussion of anti-Babylonian coalitions and the like were customary, Hananiah's prophecy was not "out of the blue."[147] Hananiah too appealed to tradition.

Duhm treats Jeremiah's response in 28:5-9 in greater detail and in a manner, as we shall shortly see, which will come to dominate subsequent interpretation of this text. Noting Jeremiah's doubt, Duhm observes at v7 that Jeremiah's response did not claim the auspicious title of the "word of the Lord," rather it was merely Jeremiah's word.[148] Jeremiah was setting about explaining things as he understood them. Instead of responding to Hananiah's claims with charges of libel and calls for the death penalty, an *Erzähler*, our "narrator," paints a more plausible picture in which Jeremiah speaks with caution and marked reserve. "That shows us," Duhm writes, "that we have another source before us... an unbiased, untheological narration, in which Jeremiah has the appearance of a common man."[149] Duhm continues, "There is not any question that this portrayal of Jeremiah corresponds more to reality, than the role of 'rough-housing' saint, which later writers let him play."[150] For Duhm the actions of the 'real' Jeremiah in v11 (silently going his way) again prove that vv5-11's construal of a fair and restrained prophet paints the simple, correct picture.

---

145. "...es handelt sich aber wohl weniger um eine Schätzung der Zeit, die für die Überwältigung Babels und die Rückkehr der Geräte nötig ist, als um das Bedürfnis." Duhm, *Jeremia*, 223.
146. "...den Eindruck der Sicherheit zu erzeugen und sich Glauben zu erzwingen," Duhm, *Jeremia*, 223.
147. "...ins Blaue hinein," Duhm, *Jeremia*, 224.
148. "'Dies Wort' ist natürlich kein Wort Jahwes, sondern bezeichnet den Grund, den Jeremia für die Wahrscheinlichkeit beibringen will, dass er und nicht Hananiah im Recht sei." : "'This word' is certainly not the word of the Lord, rather it designates the reason that Jeremiah will provide in favor of the likelihood that he and not Hananiah is in the right." Duhm, *Jeremia*, 224.
149. "Das zeigt, dass wir eine andere Quelle vor uns haben,...eine unbefangene, untheologische Erzählung, in der Jer als einfacher Mensch auftritt." Duhm, *Jeremia*, 224.
150. "Es ist gar keine Frage, dass dies Auftreten Jeremias der Wirklichkeit mehr entspricht, als die Rolle des polternden Heiligen, die ihn die späteren Schriftsteller spielen lassen." Duhm, *Jeremia*, 224-225.

This brings us to the content of Jeremiah's claims in vv5-9. Jeremiah makes the grand claim that the "previous history of prophecy speaks in his favor."[151] Duhm writes,

> So if—Jeremiah obviously wants to have drawn this conclusion—prophecies of doom were the generic form of accepted prophets, like Amos, Jesaia, etc., and Jeremiah were to render his in the same way, then there is the chance for himself, that he is a true prophet and his prophecy of doom is from God.[152]

Conversely, Duhm notes, while a prophecy of peace might have been contrary to experience and the norm, it held the capacity for truth. The determinative criteria would be whether future events bore it out. Here Duhm regards Baruch's *Satz* at v9 as *unbehilflich*, "unhelpfully," representative: "if the word of the prophet arrives, then the prophet sent by the Lord has really proven himself."[153] Accordingly, seeing an oversimplification in this passage's construal of a thorny matter, Duhm turns from the prophet to the text.[154]

Duhm first notes Baruch's variance with editor(s) of the book. The postexilic editors were of the opinion, evidently in the majority, that prophecies of glad-tidings were abundant; that "at the time of Jeremiah, the *Glückspropheten* walked around by the dozens."[155] Conversely Baruch considers Hananiah, and by extension those of his ilk, an anomaly, "eine rara avis."[156] Duhm elicits Jer 5:12-13 in order to show that Jeremiah agrees with Baruch, noting that Jeremiah too considers authentic prophets to be *Uglücksraben*, rather "unlucky fellows."[157] "It is not to be denied," Duhm admits, "that since the deuteronomic reform some prophets prophesied fortune, but the editors of the book of Jeremiah all evidently proceed with their opinion of the prophets out of a postexilic mindset."[158] Had Jeremiah or Baruch lived after Deutero-Isaiah, they would have sounded different. Presumably, by this Duhm means having witnessed the exile, Jeremiah's message would have instead been shot through with more hope and the promise of peace.

---

151. "dass dies bisherige Geschichte der Prophetie für ihn spreche." Duhm, *Jeremia*, 225.
152. "Wenn also — diesen Schluss will offenbar Jer gezogen haben — die Weissagung des Unheils die allgemeine Art der anerkannten Propheten, eines Amos, Jesaia u.s.w. war und Jeremiah es ebenso macht, so hat er die Wahrscheinlichkeit für sich, dass er ein wahrer Prophet und seine Unheilsweissagung von Gott ist." Ibid.
153. "...wenn das Prophetenwort eintrifft, so bewährt sich der Prophet, den Jahwe wirklich gesandt hat." Ibid.
154. Helpfully signaled by switching to small-text.
155. "...die Glückspropheten seien zu Jeremias Zeit zu Dutzenden herumgelaufen." Ibid.
156. Ibid.
157. Ibid.
158. "Es soll ja nicht geleugnet werden, dass seit der deuteronomischen Reform manche Propheten von Glück weissagten, aber die Bearbeiter des Jeremiabuches gehen mit ihrer Ansicht von den Propheten ganz offenbar von nachexilischen Zuständen aus." Ibid.

Duhm comments on Jeremiah's manner of argument at this point. He appealed neither to an "*inneren*" (i.e., highly subjective) phenomenon of prophecy, nor were his points "*theologischen*."[159] Noting the peculiar—and most likely unexpected—nature of Jeremiah's reasoning, Duhm calls it "remarkable." Jeremiah's rationale was external and outward-focused. It was "predicated upon the sinfulness of the people."[161] It was in the act of focusing on the plight of sin afflicting the people that Duhm saw the prophet's self-identification with those who preceded him, whom he calls Jeremiah's "predecessors and models."[162] Prophecies may legitimately deviate from this, Duhm tells us, but not without an added proviso concerning a prophecy that did not overtly address the people's *Sündhaftigkeit*. The matter prophesied may indeed occur, however, this was at the cost of being granted immediate acceptance. Duhm notes that this occurs in the later pages of Jeremiah, but he does not follow this up in any substantive way throughout the remainder. He does briefly mention that the post-exilic prophets "had no luck with their promises" of fortune.

Duhm finishes this section with two rather open-ended propositions. First, he comments on the fact that prophecies of disaster have constituted "genuine seers," that is, true prophets.[163] To delve into the question of why true prophets are here harbingers of only doom and disaster would be to touch on the "*Sache* of the psychology and theory of religion."[164] These questions are foundational to the understanding of prophecy. By uncovering or excavating the central denominator inherent in messages of prophets that would in time be revered as genuine, Duhm believes we have reached the core, the fundamental thing underlying the prophetic phenomenon. He does not extrapolate further in the context of true and false prophecy, but he has perhaps hinted at what he is driving at above. Hananiah's message left unaddressed the culpability of the people on account of their sinfulness, their *Sündhaftigkeit*. As forerunners of Israel's religion, Duhm sees a handy, if not airtight, maxim (or criterion), in a prophet's message. A message of doom or disaster is one of judgment. This judgment would be inevitable due to the people's transgressions and idolatry as defined by either loose legal traditions extant at the time of said prophet, or, and perhaps more troublesomely, as defined and interpreted by the prophets themselves. That was the way it has been done, and Duhm sees in Jeremiah no otherwise.

Duhm's second proposition concerns speculation regarding Jeremiah's hypothetical assessment of Deutero-Isaiah in light of the prophet Hananiah. "Nevertheless one would gladly like to know, what Jeremiah would have judged of Deutero-Isaiah, the sole sanguinist and optimist from among the prominent

---

159. "Die Art wie Jer hier argumentiert, ist interessant und bemerkenswert. Jer trägt für die Richtigkeit seiner Weissagung keine inneren und keine theologischen..." Ibid.
161. "...auf die Sündhaftigkeit des Volkes basierten" Ibid.
162. "Vorgängern und Vorbildern," Ibid.
163. "...den echten Sehern..." Ibid.
164. "...die zu ergründen Sache der Psychologie und der Theorie der Religion ist." Ibid.

prophets of Israel."[165] According to Duhm's construal of Jeremiah's prophetic message, even a renowned predecessor such as Deutero-Isaiah cut across the grain of the prophetic trajectory in which Jeremiah firmly placed himself. For Duhm's Jeremiah, no prophet was above suspicion. Duhm wonders whether Jeremiah would have treated Deutero-Isaiah the same as Hananiah. "Would [Jeremiah], if he had lived fifty years later, have been amenable to his prophecy of peace? Or, would he have wanted to wait on that also?"[166] Pitting prophet against prophet, Duhm here exhibits irreverence towards the text with what Smend describes as nothing short of "contempt."[167] Duhm's tongue-in-cheek rhetoric signals a deeper ambiguity, for Deutero-Isaiah is far from ambivalent concerning his own message and prophetic pedigree: "Deutero-Isaiah, for his part, believes he stands in an organic connection with previous prophets."[168] The situation is further muddled when it is observed that Duhm, as will the majority of subsequent critical scholarship on the prophets, places Deutero-Isaiah after Jeremiah and Baruch. Accordingly, the late exilic Deutero-Isaiah, prophesying Israel's return and anticipating Persian dominance under Cyrus, considered himself *organically* tethered to the late seventh and early sixth-century prophet Jeremiah. We see then in Duhm a glaring ambiguity revealing itself at the textual level, one that would not be easily navigated. With this textual difficulty in mind, our study turns now to Abraham Kuenen's influential *De Profeten en de Profetie onder Israël*.[169]

Abraham Kuenen (1828-1891)

We have elected to examine Kuenen's *De Profeten* (1875), published the same year as Duhm's *Theologie der Propheten*, at this point in our study on account of two critical factors. First, throughout *De Profeten*, Kuenen's main interlocutor is Karl Köhler. We will interact with Köhler in so far as Kuenen does, due to Köhler's relative absence in subsequent scholarship. Kuenen considers Köhler

---

165. "Immerhin möchte man gern wissen, was ein Jeremia über Deuterojesaia geurteilt hätte, den einzigen Sanguiniker und Optimisten unter den bedeutenderen Propheten Israels." Ibid.
166. "Wäre er, wenn er fünfzig Jahr später gelebt hätte, dessen Friedensweissagung zugänglich gewesen? oder hätte er auch da abwarten wollen?" Ibid..
167. Smend, *Astruc*, 114. This acerbic rhetoric on the part of Duhm was most notable in his treatment of secondary or tertiary texts. And in Duhm's estimation, the present form of Jer 28, particularly vv5-11, qualifies as such.
168. "Deuterojesaia glaubt seinerseits auch mit der früheren Weissagung in organischem Zusammenhang zu stehen." Duhm, *Jeremia*, 225.
169. Abraham Kuenen, *De Profeten en de Profetie onder Israël: Historisch-dogmatische Studie* 2 vols. (Leiden: P. Engels, 1875); ET: *The Prophets and Prophecy in Israel: An Historical and Critical Enquiry*, trans. Adam Milroy, (London: Longmans, Green, and Co, 1877).

representative of a position that may be considered the 'traditional' expression of the difference between true and false prophets through the mid to late nineteenth—century (1860's and 70's).[170] Indeed similar themes can be found in the likes of Seiler, Hengstenberg, and Orelli. Kuenen is quick to note Köhler's position bears some resemblance to his own. Köhler's insistence that God's "immediate action" in Abraham's calling and the formation of Moses "approximates" Kuenen's view.[171] Along with these, Köhler also rightly sees the natural procession of prophecy from the time of Moses onward. Köhler errs, however, in his fundamental rejection of the role the prophets played in the development of Israel's religion. Köhler writes,

> In Israel, two religious tendencies, which differ, not only formally, but also essentially, are opposed to each other; the one, the heathenish, into which the people sink again after every spiritual revival, because it is their natural tendency, the other, which has been implanted in the people by a few creative minds exclusively, and is now maintained and propagated also by a similar agency, and just on that account must be called the revealed.[172]

In Köhler's estimation, true ('canonical') prophecy was derivative, that is, it was dependant upon revelation. True prophecy "could originate only *through divine revelation,* that is, it could be developed only out of a life which was not the natural life of the people, but which was implanted in the people by some persons endowed with a creative faculty."[173] This revelation is not the dogmatic loci of a Calvin or Orelli. Rather, for Köhler, the prophet spoke out of a divinely sanctioned *Gemeingeist*, a "common spirit which was implanted in the people by that creative personality (Moses)."[174] True prophets conflicted with Israel's natural *Gemeingeist*. In other words, it was the job of the true prophets to tend the flame of Israel's correct view of God entrusted to them by Moses, a spark that was increasingly in danger of being extinguished. The people and their false prophets were caught up in the flow, or natural development, of their own wayward religion. More precisely, to the degree that the true prophet pointed back to the antecedent "creative action on the part of God," one that began with Moses, a prophet could be regarded as true.[175] The rejection of false prophets by the true was the rejection of all things heathen and profane.

---

170. Kuenen, *De Profeten*, 577-579. For reasons to be discussed below, it is to be noted Kuenen employs the term 'canonical' over against the 'so-called false' prophets throughout.
171. Ibid., 579.
172. Karl Köhler, Der Prophetismus der Hebraër und die Mantik der Griechen in ihrem gegenseitigen Verhältniss, (Darmstadt: Eduard Zernin, 1860), 93-94; cf. Kuenen, De Profeten, 578n12.
173. Köhler, Der Prophetismus, 96.
174. Ibid., 70.
175 Ibid., 70.

Second, since Ewald, critical scholarship had found in Old Testament prophecy the zenith of ancient prophecy, heathen or otherwise.[176] Köhler's construal, while not wholly antagonistic to historical and literary-critical findings, appeared to Kuenen to have more in common with a traditional or perhaps a premodern understanding of the question. Kuenen's response in many ways encapsulates much of the critical school's take on true and false prophecy toward the end of the nineteenth-century.

As mentioned above, Kuenen concedes that a traditional approach does indeed have room for a type of stunted religious development. Köhler and his ilk, however, do not go far enough. Kuenen is intent on showing that the development of the prophetic was not the detraction the traditionalists construed it to be. Limiting the operative work of God in the development of Israel's religion by delimiting God's immediate work to his interactions with Abraham and Moses, in Kuenen's estimation, deprived God of his place in history.[177] The traditional view(s) were guilty of this.

Kuenen's position contra his conservative interlocutor(s) is three-pronged. First, Kuenen points to the troublesome phenomenon of unfulfilled prophecy.[178] Under the traditional view, a true prophet "takes upon himself...the obligation of neutralizing the force of the facts" brought to light by Kuenen.[179] Rationally, Kuenen argues, this neutralization cannot take place. The only result is to 'downgrade' the prophets' revelation from supernatural and immediate to mediate. Redrawing the lines in this manner reveals the slippery slope on which the traditionalists stood. Once the decision has been made to credit something other than supernatural revelation as the true prophet's source, Kuenen believes the traditionalist will still have to "go one step further, and ...seek for prophecy an explanation which lies beyond the traditional conception of 'revelation.'"[180]

Second, Kuenen is convinced that the message of the canonical prophets is not "wholly foreign to Israel's 'natural life.'"[181] There are, in fact, many points of overlap between the canonical and the opposing prophets. The traditional view of the differences between the two is guilty of failing to see the entire picture as construed in the Old Testament. Kuenen sees traditionalists focusing on passages in which the people's opposition to the canonical prophets is outright without noting the people's continued reverence and submission. The prophets

---

176. "All ancient prophecy was glorified and consummated in this nation," Ewald, *Commentary on the Prophets*, I:25.
177. Kuenen, *De Profeten*, 585.
178. Chapters V-VII of *De Profeten* (98-275) deal with Old Testament prophecies that either never materialized, or were fulfilled in other, unexpected manners. This has been a source of great contention to conservative scholars since. William H. Green, an Old Princetonian, penned a 78-page scathing rebuttal in his *Moses and the Prophets* (New York: Robert Carter and Brothers, 1883), 173-251.
179. Kuenen, *De Profeten*, 579.
180. Ibid., 580.
181. Ibid.

maintain a hold on the people amidst public rejection and opposition. Kuenen points to several prophetic narratives (including Jer 26) that illustrate just this.[182] In short, the scene that the traditional view paints of the canonical prophets' opposition from the people is overblown and distorted: "In one word: however violent the context may be now and then, it still is not of that nature... we should expect it to be."[183]

Third, Kuenen accuses the canonical prophets—and in turn, the traditionalists—with caricaturing the false prophets. It is unfair to apply to all opponents of the canonical prophets "complaints which were true only of some."[184] Kuenen warns against taking too seriously the sweeping claims reported in the canonical prophets. Undoubtedly there were prophets who were immoral or unscrupulous. However, he is quick to temper, to acknowledge that there were individuals of whom these descriptions fit is not to turn them all into "unprincipled deceivers."[185] When we read the canonical prophets telling the reader their opponents prophesied "out of their own heart," what thinking reader simply accepts this as the final word on the matter?[186] It is natural and expected for them to have attacked their opponents' most cherished claim, their divine commission. However, Kuenen writes of the readers' responsibility: "there is nothing to hinder *us* from acknowledging the good faith of both. The supposition that the 'false prophets'...were not convinced of their calling seems, in truth, the more unreasonable, the more thoroughly we consider it."[187] If the very foundation of the office of prophet was infested with deceit and malice, how can one account for its longevity?[188] Broadly categorizing the so-called false prophets as intentionally wicked and corrupt is the particularly weak point of the traditionalist's program. Not only is this bad history, Kuenen holds, but also this view is guilty of idealizing one group against another, which, at the end of the nineteenth-century, was all but unmentionable.[189] So then, what was Kuenen's "better" way forward?[190]

As noted above, the notion of religious development and the response of the prophets therein is central for Kuenen. After mentioning the narratives of Hana-

---

182. Cf. Ahaz's refusal to heed Isaiah (Isa 7:12) is "couched in as courteous terms as possible;" Hezekiah seeks Isaiah's counsel upon Jerusalem's siege (2 K 19:2; Isa 37:2f.); Jeremiah's defense at Jer 26 and Zedekiah's consultation and protection of Jeremiah (Jer 37, 38), *De Profeten*, 580.
183. Kuenen, *De Profeten*, 580.
184. Ibid., 581.
185. Ibid.
186. Ibid.
187. Ibid.
188. Ibid.
189. To this extent Kuenen writes, "It is indeed no small recommendation of our view that it relieves us from the duty of passing upon men of whom we know nothing evil—a sentence which leaves nothing good remaining in them." Ibid., 362.
190. Ibid., 582.

niah (Jer 28), Micaiah ben Imlah (I K 22), and Ezekiel (14:9), Kuenen rules out of court any reflexive attempts to label these so called 'false prophets' impostors.[191] He writes,

> The standpoint of religious development is not the same in both. The canonical prophets have struggled forward in advance of their nation and of their own fellow-prophets. In consequence of this, their view of the state of the people and their expectation regarding Jahveh's dispensations have become different, and their preaching frequently stands directly opposed to the popular spirit and its organs—for as such we have to regard the "false prophets."[192]

Therefore, the conflicting messages, signs, and actions amongst the canonical and false prophets take on an almost necessary or expected quality. They are the growing pains of religion; growing pains which Kuenen also sees traces of in his day. He likens the situation between a Jeremiah and a Hananiah to his time, finding a ready analogy in "the more highly developed" innovators and thinkers who espouse ideas and advance culture and that "great mass which lags behind."[193]

Two interwoven elements combined to constitute the religion of Kuenen's prophets. Interestingly, Kuenen believes the study of these parallel themes, the "prophetic conception[s] of Jahveh's character and attributes," will yield what others' schemes of differentiation have yet to produce.[194] Both were evident in Isaiah's phrase "the Holy One of Israel."[195] From here, according to Kuenen, two roads diverged. The first issued in a heightened sense of patriotism, a divinely sanctioned national-right-to-exist. Kuenen says false prophets took this path, subordinating their religion to "national feeling."[196] This patriotism was a result of a robust faith in Israel's status as elect.[197] Far from abandoning the notion of the Lord's righteousness, the false prophets rather "conceived of it [as] especially operative against the enemies of Israel" in judgment.[198] The second, less-traveled way was that of the canonical prophets. With an unparalleled vantage atop the crest of Israel's developing religious tide, the true prophet grounded his message and mission on the Lord's holiness.[199] As seen forcefully in

---

191. Ibid., 361.
192. Ibid., 583.
193. Ibid., 583. Kuenen does, however, see shades or degrees of a prophet's falsity. For example, Hananiah's message was shot through with a purer form of Yahwism than those opposing Isaiah and Micah.
194. Ibid., 361.
195. Ibid., 583.
196. Ibid..
197. Ibid., 361.
198. Ibid.
199. In Kuenen's accounting of the discrepancy, he not only has a cipher with which to adjudicate true and false, but also to account for the disparate messages of the canonical

Jeremiah, an honest assessment of the condition of the people left the prophet with no choice but to come to the unpopular conclusion that "even the chosen people should not be spared."[200] In either case the "enigma" which so troubles Kuenen — the self-confidence of both prophets' threats and predictions — can be laid to rest. Both were functioning out of the firmly held religious conviction of Israel's status as elect. Both spoke in the name of the Lord. The false prophets understandably believed "Jahveh's holiness and righteousness were tempered by his relation to Israel."[201] Conversely, the true prophets held that the Lord must be "manifested as the Holy and Righteous above all to the covenant people."[202]

Towards the end of his treatment of this question, Kuenen moves into what he calls the results of such an inquiry. While there was "no fixed external sign by which men could distinguish the genuine from the false prophet," he does, however, see a material distinction between the two beyond textual representations.[203]

> It is the moral earnestness combined with deep piety which forms the characteristic mark of the canonical, as distinguished from the other prophets. That is to say: if we follow attentively the contest which they maintain against the people, and especially against "the prophets," and trace it back to its principles, we see in them the representatives of the same effort which we believed that we observed in prophecy from the very first, and which seemed to us to determine the direction in which prophecy itself worked and gradually raised Yahwism to a greater elevation.[204]

For Kuenen, an acceptance of Köhler's position—and the traditional writ large—amounts to inflicting great harm to the very character of God, not to mention the historical documents. Simply attributing the actions of the prophets to supernatural revelation would be to "allow ourselves to be deprived of the belief in God's presence in history."[205] A thorough cleaning of house is in order. The notion of the developing religious consciousness of the prophets—issuing ultimately in ethical monotheism—leaves no room for other explanations or competing causes.[206]

One final word is in order concerning Kuenen's interpretation of Deut 13 and 18. It has been thoroughly demonstrated elsewhere that Kuenen, drawing on Graf, J. Popper, and Colenso's works on the Pentateuch, was formative for what would become the Wellhausian, and therefore consensus, view of the *Grund-*

---

prophets themselves over time. This will be modified and readdressed in our treatment of James Sanders' prophetic hermeneutic.
200. Ibid., 361-362.
201. Ibid., 362.
202. Ibid.
203. Ibid., 587.
204. Ibid., 584-585.
205. Ibid., 585.
206. Cf. Smend, *Astruc*, 84.

schrift (P) as wholly post-exilic.[207] A basal tenet of the traditional view held that the prophets had access to or at least knowledge of a corpus of religious laws that could be identified (if only embryonically) with the Torah with relative certainty.[208] Therefore, in the face of prophetic conflict, Deut 13 and 18 could be appealed to. Kuenen rejects the simplicity of this scheme on account of the late date of the *Grundschrift*.

Kuenen holds that this section of Deuteronomy was put into writing in some form in the seventh-century BCE and is to be associated with Josiah's reforms since there is no evidence that either were ever appealed to prior to this time. Even if they were enacted prior to Josiah they would have served only to distinguish between Israelite and non-Israelite prophets. Such was the limited utility of their function. The prophetic law of Deut 13 served its purpose in revealing and prescribing the punishment due those who would incite apostasy among the Israelites as nothing more than trials of faith sent by the Lord.[209] Deut 18 is only slightly better suited to address the issue of adjudication in intra-Israelite prophetic conflict. As for the utility of Deut 18, non-fulfilled prophecies, while spoken in the name of the Lord, were sure proof of that prophet's falsehood. Kuenen also allows that the converse must also be valid, granting the presence of two key qualifications. A prophecy's fulfillment was to be accepted as proof of that prophet's authenticity provided he spoke in the LORD's name and promoted orthodox worship of the LORD only.[210]

For Kuenen, the limitations of looking to these laws in resolving Israelite prophetic disputes are readily apparent. First, what were the people to do in the interim period between the utterance of a prophecy and its culmination (or lack thereof)? Second, who was entrusted to apply and enforce this law? Kuenen presses this point noting that if no one was going to render a definitive judgment on a prophet's veracity, there was no point in investigating the matter. It is true that a prophet who prophesied in the temple came under the jurisdiction of the temple priests and temple police.[211] However, they were more concerned with keeping order and a modicum of peace than with trying to silence every contentious prophet.[212] Also, a majority of prophesying surely took place outside the temple walls, thus outside the reach of this law. He illustrates this with an example from Jeremiah. At Jer 26, the only defenses entered on Jeremiah's behalf

---

207. Cf. especially Rogerson, *Criticism*, 259n7, 261f.; Smend, *Astruc*, 83, notes that Wellhausen believed Kuenen deserved the title of "Graf's *Goel*," since Kuenen had convinced Graf of the post-exilic date of both the narratival content and the law and thus the necessity of combining the two.
208. Cf. Calvin, Hengstenberg, inter alia.
209. Kuenen, *De Profeten*, 55-56.
210. Ibid., 56.
211. Kuenen, *De Profeten*, 58. Kueuen references 2 K 11:18.
212. In fact, leaving them alone was often the surest way to maintain tranquility, Kuenen adds.

appear to be his own reiteration that he spoke in the name of the LORD and the elders' mention of the precedent of Micaiah ben Imlah's similar anti-nationalist message.[213] Deuteronomy is nowhere mentioned. The deciding factor "was whether the prophet had protectors powerful enough to ensure his safety against the attempts of those who were exasperated by his preaching."[214]

Ever before Kuenen—and subsequent critical treatments of the prophets up through the present day—is the self-evidential truth that what we have before us (Kuenen's "historical documents") in the prophetic books is a biased, preferential treatment of the histories in question. "The authors of the prophetical books incorporated in the Old Testament can in no wise be regarded as representatives of the prophetical guild of their time."[215] It would appear to a modern sensibility that those with the last authorial or editorial word painted their opponents with too broad a brush. Much of the distinction between the two could be accounted for, in part at least, by the concept of tradition. Kuenen elaborates on the question of false prophecy's tangential relationship with tradition. He writes, "if we are to abide faithfully by the testimony of the records, then we must acknowledge that the distinctions, so simple in appearance, by the help of which the phenomena are arranged and explained, are the creations of tradition, and are maintained in its interests."[216]

Summary

We come to the close of a long and productive epoch in Old Testament interpretation. Among the more conservative interpreters we have seen a search for some internal, organic 'thread' or *res* informing the canonical, or 'true' prophets. Different interpreters saw various loci around which the true prophets gathered. Theological themes such as a messianic ideal (Hengstenberg) or an animating Spirit (Seiler) were offered as the core elements of true prophecy. Similarly, for Orelli, a high doctrine of inspiration and a fuctional principle of *sola scriptura* at work in the text made sense of the generative nature of successive prophets' oracles, particularly Jeremiah. Under no terms were conservatives prepared or willing to surrender any element of ancient prophecy that relied on or evidenced the revelatory nature of prophecy or denigrated God as the source of all divine prophecy.

At the turn of the twentieth-century, it was the obligation of the critical inquirer to objectively and soberly reconstruct the historical 'life and times' of the prophets while keeping the prejudices, dispositions, and opinions apparent at the textual level always in view. In part, the critical reflex cleaving the Law from the prophets furthered this historical impulse. This bolstered independent inquiry

---

213. Kuenen, *De Profeten*, 58-59.
214. Ibid., 59.
215. Ibid., 60.
216. Ibid., 54.

into the texts of the prophetic books, highlighting their literary (poetic) qualities along a history-of-religions vein. Scholars looked behind the text, intent on re-presenting those men of old on historically solid ground. While intent on reading Jeremiah on its own terms (GA Smith), at times critics outright denied any divine inspiration at work among the ancient prophets of Israel (Kuenen).

Rather than forcing the prophets into line with one another, their diversity and dissonance in message and emphases was increasingly highlighted by critics. At times the tradition consciousness of even the so-called 'false' prophets was mentioned (Duhm). With Kuenen, Duhm urged readers of the texts to suspend judgment on the 'false' prophets, noting, for example, Hananiah's purer form of Yahwism in the face of Jeremiah's judgments. Positive characteristics of the canonical prophets included their moralism which consistently cut across societal grains, calling for justice, mercy, and care of the marginalized in the face of abuse and cultic negligence along with their prescient cognition of God's ways in their world (Smith and Duhm). Also, canonical prophets refused patriotic tendencies that, like Isaiah, privileged the nation of Israel solely on their election. The canonical prophets will come to be heralded as the innovators of Israel's religion, visionaries whose calls for repentance most truly portrayed the will and word of a free God.

We see a burgeoning emphasis on the final form in Ewald's discussion of Jeremiah 26-29. This paved the way for Duhm and subsequent critically informed scholars to begin to make sense of the markedly deuteronomistic flavor of this portion of Jeremiah. Ewald adumbrates Sanders' prophetic hermeneutic with his discussion of the 'prophetic eye,' that distinct ability of a prophetic personality to accurately assess the geopolitical landscape and thereby situate Israel accurately along God's redemptive historical timeline.

Of lasting value will be the note sounded by Duhm and Kuenen concerning the discord between the prophecies of Isaiah (salvation) and Jeremiah (judgment) and the manner in which subsequent interpreters will explain this. Scores of additional figures could undoubtedly be made mention of, not least among whom would number de Wette, Cheyne, or Wellhausen, to name three. However, we have limited our treatment to nineteenth-century interlocutors whose works on prophets include sustained, close examinations of the question of true and false prophecy dealing with the prophet Jeremiah at the historical and textual levels. Moving into the twentieth-century, the normative role of theological motifs—a theme apparent among scholars of all ideological stripes—will be developed in the context of the rise of the phenomenon of Old Testament Theologies in the works of such giants as Gerhard von Rad and Brevard Childs.

7. True and False Prophecy and the Rise of Old Testament Theologies in the Twentieth Century (1910-1986)

Introduction

Twentieth-century Christian interpretation of true and false prophecy in the Old Testament, most notably the conflict between Jeremiah and Hananiah in Jer 28, was given its inceptive shape by Gerhard von Rad and furthered substantially by the works of James Sanders and Brevard Childs. Subsequent explorations of the question of true and false prophecy, it will be argued, have expanded upon von Rad's treatment.[1] Discussing the historical setting, textual interpretation, and some hermeneutical considerations of von Rad, Sanders, and Childs, we will note a varying degree of reliance on historical-critical findings. Recognizing a later editing of the book to what is now its present form, we will discuss the role and degree of importance attributed to the forces at work in the shaping of the book of Jeremiah. The prophets' theologies will be of central concern, as well as the application of those theologies to the prophets' present situations. And, seeing a theological intentionality in Jeremiah's portrayal of true and false prophecy, we will seek to locate and develop von Rad's methods of approach in the interpretations of Sanders and Childs. While noting their similarities, we will demonstrate different interpretative schemes, seeking to place their voices in the larger choir of contemporary Old Testament scholarship. This chapter will limit itself to scholarship falling between 1910 and 1986. Roughly thereafter the discussion becomes increasingly comprised of social and political retrievals of the prophetic characters. While not wholly peripheral to this chapter, it is our position that this era's approach to the problem is firstly theological.[2]

---

1. While von Rad was not the first in the 20th century to devote an article to the subject, it is our opinion that his would have a wide scope of influence. Cf. Sigmund Mowinckel, "Profetenes forhold til *nabiismen*," *NTT* (1910); a popular account by J. J. P. Valeton, "Prophet Gegen Prophet," in *Gott und Mensch im Lichte der prophetischen Offenbarung. Alttestamentliche Abhandlungen* (Gütersloh: C. Bertelsmann, 1911); Eduard Sachsse, *Die Propheten des A-T. und ihre Gegner*, (Berlin: Runge, 1919); and esp. Willy Staerk, "Das Wahrheitskriterium der ATlichen Prophetie," *ZSysTh* 5 (1928): 76-101, who saw the balanced message of both judgment and restoration, evidenced by the Holy Spirit, to be a positive truth criterion (83). Ultimately, the occurrence legitimated the prediction (87).
2. These treatments will be explored in detail to follow.

Gerhard von Rad (1901-1971)

Since his death many works have emerged treating the lasting impact von Rad has made on the landscape of Old Testament studies.[3] This is all the more remarkable in that it was made in the face of cultural upheaval and an increasingly sterile climate of biblical studies. This period can be characterized by the dominance of source and traditio-historical criticism's atomization of the Old Testament, particularly the prophets.[4] Von Rad was said to have battled against this approach to the Old Testament as if against some form of "evil."[5] As Christopher Seitz[6] notes, while a product of the source and form-critical school (Gunkel, Alt, Gressmann, *et al.*), von Rad's intention was self-admittedly theological: "The subject matter which concerns the theologian is, of course, not the spiritual religious world of Israel... it is simply Israel's own explicit assertions about Jahweh."[7] However, this extraction of the true Israel could not be accomplished without a myriad of sophisticated methods concerned with "seeing the literature through highly sophisticated methods."[8] These methods utilized form, literary, and traditio-historical criticism in an effort to uncover individual units' authors and their intentions.

In his work on von Rad, Joseph Groves noted that, given the status of biblical studies' developing relationship to theology in the mid twentieth—cenury,

---

3. These include: W. H. Schmidt, "Theologie des Alten Testaments' vor und nach Gerhard von Rad," in Verkündigung und Forschung, *EvThBeih* 17 (1972): 1-25; *Gerhard von Rad: Seine Bedeutung für die Theologie; Drei Reden von H.W. Wolff, R. Rendtorff, W. Pannenberg* (München: Chr. Kaiser Verlag, 1973), esp. H.W. Wolff's "Gerhard von Rad als Exeget," pp. 9-20; and James L. Crenshaw, *Gerhard von Rad* (Waco, TX: Word Inc, 1978). Recently Rudolf Smend, "Gerhard von Rad," in *Das Alte Testament und die Kultur der Moderne*, ed. Manfred Oeming, Konrad Schmid, and Michael Welker, *Beiträge des Symposiums »Das Alte Testament und die Kultur der Moderne« anlässlich des 100. Geburtstags Gerhard von Rads (1901-1971) Heidelberg, 18.-21. Oktober 2001*, Bd. 9 (Berlin: LIT Verlag, 2004), 13-24; Smend, *Astruc*, 170-197.
4. See Brevard S. Childs, "Gerhard Von Rad in American Dress" in *The Hermeneutical Quest: Essays in Honor of J. L. Mays on His 65th Birthday*, ed. Donald G. Miller, (Allison Park: PA: Pickwick Publications, 1986), 77-86; and Childs, *Struggle*,145f.
5. Crenshaw, *Gerhard von Rad*, 27.
6. Christopher R. Seitz, *Word Without End: The Old Testament as Abiding Theological Witness* (Waco, TX: Baylor University Press, 2004), 30f. See also Christopher R. Seitz, "Two Testaments and the Failure of One Tradition-History," In *Figured Out: Typology and Providence in Christian Scripture*, 1st ed., (Louisville: Westminster John Knox Press, 2001), 35-47.
7. Gerhard von Rad, *Old Testament Theology*, trans. D.M.G. Stalker, The Old Testament Library, 2 vols. (Louisville: Westminster John Knox Press, 2001), I:105; cf. Seitz, *Word Without End*, 30; and Robert Morgan and John Barton, *Biblical Interpretation*, Oxford Bible series (Oxford/New York: Oxford University Press, 1988), 98ff.
8. Seitz, *Word Without End*, 32.

any Old Testament study that would seriously consider making theological assertions about the biblical text must deal with the accepted historical—criticism of the day.[9] Many scholars proposed methods of combining the theological and the historical in the Old Testament.[10] To varying degrees, either the theological element or the historical was highlighted, resulting in the subordination of one to the other.[11] In Walther Eichrodt's treatment of the Old Testament's inherent categories, namely covenant, the two seemingly opposed interests of the interpreter, history and theology, were seen to be somewhat satisfactorily juxtaposed. However, von Rad critiqued Eichrodt's Old Testament Theology, along with the *Theologies* of Ernst Sellin and Ludwig Köhler for failing to adequately link the diachronic with the religio-developmental aspect of the Old Testament material itself.[12]

Von Rad's work is derivative of this embryonic extension of biblical studies, Old Testament theology. Critical of the romantic and idealistic formulations of J.C.K. von Hoffman's mid-nineteenth century organic form of *Heilsgeschichte* and Vischer's subsequent Christological exegesis as the means of extracting theological assertions of substance from the Old Testament in particular, von Rad was to introduce a method that would deal, fairly in his estimation, with the theological without diminishing the historical (i.e., jettisoning *Religionsgeschichte in toto*). It is to this method and its adherents that we now turn.[13]

Vergegenwärtigung, Aktualisierung, or "actualization" has been treated in detail recently by Joseph Groves' dissertation under Brevard Childs.[14] Groves' study illustrates the development of actualization as it became the center of von Rad's theological concerns. It is beyond the scope of this study to treat actualization in detail, however a working understanding of his application of this technical term to the prophets is in order. Von Rad's first formal use of the term

---

9. Joseph W. Groves, *Actualization and Interpretation in the Old Testament* (Atlanta: Scholars Press, 1987), 2ff.
10. For a survey of this history see inter alia., Emile Kraeling, *The Old Testament Since the Reformation* (New York: Harper & Bros., 1955); R. E. Clements, *One Hundred Years of Old Testament Interpretation* (Philadelphia: Westminster Press, 1976); and Robert P. Gordon, "A Story of Two Paradigm Shifts," in Robert P. Gordon, ed., *"The Place is Too Small for Us": The Israelite Prophets in Recent Scholarship*, Sources for Biblical and Theological Study; 5 (Winona Lake: Eisenbrauns, 1995): 3-26.
11. See Groves, Actualization and Interpretation, 3-5.
12. Walther Eichrodt, *Theologie Des Alten Testaments* (Leipzig: J.C. Hinrichsm, 1933). Von Rad, "Grundprobleme einer biblischen Theologie des Alten Testaments," *TLZ* 68 (1943): 225-234, esp. 227; particularly the preface to the 1965 ed. of *OT II*, xi: "The only really important question is whether Eichrodt's treatment of the material does justice to the close relationship with history which is characteristic of Old Testament utterances."
13. For a helpful synopsis of those theologians, American, British, and Continental, who, in some way, have perpetuated this method in the mid-twentieth century, see Groves, *Actualization and Interpretation*, 5.
14. Ibid.

was in 1938.[15] But it is not until the second volume of his *Old Testament Theology* that actualization was to play a more clearly discernible role in his discussion of the canonical prophets.[16] In the Old Testament, the prophets' awareness of the present historical situation and their ability to speak into it was governed by their application of the old traditions to the current situation. The prophets' task was to actualize the "old basic events of the canonical history."[17] By "basic events," von Rad was referring to those ingredient to Israel's creed: exodus, Sinai, and conquest.[18] This notion of the actualization of former traditions will come to bear in our discussion of Jer 28:8, "The prophets who came before you and me." Prophetic actualization was not only past-oriented, it also held a future element. Von Rad wrote, "[Prophets] were called forth by their conviction that Jahweh was bringing about a new era for his people," a conviction that was theological, rather than purely political, in its outlook.[19] It was in the context of prophecy that interpreters considered actualization to have been von Rad's "central hermeneutical force for the entire Old Testament."[20] This study will treat actualization to the degree it, as an interpretive strategy, informs not only von Rad's reading of prophetic conflict as seen in Jer 28, but also recent readings of the problem of true and false prophecy in the works of James Sanders and Brevard Childs.

Von Rad first handled the problem of true and false prophecy in a 1933 *ZAW* article entitled "Die falschen Propheten."[21] He would not return to the subject until 1960 in the second volume of his *Theologie*.[22] Four years later, in his commentary on Deuteronomy,[23] von Rad deals with the prophetic laws

---

15. Appearing originally in Gerhard von Rad, *Gesammlte Studien Zum Alten Testament* (München: Kaiser Verlag, 1958), reprinted in "The Form-Critical Problem of the Hexateuch," in *The Form-Critical Problem of the Hexateuch and Other Essays* (New York: McGraw-Hill, 1966), 28. In a cultic setting, actualization was a literary phenomenon: "the re-creation of the events of the cult and the re-experiencing of those events by the participants in the ceremony", Groves, *Actualization and Interpretation,* 8.
16. Cf., 105ff.
17. Von Rad, *OT* II:113.
18. Groves, *Actualization and Interpretation*, 49f.
19. Von Rad, *OT II*, 113.
20. Childs, "Gerhard von Rad in American Dress," 79, referring to von Rad, *OT I*, 155ff.
21. Studying with Albrecht Alt at Leipzig in the early 1930's, Gerhard von Rad wrote "Die Falschen Propheten." *ZAW* 51 (1933): 109-120. Staerk, who had just six years prior written on discernment and the truth criterion of Old Testament prophecy, "Das Wahrheitskriterium," would invite von Rad to join him in Jena, a town rife with anti-Semitism and national-socialism, in 1934.
22. Jer 28 is treated in passing early in *OT II* (pp. 48, 55-56, 17), but at length at 209f.
23. Gerhard von Rad, *Das fünfte Buch Mose: Deuteronomium*, Das Alte Testament Deutsch 8 (Göttingen: Vandenhoek & Ruprecht, 1964); ET: (Chatham: SCM Press, 1966), pp. 96-97 and 122-125.

found in chapter 13 and 18. Our focus will be on "Die falschen Propheten," bringing his other works to bear on the discussion when needed.

In this essay, von Rad appealed to numerous prophetic conflicts in the Old Testament between true and false prophets. These included Michaiah ben Imlah and the 400 Yahweh prophets (1 K 22), Jeremiah and Hananiah (Jer 28), and Ezekiel. These examples were relevant, von Rad maintained, only to the degree that they illustrated the attitude of the opponents.[24] Their attitude, or more specifically, the theological location from which they spoke, was of primary interest to von Rad.[25] Indeed, it was the first task of his essay.[26] Due to the off—handed way in which the opponents of the *Schriftpropheten* had been heretofore designated as "false," to penetrate the question of true and false prophets von Rad first stressed the neutrality with which the interpreter must come to these narratives.[27] An echo of von Rad's theological leaning can be heard in what may be called a qualifier of his call for objectivity. He advocated a neutral reading of the false prophets, but "without wanting to rehabilitate those opponents."[28] Von Rad was keen to locate their message, but without correcting, as it were, the tradition's view of them as having prophesied erroneously concerning Yahweh's will for Israel.

The absence of a Hebrew term for false prophet designated somewhat the nature of the historical problem as von Rad saw it. Often, the lives and messages of the true prophets had taken center stage in scholarship's treatment of the matter, with little concern for their counterparts. Von Rad accused Mowinckel of

---

24. Von Rad, "Die Falschen Propheten." 111.
25. Here von Rad makes mention of this century's four prior treatments of the issue, the "critical essays" (109, n.1): Mowinckel (1910), Valeton (1911), Sachsse (1919), and Staerk (1927).
26. Ibid., 116.
27. This objective stance which we encountered most notably in Duhm and Kuenen, would be heralded as the way forward for the next half century, to be epitomized in the works of Gottfried Quell, *Wahre und falsche Propheten; versuch einer Interpretation* (Gütersloh: C. Bertelsmann, 1952), 65f.; Frank-Lothar Hossfeld and Ivo Meyer, *Prophet gegen Prophet: Eine Analyse der alttestamentlichen Texte zum Thema, Wahre und falsche Propheten*, Biblische Beiträge; 9 (Fribourg Einsiedeln: Verlag Schweizerisches Katholisches Bibelwerk Auslfg., Benziger, 1973), 113; Gerhard Münderlein, *Kriterien wahrer und falscher Prophetie: Entstehung und Bedeutung im Alten Testament*, 2nd ed., Europäische Hochschulschriften: Theologie Bd. 33 (Bern/Frankfurt-on-Main/Las Vegas: Peter Lang, 1979). More recently Burke O. Long, "Social Dimensions of Prophetic Conflict," *Semeia* 21, (1984): 32, has seen a "canonical tilt towards ideologically drawn pictures," permeating the tradition's interpretations of prophetic conflict, from the LXX to many critics of his day.
28. "Ohne jene Gegner rehabilitieren zu wollen," Von Rad "Die Falschen Propheten," 109.

ignoring the false prophets in favor of the true.[29] Scholarship's dominant classification of false prophets at the time as backward, pathological, or categorically immoral was, to him, unacceptable.[30] The nature of the distinctions between true and false prophets took many forms. Sachsse held that true prophets spoke in the name of Yahweh, while their opponents were actually veiled prophets of Ba'al.[31] The difference for Kittel[32] and Staerk[33] was moral.[34] According to Valeton, false prophets transmitted a dogma of welfare and proclaimed unconditional intervention by Yahweh, regardless of historical reality.[35] In the coming decades, conflict among prophets would come to be seen by many as a result of the interaction between institutionally-bound cult prophets and free, charismatics. However, as von Rad approached the problem, he noted that the distinction was not centered on the cult, or some form of retaliation dogma, or social questions, or the relationship of foreigners to Yahweh.[36] Prophets were not conceptually easily distinguishable.[37] Von Rad pointed to the apparent lack of response by both Jeremiah and Micaiah as evidence of the inability to easily label false prophets as "backwards" or "immoral."[38] In fact, in the confrontation at Jer 28, Jeremiah's inability to apply a working truth criterion alerts one to the fact that there must have been none, "in respect to form and content."[39] The plethora of distinctions lends support to von Rad's assertion that the problem did not lie in any observable qualities of either prophet. Rather, the issue turned on the prophet's answer to the question of the possible outcome facing Israel or Judah in times of crisis: "welfare or judgment?"[40]

Von Rad was concerned to draw attention to the theological content of these opponents' messages.[41] Material promotion and unqualified blessing of the physical entity of Israel by Yahweh seemed to be constitutive of the message of the false prophets in question. According to von Rad, this decidedly theological

---

29. Von Rad "Die Falschen Propheten," 110n1; cf. Sigmund Mowinckel, "The '"Spirit"' and the '"Word"' in the Pre-Exilic Reforming Prophets," *JBL* 53 (1934): 199-227.
30. Von Rad "Die Falschen Propheten," 109.
31. Sachsse, 3ff., 13ff., in Eva Osswald, *Falsche Prophetie im Alten Testament*, (Tübingen: Mohr Siebeck, 1962), 8.
32. Rudolf Kittel, *Die Religion des Volkes Israel* (Leipzig: Quelle & Meyer, 1921), 106; cited in Osswald, *Falsche Prophetie*, 8.
33. W. Staerk, 84; cited in Osswald, *Falsche Prophetie*. 8.
34. Moberly, who does not treat Kittel or Staerk, expands upon this moral element, in *Prophecy and Discernment*, (Cambridge: Cambridge University Press, 2006).
35. P. Valeton, 64ff.; cited in Osswald, *Falsche Prophetie*, 8.
36. Von Rad "Die Falschen Propheten," 112. In the case of Jeremiah particularly, von Rad noted that it was interesting to see him so perplexed by Hananiah (*OT II*; 210).
37. Von Rad, "Die Falschen Propheten," 109.
38. Ibid., 109.
39. Von Rad, *OT II*, 55f., 209.
40. Von Rad "Die Falschen Propheten," 112.
41. Ibid.

purpose was also operative in Deuteronomy.⁴² Von Rad understood Deuteronomy's portrayal of a prophet as an institutional intermediary who stood between the dreaded Yahweh and the people.⁴³ This prophet was charged with executing certain ritual functions and was linked in a succession of prophets that found their head in Moses.⁴⁴ Two ritual functions that von Rad believed were of importance to the question of false prophecy were intercession (*Fürbitte*) and proclamation (*Verkündigung*).⁴⁵ The activity of intercession was linked back to the need for an intermediary, for one who would primarily fill a placating role in the people's interaction with Yahweh. Deuteronomy, for von Rad, understood the interceding prophet to be standing in linear succession to Moses. This led to the cultic ritualization of a prophet and his duties.⁴⁶ In passing, von Rad said that perhaps Hananiah was an institutionally bound, cult prophet.⁴⁷ That would explain his concern for the temple and temple items (Jer 28:3).⁴⁸ According to Deuteronomy, the true prophet's duty, far from proclaiming judgment and repentance, would be to remind the people of Yahweh's promises of peace and victory, a common theme in Deuteronomy. In light of this, von Rad said, Deut 18's prophetic law had to do with peace, and was thus inapplicable to the situation in Jer 28. Von Rad saw two completely different criteria at work in Deut 18 and Jer 28. Deut 18 pointed to a prophet's presumptuous word of doom failing to materialize, while in Jeremiah it was the word of peace that must legitimize itself. Proclamation, the second duty von Rad attributed to prophets, is the prophet's divine answer to the historical reality. For von Rad, this proclamation may have also pointed to an association with the cult.⁴⁹

In a footnote, von Rad said that it might be possible to find clues in the prophet's words that reveal whether or not they could be attributed to cultic ritual functions.⁵⁰ Here, von Rad brought in the Elohist. He stated that, over against deuteronomic cult prophets, the Elohist was interested in seeing the link to Moses as charismatic rather than purely functional. He summarized Num 11:24ff where the 70 elders are given the 'spirit' (*ruah*) and come immediately into pro-

---

42. Ibid.
43. Ibid., 113.
44. Ibid., 114; Mowinckel treated these ritual functions, but omitted the role of *Fürbitter* in his *Kulturprophetie und prophetische Psalmen* (Kristiana: Dybwad, 1923).
45. Von Rad "Die Falschen Propheten," 115; he wrote, "Das prophetischeTun besteht dann einerseits in der Fürbitte selbst, andererseits in der Verkündigung des dabar, d. h. der göttlichen Antwort."
46. Ibid., 113.
47. Quell (51f.) argued, particularly in the case of Hananiah, connection with the cult in no way ultimately designated a prophet's message as false.
48. Von Rad "Die Falschen Propheten," 115.
49. The difference in criteria noted here by von Rad will also be stressed in Childs.
50. Ibid., 115n3; a position, von Rad noted, closely dependant on the work of H. Schmidt, "Hosea 6:1-6," In *Festschriften*, (n.p.: n.p, 1927).

phetic excitation.⁵¹ He says this story is to be understood aetiologically and applies it to the discussion by noting that prophets had Moses' spirit, thus they were free and not bound to the cult.⁵² Von Rad saw these free prophets' detachment from the cult not as critique of the cult, rather as "an expression of a much deeper reorientation."⁵³ These prophets talked to Yahweh face to face. The Elohist depicted Moses conversing thus with Yahweh, and the book of Jeremiah is at pains to cast Jeremiah in the same light.

Von Rad saw Deuteronomy wanting to protect against any uneasiness brought about by so-called doom prophets. This allowed him to speculate as to the association of Hananiah with these cult-bound institutional prophets. However, he maintained that the book of Jeremiah exhibited Jeremiah's access to the divine presence, as the Elohist had shown for Moses. While the above categorizations are helpful historically for von Rad, he did not view these distinctions as the delineation between false and true. The matter was not as simple as saying that later editors of Jeremiah saw Hananiah as bound to the cult and thus his message as suspect. Or, since Jeremiah's message and life were indicative of those free prophets who share the spirit of Moses, he must have been a true prophet. No, von Rad admitted that even though doom prophets turned violently against their opponents, they still did not yield any objective, or formal, criteria for discernment.⁵⁴ Traditio-historical criticism has informed von Rad's view of the respective prophets, however, it could not definitively adjudicate between opposing prophets.⁵⁵

The last three pages of von Rad's essay deal with the narrative of Jer 28. So far, no formal criteria have emerged. In the book of Jeremiah we sense a great skepticism from Jeremiah, an almost modern questioning of the subjective nature of the actions and experiences of his opponents. Time and again Jeremiah has been persistent in his critique of the false prophets; he was not against dreams per se, just false ones.⁵⁶ The word of Yahweh was to be preferred "under any circumstance" to dreams, ecstasies, or visions.⁵⁷ The *content* rather than the *mode* of revelation was a crucial determinant of truth for Jeremiah. Perhaps intimating an association with the cult prophets, von Rad was pinpointing Hananiah's culpability. Caring more for the manners in which one received and enacted a prophetic message than for the word itself, was intolerable to Jeremiah and would have constituted falsity.

---

51. Von Rad "Die Falschen Propheten," 115f.
52. Ibid., 116.
53. Ibid., 116, n. 1.
54. Ibid., 117.
55. Cf. Georg Fohrer, "Remarks on Modern Interpretation of the Prophets," *JBL* 80 (1961): 314ff.
56. Von Rad "Die Falschen Propheten," 118.
57. Ibid.

For Jeremiah (and von Rad), this theme of 'word' could not be over theologized.[58] The point of dreams, ecstasies, and visions was to reveal the word of Yahweh. In Jeremiah's estimation, however, the word had lost its freedom in the mouths of his opponents because it was stuck in the false prophets' psychological sphere.[59] As illustrated famously in Barth's exposition of 1 K 13 in *CD II/2*, the word of Yahweh alone prescribes the means by which it was to be revealed.[60] This rather formal criterion was sounded nearly 25 years prior by von Rad: "The word of Yahweh must stand completely on its own and must, if otherwise it wants to be a transcendental revelation, dictate the recommended bridges."[61] It was here that von Rad first credited Jeremiah with striking a blow to Hananiah. He said, "Jeremiah has…cornered his opponent with regard to the absolute transcendence of revelation."[62] The true prophet was concerned with Yahweh's word being effectively communicated to his people, whatever bridge by which its locutor sent it.

Von Rad next addressed the question of history and the historical situation as perceived by Jeremiah and Hananiah. It is in this context that the office of the true prophet will be further revealed. Jeremiah, in his responses to Hananiah, raised the question concerning the relationship of correspondence between prophet and history.[63] History, the "place at which the doings of Yahweh become recognizable," will read Hananiah in passing and "discredit" him.[64] In von Rad's estimation, Hananiah was too certain. Martin Buber would echo this in 1947, saying that Hananiah spoke like one who "knows it all."[65] Opposed to this surety, a true prophet was one who stood before a concrete historical activity in "absolute uncertainty."[66] With Duhm and Volz, von Rad asserted the freedom of a God far off.[67] God's plans were not to be forecast so easily. Yahweh's plans for Israel were unknown. In the face of such uncertainty, a prophet had an obligation to recognize if and when Yahweh was altering his plan. Von Rad's point

---

58. Ibid.
59. Ibid.
60. Karl Barth, *CD* II/2, 393-409; cf. R.W.L. Moberly, *Prophecy and Discernment*,105n10. Cf. also Thomas B. Dozeman, "The Way of the Man of God from Judah: True and False Prophecy in the Pre-Deuteronomic Legend of 1 Kings 13," *CBQ* 44 (1982): 379-393; Walter Gross, "Lying Prophet and Disobedient Man of God in 1 Kings 13: Role Analysis as an Instrument of Theological Interpretation of an Old Testament Narrative Text," *Sem* 15 (1979): 97-135.
61. Von Rad "Die Falschen Propheten,",118.
62. Ibid.
63. Ibid., 119.
64. Ibid.
65. Martin Buber, "Falsche Propheten," *Die Wandlung* 2 (1947): 277-283, translated and reprinted in *On The Bible; Eighteen Studies by Martin Buber,* ed. Nahum N. Glatzer, Pages 166-171, (New York: Schocken Books, 1982), 166f.
66. Von Rad "Die Falschen Propheten.,",119.
67. Ibid.

was that a prophet's uncertainty in the face of crisis did not guarantee his or her veracity. It did, however, put them in a place to listen.

In von Rad's estimation then, Hananiah failed. His failing consisted of his appropriating a message that, at one time, had rung true. 2 K 19 reports Isaiah's message of deliverance for Jerusalem in the face of Assyrian threat. But, over a century later, the historical situation had changed. Hananiah's message of an expeditious return echoed Isaiah's.[68] However, what had at one time been an "examination of faith" for Isaiah and the people of Israel was now perhaps better understood as a "temptation."[69] A temptation to extract what had been true of Yahweh and apply it to what was currently underway. This, von Rad saw, was the grievous flaw of false prophecy: an inability to grant the creating God freedom to act. With Kuenen, von Rad holds that there were no easily recognizable criteria by which to determine the veracity of a prophet's words. What determined the ability of a prophet to speak truth was their view of Yahweh's sovereignty. A prophet "completely arrested by the hour of history which Yahweh let his people experience; a prophet who hung in complete immediacy with the creating God," was the prophet that was able to speak truly about Yahweh's plan for his people.[70] For von Rad, a prophet's ability to speak truth lay in that prophet's relationship to Yahweh and subsequently in his ability to discern present reality, a privilege afforded by the immediacy of that relationship. But, while the proclamation of truth was the duty of all who would call themselves prophets of Yahweh, discernment was also ingredient to the office.

In the confrontation with Hananiah, Jeremiah himself indicted Hananiah as false (Jer 28:12-17). Von Rad, and later Quell, viewed this as integral to the evaluation of true and false prophecy.[71] In his discussion in *OT II* of Deuteronomy's failure to produce an all-encompassing criterion, von Rad noted that true prophets often viewed a message of salvation with skepticism and that judgment was solely the prerogative of those true prophets.[72] It was in the true prophet's critique of his opponent that discernment lay. He wrote:

> The falsity cannot be seen either in the office itself, or in the their words themselves, or in the fallibility of the man who spoke them. It could only be seen by the person who had true insight into Jahweh's intentions for the time, and who, on the basis of this, was obliged to deny that the other had illumination.[73]

---

68. In Moberly's recent treatment (*Prophecy*, 104n6), he notes Osswald (*Falsche Prophetie*, 20) tracing Hananiah's dependance on Isaiah to the end of the 19th century with B. Stade, "Deuterosacharja. Eine kritische Studie. 1 Theil," *ZAW* 1 (1881): 1-96.
69. Von Rad "Die Falschen Propheten," 120n1, with Valeton, 56.
70. Von Rad "Die Falschen Propheten," 120.
71. Quell, 66.
72. Von Rad, *OT II*, 210n27, (he lists 1 K 12:11ff; Mic 3:5ff; Jer 6:14, 14:13; 13:9ff., 18:5-9; Ezek 13:16).
73. Ibid., 210n27.

In the case of Hananiah, this lack of illumination was replaced with what von Rad called a *liebgewordenes Dogma*, a "much-beloved dogma," that Hananiah had passed down.[74] This dogma was unable to distinguish the *will* of Yahweh from his *character*.

Von Rad saw true prophets as those privileged few who, through unmediated access to Yahweh, were granted the ability to discern his ever-changing plan. Insight that was to be proclaimed and, if need be, corrected by Yahweh himself. Along with being privy to divine council, von Rad saw Jeremiah in a succession and "completely conscious of his spiritual ancestry."[75] Whether this ancestry could be readily identified with the free prophets as portrayed by the Elohist or with Deuteronomy's institutional, cult-bound prophets was of secondary concern to von Rad. So too were the social aspects of this narrative. In this we see him distancing himself from the strict rationalism of Kuenen and Duhm. His concern was to demonstrate that the determination of prophetic truth in Jeremiah's confrontation with Hananiah, although finally unyielding to objective criteria, was approachable once the interpreter recognized the issue turned on a prophets' ability to accept and adapt to the uncertain out-workings of Yahweh's will while remaining confident in the guidance and protection of one far off.

We would be remiss if we failed to briefly mention Gottfried Quell's 1952 *Wahre und falsche Propheten* which built upon and developed many aspects of von Rad's early work, "Die falschen Propheten." Quell's extensive influence can be seen throughout the remainder of the twentieth-century in the works of Crenshaw, Sanders, Brenneman, and Brueggemann. In his later (1960) discussion of true and false prophecy in Jeremiah, von Rad, in turn, references Quell approvingly.[76] Among the more noticeable overlaps between von Rad and Quell that Armin Lange sees are the presence of no absolute criteria in the accounts as they are reported in the Old Testament; the conditionality of Deut 13 and 18's criteria along with their lack of applicability to the late canonical prophets; and the name false prophet as a perjorative term which was only 'recently' imported through ancient Jewish translations and interpretations.[77] Other points of conti-

---

74. Von Rad "Die Falschen Propheten," 120. Cf. the roughly contemporaneous Neo-modern Frankfurt School's works of Adorno and Horkheimer on a 'negative dialectic' principle. Interestingly, it was not until 1993 that a Marxist reading of the problem featured prominently in Henry Mottu, "Jeremiah vs. Hananiah: Ideology and Truth in Old Testament Prophecy," in *The Bible and Liberation: Political and Social Hermeneutics*, ed. Norman K. Gottwald and Richard A. Horsley, (Maryknoll, NY: Orbis, 1993): 313-328. See Stephen Chapman's citation of Barr's scathing comments on the ready purchase Marxist readings retain at present among socio-theological Christian interpreters, in his *The Law and the Prophets: A Study in Old Testament Canon Formation* FAT 27, (Tübingen: Mohr Siebeck, 2000), 86n70.

75. Gerhard von Rad, *The Message of The Prophets* (New York: Harper & Row, 1972), 175.

76. Von Rad, *OT II*, 209f.

77. Lange, Vom prophetischen Wort zur prophetischen Tradition, 35.

nuity we see between von Rad and Quell include prophets' singular ability to discern the truth and divine commission of another prophet;[78] prophets' charismatic ability to apprehend and read the times;[79] and (with Duhm) the resistance of an easy association between false prophets and a readily identifiable party, be it cult-prophets or the people.[80]

Quell's treatment of false prophecy is somewhat unique in its appreciation of historical figures' readings throughout. In his discussion of Hananiah and a modern's need to assume a prophet innocent before being proven guilty, Quell notes that even for a lawyer such as Calvin, Hananiah would have gained an "acquittal for lack of proof" of guilt.[81] Quell opts for a more positive assessment of Hananiah, agreeing with Luther that, had he been there to hear Jeremiah rail against the temple, he "would have knocked [Jeremiah's] head off!"[82] In his conclusion Quell notes the philosophical formulation of Spinoza concerning the notion of prophetic truth.[83]

James A. Sanders

Von Rad's influence would continue to exert itself.[84] A reliance on his understanding of the transmission of tradition complexes with the explicit intent of uncovering the religious witness therein can be seen with the emergence of the study of those tradition complexes' final form.[85] The traditio-historical criticism embodied by von Rad would be succeeded and subsumed into Old Testament studies' emerging field of canon-criticism. Among Americans, James Sanders was one of the earliest that would seek to understand biblical prophecy from a canonical perspective. While differing from von Rad in his understanding of the canon's flexibility, Sanders, like von Rad, sought to exhibit biblical tradents reinterpreting traditions in the face of ever-changing contexts.[86] In this light,

---

78. Quell, 45.
79. Ibid., 206. By 1971, James L. Crenshaw, *Prophetic Conflict*, (Berlin: De Gruyter, 1971), 47-48, considers this "the ultimate criterion to which contemporary scholarship appeals."
80. Quell, 217.
81. Quell, 66.
82. Ibid.; Cf. Eric W. Heaton, *The Old Testament Prophets* 2nd ed. (London: Darton Longman & Todd, 1977), 36.
83. Quell, 217; Spinoza, *Ethics*, prop. 43.
84. Particularly in the works of Quell, Osswald, and Hossfeld/Meyer.
85. Michael Fishbane, "Inner-Biblical Interpretation and the Development of Tradition," in *Das Alte Testament und die Kultur der Moderne,* ed. Manfred Oeming, Konrad Schmid, and Michael Welker, Beiträge des Symposiums »Das Alte Testament und die Kultur der Moderne« anlässlich des 100. Geburtstags Gerhard von Rads (1901-1971) Heidelberg, 18.-21. Oktober 2001, Bd. 8, (Berlin: LIT Verlag, 2004), 25-26.
86. See Francis Watson's helpful comments in *Text and Truth: Redefining Biblical Theology* (Grand Rapids: Eerdmans, 1997), 222n34.

prophecy's role was to "insist that history, especially the current events of their day, had to be perceived through Israel's historic faith."[87] This faith found voice in tradition complexes such as the Davidic Torah, the Mosaic Torah, and the exodus and conquest. In the introduction to *Torah and Canon* Sanders relates questions of canon criticism to the question regarding true and false prophecy: In which capacities did the traditions evident in the prophetic books function? For example, when the exodus and conquest of Canaan tradition appears throughout the prophets, canon criticism's intent was to "measure the authority that the ancient tradition exercised in the context where cited."[88]

That the canonically portrayed true prophets used these traditions is evident. Sanders was interested to see where and how the so-called false prophets employed them.[89] Recognizing that they too drew from a common well of traditions, most notably the Torah story, Sanders sought to uncover these false prophets' principles of interpretation and manners of faith.[90] Along with the prophets' canonical monotheizing, Sanders' major contribution to the study of true and false prophecy can first be detected here. He writes, "The difference [between true and false] must lie in the hermeneutic axioms and rules they employed."[91] It is to Sanders' prophetic hermeneutics and his contribution to the study of true and false prophecy that we now turn.[92]

In 1972 Sanders raised the double-sided issue of how the canonical prophets survived the canonical process and, correspondingly, why we lack the entire message of the false prophets.[93] This was a setting into which, he believed, can-

---

87. James A. Sanders, *Torah and Canon* (Philadelphia: Fortress Press, 1972), 55.
88. Ibid., xvii.
89. Sanders is at great pains to remain sympathetic to the opponents of those the church has deemed true. In "Jeremiah and the Future of Theological Scholarship," *ANQ* 13 (1972): 138, Sanders noted that in order to "grasp the situation, we must *not* assume that Isaiah's antagonists in the debate were "false" prophets." Because, "Psychologically these inherited terms ['false' and 'true'] prevent us today from fully recovering the point." Sanders interestingly went on to say that "like any good historian," embracing the "ambiguity of reality," we are to resist the urge to assume the conclusion, implicitly indicating that the interpretive task was to be undertaken first and foremost as an *historical* endeavor.
90. Sanders, *Torah and Canon*, xvii.
91. Ibid., xviii.
92. This study will focus on Sanders' two essays devoted to the study of false prophecy: "Jeremiah" *op. cit.* (n. 298) and "Hermeneutics in True and False Prophecy," in *Canon and Authority: Essays in Old Testament Religion and Theology*, ed. George W. Coats and Burke O. Long, Pages 21-41, (Philadelphia: Fortress Press, 1977), reprinted in *From Sacred Story to Sacred Text: Canon as Paradigm*, Pages 87-105, (Philadelphia: Fortress Press, 1987). Particularly helpful is the reprint's introduction in which he recounted the development of his thought in response to Crenshaw and van der Woude's work. We will be referencing the 1977 article as no substantial alterations have occurred in the 1987 reprint. His other works will be consulted as needed.
93. Sanders, "Jeremiah," 135.

on-criticism could speak, particularly regarding the recovery of the messages of true and false prophets.[94] Before turning to the confrontation between Jeremiah and Hananiah in Jer 28 in his first extended treatment of false prophecy, he discusses Isaiah's assumed disputation in Isa 28:20-22. In this passage Sanders believes Isaiah is interacting, albeit one—sidedly, with false prophets and employing two different traditions of the Davidic Torah story.[95]

In the Isaiah passage, the false prophet is identified as a "good Davidic theologian."[96] Recounting Yahweh's victories on behalf of king David at Mt Perazim (2 Sam 5:17-22) and the Valley of Gibeon (1 Chr 14:16)[97] in Isa 28:21a, Isaiah repeated the anonymous Davidic theologian's inference that, in the face of Assyrian siege and the impending destruction of Israel, Yahweh would act to save his people again. Sanders sees the false prophet appealing to the same tradition as the true. He says of the false prophet's reference to the rescue of David: "to be true to the story we have to say, by analogy, [Yahweh] would save again."[98] Such a response, Sanders admits, would have held great appeal.[99] 28:21b records Isaiah's response, in similar Davidic tradition fashion. The LORD would indeed rise up, but not as imagined, rather, it would be strange and alien. Sanders attributes Isaiah's response and message of judgment to his theology.[100] The prophets' views of God dictate the application of their respec-

---

94. A detailed study of Sanders' contribution to the growth of 'canon criticism' is outside the scope of this thesis. See the recent *Festschriften*: Craig A Evans and Shemaryahu Talmon eds., *The Quest for Context and Meaning : Studies in Biblical Intertextuality in Honor of James a. Sanders*, Biblical interpretation Series 28 (Leiden ; New York: Brill, 1997) and David M. Carr and Richard D. Weis, *A Gift of God in Due Season: Essays on Scripture and Community in Honor of James A. Sanders*, JSOTSupp 225, (Sheffield, England: Sheffield Academic Press, 1996).
95. Sanders, "Jeremiah," 137. Significant interest in the recovery of such one-sided disputations (*Disputationswörter*) was seen in the years surrounding this publication. See Osswald, *Falsche Prophetie*; Rolf Rendtorff, "Erwägungen zur Frühgeschichte des Prophetentums in Israel," *ZThK* 59 (1962): 145-167; Adam S. van der Woude, "Micah in Dispute with the Pseudo-Prophets," *VT* 19 (1969): 244-260, and "Micah IV 1-5: An Instance of the Pseudo-Prophets Quoting Isaiah," in *Symbolae Biblicae et Mesopotamicae Francisco Mario Theodoro de Liagre Böhl Dedicatae*, ed. M.A.   Beek et al., Pages 396-402, (Leiden: Brill, 1973). While appreciative of this approach, Sanders expressed reserve regarding van der Woude's claim that the difference between true and false prophecy lay in theological doctrines themselves; that, for example, the prophets presented Zionism or a royal theology as categorically false; cf. Sanders, *Sacred Story*, 87.
96. Sanders, "Jeremiah," 138.
97. Concerning the Valley of Gibeon, cf. Josh 10:6-13.
98. Sanders, "Jeremiah," 138.
99. "Frankly, I think, if I had been there...I would have agreed with the so-called false prophet." Ibid., 138; recall Luther and Quell, *op. cit.*
100. Ibid., 139; "theology" here is used to denote Isaiah's over-arching understanding of the ways of Yahweh with his people. A distinct "Zionist" or "establishment" theology is not in Sanders' purview.

tive hermeneutics. However, against van der Woude, it is not the theologies of the prophets themselves that were right or wrong, rather the suitable appropriation of them within the given context. Sanders calls the prophets' foundational understanding of the character of Yahweh their "hermeneutical axiom."[101] In the case of Isaiah 28's theology, the false prophet believes that Yahweh will keep his promise, while Isaiah's God is free to correct his people because he has not been "reduced to a guiding, protecting deity who was obliged to preserve them."[102]

Sanders then moves to the prophet Jeremiah. Prior to chapter 28, Jeremiah has made numerous references to the Exodus Torah story (tradition). While those responsible for the final shape of the narrative have not explicitly said so, Sanders assumes the same tradition shaped Jeremiah's argument in his confrontation with Hananiah.[103] Sanders understands Jer 28:8-9 as Jeremiah's hermeneutical appeal to a commonly held tradition; a tradition in which prophets rightly "read current events in the light of Israel's self-understanding in the covenant."[104] By reminding Hananiah of this tradition's standard prophetic message, one in which peace and war (28:8) stood rather for status quo and disruption, Jeremiah was affirming that "at the heart of prophetic hermeneutics is judgment, or challenge to things as they are."[105] To appeal to the Torah story in the face of Babylonian conquest means to examine the covenantal relationship in light of the present reality and act accordingly. Prophecy regarding the present or future, Sanders says, must be oriented towards God as judge.[106] Here a divergence from von Rad can be noted. Sanders holds that the prophets' guiding hermeneutic was the covenant story. Conversely, von Rad maintained the covenant, along with the current historical reality, must be read in light of Yahweh's will, the final governing hermeneutic.

Sanders notes that it is little wonder Jeremiah was imprisoned three times for treason given the people of Judah subscribed to a divine providence in which God fostered unblinking continuity and "willy-nilly" forgiveness and support.[107] Alongside Jeremiah's superior hermeneutic of tradition in the face of crisis, Sanders notes the theme of Yahweh as creator to be another means by which Jeremiah combated false prophets.[108] Citing the Torah story time and again throughout the book, Jeremiah stressed the universalism of Yahweh's rule, wherein Yahweh was "free enough of his own people to engage in purposeful

---

101. Ibid.
102. Ibid.
103. Ibid., 139.
104. Ibid., 140.
105. Ibid., 141.
106. Ibid.
107. Ibid.
108. See J. van Seeters, "The Doctrine of Creation in the Old Testament: A Prolegomenon," PhD dissertation (Princeton Seminary, 1962).

discipline of them, in a transforming act which would extricate the covenant relationship from the falsehood of narrow views of divine providence."[109]

Similarly, Sanders notes, true prophets exhibit real faith. As opposed to falsehood (*sheqer*),[110] faith is a major hallmark of the true prophet as portrayed in Jeremiah. With Gese,[111] Sanders sees true prophets' faith as "being able to affirm the sovereignty of the one God of all over the adversity which befalls Israel: it specifically excludes narrow views of a divine obligation to prosper his people."[112] This is evidenced by Jer 1:5's use of the verb *yotser* ("to create, form"), denoting Yahweh's all-powerful creating might. It is this aspect of the character of Yahweh that Jeremiah used to combat false prophets. Jer 23:23f. was given as the grounds of Jeremiah's position as a true prophet. Jeremiah's view of Yahweh was a view informed by faith; a faith not in Yahweh's unquestioning promotion of an undeserving people, for that would be *sheqer*. Rather his was a faith that, come what may, was confident of Yahweh's guidance and ultimate deliverance. In the midst of a collapsing view of the Torah's portrayal of a creating, judging God, Sanders credits Jeremiah (and other prophets) of exhibiting a faith that challenged the stymied popular view of God and redeemed "the authority of the Torah story."[113] Exilic Israel was in need of faith. Sanders sees canonical criticism as the lens through which the interpreter can best grasp the prophets' "hard" message of judgment. Through it one can see that the prophets "provided the remnant in exile with the faith, the theological perspective, to be able to affirm their identity as Israel, all 'historical evidence' to the contrary notwithstanding."[114]

Moving to his 1977 essay, we can see a more developed exploration of prophetic hermeneutics as it relates to the nature of false prophecy. He begins by claiming that prophecy in general can be better grasped by examining three elements: ancient traditions (texts), situations (contexts), and hermeneutics.[115] A prophet's hermeneutic is extracted by examining the prophet's appeal to "the authoritative forms of speech" and "epic-historic traditions" and how these are related by the prophet to his or her "full, three-dimensional situation in antiquity."[116]

---

109. Sanders, "Jeremiah," 142; Sanders references Jer 18:1-11 and Jer 1:5 as passages in which Yahweh's current activity as *yotser* is reminiscent of his dealings with the old Israel.
110. See Thomas W. Overholt, *The Threat of Falsehood*, (London: S.C.M. Press, 1970), 86-104, for a detailed discussion of the role *šheqer* played in Jeremiah.
111. Hartmut Gese, "The Idea of History in the Ancient Near East and the Old Testament," *JTC* (1965): 49-64.
112. Sanders, "Jeremiah," 142.
113. Ibid.
114. Ibid., 143.
115. Sanders, "Prophetic Hermeneutics," 21.
116. Ibid., 21f.

Sanders begins by tracing those most influential in his understanding of the problem.[117] He expresses affinity to Quell's approach, noting particularly Quell's achievements of freeing Hananiah from the label of "false" and his success at abolishing the prophets' "intentionality" as a determinative criterion.[118] Recognizing Buber's positive emphases of the sovereign freedom of God as opposed to the false prophets' materialism and political ideology, Sanders wants to move beyond his negative characterizations.[119] Sanders considers much of the research since Quell to be marked by the influence of ambiguity and pluralism, both factors that resulted in skepticism becoming the mark of serious scholarship. Crenshaw's thesis that false prophecy inevitably brought about prophecy's demise due to the prophets' inability to distinguish the *vox populi* from the *vox dei*, in Sanders' opinion, most fully embodies this trademark skepticism.[120] And, although Eva Osswald is seen to have contributed the criterion of judgment, it is her development of von Rad's notion of 'history' that Sanders sees to be her primary contribution.[121] Concerning it he writes:

> It is in the canonical process that the so-called criterion of "history" (Jer 28:9; Dt 18:22) or fulfillment of prophecy should be understood, rather than in the simpler sense of specific prediction coming to pass or not; and it is in this sense that the emphases of von Rad, Buber, and Osswald on "history" as the vehicle of true revelation can be retained.[122]

Sanders affirms his emphasis on the freedom and dynamic nature of the divine will as the Bible in various cultural and social situations construes it.[123] The true prophets were those who could accurately discern and apply traditions to the current situations. They must have had an "intimate knowledge of the traditions...and a dynamic ability to perceive the salient facts of one's own moment in time."[124] They must have possessed the ability to discern where the historical hour stood,[125] an activity that the false prophets, due to their static understanding of "texts" and traditions, failed to accomplish.

Given recent scholarship's lack of a "serious attempt to extrapolate from the disputation passages the hermeneutics of the debating colleagues," Sanders tries

---

117. Ibid., 22ff.
118. Quell, 65.
119. Buber, 282f.
120. Crenshaw, *Prophetic Conflict*, 24-35 and 62-74. For the *vox populi* as a positive factor of discernment by implicating it in the later canonical process, see Francis Lèon Ramlot, "Les faux prophètes," *DBSup* 8 (fasc. 47, 1971): cols. 1047-1048, in Sanders, "Prophetic Hermeneutics," 24.
121. Sanders, "Prophetic Hermeneutics," 24. Cf. Renate Brandscheidt, "Der prophetische Konflikt zwischen Jeremia und Hananja," *TThZ* 98 (1989): 73-74.
122. Sanders, "Prophetic Hermeneutics," 24.
123. Ibid., 27.
124. Ibid., 27.
125. Ibid., 27, in Osswald, *Falsche Prophetie*, 22; cf. Crenshaw, *Prophetic Conflict*, 54.

to do just that. While expressing dependence on the prior fifty years of research in the area, he critiques scholarship's over-realized emphasis on the location and labeling of the false prophets' *theologies*.[126] This method of approaching the problem does not sufficiently address the comparative aspect of the prophets' dependence on extant traditions. To this he asks, "When the ancient biblical thinkers rendered the old traditions relevant to their day, what hermeneutics did they employ?"[127]

Sanders is in partial agreement with von Rad, Quell, and Hossfeld/Meyer concerning the lack of clarity surrounding a prophet's authority at any given time. He posits hermeneutics' status as the "mid-term" between the canon's stability and its adaptability. "Before stabilization of forms had become a dominant feature...prophets, psalmists, and others frequently made allusion to Israel's *mythos* traditions in order to legitimate their thoughts and messages."[128] As evidence of this phenomenon, Sanders credits von Rad with having shown this taking place in the prophets. Approaching the prophetic literature in this fashion, the legitimacy of what the false prophets actually said could be seen. They were drawing on accepted, ancient traditions in an effort to communicate on behalf of Yahweh. Therefore, false prophets were not to be dismissed off-handedly. The interpreter was now free to examine the whole of the false prophets' activity.[129] Scholars agreed that true and false prophets both appealed to Israel's traditions. However, it is here that Sanders saw a major problem inherent in the current approach. In focusing on the theologies of the opponents and their misapplication of them, scholarship had been content merely to resolve the problem in terms of good or bad theological timing.

In response to this stalemate, Sanders puts forth several test cases in which he argues that what constituted false prophecy was not who spoke or what was spoken, rather *when*. Comparing Ezek 33:23-29 (a text heretofore not associated with the discussion regarding true and false prophecy) with Isa 51:1-3 in order to demonstrate the importance of "context," Sanders notes that both the exiles in Ezekiel's and Deutero-Isaiah's day made use of the hermeneutical tools of typology and *argumentum a fortiori* in analogizing God's prior work of bringing Abraham out of Babylonia to their respective current realities. Sanders sees the

---

126. Sanders, "Prophetic Hermeneutics," 30; these include: royal theology (E. Jacob, "Quelques remarques sur les faux prophètes," *TZ* 13 (1957): 479-486.), establishment theology (J. Bright, *Jeremiah* (Garden City, N.Y: Doubleday & Co. Inc, 1965), 197-203.), Zionist theology (van der Woude and Weber), *vox populi* (Gunkel and Crenshaw), and a fanatical patriotism and political ideology (Buber).
127. Sanders, "Prophetic Hermeneutics," 30.
128. Ibid., 29.
129. Sanders (ibid, 30) notes scholarship's acceptance of Koch's redactional—criticism, and therefore, a responsibility to move beyond the forms employed by the false prophets; cf. Klaus Koch, *The Growth of the Biblical Tradition: The Form-Critical Method* (London: Black, 1969), 200-210.

falsity in the people's (Ezek 33) "assumption of consistency" of Yahweh.[130] "The hermeneutic principle of the "false prophecy" in Ezekiel and of the true in Isaiah was the same: they both cited the tradition *constitutively*, as a support to what the people felt they needed."[131] With Duhm, what was right for Deutero-Isaiah will be renounced 50 years later by Ezekiel.[132] Not only was the context's importance seen in the text itself, but also in the theology supporting it. Alluding to von Rad's work on Genesis,[133] Sanders sees nearly three-quarters of the biblical text as being representative of a prevenient grace: "God's grace works through human sinfulness."[134] This grace, which was foundational for the Torah story, was, at times, crucial for survival and at others considered falsehood.[135] Sanders believes the period between the Northern and Southern kingdom's exiles was indicative of the latter. Appealing to Isa 29:1-8 (Yahweh's campaign against Jerusalem), Sanders asserts a misapplication of this grace in the form of a message of deliverance constituted false prophecy in this context. For Sanders, false prophets often exhibited "right" theology at the "wrong" moments. This begs the question: Why? Were they evil? Faithless? Sanders seems to say the false prophets were half-right; their theologies were incomplete.

It was not the true prophets' appeal to commonly held authoritative traditions that made them true; rather, that Yahweh was LORD of all peoples. Sanders sees Amos' reply to the people in 9:7 as illustrative of this point. At the people's supposed appeal to the Exodus tradition as grounds for an expected deliverance, Amos replied, "Did I not bring up Israel from the land of Egypt, and the Philistines from Caphtor and the Syrians from Kir?" Sanders reads Amos as implying, "If the Philistines and Syrians migrated…then Yahweh as creator of all peoples had been their guide as well."[136] The Israelites were not the only people group with an Exodus story. It is in the context of Yahweh's sovereignty over all peoples that Sanders raises an issue undeveloped in the 1972 article. In his discussion of Hananiah's breaking the yoke and returning it to Jeremiah, Sanders pays close attention to 28:14's reference to Nebuchadnezzar as having been given all the beasts of the field by Yahweh. Linking this to 27:5-7, Sanders sees this as Jeremiah's polemic of Yahweh as creator, sustainer, and redeemer of all, not just Israel.[137]

---

130. Sanders, "Prophetic Hermeneutics," 32.
131. Ibid.
132. Ibid., 32.
133. Gerhard von Rad, *Genesis* (Philadelphia: Westminster, 1961), 13-42.
134. Sanders, "Prophetic Hermeneutics," 33-34; *Errore hominum providentia divina*.
135. Ibid., 34.
136. Ibid., 38.
137. Ibid., 39; Sanders notes the question of the reliability of the source in 27:5-7, referring to Helga Weippert, *Die Prosareden des Jeremiabuches*, BZAW 132 (Berlin: de Gruyter, 1973); and William L. Holladay, "A Fresh Look at "Source B" and "Source C" in Jeremiah," *VT* 25 (1975): 394-412, concerning this passage's thematic similarity with other recognized "C", Deuteronomic sources throughout the book (39n39).

There is something more at work, Sanders notes, than contexts and the application of traditions. The prophets' theologies were considerable factors in and of themselves. He sees the false prophets' inability to admit Yahweh's Lordship over all peoples as their refusal to take part in the process of canonical monotheizing, the "fundamental canonical thrust of the Bible."[138] If a prophet did not recognize the work of Yahweh on behalf of other nations besides Israel, Sanders sees this as partly constitutive of their failure. Drawing on Crenshaw's notion of God's testing of Israel,[139] Sanders sees the true prophets as those who "consciously contributed" to Yahweh's work on behalf of his, and all, people. This work was painful at times, but, at its completion, it will bring forth a new Israel.[140]

Brevard S. Childs (1923-2007)

Given the breadth and scope of literature elsewhere that is busy recovering or critiquing Brevard Childs' contribution to Old Testament theology and to canonical interpretation, this study will chiefly be concerned with his navigation of true and false prophecy.[141] Brief comments regarding the history of the discipline as it relates to Childs are in order. Childs witnesses many major gains in the field of Old Testament theology in the years between 1930 and the 1960's. Chief among these was Old Testament theology's renewed independence over against the critical history-of-religions emphasis prevalent in biblical studies in

---

138. Sanders, "Prophetic Hermeneutics," 40.
139. Crenshaw, *Prophetic Conflict*, 77-90.
140. Sanders, "Prophetic Hermeneutics," 40-41.
141. See Leo G. Perdue, *The Collapse of History: Reconstructing Old Testament Theology*, (Minneapolis: Augsburg Fortress Press, 1994), 153-196, esp. 155, n. 4. Weighty, and perhaps at times splenetic, critiques of Childs' approach were leveled by both James Barr, *Holy Scripture: Canon, Authority, Criticism*, (Philadelphia: Westminster Press, 1983), esp. 130-171, and John Barton, *Reading the Old Testament: Method in Biblical Study*, (London: Darton Longman and Todd, 1984); cf. Daniel Driver's *Brevard Childs, Biblical Theologian; For the Church's One Bible*, FAT II 46 (Tübingen: Mohr Siebeck, 2010). The most formative treatment of true and false prophecy from an admittedly canonical perspective was that of Childs in his *Old Testament Theology in a Canonical Context* (Philadelphia: Fortress Press, 1985; First Fortress Press paperback, 1989), 133-144. Childs' literary analysis of Jer 27-28 relies heavily on the work of Overholt, *Threat*, 33ff. Other 'canoically-oriented' readings of true and false prophetcy would include: the recent, less in-depth treatment of Gerald T. Sheppard, "True and False Prophecy Within Scripture," in *Canon, Theology, and Old Testament Interpretation*, ed. Gene M. Tucker, David L. Petersen, and Robert R. Wilson, 262-282, (Philadelphia: Fortress Press, 1988); a PhD dissertation submitted under G. Sheppard by Jacob Daniel Epp-Tiessen, "Concerning the Prophets: True and False Prophecy in Jeremiah 23:9-29:32," University of St. Michael's College (Canada), 1994; and recently James Brenneman's somewhat canonical treatment of the issue, *Canons in Conflict*, 1997.

the late nineteenth and early twentieth centuries. He attributed this positive advance in large part to von Rad and Eichrodt, along with Köhler,[142] Vriezen,[143] and Zimmerli[144] on the continent and H. W. Robinson[145] in Britian. In their work, particularly von Rad's, Childs noted a growing trend to use the findings of historical-critical scholarship in the construction of positive theological asertions.[146]

Alongside this, Old Testament theology was making its presence felt in Old and New Testament exegesis, especially von Rad and Bultmann, respectively. In spite of these 'gains,' Childs perceived a stalemate having occurred due to a myriad of reasons. These included the confusion as to whether or not the discipline of OT Theology was to be considered an extension of the history of the religion of Israel. Also there appeared to be a lack of coherence in a body of literature fraught with inconsistencies and seemingly opposing religious elements. Add to these an exegetically 'false' assumption that meaning can be derived from somewhere outside the text itself. Finally, obvious to anyone in the field, Old Testament theology's relationship with both Judaism and the New Testament lacked clarity.[147] It was in response to this quagmire that Childs proposed his canonical method.[148] Before examining Childs' interpretation of Jer 28, a look at his understanding of prophecy and fulfillment as Old Testament phenomena is in order. Childs saw in the early church's interpretation of prophecy a struggle to make sense of the fulfillment of prophecy. Used apologetically by such fathers as Justin[149] and Cyprian,[150] prophecy was interpreted both literally and allegorically.[151] Moving into the period of the Reformation, Luther's Christological interpretation of prophecy and, subsequently, Calvin's view of history moving towards a goal that saw the Old Testament's prophecies as shad-

---

142. Ludwig Köhler, *Old Testament Theology* (Philadelphia: Westminster Press, 1957).
143. T.C. Vriezen, *An Outline of Old Testament Theology* (Oxford: Blackwell, 1958; 2nd ed., revised and enlarged ed., 1970).
144. Walter Zimmerli, *Old Testament Theology in Outline*, 2nd ed., (Atlanta: John Knox Press, 1978).
145. H. Wheeler Robinson, *Inspiration and Revelation in the Old Testament* (Oxford: Clarendon Press, 1953).
146. Childs, *OTTCC*, 4.
147. See Childs' helpful survey of the discipline in *OTTCC*, 4ff. and "Prophecy and Fulfillment: A Study of Contemporary Hermeneutics," *Interpretation* 12 (1958): 259-271, esp. 259-263.
148. In response to Sanders' accusation that Childs' canonical approach is just another critique alongside historical, literary, or form-criticism, Childs protests that the canonical approach is to be understood rather as, "a stance from which the Bible is to be read as Scripture" in "Canonical shape of the prophetic literature," *Interpretation* 32/1 (1978): 55. See also Childs, *Biblical Theology in Crisis* (Philadelphia: Westminster Press, 1970).
149. *Dialogue with Trypho*, in Childs, "Prophecy and Fulfillment," 259.
150. *Testimonies against the Jews*, in Childs, "Prophecy and Fulfillment," 259.
151. Ibid., 259ff.

ows to be given form by Christ in the New, was the dominant method of approach. In the years following, prophecy in the Old became intrinsically associated with the notion of prediction, largely through the work of Vitringa. Prophecy's relation to its fulfillment came to be understood rationally. The result of which, Childs claimed, was the divorcing of prophecy from "the purpose of God in history."[152] With Schleiermacher's distinction between "special prediction" and "Messianic prophecy," Childs saw a positive contribution from the non-Orthodox side of interpretation.[153] Schleiermacher's influence would be felt in Hengstenberg's similar delineation between the "general truths" of the prophets and the "incidental particulars" of their prophecies employed to convey a message.[154] Discussing the contributions of von Hofmann (*Heilsgeschichte*), Vischer (Christ was actually at work in the OT community), Eichrodt (prophecy and fulfillment unfold in history), and von Rad (typological), Childs then went on to offer a correction of the modern notion of fulfillment by exploring the Old Testament's distinct Hebraic usage.[155]

In his early (1958) work on prophecy and fulfillment, Childs notes that the Hebrew term *ml'* ("fill" or "to be full") was used in the Old Testament to denote temporality and most often referred to days or years having passed, thus designating the completion of time. To most accurately describe the Hebrew concept, Childs said that time was to be known by its content. It was with this distinction that the term had bearing on the discussion of prophecy, for *ml'* referred to the filling of words.[156] In the Old Testament this could be seen in instances where the prophets', or Yahweh's, words were filled when the completion of the event spoken of occurred. Childs claimed this touched on the Hebrew notion of truth and reality. Citing numerous scriptural examples, he noted that false words spo-

---

152. Ibid., 260. While appreciative of his contribution to the interpretation of prophecy, Childs, in *Struggle,* 249-50, offers two sustained critiques of Vitringa: (1) by placing the biblical events in a "single historical trajectory", Vitringa negated any "dialectical tension within the biblical story" thereby losing the element of *Heilsgeschichte*, and (2) Vitringa's interpretations largely failed to serve the contemporary community of faith because there was "no sense of a vertical imperative in receiving a Word of God."
153. Ibid., 260f. According to Schleiermacher, *The Christian Faith,* ed. James S. Stewart and Hugh R. Mackintosh, English trans. of 2nd German ed., (Edinburgh: T&T Clark, 1928), 446, Old Testament prophecies fell into one of two categories. First, "special prediction," was intended for a specific historical situation. Built on the Old Testament themes of election and divine retribution, it "formed an addition to teaching which conveyed warning, encouragement, and comfort, in accordance with the spirit of the law." Being "strictly foretelling," this type of prediction exhibited varying degrees of accuracy. The second type, "Messianic prediction," "rose above the individual event to an exposition of the universal." Therein lay this type's value — "it spoke of the future of God's true messenger."
154. Childs, "Prophecy and Fulfillment," 261.
155. Childs, "Prophecy and Fulfillment," 263ff.
156. Ibid., 264f., i.e., Jer 44:25; 1 Kgs 2:27; 2 Chr 36:21.

ken have no reality because they never possessed a reality.[157] Conversely, true words were filled because they already shared in reality. Therefore, biblical fulfillment was not in terms of "identical correspondence" between two identical entities.[158] Rather, prophecy and fulfillment belonged to the same event. The word set into motion an event that was then "filled up" (i.e. reaches wholeness). The *kairos* of the word and event were the same, but the *chronos* was different, "and it is during this time that the creative word strives for its filling."[159] There were no criteria for whether or not a prophecy was fulfilled, only for its truth or falsity.[160] Understandably then, there was no simple wait-and-see criterion for the truth of a prophecy. An event with which a given prophecy was concerned was "fulfilled when it is full."[161] The problem, then, was with the truth of the not-yet filled prophecy. Here was where Childs saw Deut 18:22 coming into play. For Childs, this prophetic law was a regulatory statute intended to protect the people from bully-prophets, not a mechanism of discernment whereby a prophet could be accurately accused as false at the scene of the prophesying.[162] Similar to von Rad, Childs saw two operative criteria in Deut 18 and Jer 28 concerning the truth of a prophecy. First, if a word did not maintain itself by filling, then it was not sent from Yahweh. Second, utilizing a "correspondence theory," Childs held that if the word and the fulfillment belonged to the same reality (i.e., are true), there must be a correspondence between them "in order to form a totality."[163] Having sketched Childs' understanding of the Old Testament's construal of prophecy and fulfillment's relationship to truth, we now turn to Childs' approach to prophetic truth versus falsity in Jeremiah's confrontation with Hananiah.

Childs saw significant Deuteronomistic shaping evident in the book of Jeremiah.[164] This resulted in a canonical portrayal of Jeremiah's words linking him to a line of faithful prophets who found their roots in Moses and whose messages were often characterized as warnings of the coming destruction of Jerusalem.[165] Canonically, the present (final) "ordering of Jeremiah's message within

---

157. Ibid., 266; Ps 4:3; Jgs 9:4; Ruth 1:13; Is 51:58; 65:23.
158. Ibid., 267.
159. Ibid., 267f.
160. Ibid., 268; Childs here referenced Deut 13:1ff., 18:22, and Jer 28:9 in relation to a prophecy's fullness authenticating itself.
161. Ibid., 268.
162. Brevard S. Childs, *Isaiah and the Assyrian Crisis* (London: S.C.M. Press, 1967), 92-93.
163. Childs, "Prophecy and fulfillment," 268.
164. *IOTS*, 347f.
165. Ibid.; see esp. Mowinckel, *Prophecy and Tradition*, 61ff.; cf. John Skinner, *Prophecy and Religion: Studies in the Life of Jeremiah*, Cunningham lectures; 1920 (Cambridge: Cambridge University Press, 1948), esp. 89-107; H.H. Rowley, "The Prophet Jeremiah and the Book of Deuteronomy," in *Studies in Old Testament Prophecy; studies presented to Professor Theodore H. Robinson*, ed. H.H. Rowley, Pages 157-174, (Edinburgh: T & T

the tradition of the preachers of the law provides the later community with a prophetic interpretation of how the law properly functions within the divine economy."[166] Childs thus sees theological intentionality as characteristic of the editorial shaping of the book.[167] It is with this intentionality in mind that Childs touches first upon the history of research surrounding the confrontation of Jeremiah and Hananiah and then offers his own reading of the problem, making conspicuous use of Jer 28.

Childs saw in the majority of scholarship insufficient attention devoted to the theological freight of Jer 28 as it stands in relation to the book of Jeremiah and the post-exilic Jewish community of faith at large. As illustrative of this, Childs highlights Zimmerli in particular. Childs found Zimmerli's notion of fulfillment, in which the determinative criteria rested in Yahweh's divine presence in history rather than in some demonstration of that truth, to be helpful but inconclusive in relation to true and false prophecy.[168] Fulfillment for Zimmerli was not authenticated by a message's "correspondence to a predicted set of facts," rather it was entirely dependant on Yahweh's personal fulfillment of his word. This fulfillment was then publicly demonstrated in the coming to pass of the previously spoken words.[169] Childs labeled Zimmerli's approach, along with Buber and von Rad's, *existential*, seeing several common characteristics therein. First, Jeremiah was in a running battle with prophets who preached peace. Second, the yoke and thong symbols actualized his message of coming destruction. Third, Jeremiah retreated meekly upon Hananiah's breaking of the yoke, content to wait-and-see. Finally, they conclude that Jeremiah had no authoritative refutation deriving from the past, rather, only through a new word from Yahweh could he oppose Hananiah. Of this existential interpretation Childs wrote, "There was no horizontal continuity in prophecy...The criterion of truth resides alone in a fresh word from God *hic et nunc*."[170]

Clark, 1950); Robert Davidson, "Orthodoxy and the prophetic word: a study in the relationship between Jeremiah and Deuteronomy," *VT* 14 (1964): 407-416; and Christopher R. Seitz, "The Prophet Moses and the Canonical Shape of Jeremiah," *ZAW* 101 (1989): 3-27.
166. Childs, "Shape," 50.
167. Contra Hyatt's or Bright's treatment of the book as a "referential source for historical reconstruction," Childs, *Introduction to the Old Testament as Scripture* (Philadelphia: Fortress Press, 1979), 354.
168. *OTTCC*, 134f.
169. Walter Zimmerli, "Verheissung und Erfüllung," *EvT* 12 (1952-3): 6ff., reprinted as "Prophecy and Fulfillment," in *Essays on Old Testament Hermeneutics*, ed. Claus Westermann, Eng. trans. James Wharton, Pages 89-122, (Richmond: John Knox Press, 1963), 107, n. 64, saw Jer 28:9's criterion as the same criterion found in Dt 18:21f., which was relativized in 13, a criterion which was present in Jeremiah but never utilized, because to do so would be to subject Yahweh and his word to an "objective test-case."
170. *OTTCC*, 136.

Childs saw Sanders' approach to the problem as an expansion of this existential method. Positively, Sanders' approach appeared to be driven by strong theological concerns and would have been attractive as it offered an alternative to a "sterile, historicist" reading of the Bible. While certainly not wholly devoid of merit, Childs did, however, see Sanders' method as critically flawed in its theology.[171] Believing a fundamental role of canon was to "establish theological continuity between the generations by means of the authority of sacred scripture,"[172] Childs saw in Sanders' view of history as the final arbiter of Hananiah and Jeremiah an example of a use of canon that was inherently foreign to biblical interpretation until after the Enlightenment.[173] Sanders believed that the task of the current interpreter was in some way analogous to that of the prophets of Israel as they sought to apply an old tradition afresh. To this Childs can be understood to say, from an admittedly entrenched theological position, "We are not prophets nor apostles, nor is our task directly analogous."[174] Childs began his own exposition of the confrontation between Jeremiah and Hananiah noting that considerable confusion would have inevitably been present in early post-exilic Jewish communities. With prophets offering opposing messages, appealing to the same authority, and employing similar, if not identical, vocabularies, the threat of false prophecy was an immediate problem. A means of discernment would have surely been sought. As mentioned above, concerning Deuteronomy's proposed solution, Childs largely followed von Rad. Deuteronomy's prophetic laws (Deut 13 and 18) forbid polytheistic prophecy and protected against the unwarranted fear of doom prophets, while in Jeremiah, the burden of proof was on the prophet proclaiming peace. Like von Rad, Childs too saw here two separate criteria whose differences were "in kind."[175]

For the present discussion, Childs' own interpretation can be seen as consisting of three sections: literary, theological, and canonical. We will treat them in that order. Literarily, Childs, like the majority of interpreters, placed chapter 28 in the editorial section beginning in 23:9 and ending in 29:32. Of particular importance to Childs was chapter 27. He saw 27 as being comprised of three oracles (vv. 1-11, to the nations; vv. 12-15 to Zedekiah; vv. 16-22 to the priests and the people), each with four components (vv. 5-8 and 17, serve Nebuchadnezzar; vv. 9, 14, 17, do not listen to your prophets; vv. 10, 14, 16, the prophets prophesy a lie; vv. 11, 15, 22, if disobedient, you will be removed from the land).[176] Childs saw the later editor's construal of 28 as illustrative of this

---

171. Ibid., 137.
172. Ibid.
173. Ibid.
174. Ibid.
175. Ibid., 133; von Rad, "Die Falschen Propheten," 115.
176. Ibid., 137f.; this is heavily dependant on the earlier work of Overholt, *Threat*, 33ff. In the context of political allegiance, Overholt saw chapter 27 divided into three sections

scheme,[177] thereby showing Jeremiah's to-be-fulfilled words to Hananiah to be consistent with his prophetic message writ large. Childs wrote, "Jeremiah's confrontation with Hananiah functions to provide a concrete illustration of the one message against false prophets."[178]

Next, Childs took up the question of 28:5-9, which he granted could have had a life "independent of the later editorial framework into which it has been placed."[179] But if that were the case, Childs noted, his disagreement with von Rad and Zimmerli would revolve around their attempt to recover an "original historical situation in which Jeremiah is thought to reflect great uncertainty and to seek a fresh existential confirmation."[180] Psychologizing the text in this way, discounting whatever continuity between past and present existed, would be to call into question Jeremiah's certainty as to his previous message, something Childs, following Duhm, was not willing to do. Childs disagreed with any interpretation that would sideline the theological emphases present throughout Jeremiah's messages. Jeremiah was not uncertain regarding his previous message. Rather, he was "uncertain regarding God's plan."[181] For Childs, the exegetical issue, which verses 5-9 fully supported, was theocentric in the sense of God's actions in history and concerned "God's will for the nations under the rule of Nebuchadnezzar."[182]

For Childs, the editorial shape signposted the narrative's theological focus. Jeremiah's concern was God's purpose for Israel under Babylonian rule. Childs saw the major difference between Jeremiah and Hananiah's theological viewpoints to be Jeremiah's unwillingness to deny Yahweh the "freedom of changing his mind."[183] According to Childs, Jeremiah allowed that Hananiah might have been right; Yahweh may have had a different purpose. And, in case he did, Jeremiah set up a criterion by which to judge Hananiah's message, basing it on the following 'precedent': "God has in the past always spoken of judgment. If he now changes his plan, he will demonstrate it in history."[184] For Childs the issue

---

each having a two-part exhortation: (1) do not believe the šheqer spoken by the prophets promising peace or urging rebellion against Babylon and (2) serve Nebuchadnezzar (35).
177. In 28, the scheme is as follows: 28:14 — the nations will serve Nebuchadnezzar; 28:15 — Hananiah has spoken a lie; 28:16 — Yahweh will remove Hananiah from the land. Childs explains the absence of 27:9, 14, 16 ("do not listen to your prophets") from 28 by saying that Hananiah was the aforementioned liar and was being personally addressed, Childs, *OTTCC*, 138, as Mowinckel, *Prophecy and Tradition*, 63.
178. *OTTCC*, 138.
179. Ibid., 138. For an alternative position, cf. H. Seebass, "Jeremias Konflikt mit Chananja: Bemerkungen zu Jer 27 und 28," *ZAW* 82 (1970): 451-452, who held that 28:8f. addresses the oracles against the nations.
180. Ibid., 138.
181. Ibid., 139.
182. Ibid.
183. Ibid.
184. Ibid.

was theological rather than psychological. Jeremiah was more concerned with determining God's purpose than with whether his message constituted the more accurate 'doctrine of God.' For both the original and the redacted layers of 23-29, the theological issue was the same: false prophets speak lies. The differences lay not in hermeneutics or timing, but concerned the "objective word of God."[185] Concerning the presence of criteria Childs's remarks were brief. The canonical shape of Jer 23-29 left subsequent readers with no less than two 'criteria'. First, the true prophet has stood in the council of the LORD (Jer 23:18). Second, citing Jer 26:5, 25:3, 26:4, and 23:22, Childs contended that the prophets have consistently spoken a message of repentance, thus signifying a univocal message that spanned the life of the office.[186]

Childs saw the entire book of Jeremiah as uniform in its depictions of the roots of false prophecy in relation to the source of a prophet's message. Childs wrote:

> The test of the truth lies in God who makes known his will through revelation. The contrast is not an existential one between a past, horizontal tradition about God and a present, vertical word from God. Rather, the truth of prophecy is determined by God's confirmation in action.[187]

The canonical shape of Jeremiah was an answer to the problem of true and false prophecy. By this Childs meant that the editing of the book of Jeremiah, particularly 23-29, addressed the question both descriptively and prescriptively.[188]

Summary

In the preface of the third Dutch edition of his *An Outline of Old Testament Theology*, Vriezen explained some recent additions. Due to the current climate of Old Testament studies, the role of faith in the Old Testament testimonies, he said, should now (1966) be more prominently central. However, in relation to our preceding discussion, his next point was indicative of the attitude of the mid-20th century scholarship regarding von Rad's influence on subsequent Old Testament work, whether theological or otherwise. Vriezen wrote:

---

185. Ibid., 143.
186. Ibid., 141. Childs also mentioned the moral test set forth by the book of Jeremiah (23:13f. and 29:23).
187. Ibid., 139; cf. similarly Zimmerli, "Prophetic Proclamation and Reinterpretation," in *Tradition and Theology in the Old Testament,* ed. Douglas A. Knight, Pages 69-100, (London: SPCK, 1977).
188. Ibid., 140. See Crenshaw's treatment of the demise of prophecy and the growth of wisdom and apocalyptic literature in post-exilic Judaism due to the lack of criteria for discerning true prophecy, in relation to the descriptive function of the book of Jeremiah. Crenshaw, in Childs' opinion, "does not reckon with the formation of the Old Testament canon."

> [A]fter the appearance of the former edition discussion concerning the character of Old Testament Theology revived so strongly, especially in Germany, that is was impossible to ignore either the discussion or the book that came so much to be the centre of the discussion, namely G. von Rad's *Old Testament Theology*.[189]

That von Rad's influence was and is still felt throughout Old Testament studies is not nor could be adequately dealt with in the scope of the present study. His influence, however, on the direction taken in the latter half of the 20th century by those who would seek to hear afresh the Old Testament's portrayal of true and false prophecy, was considerable.

It appears that two streams of interpretation have emerged in the last century. Recognizing von Rad as influential, Sanders and Childs have both drawn substantially on his findings with differing, and at times conflicting, results. In Sanders we saw von Rad's emphatic insistence on the need for prophetic timing. Von Rad understood that a message in the mouth of Isaiah could have been a measure of strengthening and testing the faith of Israel for one generation, but nearly a century later, that same word may lead to death. Proper timing, or hermeneutics, for von Rad, was not the mark of a true prophet. Sounding more like a dogmatician than a professor of Hebrew, von Rad saw the absolute transcendency of Yahweh's word and a prophet's ability and willingness to submit to it as irrefutable evidence of true prophecy. It appeared von Rad's insistence on the divine would be muted considerably in the coming generation's increasingly existentialistic and psychological interpretations of the conflict in Jer 28. This can largely be attributed to the work of Quell and subsequently Sanders. In seeking to make relevant to a modern readership seemingly alien encounters between prophets, Sanders has reverted to an approach to the prophets that appears to be more at home in post-Enlightenment, Idealistic nineteenth-century Germany.

Agreeing with von Rad regarding the transcendency of the divine word, Childs' approach also paralleled von Rad's in its hesitancy to simply apply a deuteronomistic prophetic law to the situation in Jer 28. Therein also lay a distinct difference. Childs' commitment to the shape of the canon constrained him to see some relation present between the prophets and the law that von Rad was reticent to spotlight. Von Rad linked Jeremiah with those before him by observing similarities in literary sources and his execution of certain offices or functions, but saw no horizontal continuity. Childs, however saw something more concrete. A prophet's message was true if sent from Yahweh. Its legitimation was proof of its veracity. Echoing Calvin, prophecy and fulfillment were thought to be ontologically linked. That was the manner in which prophecy had functioned at its Mosaic inception and, Childs believed, it still functioned that way on the eve of the destruction of Jerusalem.

---

189. Vriezen, *Old Testament Theology*, preface.

8. A WAY FORWARD: SINCE 1986

Introduction

In the main, the last quarter of the twentieth—century saw a decline in the treatment of true and false prophecy.[1] Articles appeared intermittently in which the question of true and false prophecy was broached in so far as it contributed to a fuller historically oriented (diachronic) understanding of the prophetic activity of Israel's surrounding nations.[2] Interestingly, just as Childs and Sanders furthered the work of von Rad in relation to this question, students of both Sanders and Childs expanded upon and refined their work on false prophecy as well. And, the issue was necessarily treated in passing in several commentaries of the latter twentieth-century, but it was not until 1997 that any substantial interest revived in the hermeneutical implications of false prophecy.

The total literature of this period treating the prophets, even that limited to the prophet Jeremiah, is beyond the scope of our study. In an effort to focus the discussion by surveying representatives of various approaches, the remainder of this study will examine the monographs of Brenneman (1997), Lange (2002), and Moberly (2006), incorporating articles, commentaries, and other works when relevant. In conclusion, we will show that acceptable schemes of reading the prophets with an eye to discernment have been ingredient to the Christian tradition's interpretation of prophetic conflict.

---

1. Cf. Simon J. de Vries's work, *Prophet Against Prophet: The Role of the Micaiah Narrative (I Kings 22) in the Development of Early Prophetic Tradition* (Grand Rapids: Eerdmans, 1978), written several years after Crenshaw, advanced the question in but a limited fashion. With Crenshaw, De Vries broadly viewed conflict and the inability to discern not simply as a symptom of Israel's decline, but a cause. Coupled with this, de Vries saw true prophecy to be signposted philosophically by the presence of biblical personalism, which, for the prophet, meant, "the interaction of divine and human integrity in purposeful cooperation for the spiritual enrichment of mankind" (de Vries, 145). Cf. the reviews of Craghan, *CBQ* 42 (1980): 234-235; Willis, *ResQ* 23 (1980): 45-46; Birch, *JBL* 98 (1979): 594-595; and J. Bright, *Them* 5 (1981): 17. Particularly helpful was a review by Carroll Stuhlmueller (*Hor* 7 (1980): 323-325) of De Vries' work alongside Robert Carroll's *When Prophecy Failed* (New York: Seabury Press, 1979).
2. Representatives of this approach include Martti Nissinen, "Falsche Prophetie in neuassyrischer und deuteronomistischer Darstellung," in *Das Deuteronomium und seine Querbeziehungen,* ed. Timo Veijola, Schriften der Finnischen Exegetischen Gesellschaft 62 (Göttingen: Vandenhoeck & Ruprecht, 1996); Hans-Jürgen Hermisson, "Kriterien »wahrer« und »falscher« Prophetie im Alten Testement," *ZThK* 92 (1995); and Evangelia G. Dafni, *"ruah sheqer* und falsche Prophetie in I Reg 22," *ZAW* 112 (2000); cf. Lange, 19—33.

James E. Brenneman

Brenneman's *Canons in Conflict* is as much a reader on post-modern hermeneutical theory as it is an exegetical "negotiation [of] texts in true and false prophecy," as the subtitle indicates. Brenneman juxtaposes the message of Isa 2:4, "They shall beat their swords into plowshares and their spears into pruning hooks," with Joel 4:10 (ET 3:10), "Beat your plowshares into swords and your pruning hooks into spears." Before he turns to the question of true and false prophecy outright, Brenneman lays out his prolegomena. He largely sees canon as a construct to be restrictive. The product of power brokers, the canon's central message has been usurped.[3] Appealing to a canonical (in the broadest sense) approach to interpretation, Brenneman is heavily dependant on James Sanders' monotheizing process throughout.[4] Believing that the reader is left with no alternative but to turn from the text itself to the reading community (Sanders)[5] for authority, Brenneman sees ethics, or determinative "norms for living,"[6] as the way to get at the question of which message to prefer. As a Mennonite, and thereby a member of a non-violent reading community, one is not surprised at the prophetic message for which Brenneman ultimately inveighs.[7] "The biblical canon is a canon whose authority derived from its ethical *performance*...The implication of such an observation insists on nonviolence as a first principle (rule of order) in any canonical dispute."[8] Brenneman makes this statement, however, after electing to prefer canon's role as *function* to its role as *shape*, which was comprised of older, outmoded ontological views of canon "that have relied on the determinacy of texts, authorial intentions, and other foundations."[9] Swords and spears are destined, in the end, to become plowshares and pruning hooks (Isaiah).

What better place, Brenneman intones, to see the function of canon at work, for better or worse, than in prophetic conflict and its derivative alternative readings? Before offering his own, relatively thin, reading of the problem, Brenneman recaps the findings of the last century (and a half?).[10] Through a wide-angle lens, Brenneman sees the nineteenth-century to be characterized by a fo-

---

3. Brenneman, 69-76.
4. Ibid., 76.
5. Ibid., 34.
6. Ibid., 6.
7. Cf. Lionel Basney's insightful and critical review in *ChrLit* 48 (1999): 213-214.
8. Brenneman, 140.
9. Ibid., 6. For Brenneman (i.e., Sanders), this role of canon was, at least initially (until 1977), associated with a historical-critical program in crisis (150n9). Cf. Sanders, "Canon (Hebrew Bible)," *ABD*, 1:847; cited in Brenneman, 151n12.
10. As the concerns of this study are historically oriented, we will only briefly treat Brenneman's exegesis. Our main intent is to demonstrate the extent to which Brenneman deviated from or adhered to the stream of scholarship at the end of the twentieth—century.

cus on the prophet.[11] This individual focus gives way to increased attention paid to the prophets' messages, culminating in the work of von Rad (for whom Prophet was 'law preacher').[12] Finally, overlapping literary theory's "paradigm shift"[13] of the latter twentieth-century, the focus is transferred yet again, this time to the prophet's audience, as seen in Crenshaw. Brenneman's account is highly, and understandably, selective.

First, Brenneman views Quell's 1952 *Wahre und falschen Propheten* as the death knell for this first phase of individualistic research on the prophets. Arguing for Hananiah's moral rectitude, Quell "put an end" to those who saw an easy criterion for discernment in the identifying of canonical prophets' opponents' intentions.[14] Until Quell, late nineteenth- and early twentieth-century scholars had erroneously placed too high a value on the excavating of the so-called false prophets' "cultic and nationalistic tendencies, fanatic demagoguery, moral looseness, primitive spirit, and so on."[15] Brenneman credits Duhm with influencing not only Ewald, but also Herder's approach to the prophetic individuality.[16] Chronological errors notwithstanding, Brenneman's thesis might perhaps be well served by a fuller understanding of this period's reception of true and false prophecy; particularly Duhm's work at the textual level and Kuenen's understanding of prophetic development. As evinced above, Duhm was interested as much in the text of Jeremiah as he was the prophet concerning this question of false prophecy. By posing the question "what would Jeremiah have made of Deutero-Isaiah's message of restoration?," Duhm admits of legitimate conflict between the messages of two canonical prophets, akin to Brenneman's Joel and Isaiah. There would surely be much fodder in Duhm's commentary for a thesis such as Brenneman's. Kuenen's notion of prophetic development might also come into play, since Kuenen saw the authentic prophet as the one most in tune with the original prophetic ethic, the Mosaic. At the least, Kuenen sounded the alarm against the caricaturing of the opposing prophets 77 years prior to Quell. Not only was Kuenen prepared to give the false prophets a fair hearing for fairness' sake; he was convinced they spoke out of firmly held religious convictions.

Criteria, if any were to be found, would have to be sought for elsewhere. Next, Brenneman sees the prophetic message as the locus under consideration. Mentioning Westermann and Mowinckel briefly, Brenneman sees von Rad's 1933 "Die falschen Propheten," as representative of this period's fascination

---

11. Ibid., 84-85.
12. We will return to his assessment of von Rad below.
13. This shift in literary theory was from author to text/tradition to audience response, Brenneman, 84; 51n14
14. Ibid., 5
15. Ibid., 85.
16. Brenneman, 174n5.

with the prophetic message.[17] Brenneman engages von Rad at closer range when he makes the case that von Rad's insistence on a criterion of weal was due in large part to his (over—) commitment to a scheme of historical fulfillment: if it happened, it was true. Thus, postexilic Deuteronomy's warnings (13 and 18) are directed toward weal, because woe occurred. Von Rad may have been better served, Brenneman offers, had he pointed out that after the exile, as far as the Hebrew Bible's canon was concerned, Deuteronomy's message was anything but false. Just the opposite: it was formative. Brenneman writes, "History may be the final arbiter but only in its *telos*, not any particular moment in between."[18] However, this qualification to von Rad's approach seems to undercut Brenneman's central thesis of the canon's role as function, opting instead to render value judgments on the utility of a biblical text based on its final form Also, as noted by Childs, von Rad's focus was on the historical situation of Jeremiah, not the canon as it now stands (or stood post exile).[19] He was working on a different level of the text. To render a judgment on the suitability of such an approach is another matter.

Buber, Osswald, and Koch also receive passing mention before he turns to Crenshaw and audience/reader response. Seeing a throwback to Gunkel's *vox populi*, Brenneman rehearses Crenshaw's well-known thesis for the post-exilic dissolution of prophecy due to the lack of discernible criteria and the prophets' "embellished account of Israel's history."[20] Having reached the "denouement" of scholarship's inquiry into false prophecy with Crenshaw in 1971, Brenneman directs the reader to Sanders' prophetic hermeneutic as the optimal of available options by which to advance the question. That is, given the canonical approaches of Childs and Sanders, Brenneman opts for the latter, since Childs "rests on the assumption that it is the text as scripture, and not its readers, that provides the primary role for theological continuity."[21] Brenneman notes Childs' contributions to the question, namely the differentiation between the original setting and later redactional construals. However, in focusing on the text in its final form, Childs has rendered the function of canon void. Brenneman extends the same critique to Childs' student Sheppard.[22] Noting approvingly Sheppard's 'flexible' criteria for discerning true and false prophets, along with his view (contra Childs) of the constantly shifting "politics of truth" in a given reading community, Brenneman nonetheless sees the same fatal flaw in Sheppard as in

---

17. Cf. von Rad above.
18. Brenneman, 175n12.
19. Childs, *OTTCC*, 138.
20. James L. Crenshaw, *Old Testament Wisdom: An Indroduction* (Atlanta: John Knox, 1981), 202; cited in Brenneman, 175n16.
21. Brenneman, 90. Cf. Chapman, *The Law and the Prophets*, 111n5, on Child's take on the community's conformity to its "received traditions" over against a reading that exerts a pressure on the text.
22. Sheppard, "True and False Prophecy Within Scripture," 262-282.

his teacher and, to a degree, Sanders. Brenneman sees in the self-defensive stances of both Childs' final form and Sanders' canon-criticism, "the very dynamic that is played out between conflicting prophets within the biblical texts themselves."[23] In arguing for the primacy of one's approach, that same persuasive, political struggle is analogously enacted in which the prophets and their subsequent reading communities engaged. Admittedly, one is left wondering where this will all end.

Admitting that he has extended his model farther than Sanders himself, Brenneman argues this is warranted. Seeing the reading community, not the text itself, to be the adhesive connecting generations of the faithful, the intertwining of "text to context to hermeneutics to the reading community" is a logical premise.[24] Against Knierim, Brenneman believes the question of discernment, as it can be grasped canonically, has less to do with adjudication than with "whether it is possible to define criteria in such a way as to claim a universality for those criteria beyond one's own peculiar claims to their universality."[25] As mentioned above, in a postmodern era, Brenneman draws on ethics as the grounds for adjudication. Here his thesis is clearly on display. Postmodern canonical-critical interpretation is in a particularly advantageous position, Brenneman argues, for it is readily observable that "the formation and content of the canon are vey much political activities spawning conflicts over power."[26] Understanding this allows the reader to keep in mind that what has been dressed up as "objective" truth, was always merely "rhetorical art within competing discursive communities."[27] Prophets argued their cases from within the community of Israel. Falling broadly along two lines, they preached either change (prophetic critique) or the status quo (constitutive hermeneutics).[28] There are (were) derivative benefits to the interpretive community from either stance. Conflict (prophetic critique) has trained the reader to recognize the self-correcting mechanisms built into the function of canon, thereby allowing them to "choose the constraints to which they are willing to submit."[29] Constitutive hermeneutics bolstered diplomacy and fostered an environment in which sober evaluation of competing messages could transpire.[30]

A reading of the question of true and false prophecy that bridges Brenneman and our next interlocutor, Armin Lange, can be found in Walter

---

23. Brenneman, 92.
24. Ibid., 90.
25. Cf. Rolf Knierim, "The Task of Old Testament Theology," *HBT* 6 no. 1 (1984): 25-57; and "On the Task of Old Testament Theology: A Response to W. Harrelson, S. Towner, and R. E. Murphy," *HBT* 6 no. 2 (1984): 91-128; cited in Brenneman, 94.
26. Ibid., 94.
27. Ibid.
28. Ibid., 105.
29. Ibid., 106.
30. Ibid.

Brueggemann's *Theology of the Book of Jeremiah*.[31] Seeing heavy Deuteronomistic shaping evident throughout Jeremiah, Brueggemann locates the prophet Jeremiah, along with Baruch, within an internal opposition party operative in Jerusalem.[32] In Jer 28 the prophet Jeremiah meets Hananiah, a prophet of the existing power structure spinning the deportation of 598 as a temporal setback. With Sanders, Crenshaw, and Overholt, Brueggemann attributes Hananiah's message to an erroneous adherence to an outdated tradition of unconditional election. Jeremiah and Hananiah have presented two competing accounts of "public reality."[33] Jeremiah's *shalom* is contingent upon the people's repentance; Hananiah's message echoes Isaiah in its reliance upon the merciful election of the LORD and his foregoing protection. Brueggemann notes that those present had no way of knowing based on prophetic performances per se. And, most likely, the conclusory death sentence and occurrence served the narrative, not history. Rather, the Deuteronomic impulses at work later added the morbid conclusion to underscore the severity of Jeremiah's true message.[34] In Brueggemann, then, the book of Jeremiah is an aide in our contemporaneous quest for truth "in the face of the abyss."[35] However, when treated this way, the question of discernment is left inadequately addressed. Jeremiah was right in so far as his group achieved their desired power or his message comported with a party line. When faced with competing truth claims in the present, it appears Brueggemann's handling of prophetic dispute renders the book of Jeremiah *less* rather than *more* helpful as an aide to truth in the face of an impending abyss. Next we will consider Lange's historical reconstruction of the situation out of which Jeremian and contemporaneous prophetic messages came to be considered true.

Armin Lange

Lange's Tübingen *Habilitationsschrift* under Bernd Janowski (2000), *Vom prophetichen Wort zur prophetischen Tradition*,[36] represents a return of sorts to a historical, literary, and redactional-critical approach to the prophets. In order to reassess the question of true and false prophecy in light of the post-exilic decline in prophecy, Lange's work is driven by the question 'what accounts for the sub-

---

31. Walter Brueggemann, *The Theology of the Book of Jeremiah* (Cambridge: Cambridge University Press, 2007).
32. Ibid., 142f. Cf. Robert R. Wilson, *Prophecy and Society in Ancient Israel* (Philadelphia: Fortress Press, 1980), 231-251.
33. Brenneman, 69.
34. Ibid., 70.
35. Ibid., 192.
36. Lange, *Vom prophetischen Wort zur prophetischen Tradition: Studien zur Traditions und Redaktionsgeschichte innerprophetischer Konflikte in der Hebräischen Bibel*, FAT 34 (Tübingen: Mohr Siebeck), 2002.

ordination of prophecy as it had been known and transmitted to the exegesis and interpretation of authoritative, redacted prophetic texts?' Lange's thorough monograph begins with an extensive taxonomy. He divides the *Forschungsgeschichte* into three periods: from Matthes (1859) through Tilson (1951); from G. Quell (1952) through Crenshaw (1972); and Hossfeld/Meyer (1973) through Bergen (1999).[37] Useful to our present study as a primer, we will briefly survey Lange's history of research before moving into his work on the subject.

The first phase can be characterized by an overarching interest in the prophets' morality and its impact on the search for criteria of discernment. For Matthes, criteria of truthfulness were based loosely on the morality of a prophet's preaching. However, the lack of a prophecy's fulfillment, the inability to work signs, or a message consisting of empty promises of peace and restoration nonetheless signaled a false prophet.[38] The second phase is marked by a rise in the historical interest surrounding the prophets, particularly prophets who were termed *Nebiim* or *Kult* prophets over against the free, or so-called true prophets. Having a relatively brief life span, this phase drew heavily on its incipient voice, Quell. Also in this period, Lange highlights the change in terminology framing the question of true and false prophets. No longer are the canonical prophets' opponents off-handedly referred to as false. Instead, the situation will increasingly become described as the squaring off of two well-intentioned prophets, or "inner-prophetic conflict." The position that Brenneman termed traditional was gradually marginalized.[40] Culminating in Crenshaw, this age of research came to consider the search for true and false criteria as a means of exposing false prophecy "inadequate."[41]

Having sounded the call to abandon the search for criteria via any previous mode, scholarship, again following Quell, turned to "der gesellschaftliche Ort der falschen Prophetie."[42] "Quells Ergebnis, daß es in Israel keine wirklich praktikablen Kriterien wahrer und falscher Prophetie gab, findet auch in jenen Arbeiten Zustimmung, die die falschen Propheten soziologisch zu verorten suchen."[43] In 1965 D.E. Stevenson postulated that false prophecy could be a

---

37. Lange, *Vom prophetischen Wort*, 4-35.
38. For example cf. P. Volz: "The prophet detects spurious prophets by two criteria: the contents of their message, and their own moral character," *EB(C)* (1902): 3875; cited in Lange, 7.
40. Cf. Lindblom (false prophets drew inspiration from a syncretistic cult; *Prophecy in ancient Israel* (Oxford: Blackwell, 1963); JTE Renner (false prophets were simply selfish and malicious; "False and True Prophecy," *RTR* 25 (1966); and Overholt (false prophets were irresponsible towards the Lord and their own message damned them; *Threat*).
41. Crenshaw, *Prophetic Conflict*, 61; cited in Lange, 16.
42. "The social locatedness/locality of false prophecy." Lange, *Vom prophetischen Wort*, 17.
43. "Quell's accomplishment—that in Israel, no workable, practicable criteria of true and false prophecy were given—also finds agreement in those works that seek to locate the false prophets sociologically." Lange, *Vom prophetischen Wort*, 17.

"distortion within institutionalized religion."[44] The true prophet lived in constant "creative tension" with his culture, while, presumably, the false saw no grounds to object.[45] While there was a mounting consensus concerning the lack of definitive criteria present in the text, the consistency of a prophet's ethic could still be considered proof of true prophecy.[46] Lange also points the rise of the association between *Kultprophetie* and false prophecy, particularly in the work of Jörg Jeremias.[47] This thesis was to be adopted by such notables as (later) von Rad, Clements, and Zimmerli.

The phase from Hossfeld and Meyer up through the submission of Lange's *Habilitationsschrift* was marked by a shift from seeking strands of theological homogeneity to an analysis based on historical differentiation. Differences between the original and the redacted texts proved fertile grounds for Hossfeld and Meyer. While acknowledging no "litmus-paper quality"[48] criteria, certain periods in prophetic history seemed to be characterized by rather clear differentiations between true and false, such as the pre-classical distinction between *Hofpropheten* and the free or the clear recognition of the eighth-century's paid, status-seeking prophets.[49] In the late seventh- and early sixth-centuries, Jeremiah was to contend with *Heilspropheten*, prophets of weal. Lange also sees in Hossfeld and Meyer the beginnings of the critical application of the work of the deuteronomistic redaction of Jeremiah (=DtrJer) to the question of false prophecy. As the value and function of prophecy were respected to an ever-lessening degree after the exile, Hossfeld and Meyer noted that since the DtrJer's time, a prophet's veracity could most reliably be apprehended retrospectively. Followed by Münderlein, Carroll, and to a degree, Lange, this position saw competing interest groups developing criteria post-exile in order to vindicate respected prophetic figures and vilify the *Heilspropheten* by pinning the blame for the exile on their shoulders.[50] It is here that we turn from Lange's review of scholarship to his contribution.

---

44. D.E. Stevenson, *The False Prophet* (New York/Nashville: 1965), 8; cited in Lange, 18.
45. Lange, *Vom prophetischen Wort*, 18.
46. Cf. Stevenson, 130; cited in Lange, *Vom prophetischen Wort*, 18.
47. J. Jeremias, *Kultsprophetie und Gerichtsverkündigung in der späten Königszeit Israels* WMANT 35, (Vluyn: Neukirhen, 1970).
48. Hossfeld/Meyer, *Prophet gegen Prophet*, 163; cited in Lange, *Vom prophetischen Wort*, 19.
49. Cf. Samuel Meier, *Themes and Transformations in Old Testament Prophecy*, (Downer's Grove: IVP Academic, 2009), 180-193.
50. Cf. Carroll, *Chaos to Covenant*, 196; referenced in Lange, *Vom prophetischen Wort*, 22. Lange notes that Carroll softens on this view in his later "Night without Vision: Micah and the Prophets," in *The Scriptures and the Scrolls,* ed. F.G. Martínez, A. Hilhorst, and C. J. Labuschagne, (Leiden: Brill, 1992).

Lange looks first at three passages: Jer 28; 23; and 29. Literarily, Jer 28 looks to be authentic; it appears an eyewitness recorded it soon after the fact.[51] Jeremiah was most likely as impressed by Hananiah's death as was his audience. For Lange, in making sense of this historical reality in light of Jeremiah's prediction and its occurrence, the issue turned on Jeremiah's expectations as mediated by the ever-present DtrJer. "In dieser Erfahrung des Propheten könnte der Grundstein dafür zu suchen sein, daß Jeremia späterhin Tod und Untergang als die Konsequenz falscher Heilsprophetie verstand."[52] The DtrJer has cosiderably expanded that which was witnessed by the eyewitness into a criterion for false prophets.[53] At Jer 23, Lange sees vv 16, 17, 18, 21-24, and 28b-31 (the *Grundschicht* of Jer 23), as prophecies most likely directed against a guild or specific group of prophets "die beanspruchten, am himmlischen Thronrat JHWHs teilzunehmen."[54] Jeremiah, operating later than Micah or Amos, is reported to have shifted the style of prophetic invective employed against his opponents from an ad hominem attack to a general rejection of those prophetic schools whose message purported peace, *Heilsprophetie*.[55] Lange next mentions Ahab and Zedekiah's deaths at the hand of Nebuchadnezzar at Jer 29:22. After the first deportation (597), it is reasonable to assert that messages of dissent and *Heils* were less than safe. Alongside this, Lange posits, Jeremiah's influence was growing. Like Kuenen, while the people may not have preferred prophets like Jeremiah around, they couldn't entirely rid themselves of them. With the benefit of hindsight, the DtrJer intensifies and codifies the prophecies of Jeremiah, employing them afresh amidst its own climate of prophetic conflict.[56]

In order to fill in the time between Jeremiah's prophesying and the DtrJer, Lange looks at Ezekiel. Lange sees Ezek 13 as the *Grundschicht* of Ezekiel's

---

51. It is interesting, given the current climate of literary— and redaction-—criticism in the prophets, especially Jeremiah, that Lange would assert throughout that many of the later editorial words and phrases of the prophet are more or less identical with the words spoken by the prophet, a point noted in Aaron Schart's review, *TLZ* 129 (2004): 161. Cf. also the reviews of A.C. Hagedorn, *VT* 54 (2004): 283; H.G.M. Williamson, *JSOT* 27 (2003): 134-135; A.A. Fischer, *BZAW* 116 (2004): 465.
52. Lange, *Vom prophetischen Wort,* 87; cited in Schart, 159. "In this experience of the prophet, the underlying foundation that would have to be was that Jeremiah understood death and downfall was the consequence of false Weal-prophecy." Cf. Lange, 263, where he similarly writes, "Das Schicksal der Propheten Hanaja (Jer 28), Ahab und Zedekia (29: 15, 21-23) sowie die Person des erst von einem dtr Radaktor zum Propheten ausgesalteten Schemaja (29:24-32) bewähren die Wahrheit von Jeremias Vorhersage, dass die Propheten mit dem ihrer Führung folgenden Volk umkommen werden (Jer 27:15)."
53. Cf. Schart, 159-160.
54. Lange, *Vom prophetischen Wort,* 123. "…who stressed the participation in the divine council in Yahweh's throne room."
55. Ibid., 131.
56. Lange, *Vom prophetischen Wort,* 130.

invectives against his opponents. Like Jeremiah, Ezekiel's opponents preached hasty restoration. In an excursus on "Deuteronomy and Prophecy," Lange looks at Dt 13 and 18, focusing on the role of prophecy in the DtrG and Moses' *Überordnung* above all other prophets.[57] Here E. Otto's work on Deuteronomy has proven foundational not only for Lange, but for Veijola and Nissesen as well.[58] With Otto, Lange reconstructs and dates the proto-Dtr to the time of Josiah. It was there associated with the Assyrian Loyalty Oath Asarhaddon demanded for his people. Lange points to the contract's text as warrant for the assertion that prophets wielded considerable influence, particularly for ill.[59]

Lange identifies three blocks of DtrJer material, 14:13-16; 23:9-32; 27-29[60] with which the DtrJer confronts *Heilsprophetie*. In his review, Schart helpfully delineates the three steps of argument Lange examines. First, the DtrJer presents the prophets as reproaching the people. Therefore a message of comfort would have brought about the opposite of repentance. Second, since the *Heilspropheten* issue the wrong message, they are represented as reliant on their "own thinking, speeches, and acts," rather than solely on the word of the LORD.[61] Third, there is historical evidence that those prophets who led the people astray in fact died (27:15 and 28:17). Chapter 28's stark recounting of Hananiah's death shows that the DtrJer took seriously the charge of prophesying a word not derivative of the LORD. Therefore, the DtrJer 'arms' the true prophets—those whom God deems his "servants"—with messages contra false *Heils*—prophets.[62] Lange sees in the resonating messages of the exilic and post-exilic prophets a succession or catena (*Kette*) of prophets which the DtrJer has reconstructed. And, in light of the diminishing reception of post-Jeremianic prophecy, Lange sees the DtrJer as designating Jeremiah "der letzte Prophet in dieser Kette Gott."[63] However, moving forward along this prophetic trajectory, Lange sees in the DtrJer a rejection of the *Heils*-prophecies of Haggai and Zechariah, since they promulgated the message of Jeremiah's opponents. According to Lange, emphases such as "Tempelkult und Opfertheologie" would have received a less than inviting welcome in DtrJer's theology.[64] It is here that an answer to the question posed at the

---

57. Lange, *Vom prophetischen Wort*, 163-184.
58. For a respective list of critical works on Deuteronomy and prophecy, cf. Lange, *Vom prophetischen Wort*, 163n365.
59. Lange, *Vom prophetischen Wort*, 165.
60. Cf. Lange's footnotes esp. on 185-186 and throughout chapter 3 for a detailed representation of scholarship on the DtrJer.
61. Lange, *Vom prophetischen Wort*, 263.
62. Lange, *Vom prophetischen Wort*, 266; cited in Schart, 160.
63. Lange, *Vom prophetischen Wort*, 266; cited in Schart, 161.
64. Lange, *Vom prophetischen Wort*, 267; cited in Schart, 161. Schart brings forward three critiques of Lange's thesis at this point that are worth further consideration. First, what of Deutero-Isaiah's exilic *Heils*—prophecies? Related to the first, Schart finds it difficult to fathom that Deutero—Isaiah could have so obtusely misconstrued the current events taking place around him as to render him culpable of the same fate as Hananiah.

beginning takes clearer form. For Lange, the DtrJer saw no distinction between true and false prophets among those operative in its day. Passages such as Ez 22:28, Jer 23:22-40, and Zech 13:2-6, according to Lange, "each deny current and future [true] prophetic practice."[65] Instead, a backwards-looking exegesis of a steadily increasing corpus of older authoritative prophetic texts came to supplant any efforts at real-time criterion identification on the part of the DtrJer.[66]

R. W. L. Moberly

Walter Moberly's recent *Prophecy and Discernment* is an avowedly theological work written to those within and without the academy.[67] Following his *The Bible, Theology, and Faith*,[68] this work on prophecy is situated as a "sequel" that will "extend the thesis of the first book by showing how a key issue within Christian theology and spirituality—the critical discernment of claims to speak on God's behalf—might be articulated and developed within the context of Christian Scripture as a whole, with a view to its contemporary appropriation."[69] Moberly's concerns are shared by H. W. Wolff, who believes (in much the same manner as von Rad and Carroll) it is in humanity's best interest to take the issue of true and false prophecy seriously. Wolff writes "the whole future of mankind depends on the clear distinction between true and false prophecy."[70] To this end he gives five criteria that he believes are applicable at present through attentive comparison of competing prophets' claims. The true prophet: 1) is attentive to history, that is the tradition's message of judgment over time; 2) "shows no trace of *self—confidence*;" 3) is not dependant upon his listeners; 4) possesses a high sense of morality or ethics; 5) possesses the "*charismatic*" ability to discern amongst other prophets by the operation of the Spirit of the Lord.

Finally, one would be almost forced to admit to the canon's inclusion of (at least) two prophets who, according to DtrJer, spoke false prophecy.
65. Lange, *Vom prophetischen Wort*, 308.
66. Lange, *Vom prophetischen Wort*, 267-268.
67. R.W.L. Moberly, *Prophecy and Discernment*, xii-xiii.
68. R.W.L. Moberly, *The Bible, Theology, and Faith* (Cambridge: Cambridge University Press, 2000).
69. Moberly, *Prophecy*, xi.
70. Hans Walter Wolff, *Prophetische Alternative: Entdeckungen des Neuen im Alten Testament* (München: Chr. Kaiser-Verlag, 1982); ET: Hans Walter Wolff, *Confrontations with Prophets* (Philadelphia: Fortress, 1983), 63-76. Another recent effort is Anthony Osuji's *Where is the Truth?* (2010). Cf. the reviews of Strine, *JSOT* 35 (5) 2011: 109-110; Fischer, *CBQ* 73 (4) 2011: 838-840; and Stipp, *ZAW* 123 (3) 2011: 478. Osuji's synchronic, narratival approach seeks to deal with the final form of the text in an effort to extract workable criteria from Jeremiah with which to discern true from false. Osuji breaks no new, discernible methodological ground as others (Freitheim, Stulman, Lundbom, to name a few) also utilize—to varying degrees—a synchronic approach.

It is mainly a series of exegetical remarks on those passages in both the Hebrew Bible and New Testament that, according to Moberly, touch on the issue of discernment in an effort to aid the reader. To the degree it aids in the "moral—theological understanding and appropriation" of those biblical passages touching on discernment, it may be, according to Moberly, considered heuristically valuable.[71] In his concluding remarks Moberly analogizes what he has been after in the preceding pages to the reformulation of a game requiring "skill, learning, and discipline," rather than relying on blind luck.[72] Previous models of evaluation of criteria of discernment have viewed such an endeavor as: doubtful at best;[73] a veiled attempt at coercion of some kind;[74] or perhaps necessary yet ultimately unworkable.[75] Moberly, however, is offering a litany of readings in an effort to aid both the ecclesiastically affiliated and the skeptic to better discern "Whom should I trust?"[76]

In light of the above, Moberly says that he will be posing the question differently than Lange's "putative" diachronic reconstruction.[77] At the outset of the chapter on Jeremiah,[78] the longest chapter in the book, Moberly notes that his

---

71. Moberly, *Prophecy*, 41n1.
72. Moberly, *Prophecy*, 253.
73. As representative of sociologically oriented readings of prophetic conflict Moberly references Maxine Rodinson, *Mohammed,* trans. Anne Carter, (London: Penguin, 2002). For similar readings see Burke O. Long, "Social Dimensions of Prophetic Conflict," *Semeia* 21 (1984): 31-53; and Henri Mottu, "Jeremiah vs. Hananiah: Ideology and Truth in Old Testament Prophecy," in *The Bible and Liberation: Political and Social Hermeneutics,* ed. Norman K. Gottwald and Richard A. Horsley, (Maryknoll, NY: Orbis, 1993): 313-328.
74. The perception of competing ideologies and manipulation at work in the development of evaluative criteria is a calling card of such critical approaches as Carroll, *Chaos to Covenant.* Carroll's formative treatment of true and false prophecy was built upon a late date of Jeremiah as it stands in the canon, having undergone heavy redaction at the hands of the DtrJer (158). Enjoying the purview of hindsight, the redactors have shaped Jerrmiah in such a way as to clean up the mess of competing claims postexile (159) by simplifying the discernment process (164). In Carroll's estimation, however, they have dumbed it down too far (188-189). Jer 28's narrative's silence concerning the audience is evidence that discernment is not thethe issue. For Carroll, talk of "criteriology is futile" (192) since any criteria that may appear to be operative, in light of the laws of Deut 13 and 18, while appearing criteriologically normative, are subsumed into the Torah and the preeminence of Moses as prophet. These factors virtually negate any operative means of discernment on the part of the people. Cf. Moberly's well-sounded critique of Carroll's flat handling of Jer 23:22 in *Prophecy and Discernment*, 83-95.
75. William McKane, *Jeremiah,* ICC, 2 vols. (Edinburgh: T. & T. Clark, 1986, 1996); and *A Late Harvest* (Edinburgh: T. & T. Clark, 1995).
76. Moberly, *Prophecy*, 254.
77. Ibid., 41n1; 14n26; 17n37.
78. Which, oddly, contains close readings of the standard passages within the book minus that one which has been seen by most of the tradition as its locus classicus, Jer 28.

exegesis of Jer 1:1-10; 18:1-12; 3:6-11 and 4:3-4; 7:1-15; 6:13-15; 8:10b-12; and 22:13-19 is merely spadework. The programmatic passage of Jer 23:9-22 contains "the explicit discussion of criteria for critical discernment of prophetic authenticity."[79] Moberly delays his treatment of Jer 28 due to its lack of any constitutive contributions to the question of criteria of discernment. Not content with relegating it to the level of illustration, as he does positively with 1 K 22, Moberly insists traditional readings have erred and in the introduction to the following chapter on Micaiah ben Imlah Moberly offers a corrective. But we will first survey his treatment of Jer 23:9-22, since for Moberly, the "pattern of thought" therein is "foundational for the thesis of this book."[80]

At the outset, Moberly seeks to dispense with what he would most likely consider obtrusive critical divisions within this passage by alerting us that he is relying on the final form of the received MT in joining v9 to vv10-22. The "Holy words" which have crushed Jeremiah's heart within him, are of the LORD and are recounted in vv10-22; they are not restricted to v12.[81] Focusing throughout on the false prophets' *sheqer* and the ingredient concept of *shuv* as it relates to the prophetic office,[82] Moberly extracts evaluative emphases useful in locating criteria for discernment.[83] The first two—a lack of character in the life of the prophet (vv10, 11, 14a) and a failure to urge repentance which results in an endorsement of moral complacency (vv14b, 17, 22)—are drawn into sharp relief by the book of Jeremiah's construal of the life of the prophet Jeremiah himself. Interestingly there is no mention here of any intentional shaping of the final form of the text in order to convey this portrait. Moberly does mention the text's portrayal of Jeremiah as it relates to his suffering in his conclusion, noting that the modern proclivity to side with the losers has in fact been inverted in the book of Jeremiah; Jeremiah, Micaiah, and Paul's eventual demises are the very antitheses of "winning."[84] Therefore, the canonical shaping forces at work—when and wherever Moberly wants to credit them as operative—appear to have

---

79. Moberly, *Prophecy*, 42.
80. Moberly, *Prophecy*, 42.
81. Those who (contra Moberly) see vv9-12 as a single textual unit with another following at v13 include Holladay, *Jeremiah,* 624-625; Clements, *Jeremiah* Interpretation, (Atlanta: John Knox, 1988), 140; Leslie C. Allen, *Jeremiah* OTL, (Louisville: Westminster John Knox, 2008), 263, who sees vv9-24 as a poetic collection divided into four units, which are the standard divisions: vv9-12; 13-15; 16-20; and 21-24. Allen's proposal best accords with Moberly's limiting the relevant material in Jer 23 to v22, since, by this verse, "the basic logic and pattern of Jeremiah's critique are already apparent," (*Prophecy*, 70n76).
82. Cf. Moberly, *Prophecy*, 52-53, on the axiomatic relationship of repentance to prophecy as "response-seeking speech": "…in the first instance the purpose of pronouncing impending disaster is that the sinful respond by turning to God, but there is the further prospect that God may then respond by withholding the disaster."
83. Moberly, *Prophecy*, 75-76.
84. Moberly, *Prophecy*, 252.

had a hand in some fashioning of the polarity Moberly rightly highlights. Seitz's critique in *Theology* perhaps overstates the absence of any overt canonical portrayals of the prophets.[85] The third, and Moberly admits, more contentious criterion of 23:9-22, is a false prophet's absence from the divine council (vv16, 18, 21, 22). Moberly here engages modern scholars who have found the notion of the divine council at best unknowable and at worst patently misleading.[86] Efforts to attribute divine council critiques to the hindsight of the DtrJer (Carroll, et al.; see above) still do not address the question of discernment at the historical moment, the horizon Moberly consistently has in view in his treatments of the relevant Old Testament texts.

In a section on Calvin's reading of the divine council, Moberly, following McKane, characterizes Calvin's "derivative" prophecy as "unhelpful."[87] Simply functioning as "interpreters of the law," Calvin's prophets are easily (for Moberly and McKane) separated into sheep on one side and goats on the other.[88] Calvin's comments at Jer 28 on the expansion of the criteria of prophetic authenticity as it was to be applied to sixteenth-century preachers, go too far for McKane and Moberly. Moberly says this is "more a transposition into a different frame of reference than it is a substantive engagement with the subject matter of the text."[89] Moberly's assertion that Calvin has shifted frames of reference without warrant only stands to the degree one accepts Moberly's thesis that one need look elsewhere than Jer 28 for an illustration of prophetic criteria in operation. Also, as Moberly has conceded, the passage quoted by Calvin is but a summation. I have argued in chapter four for the complexity of Calvin's notion of what does and does not constitute true prophecy. However, Moberly's critique of both Calvin and the historical-critics' inability to abandon the benefit of hindsight and put themselves sympathetically in the shoes of those who lived at that moment of discernment is accurate.

---

85. Christopher R. Seitz, review of *Prophecy and Discernment*, by Walter Moberly, *Theology* 111 (2006): 33-34.
86. Moberly disagrees with Overholt's (*Threat*, 61) claim that Jeremiah was not negatively critiquing his opponents' call, but the content of their message. Stressing the interrelatedness of prophetic call and message, Moberly argues that both necessarily constitute prophet (in—) authenticity. However, since Overholt's theory locates the false prophets' culpability in their inability to 'read' the times or adequately apply prophetic traditions to them, Moberly credits him with misreading the sense of 23:9-22. Moberly also disapprovingly notes the detracting statements of Lester Grabbe, *Priests, Prophets, Diviners, Sages: A Socio—Historical Study of Religious Specialists in Ancient Israel* (Valley Forge, PA.: 1995), 84; and Marvin A Sweeney, "The Truth in True and False Prophecy," in *Truth: Interdisciplinary Dialogues in a Pluralist Age,* ed. Christine Helmer and Kristin De Troyer, Studies in Philosophical Theology 22 (Leuven: Peeters, 2003), 11.
87. Moberly, *Prophecy*, 77-78.
88. Cf. McKane, *Harvest*, 48.
89. Moberly, *Prophecy*, 77.

Coming to Moberly's treatment of Jer 28's narrative, we observe first Moberly's construal of the traditional reading, and then his rereading. Moberly sees no criteria in development at Jer 28. Rather, it is simply a prophetic conflict story whose aim is "to portray the opposition to, and consequent suffering of, the faithful prophet, but also to show his vindication."[90] Against Childs and Sheppard, Moberly believes a narrative concerning prophetic conflict could be, and in the case of 28 was, just that and no more.[91] Moberly first raises the question of audience. While an audience was reported to have witnessed the interchange (28:1, 5, 7b, 11a), no mention is made of a pervading ambivalence or uncertainty. Since v15 appears to indicate Hananiah had gained a substantial hearing, the text can best be understood as an example of Jeremiah's suffering and ultimate vindication. Next Moberly addresses the issue of Jeremiah's seemingly irenic reply to Hananiah at vv6-9. Moberly envisions Jeremiah's response to be delivered out of a stance in which "nobody is heeding him anyway,"[92] and as such, believes it to be a caveat rather then a criterion.[93] To this end Moberly asks an insightful question relating to Jeremiah's second response to Hananiah. If Jeremiah meant what he said in vv5-9, why disregard it and return with a more stringent invective? Why not let it play out? An understanding of Jeremiah's words in vv6-9 as caveat rather than criterion bear out Jeremiah's actions in vv15-16. Jeremiah has no need to say anything further. Finally, Jeremiah's wording at v15, "made this people trust in a lie," echoes the language of 7:4, 8. Moberly sees Jeremiah in this way accusing Hananiah of promoting the LORD's blessing without the required repentance. Here, according to Moberly, is where Hananiah's falsity lies, not in his message of peace alone.

Summary

In conclusion, we see that Brenneman argues that canonical criticism most ably gets at the problem of true and false prophets/prophecy at several points. First, seeing "truth itself [as] a contingent value" with its own history, Brenneman sees criteria ultimately determined by the reader and interpretive community.[94] Here his work is heavily dependant on Rendtorff, seeing the prophetic litera-

---

90. Moberly, *Prophecy*, 105.
91. Cf. Childs, *OTTCC*, 135-139; and Sheppard, "True and False Prophecy Within Scripture," esp. 272-273.
92. Moberly, *Prophecy*, 107.
93. Cf. Lange, *Vom prophetischen Wort*, 87, 173.
94. Sweeney's chapter, "The Truth in True and False Prophecy," in Helmer, Christine, et al. *Truth*, 9-26, also extrapolates on the contingency of truth in the prophetic tradition. For him the issue turns on Jeremiah's flexible relationship to the Isaianic tradition of restoration: "Truth in prophecy lies therefore not simply in the question of whether or not it will be fulfilled, but when and how" (26).

ture's focus shifting roughly along the same lines of the history of research.[95] Second, Brenneman's particularly postmodern brand of canonical criticism transferred the location of criteria from the tradition (text-bound and static) to its use therein. Preempting critiques, Brenneman claims this utilization of canonical criticism allows for the necessary application of truth claims to the politic, or *ethos*, of a community of readers, whether they be post-exilic or contemporary.[96] Third, contemporary interpretation of competing truth claims is by no means a spectator event. Rather than relegating truth to the historically derived past, or opting for a purely explicative meaning that says only current relevance is of value, canonical criticism connects today's readers with those down through the previous generations. Fourth, making bedfellows of Robert Carroll and Nietzsche,[97] Brenneman advocates a kind of pluralism constrained by the canon's monotheism. While admitting that no prophet cornered the market on truth, canonical criticism stops short of postulating that, therefore, "there is no truth that is true."[98] Finally, Brenneman seems to be asserting that canonical criticism best addresses the problem, since, in light of the above, ultimately a community ethic must be self-preserving. Thus, canonical criticism accords with Brenneman's insistence that a prophetic promise of non-violence (Isaiah) must necessarily be true.[99]

With Crenshaw, Lange sees the displacement of prophecy in the period after the exile. However, Lange breaks with Crenshaw's long-respected thesis that prophecy failed and lost its place to the writings due to its inability to offer functional criteria for discernment. Believing that standard prophecy has been relegated to the periphery after the exile in favor of the text, Lange argues that by the time of the DtrJer, *kerygmatische-prophetie* had not simply run its course, rather those prophets who announced prophecies of this kind were considered de facto false. Texts that historically had been looked to concerning the question of true and false prophets (1 K 13, Num 22:22-24, and Neh 6:10-14) had become

---

95. Rolf Rendtorff, *Men of God,* trans. Frank Clarke, (London: SCM Press, 1968), 71; cited in Brenneman, 174n4.
96. Ibid., 107-108.
97. Carroll, in "A Non-cogent Argument in Jeremiah's Oracles," *ST* 30 (1976): 51(cited in Brenneman, 182n100), writes, "Every attempt to delineate true and false criteria would render every prophet false;" and Nietzsche's famous, "There is no truth, only an array of interpretations."
98. Brenneman, 110.
99. Cf. the reviews of Barton, Basney, and Davies. Lange makes no mention of Brenneman's work in his. Brenneman only makes a cursory appearance in Moberly's recent work (*Prophecy and Discernment*, 19n41). While Brenneman's work is a helpful reminder of the increasingly reader-oriented stance gaining ground in OT/HB scholarship, Moberly does not include Brenneman for at least two reasons. First, his lack of interaction with the question as seen in the New Testament leaves his treatment, in Moberly's estimation, lopsided. Second, Moberly laments the lack of any sustained exegesis of the controversial texts (i.e., Jeremiah or 1 Kings).

"transfigured into…theological didactic drama[s] with the theme of 'true and false' prophecy"[100] by the time of their final redaction. Along with Jeremiah, Lange sees a common theme running among the books of Amos, Micah, Isaiah, and Zephaniah. In seeking the favor of benefactors (real or potential) and prophesying to please the people, the false prophets led to—rather than slowed—the downfall of the people.[101]

In sum, Moberly's criteria for the discernment of true and false claims to speak for God "can be meaningfully tested both in terms of the moral character, disposition, and behaviour of the speaker and in terms of the moral and theological content of the message."[102] While appearing simplistic, Moberly asserts such an assessment is intellectually rigorous.[103] In anticipation of the charge of moralism, Moberly devotes four pages to qualifying his use of the all too woodenly apprehended term "moral."[104] At the heart of his qualification Moberly calls for a serious grappling with the moralistic language of Jeremiah, Paul, or Jesus, while retaining flexibility in its contemporaneous application.[105]

---

100. Lange, *Vom prophetischen Wort*, 48.
101. Lange, *Vom prophetischen Wort*, 83.
102. Moberly, *Prophecy*, 225.
103. Even if much to the chagrin of his reviewers; cf. Kurt Noll *RBL* (2007). Cf. Collin's critiques in his "Critical Reflections on New Trends in Theological Interpretation," paper delivered at the Annual Society of Biblical Literature Meeting (November 2008), esp. 6ff.
104. Moberly, *Prophecy*, 236-239.
105. A trajectory along the lines of J. Hibbard, "True and False Prophecy: Jeremiah's Revision of Deuteronomy." *JSOT* 35, no. 3 (2011): 339-358.

9. General Conclusions

A history of Christian interpretation of true and false prophecy, this study has sought to point out common features that have emerged throughout the literature and in doing so, has brought to light elements from which subsequent studies of prophecy may perhaps benefit. It is worth noting that throughout the latter portion of our survey (chapters five through eight) few modern exegetes have dealt with the tradition of interpretation in any substantive fashion. Quell devoted a sentence each to Luther, Calvin, and Spinoza while Lange's detailed *Forschungsgeschichte* reached no further back than the mid-nineteenth century. Crenshaw obliquely notes Origen and McKane dispenses fairly quickly with Calvin. We should hastily point out that, far from a 'rehabilitation' of a precritical approach to the interpretation of prophecy, our study has sought to demonstrate the value of these early readings. In other words, we have identified in the Christian tradition a series of interpretive markers or signposts for the interpretation of Old Testament prophecy of which current readers should be aware.

Origen's circuitous definition of a true prophet in our introduction spotlights one of the issues that has occupied much of the Christian traditions' interpretive energies. Exegetes have sought in myriad fashions to dissect the phenomenon of prophecy in the hope of excavating the ontological reality of true prophecy from its epistimological bedding. When the former proved too 'loaded,' the attention of scholars turned to the latter. That the pre-moderns' search for criteria was subsumed into a modern historical reconstruction of the prophetic conflict illustrates this shift. Duhm mentions approaching the *Sache* of prophecy when broaching the subject of true versus false prophecy. After touching upon its presence, however, Duhm—and many moderns—promptly turn to other matters, matters that *are* discoverable by the exegete. Much of Duhm's discussion of the problem at the textual level appears to be an attempt to regain entry or access to the nucleus of prophecy. However, when one sees prophecy and fulfillment connected by a self-same reality, as in Childs, the function of the prophetic book in question becomes more than a reconstruct—able source; it is operating as Scripture, Christian or Jewish. For Childs, history had legitimated Jeremiah's message and the canonical shape of the book bearing his name made it possible for later communities to distinguish between true and false. "If there had been confusion during Jeremiah's lifetime, there need be no longer."[1]

When an exegete held that biblical texts brokered reality in some way, be it the actual word of God, predictions concerning the future, or accurate political appraisals, the critical issue of true and false prophecy turned on getting at the text's truth. Not surprisingly, an urgency of sorts marked many of these early

---

1. Childs, *OTTCC*, 141.

interpretations. Numerous examples abound. From Tertullian's defense of the New Prophecy of Montanism to Lucian of Samosata's *Alexander the False Prophet*,[2] the threat of false speech on behalf of the divine was meticulously scrutinized and attacked from both secular and religious fronts. Jerome's sharp remarks for Origenists who saw in a doctrine of the transmigration of souls a ready—made escape from judgment in his comment at Jer 28:17 illustrates well the defensive posturing of the early Christian traditions against perceived corruptions aided by examples set forth in biblical accounts of seemingly analogous situations, such as Jeremiah. And, it is worth bearing in mind that the actual occurrence (historical referent) of Hananiah's death figured prominently in Jerome's reading.

Various interpreters' quests for criteria of discernment subsequently emerge in response to a societal need, as in Calvin and the other Reformers' battle against dissenting voices claiming divine origin both from outside their particular theological persuasions and within. Believing Scripture itself to be paradigmatic for reality as it was known, many pre-moderns, as Frei has argued, understood their lives in light of Scripture; the text absorbed their world.[3] Therefore, with their present hour's need consisting largely of functional apparatuses for delineating between those who truly speak for God and the spurious, these were naturally sought after in the text. And, without recourse to various proposals of, say, Jeremiah's editorial shaping and the ideologies inherent therein or the direction of intertextual dependence between Jeremiah and Deuteronomy,[4] the criteria of discernment proposed by Aquinas or even Ewald sound somewhat simplistic or naïve to a twenty first-century ear.

This supposed naïvete suggests another element of value early interpretations bring to bear on modern discourse. Portions of current modern readings, it

---

2, Lucian, *Alexander the False Prophet*, ann. A. M. Harmon, Loeb Classical Library 3/8, (1936). Cf. the excellent work by Hvidt, *Christian Prophecy*, in which various manifestations of Christian prophetic movements are traced through church history.
3. Frei, *Eclipse*, 24.
4. Christl Maier, *Jeremia als Lehrer der Tora: Soziale Gebote des Deuteronomiums in Fortschreibungen des Jeremiabuches* (Göttingen: Vandenhoeck & Ruprecht, 2002), 154n112, following Gunther Wanke, *Untersuchungen zur sogenannten Baruchschrift* BZAW 122, (Berlin: de Gruyter, 1971), 30, 35, considers the directions of the texts upon one another as "hardly discernible" ("kaum bestimmbar"; 154n112). Similarly G. Fischer, *Jeremia II* HThK AT, (Freiburg im Breisgau: Herder, 2005), 82, notes Jer 28 "kennt 'Gesetz und Propheten' (Tora und dtrG) und vermag blenden damit umzugehen." Cf. also Seiko Sekine, "The Emergence of the Text in the Redaction History of the Book of Jeremiah: On the Question of Authenticity," in *Schriftprophetie: Festschrift für Jörg Jeremias zum 65. Geburtstag*, ed. Friedhelm Hartenstein, Jutta Krispenz, and Aaron Schart, (Neukirchen-Vluyn: Neukirchener, 2004), 163ff, for a helpful taxonomy of the alternative redaction-critical approaches of Thiel (*Die deuteronomistische Redaktion von Jeremia 1-25*, WMANT 41 (Neukirchen-Vluyn: Neukirchener, 1973), and *Jeremia 26-45* WMANT 52 (Neukirchen-Vluyn: Neukirchener, 1981), and McKane (*Jeremiah*, ICC).

can be argued, find embryonic traces much earlier in the tradition than one might suspect. For example, Aquinas' shift from the prophet's role as foreteller to one of judgment requires a textual foundation, the law. This is picked up again clearly in Calvin as he fashions the prophets as attentive students of the law, its interpreters. When this development of prophetic function begins to take shape and the prophet is increasingly bound to something outside his own subjectivity (i.e., the law or the 'goodly fellowship of prophets'), glimpses of programs such as Crenshaw's, and more explicitly Lange's, begin to take shape.[5] Similary, Moberly's critierion of a prophets' moral fortitude is inceptively present in both Maimonides' prophetic ethic and Spinoza's assertion that true prophets' messages comported with universal moral law. Also, the existential uncertainty Duhm, Buber, and von Rad are eager to point out was touched upon centuries earlier by Aquinas.

Reappraisals also figure heavily in modern discussions of this problem, particulary concerning Hananiah. In an effort to render an objective reading unencumbered by Christian dogmatic constraints, modern interpreters have sought in varying degrees to all but do away with any villification of Hananiah in the book of Jeremiah. Quell, Buber, Sanders, and Carroll all in some form relate that had they been there, they too would have sided with Hananiah, as did the crowd present. This willingness to actively combat prejudiced readings of the false prophets, namely Hananiah—who presumably has been wrongly labeled false because his ideological party lost—are standard in many modern interpretations, and have merit.

Traditional readings from Seiler, Orelli, and Keil staked much of their interpretive ground on the exclusivity of a true prophet's revelation. Seeing the rising historical-critical school's reconstructions as dissections of a unified whole, the notion of true and false prophecy became a tool of historical association among the prophetic books. Identifying similarities between their opponents and responses, Hengstenberg argued the question from the historically conservative preexilic date for the books of both Jeremiah and Ezekiel. Similarly, Orelli used the shared characteristics of Zechariah and Jeremiah's opponents to grant an early date to Zech 12-14. However, this period sees the gradual loosening of any straightforward use of Deuteronomy by Jeremiah once the law is dated later; a loosening which had begun a century earlier with Newton. With the nature of prophets shifting from foreteller and interpreter of the law to religious innovator, poet, and/or moralist, the ethical thrust of Spinoza's and Hobbes' prophets is realized.

---

5. This new prophetic role of interpreter of scribal traditions as revelatory was sounded by Joseph Blenkinsopp, *Prophecy and Canon* (Notre Dame, Ind.: University of Notre Dame Press, 1977), 129. Conversely, John Barton, *Oracles of God* (London: Darton, Longman and Todd, 1986), sees the disparate oracles that where collated into a common source as lending themselves to various ideological distortions amongst postexilic communites; cf. the critique of Childs, *BTONT*, 172-173.

Hananiah's message, often identified with Deutero-Isaiah's, has drawn much attention as well (most notably in Duhm; also Sanders, Carroll, and Lange). The contrasting reconstructions of hypothetical interactions among prophets over time offered by Newton and Duhm illustrate the often diametrically opposed positions concerning redaction-criticism and its results. On the one hand, Newton sees a harmonious coherence between Isaiah's message, uttered to Israel in the late eighth-century and Jeremiah a century and a half later. Duhm pits prophet against prophet with markedly different results. First, the prophet Jeremiah's activity (which still forms the basis for much of the book's material in Duhm's day) is situated between Isaiah and Deutero-Isaiah. Second, Duhm says that, if Jer 28 is an instance of the execution of the prophetic law of Deut 18, then far from tacit acceptance, Jeremiah would have responded to Deutero-Isaiah's message with the same hesitancy and incredulity he displayed towards Hananiah.

It is this study's position that a purely objective analysis of what 'actually' took place at a given moment of confrontation between true and false prophets will yield a result other than that intended by the Bible itself.[6] As far as can be literarily and historically reconstructed, at some point in Israel and Judah's history (presumably post-exilic) redaction of Jeremiah's interaction with contemporaneous prophets (real or otherwise) took place. In this shaping, as Childs and Sheppard have noted, the normative utility of the final form that consists in part of Jeremiah and Deuteronomy comes to bear on the interpretation of such passages as Jer 23:27-29. That pre-moderns such as Jerome, Aquinas, and Calvin saw movement between texts like Jeremiah and Deuteronomy is not in question. In light of texts that apparently did not adhere so 'neatly,' contradictions were embraced by many pre-moderns as paradoxes. At present, from among the numerous 'ways forward' concerning the question of true and false prophecy as it has been and is heard from the Old Testament/Hebrew Bible in the Christian church (i.e, the strict diachronic reconstructions of Nisissen, Lange, and Maier, or the sociological existentialism of Sanders, Brenneman, and Brueggemann), the canonical approach of Childs and Sheppard appears to grapple most ably with both the claims of the Christian church's tradition and the pressures and constraints of sober, responsible exegesis at present. In making use of redaction–criticism's observations concerning the lack of harmonization among prophetic books, Childs et al. asks questions of the text which pre-moderns never asked. However, in reaffirming the dialogical model of canonical relationships between texts that may not be used in precisely the same way that they once were by, say Theodoret or Tertullian, Childs' approach can be seen to be attempting, at least, to improve upon pre–modern readings of the problem.[7] In this way we can move away from valuing pre-modern interpretations of prophetic conflict to the degree

---

6. Cf. Brevard S. Childs, *Isaiah*, OTL (Louisville: Westminster John Knox Press, 2001), 440f.
7. Childs, *Struggle*.

that they adumbrate modern interpretation. Readings of true and false prophets that display a resemblance with pre-moderns are not to be adopted simply on the grounds that they lack the scepticism of many modern reconstructions.[8] Rather, in much the same way as the religious communites of faith of post-exilic Israel "shaped their identity by those very writings which they acitvely transmitted,"[9] what we are calling for is the recognition of a long history of interpretations springing from a myriad of doctrinal (and *a*doctrinal) positions that have exerted—and continue to exert—immense pressure on subsequent generations of interpreters for whom the texts function as Scripture. It can be hoped that subsequent readings of these and similar texts will seek to offer interpretations that diligently attempt to negotiate the complexities inherent in the traditions' struggle to read the text both accurately and in such a way that the *viva vox Dei* may continue to be heard by the Christian church.

---

8. Steinmetz, *Calvin in Context*, 107.
9. Childs, *BTONT*, 173.

Bibliography

Ages, Arnold. "Calmet and the Rabbis" in *Jewish Quarterly Review* 55, (1965): 340-349.
Allen, Leslie C. *Jeremiah*. OTL, Louisville: Westminster John Knox, 2008.
Ashby, Godfrey W. *Theodoret of Cyrrhus as Exegete of the Old Testament*. Grahamstown: Rhodes University, 1972.
⎯⎯⎯⎯⎯. "The Hermeneutic Approach of Theodoret of Cyrrhus to the Old Testament" in *Studia Patristica* 15, ed. Elizabeth A. Livingston, 131-135. Berlin: Akademie Verlag, 1984.
Augustijn, Cornelis, Christoph Burger, and Frans P. van Stam. "Calvin in the Light of the Early Letters" in *Calvinus Praeceptor Ecclesiae*, ed. Herman J. Selderhuis, Geneva: Librairie Droz S.A, 2004, 139-158.
Bachmann, Johannes. *Ernst Wilhelm Hengstenberg. Sein Leben und Wirken*. 2 vols. Gutersloh: Bertelsmann, 1876.
Baglow, Christopher T. *"Modus et Forma": A New Approach to the Exegesis of Saint Thomas Aquinas With an Application to the Lectura Super Epistolam Ad Ephesios*. Rome: Pontificio Istituto Biblico, 2002.
Bardy, G. "Commentaires Patristiques De La Bible" in *Dictionnare De La Bible: Supplément*, vol. 2, ed. L. Pirot, and A. Robert, 75-103. Paris: Letouzey et Ané, 1928.
⎯⎯⎯⎯⎯. "Interprétation. Chez Les Pères IV" in *Dictionnare De La Bible: Supplément*, vol. 4, ed. L. Pirot, and A. Robert, 569-591. Paris: Letouzey et Ané, 1949.
Barr, James. *Holy Scripture: Canon, Authority, Criticism*. Philadelphia: Westminster Press, 1983.
⎯⎯⎯⎯⎯. "Typlogy and Allegory" in *Old and New in Interpretation: A Study of the Two Testaments*, 103-148. London: SCM Press Ltd, 1966.
Barth, Karl. *Church Dogmatics II/2*. Translated by G. W. Bromiley, and T. F. Torrance. Edinburgh: T. & T. Clark, 1957.
Barton, John. *Oracles of God: Perceptions of Ancient Prophecy in Israel After the Exile*. London: Darton, Longman and Todd, 1986.
⎯⎯⎯⎯⎯. *Reading the Old Testament: Method in Biblical Study*. Philadelphia: Westminster Press, 1984.
⎯⎯⎯⎯⎯. *The Nature of Biblical Criticism*. Louisville: Westminster John Knox Press, 2007.
Bartusch, Mark W. "From Honor Challenge to False Prophecy: Rereading Jeremiah 28's Story of Prophetic Conflict in Light of Social-science Models" in *Currents in Theology and Mission* 36 (2009): 455-463.
Battles, Ford Lewis. "God Was Accomodating Himself to Human Capacity" in *Interpretation* 31, (1977): 19-38.

Begg, C. T. "Orelli, Conrad Von (1846-1912)" in *Dictionary of Biblical Interpretation*, ed. John H. Hayes, 224-225. Nashville: Abingdon Press, 1999.

Berchtold, Christoph. *Manifestatio Veritatis: zum Offenbarungsbegriff bei Thomas von Aquin.* Dogma und Geschichte; Bd. 1. Münster: Lit, 2000.

Blacketer, Raymond A. "Calvin as Commentator on the Mosaic Harmony and Joshua" in *Calvin and the Bible*, ed. Donald K. McKim, 30-53. Cambridge: Cambridge University Press, 2006.

Blenkinsopp, Joseph. *Prophecy and Canon.* Notre Dame: University of Notre Dame Press, 1977.

Booth, Alan D. "The Date of Jerome's Birth" in *Phoenix* 33, (1979): 346-353.

Boucher, Wayne I. *Spinoza in English: A Bibliography From the Seventeenth Century to the Present.* 2nd ed. Bristol: Thoemmes, 1999.

Brandscheidt, Renate. "Der prophetische Konflikt zwischen Jeremia und Hananja" in *Trierer theologische Zeitschrift* 98, (1989): 61-74.

Braverman, Jay. *Jerome's Commentary on Daniel: A Study of Comparative Jewish and Christian Interpretations of the Hebrew Bible.* Washington D.C.: Catholic Biblical Association of America, 1978.

Bray, Gerald L. "Campegius Vitringa" in *Biblical Interpretation: Past and Present*, 238. Downer's Grove: IVP, 1996.

Brenneman, James E. *Canons in Conflict: Negotiating Texts in True and False Prophecy.* New York: Oxford University Press, 1997.

Bright, John. *Jeremiah.* Anchor Bible, Garden City, N.Y: Doubleday & Co. Inc, 1965.

Brown, George H. *A Companion to Bede.* Woodbridge: Boydell Press, 2009.

Brueggemann, Walter. *A Commentary on Jeremiah: Exile and Homecoming.* Grand Rapids: Eerdman's, 1998.

_____. *The Theology of the Book of Jeremiah.* Cambridge: Cambridge University Press, 2007.

Bruns, P. "Theodoret Von Cyrus" in *Lexikon der antiken christlichen Literatur*, ed. Wilhelm Geerlings, and Siegmar Döpp, 683-685. Freiburg: Herder, 2002.

Buber, Martin. "False Prophets (Jeremiah 28)" in *On the Bible; Eighteen Studies by Martin Buber*, ed. Nahum N. Glatzer, 166-171. New York: Schocken Books, 1982.

_____. "Falsche Propheten." *Die Wandlung* 2, (1947): 277-283.

Bullinger, Henry. *The Decades of Henry Bullinger.* 5 vols. in 4. Cambridge: Cambridge University Press, 1849.

Bultmann, Rudolf Karl. "Ursprung und Sinn der Typologie als hermeneutischer Methode" in *Theologische Literaturzeitung* 75, (1950): 205-212.

Calmet, Augustin. *Dictionnaire Historique, Critque, Chronoligique, Gèographie Et Littèral De La Bible.* 2 vols. Paris, 1720.

_____, ed. *Calmet's Dictionary of the Holy Bible.* American Edition, Boston: Crocker and Brewster, 1832.

Campbell, Iain D. *Fixing the Indemnity: The Life and Work of Sir George Adam Smith (1856-1942)*. Carlisle: Paternoster, 2004.
Carr, David M., and Richard D. Weis. *A Gift of God in Due Season: Essays on Scripture and Community in Honor of James A. Sanders*. JSOTSupp 225, Sheffield: Sheffield Academic Press, 1996.
Carroll, Robert P. "A Non-Cogent Argument in Jeremiah's Oracles" in *Studia Theologica* 30, (1976): 43-51.
_____. *When Prophecy Failed*. New York: Seabury Press, 1979.
_____. "Night Without Vision: Micah and the Prophets" in *The Scriptures and the Scrolls*, ed. F.G. Martínez, A. Hilhorst, and C.J. Labuschagne, 74-84. Leiden: Brill, 1992.
_____. *Jeremiah*. London: T. & T. Clark International, 2004.
Cavallera, Ferdinand. *Saint Jérôme, sa vie et son oeuvre*. Louvain: "Spicilegium Sacrum Lovaniense" Bureaux, 1922.
Chapman, Stephen B. *The Law and the Prophets: A Study in Old Testament Canon Formation*. FAT 27, Tübingen: Mohr Siebeck, 2000.
_____. "Ewald, Georg Heinrich August (1803-1875)" in *Dictionary of Major Biblical Interpreters*, ed. Donald K. McKim, 426-429. Downer's Grove: IVP Academic, 2007.
Childs, Brevard S. "Prophecy and Fulfillment: A Study of Contemporary Hermeneutics" in *Interpretation* 12, (1958): 259-271.
_____. *Isaiah and the Assyrian Crisis*. London: SCM. Press, 1967.
_____. "Canonical Shape of the Prophetic Literature" in *Interpretation* 32, (1978): 46-55.
_____. *Introduction to the Old Testament as Scripture*. Philadelphia: Fortress Press, 1979.
_____. "Gerhard von Rad in American Dress" in *Hermeneutical Quest*, ed. Donald Miller, 77-86. Allison Park, PA: Pickwick Publications, 1986.
_____. *Old Testament Theology in a Canonical Context*. Philadelphia: Fortress Press, 1986.
_____. "Hermeneutical Reflections on Campegius Vitringa, Eighteenth-Century Interpreter of Isaiah" in *In Search of True Wisdom*, ed. Edward Ball, 89-98. Sheffield: Sheffield Academic Press, 1999.
_____. "Allegory and Typology Within Biblical Interpretation." Paper Presented at St. Mary's College, University of St. Andrews: 2000.
_____. *The Struggle to Understand Isaiah as Christian Scripture*. Grand Rapids: Eerdmans, 2004.
_____. *Biblical Theology of the Old and New Testaments: Theological Reflection on the Christian Bible*. Minneapolis: Fortress Press, 1992.
Clayton, Paul B. *The Christology of Theodoret of Cyrus: Antiochene Christology From the Council of Ephesus (431) to the Council of Chalcedon (451)*. Oxford Early Christian Studies. Oxford: Oxford University Press, 2007.
Clements, Roland E. *One Hundred Years of Old Testament Interpretation*. Philadelphia: Westminster Press, 1976.

_____. "Messianic Prophecy Or Messianic History" in *Horizons in Biblical Theology* 1 (1979): 87-104.
_____. *Jeremiah*. Interpretation, Atlanta: John Knox, 1988.
Collins, John J. "Critical Reflections on New Trends in Theological Interpretation." Paper Presented at the Annual Meeting for the Society of Biblical Literature: 2008.
Condren, Conal. *Thomas Hobbes*. Twayne's English Authors Series. New York: Twayne Publishers, 2000.
Cooke, Paul D. *Hobbes and Christianity: Reassessing the Bible in Leviathan*. Lanham, MD: Rowman & Littlefield, 1996.
Cottret, Bernard. *Calvin: A Biography*. Translated by M. Wallace McDonald. Grand Rapids; Edinburgh: Eerdmans ;T. & T. Clark, 2000.
Crenshaw, James L. *Prophetic Conflict: Its Effect Upon Israelite Religion*. Berlin: De Gruyter, 1971.
_____. *Gerhard Von Rad*. Waco: Word Books, 1978.
_____. *Old Testament Wisdom: An Indroduction*. Atlanta: John Knox, 1981.
Curley, Edwin. "Calvin and Hobbes, Or, Hobbes as an Orthodox Christian" in *Journal for the History of Philosophy* 34, (1996): 257-271.
Dafni, Evangelia G. "*ruah sheqer* und falsche Prophetie in I Reg 22" in *Zeitschrift für die Alttestamentliche Wissenschaft* 112, (2000): 365-385.
Daniélou, Jean. *Sacramentum Futuri; Études Sur Les Origines De La Typologie Biblique*. Études de théologie historique. Paris: Beauchesne, 1950.
_____. *From Shadows to Reality: Studies in the Biblical Typology of the Fathers*. London: Burns and Oates, 1960.
Davidson, Robert. "Orthodoxy and the Prophetic Word: A Study in the Relationship Between Jeremiah and Deuteronomy" in *Vetus Testamentum* 14, (1964): 407-416.
Dawson, John David. *Christian Figural Reading and the Fashioning of Identity*. Berkeley: University of California Press, 2002.
de Boer, Erik A. *John Calvin on the Visions of Ezekiel John Calvin on the Visions of Ezekiel: Historical and Hermeneutical Studies of John Calvin's Sermons Inédits, Especially on Ezek. 36-48*. Kerkhistorische Bijdragen, Vol. 21. Leiden: Brill, 2004.
de Jonge, H. J. "Hugo Grotius: Exégète du Nouveau Testament" in *The World of Hugo Grotius (1583-1645)*, 97-115. Amsterdam: Maarssen, 1984.
de Lang, M. H. "Excurs IV, Hugo Grotius" in *De Opkomst Van De Historische En Literaire Kritiek in De Synoptische Beschouwing Van De Evangeliën Van Calvijn (1555) Tot Griesbach (1774)*, 125-135. Leiden: Diss. University of Leiden, 1993.
de Vries, Simon J. *Prophet Against Prophet: The Role of the Micaiah Narrative (1 Kings 22) in the Development of Early Prophetic Tradition*. Grand Rapids: Eerdmans, 1978.
de Wette, Wilhelm Martin Leberecht. *Beiträge Zur Einleitung in das Alte Testament*. Halle: Schimmelpfennig, 1806.

Diestel, Ludwig. *Geschichte des Alten Testamentes in der Christlichen Kirche*. Jena: Mauke, 1869.
Dozeman, Thomas B. "The Way of the Man of God From Judah: True and False Prophecy in the Pre-Deuteronomic Legend of 1 Kings 13" in *Catholic Biblical Quarterly* 44, (1982): 379-393.
Driver, Daniel R. *Brevard Childs, Biblical Theologian: For the Church's One Bible*. FAT II 46. Tübingen: Mohr Siebeck, 2010.
Duffield, G. E., ed. *John Calvin: A Collection of Distinguished Essays*. Grand Rapids: Eerdmans, 1966.
Duhm, Bernhard. *Die Theologie der Propheten*. Bonn: Adolph Marcus, 1875.
———. *Das Buch Jeremia*. Vol. 11. Kurzer Hand-Commentar Zum Alten Testament, Tübingen: Mohr Siebeck, 1901.
———. *Israels Propheten*. 2nd ed. Tübingen: Mohr Siebeck, 1922.
Eichhorn, Johanne G. *Die Hebräischen Propheten*. Göttingen: Vandenhoeck & Ruprecht, 1819.
Eichrodt, Walther. *Theologie des Alten Testaments*. Leipzig: J.C. Hinrichsm, 1933.
———. "Ist Die Typologische Exegese Sachgemäße Exegese?" in *Theologische Literaturzeitung* 11, (1956): 641-654.
Elliger, Walter. *150 Jahre theologische Fakultät Berlin. Eine Darstellung ihrer Geschichte von 1810 bis 1960 als Beitrag zu ihrem Jubiläum*. Berlin: 1960.
Elliott, Mark. "Ernst Wilhelm Hengstenberg" in *Dictionary of Major Biblical Interpreters*, ed. Donald K. McKim, 517—520. Downers Grove: IVP Academic, 2007.
———. *Isaiah 40—66*. Ancient Christian Commentary on Scripture, Old Testament XI, ed. Thomas C. Oden. Downers Grove: InterVarsity Press, 2007.
Epp-Tiessen, Daniel Jacob. "Concerning the Prophets: True and False Prophecy in Jeremiah 23:9-29:32." PhD diss. University of St. Michael's College (Canada), 1994.
Evans, Craig A, Shemaryahu Talmon, and James A Sanders. *The Quest for Context and Meaning: Studies in Biblical Intertextuality in Honor of James A. Sanders*. Biblical Interpretation Series 28, Leiden: Brill, 1997.
Ewald, Heinrich. *Die Propheten des Alten Bundes Erklärt*. 3 vols. Neue Bearbeitung, Göttingen: Vandenhoeck & Ruprecht, 1867.
———. *Commentary on the Prophets of the Old Testament*. Translated by J. Frederick Smith, 5 vols. London: Williams and Norgate, 1875.
Farrar, Frederic W. *History of Interpretation*. London: E. P. Dutton, 1886.
Feldman, Seymour. "Maimonides—a Guide for Posterity" in *The Cambridge Companion to Maimonides*, ed. Kenneth Seeskin, 324-360. Cambridge: Cambridge University Press, 2005.
Fischer, G. *Jeremia II*. HThK [AT], Freiburg im Breisgau: Herder, 2005.

Fishbane, Michael. "Inner-Biblical Interpretation and the Development of Tradition" in *Das Alte Testament und die Kultur der Moderne*, ed. Manfred Oeming, Konrad Schmid, and Michael Welker, Bd. 8, 25-35. Berlin: LIT Verlag, 2004.

Fohrer, Georg. "Remarks on Modern Interpretation of the Prophets" in *Journal of Biblical Literature* 80, (1961): 309-319.

Forstman, H. Jackson. *Word and Spirit: Calvin's Doctrine of Biblical Authority*. Stanford: Stanford University Press, 1962.

Frampton, Travis L. *Spinoza and the Rise of Historical Criticism of the Bible*. New York: T.&T. Clark, 2006.

Frei, Hans W. *The Eclipse of Biblical Narrative: A Study in Eighteenth and Nineteenth Century Hermeneutics*. New Haven: Yale University Press, 1974.

Froehlich, Karlfried. *Biblical Interpretation in the Early Church*. Philadelphia: Fortress Press, 1984.

_____. "The Printed Gloss" in *Biblia Latina Cum Glossa Ordinaria: Facsimile Reprint of the Editio Princeps Adolph Rusch of Strassburg 1480/81*, XXII-XXVI. Turnhout, 1992.

Fuhrmann, Paul T. "The Interpreter At Work: Calvin, the Expositor of Scripture" in *Interpretation* 6, (1952): 188-209.

Fullerton, Kemper. "The Reformation Principle of Exegesis and the Interpretation of Prophecy" in *The American Journal of Theology* 12.3, (1908): 422-442.

Gadamer, Hans-Georg. *Truth and Method*. 2nd, rev. ed. New York: Crossroad, 1989.

Ganoczy, Alexandre, and Stefan Scheld. *Die Hermeneutik Calvins: Geistesgeschichtliche Voraussetzungen und Grundzüge*. Wiesbaden: F. Steiner, 1983.

Gese, Hartmut. "The Idea of History in the Ancient Near East and the Old Testament" in *Journal for Theology and Church* (1965): 49-64.

Gibson, Margaret T. "The Twelfth-Century Glossed Bible" in *Studia Patristica* 23, ed. Elizabeth A. Livingston, 232-244. Leuven: Peeters Press, 1989.

_____. "The Glossed Bible" in *Biblia Latina Cum Glossa Ordinaria: Facsimile Reprint of the Editio Princeps Adolph Rusch of Strassburg 1480/81*, VII-XI. Turnhout, 1992.

_____. "The Place of the Glossa Ordinaria in Medieval Exegesis" in *Ad Litteram: Authoritative Texts and Their Medieval Readers*, ed. Mark D. Jordan, and Kent Emery Jr., 5-27. Notre Dame: University of Notre Dame Press, 1992.

Goppelt, Leonhard. *Typos. Die typologische Deutung des Alten Testaments im Neuen*. Darmstadt: Wissenschaftliche Buchgesellschaft, 1969.

_____. *Typos, the Typological Interpretation of the Old Testament in the New*. Grand Rapids: Eerdmans, 1982.

Gordon, Robert P. "A Story of Two Paradigm Shifts" in *The Place is Too Small for Us: The Israelite Prophets in Recent Scholarship*, ed. Robert P. Gordon, 3-26. Winona Lake: Eisenbrauns, 1995.

Grabbe, Lester L. *Priests, Prophets, Diviners, Sages: A Socio-Historical Study of Religious Specialists in Ancient Israel*. Valley Forge, PA.: Trinity Press International, 1995.

Graves, Michael. *Jerome's Hebrew Philology: A Study Based on His Commentary on Jeremiah*. Supplements to Vigiliae Christianae 90, Leiden: Brill, 2007.

Greef, Wulfert. de. *The Writings of John Calvin: An Introductory Guide*. Translated by Lyle D. Bierma. Grand Rapids: Baker Books, 1993.

Greene-McCreight, Kathryn. *Ad Litteram*. New York: Peter Lang, 1999.

Greer, Rowan A. *Theodore of Mopsuestia: Exegete and Theologian*. London: Faith Press, 1961.

Gross, Walter. "Lying Prophet and Disobedient Man of God in 1 Kings 13: Role Analysis as an Instrument of Theological Interpretation of an Old Testament Narrative Text" in *Semeia* 15, (1979): 97-135.

Groves, Joseph W. *Actualization and Interpretation in the Old Testament*. Atlanta: Scholars Press, 1987.

Grützmacher, Georg. *Hieronymus. Eine biographische Studie zur Alten Kirchengeschichte*. Aalen: Scienta, 1969.

Guggisberg, H. R. "Grotius, Hugo (1583-1645)" in *Theologische Realenzyklopädie*, 277-280. Berlin: de Gruyter, 1985.

Guinot, Jean-Noël. *L'exégèse De Théodoret De Cyr*. Théologie historique 100. Paris: Beauchesne, 1995.

_____. "Theodoret of Cyrus" in *Handbook of Patristic Exegesis: The Bible in Ancient Christianity*, Vol. 2, ed. Charles Kannengiesser, 885-918. Leiden: Brill, 2004.

_____. "L'importance De La Dette De Théodoret De Cyr À L'égard De L'exégèse De Théodore De Mopsueste" in *Orpheus* 5, (1984): 68-109.

Harrisville, Roy A., and Walter Sundberg. *The Bible in Modern Culture: Baruch Spinoza to Brevard Childs*. 2nd ed. Grand Rapids: Eerdmans, 2002.

Hartmann, Louis N. "St. Jerome as an Exegete" in *A Monument to Saint Jerome*, ed. Francis Xavier Murphy, 35-82. New York: Sheed & Ward, 1952.

J. H. Hayes, ed. *Dictionary of Biblical Interpretation*. Vol. 1, Nashville: Abingdon, 1999.

Hayward, Robert. *Jewish Traditions in Jerome's Commentary on Jeremiah and the Targum of Jeremiah*. Vol. 9. Proceedings of the Irish Biblical Association, 1985.

Healy, Nicholas M. "Introduction" in *Aquinas on Scripture: An Introduction to his Biblical Commentaries*, ed. Thomas G. Weinandy, Daniel A. Keating, and John Yocum, London: T. & T. Clark International, 2005.

Heaton, Eric William. *The Old Testament Prophets*. 2nd ed. London: Darton Longman & Todd, 1977.

Hengstenberg, Ernst Wilhelm. *Christologie des Alten Testamentes und Commentar über die messianischen Weissagungen.* Berlin: 1829.

_____. *Commentary on Ecclestiastes, With Other Treatises.* Translated by D. W. Simon. Philadelphia: Smith, English, & Co, 1860.

_____. *The Prophet Ezekiel Elucidated.* Translated by A. C. Murphy, and J. G. Murphy. Edinburgh: T. & T. Clark, 1869.

_____. *Christology of the Old Testament* 4 Vols. Translated by T. Meyer, and J. Martin. Edinburgh: T. &T. Clark, 1871.

Hermisson, Hans-Jürgen. "Kiterien »wahrer« und »falscher« Prophetie im Alten Testament" in *Zeitschrift für Theologie und Kirche* 92, (1995): 121-139.

Hibbard, J. Todd. "True and False Prophecy: Jeremiah's Revision of Deuteronomy." *JSOT* 35 (3) (2011): 339-358.

Hidal, Sten. "Exegesis of the Old Testament in the Antiochene School With Its Prevalent Literal and Historical Method" in *Hebrew Bible/Old Testament: The History of Its Interpretation. Volume I: From the Beginnings to the Middle Ages (Until 1300).* Part 1: Antiquity, ed. Magne Sæbø, 543-568. Göttingen: Vandenhoeck & Ruprecht, 1996.

Hill, Robert C. *Reading the Old Testament in Antioch.* Leiden: Brill, 2005.

Holder, R. Ward. *John Calvin and the Grounding of Interpretation: Calvin's First Commentaries.* Leiden: Brill, 2006.

Holladay, William L. "A Fresh Look At "Source B" and "Source C" in Jeremiah" in *Vetus Testamentum* 25, (1975): 394-412.

_____. *A Commentary on the Book of the Prophet Jeremiah.* 2 vols. Hermeneia, Philadelphia: Fortress Press, 1986.

Horbury, William. "Old Testament Interpretation in the Writings of the Church Fathers" in *Mikra*, ed. Martin J. Mulder, 727-789. Philadelphia: Fortress Press, 1988.

Hossfeld, Frank-Lothar, and Ivo Meyer. *Prophet gegen Prophet: Eine Analyse der alttestamentlichen Texte zum Thema, wahre und falsche Propheten,* Biblische Beiträge 9. Fribourg Einsiedeln: Verlag Schweizerisches Katholisches Bibelwerk Auslfg., Benziger, 1973.

Hurter, H. *Nomenclator Literarius Recentis Theologiae Catholicae,* Tom. I. Innsbruck: Libraria academica Wagneriana, 1892.

Hvidt, Niels Christian. *Christian Prophecy: The Post-biblical Tradition.* Oxford: Oxford University Press, 2007.

Jacob, Edmond. "Quelques Remarques sur les Faux Prophètes" in *Theologische Zeitschrift* 13, (1957): 479-486.

Jay, Pierre. "Jerome (Ca. 347-419/420)" in *Handbook of Patristic Exegesis: The Bible in Ancient Christianity,* Vol 2, ed. Charles Kannengiesser, 1094-1133. Leiden: Brill, 2004.

_____. *L'exégèse de Saint Jérôme: D'après son "Commentaire Sur Isaïe".* Paris: Études augustiniennes, 1985.

Jeremias, Jörg. *Kultprophetie und Gerichtsverkündigung in der Späten Königszeit Israels.* WMANT 35. Vluyn: Neukirchen, 1970.

Kamesar, Adam. *Jerome, Greek Scholarship, and the Hebrew Bible: A Study of the* Quaestiones Hebraicae in Genesim. Oxford: Clarendon Press, 1993.

Kappeler, Ernst. *Conrad von Orelli: Sein Werden und Wirken aus dem schriftlichen nachlass Dargestellt*. Zurich: Art. Inst. Füßli, 1916.

Kedar-Kopfstein, Benjamin. "Jewish Traditions in the Writings of Jerome" in *The Aramaic Bible: Targums in Their Historical Context*, ed. David J. A. Clines, and Philip R. Davies, 420-430. Sheffield: Sheffield Academic Press, 1994.

Keil, Karl Friedrich. *The Prophecies of Jeremiah*. Edinburgh: T. & T. Clark, 1874.

_____. *The Pentateuch*, vol. III. Grand Rapids: Eerdmans, 1971.

Kelly, J. N. D. *Jerome: His Life, Writings, and Controversies*. New York: Harper & Row, 1975.

Kieffer, René. "Jerome: His Exegesis and Hermeneutics." In *Hebrew Bible / Old Testament. The History of its Interpretation. I: From the Beginning to the Middle Ages (Until 1300)*. Part 1: Antiquity, ed. Magne Sæbø, 663-681. Göttingen: Vandenhoeck & Ruprecht, 1996.

Kihn, Heinrich. "Über 'Theōria' und 'Allegoria' nach den Verlorenen hermeneutischen Schriften der Antiochener" in *Theologische Quartalschrift* 20, (1889): 531-582.

Knierim, Rolf. "The Task of Old Testament Theology" in *Horizons in Biblical Theology* 6, (1984): 25-57.

_____. "On the Task of Old Testament Theology: A Response to W. Harrelson, S. Towner, and R. E. Murphy" in *Horizons in Biblical Theology* 6, (1984): 91-128.

Koch, Klaus. *The Growth of the Biblical Tradition: The Form-Critical Method*. London: Black, 1969.

Köhler, Karl. *Der Prohetismus der Hebraër und die Mantik der Griechen in ihrem gegenseitigen Verhältnis*. Darmstadt: Eduard Zernin, 1860.

Köhler, Ludwig. *Old Testament Theology*. Philadelphia: Westminster Press, 1957.

Kovacs, J., and C. Rowland. *Revelation*. Blackwell Bible Commentaries, Oxford: Blackwell Publishers, 2004.

Kraeling, Emil G. H. *The Old Testament Since the Reformation*. 1st Edition. London: Lutterworth, 1955.

Kraus, Hans Joachim. "Calvins Exegetische Prinzipien" in *Zeitschrift für Kirchengeschichte* 79, (1968): 329-341.

_____. *Geschichte Der Historisch-Kritischen Erforschung Des Alten Testaments*. 2nd ed. Neukirchen-Vluyn: Neukirchener Verlag, 1969.

_____. *Die biblische Theologie. Ihre Geschichte und Problematik*. Neukirchen-Vluyn: Neukirchener Verlag, 1970.

_____. "Calvin's Exegetical Principles" in *Interpretation* 31, (1977): 8-18.

Krauss, S. "The Jews in the Works of the Church Fathers" in *Jewish Quarterly Review* 6, (1894): 225-261.

Krueger, Derek. "Typological Figuration in Theodoret of Cyrrhus's Religious History and the Art of Postbiblical Narrative" in *Journal of Early Christian Studies* 5, (1997): 393-419.
Kuenen, Abraham. *De Profeten en de Profetie onder Israël: Historisch-dogmatische Studie*. 2 vols. Leiden: P. Engels, 1875.
──────. "Hugo Grotius als Ausleger des Alten Testaments" in *Gesammelte Abhandlungen zur biblischen Wissenschaft von Abraham Kuenen*. 161-185. Freiburg: Mohr Siebeck, 1894.
──────. *The Prophets and Prophecy in Israel: An Historical and Critical Enquiry*. Translated by Adam Milroy. London: Longmans, Green, and Co, 1877.
Lampe, G. W. H., and K. J. Woollcombe. *Essays on Typology*. SBT 22. London: SCM Press Ltd, 1957.
Lange, Armin. *Vom prophetischen Wort zur prophetischen Tradition: Studien zur Traditions und Redaktionsgeschichte innerprophetischer Konflikte in der Hebräischen Bibel*. FAT, 34. Tübingen: Mohr Siebeck, 2002.
Legaspi, Michael C. *The Death of Scripture and the Rise of Biblical Studies*. Oxford Studies in Historical Theology. Oxford: Oxford University Press, 2010.
Lenz, Max. *Geschichte der königlichen Friedrich-Wilhems Universität zu Berlin*. 4 vols. Halle: 1910.
Lessay, Franck. "Hobbes' Covenant Theology and Its Political Implications." In *The Cambridge Companion to Hobbes' Leviathan*, ed. Patricia Springborg, 243-270. Cambridge: Cambridge University Press, 2007.
Levenson, Jon D. *The Hebrew Bible, the Old Testament, and Historical Criticism*. Louisville, KY: Westminster John Knox Press, 1993.
Lindblom, Johannes. *Prophecy in Ancient Israel*. Oxford: Blackwell, 1963.
Long, Burke O. "Social Dimensions of Prophetic Conflict" in *Semeia* 21, (1984): 31-53.
Louth, Andrew. *Discerning the Mystery: An Essay on the Nature of Theology*. Oxford: Clarendon Press, 1983.
Lowth, Robert. *De Sacra Poësi Hebræorum Prælectiones*. 2 vols. London: E Typographeo Clarendoniano, 1753.
Lubac, Henri de. *Histoire et Esprit. L'intelligence de L'Écriture D'après D'origène*. Paris: Aubier, 1950.
Lucian. *Alexander the False Prophet*. Loeb Classical Library 3/8, ed. A. M. Harmon. 1936.
Maier, Bernhard. *William Robertson Smith: His Life, His Work, and His Times*. FAT 67. Tübingen: Mohr Siebeck, 2009.
Maier, Christl. *Jeremia als Lehrer der Tora: Soziale Gebote des Deuteronomiums in Fortschreibungen des Jeremiabuches*. Göttingen: Vandenhoeck & Ruprecht, 2002.
Martinich, Aloysius P. *The Two Gods of Leviathan: Thomas Hobbes on Religion and Politics*. Cambridge: Cambridge University Press, 1992.

———. *Hobbes; A Biography*. Cambridge: Cambridge University Press, 1999.
———. "The Bible and Protestantism" in *The Cambridge Companion to Hobbes' Leviathan*, ed. Patricia Springborg, 375—391. Cambridge: Cambridge University Press, 2007.
Matter, E. Ann. "The Church Fathers and the Glossa Ordinaria" in *The Reception of the Church Fathers in the West*, Vol. 1, ed. I. Backus, 83-111. New York: Brill, 1997.
McKane, William. "Prophet and Institution" in *Zeitschrift für die alttestamentliche Wissenschaft* 94, (1984): 251—266.
———. *Jeremiah*. ICC, 2 vols. Edinburgh: T. & T. Clark, 1986.
———. *A Late Harvest*. Edinburgh: T. & T. Clark, 1995.
McKim, Donald K. *Calvin and the Bible*. Cambridge: Cambridge University Press, 2006.
Meier, Samuel A., *Themes and Transformations in Old Testament Prophecy*. Downer's Grove: IVP Academic, 2009.
Moberly, R.W.L. *The Bible, Theology, and Faith*. Cambridge: Cambridge University Press, 2000.
———. *Prophecy and Discernment*. Cambridge: Cambridge University Press, 2006.
Moon, Joshua N. *Jeremiah's New Covenant: An Augustinian Reading*. Journal of Theological Interpretation Supplement 2. Winona Lake, Ind.: Eisenbrauns, 2011.
Morgan, Robert, and John Barton. *Biblical Interpretation*. Oxford Bible Series. Oxford: Oxford University Press, 1988.
Mottu, Henri. "Jeremiah Vs. Hananiah: Ideology and Truth in Old Testament Prophecy" in *The Bible and Liberation: Political and Social Hermeneutics*, ed. Norman K. Gottwald, and Richard A. Horsley, 313-328. Maryknoll, NY: Orbis, 1993.
Mowinckel, Sigmund. *Kulturprophetie und Prophetische Psalmen*. Kristiana: Dybwad, 1923.
———. "The 'Spirit' and the 'Word' in the Pre-Exilic Reforming Prophets" in *Journal of Biblical Literature* 53, (1934): 199-227.
———. *Prophecy and Tradition*. Oslo: I kommisjon hos J. Dybwad, 1946.
———. "Profetenes Forhold Til Nabiismen." *Nordsk Teologisk Tidskrift* (1910): np.
Muller, Richard A. "The Hermeneutic of Promise and Fulfillment in Calvin's Exegesis of the Old Testament Prophecies of the Kingdom" in *The Bible in the Sixteenth Century*, ed. David Curtis Steinmetz, 68-82. Durham: Duke University Press, 1990.
———. *The Unaccommodated Calvin*. Oxford: Oxford University Press, 2000.

Münderlein, Gerhard. *Kriterien wahrer und falscher Prophetie: Entstehung und Bedeutung im alten Testament*. 2nd ed., Europäische Hochschulschriften: Theologie Bd. 33. Bern/Frankfurt-on-Main/Las Vegas: Peter Lang, 1979.

Nadler, Steven. "The Bible Hermeneutics of Baruch De Spinoza" in *Hebrew Bible/Old Testament, the History of its Interpretation. Volume II: From the Renaissance to the Enlightenment*, ed. Magne Sæbø, 827-837. Göttingen: Vandenhoeck & Ruprecht, 2008.

―――――. *Spinoza: A Life*. Cambridge: Cambridge University Press, 1999.

Nassif, Bradley. "The 'Spiritual Exegesis' of Scripture: The School of Antioch Revisited" in *Anglican Theological Review* 75, no. 4 (1993): 437-470.

Nautin, Pierre. "Hieronymus" in *Theologische Realenzyclopädie*, 304-315. Berlin: Walter de Gruyter, 1986.

―――――. "Études De Chronologie Hiéronymienne (393-397)." *Revue des études augustiniennes* 18, (1972): 209-218.

―――――. "Études De Chronologie Hiéronymienne (393-397) (Suite)." *Revue des études augustiniennes* 19, (1973): 69-96.

Nellen, H. J. M. and E. Rabbie, eds. *Hugo Grotius, Theologian. Studies in the History of Christian Thought*; 55. Leiden: E.J. Brill, 1994.

Nellen, H.J.M. "Growing Tension Between Church Doctrines and Critical Exegesis of the Old Testament" in *Hebrew Bible/Old Testament, the History of its Interpretation. Volume II*, ed. Magne Sæbø, 802-826. Göttingen: Vandenhoeck & Ruprecht, 2008.

Newton, Thomas. *Dissertation on the Prophecies, Which Have Been Remarkably Fulfilled, and Are At This Time Fulfilling in the World*. London: J. F. Dove, 1832.

Nicholls, Rachel. "Is Wirkungsgeschichte (Or Reception History) a Kind of Intellectual Parkour (Or Freerunning)?" Conference Paper, Society for the Study of the New Testament (2005). Online: http://www.bbibcomm.net/news/nicholls.pdf. Last accessed: 26 May 2009.

Nissinen, Martti. "Falsche Prophetie in Neuassyrischer und Deuteronomistischer Darstellung" in *Das Deuteronomium und seine Querbeziehungen*, ed. Timo Veijola, 172-195. Göttingen: Vandenhoeck & Ruprecht, 1996.

―――――. "Prophets and the Divine Council" in *Kein Land für sich Allein*, ed. M. Weippert, 4-19. Göttingen: Vandenhoeck & Ruprecht, 2002.

Noll, Kurt. Review of "Moberly, R.W.L.: *Prophecy and Discernment*." *Review of Biblical Literature* (2007): online: www.bookreviews.org/pdf/5292_5572.pdf. Last accessed: 28 November 2012.

O'Keefe, John J. "'A Letter That Killeth': Toward a Reassessment of Antiochene Exegesis, Or Diodore, Theodore, and Theodoret on the Psalms" in *Journal of Early Christian Studies* 8, (2000): 83-104.

———. "Rejecting One's Masters: Theodoret of Cyrus, Antiochene Exegesis, and the Patristic Mainstream." in *Syriac and Antiochian Exegesis and Biblical Theology for the 3rd Millennium*. Ed. Robert D. Miller, 243-63. Piscataway, NJ: Gorgias Press, 2008.

Oden, Thomas, ed. *Ancient Christian Commentary on Scripture*. Downers Grove: IVP, 1998.

Opitz, Peter. *Calvins Theologische Hermeneutik*. Neukirchen-Vluyn: Neukirchener, 1994.

———. "The Exegetical and Hermeneutical Work of John Oecolampadius, Huldrych Zwingli and John Calvin" in *Hebrew Bible/Old Testament; Volume II; From the Renaissance to the Enlightenment*, ed. Magne Sæbø, 407-451. Göttingen: Vandenhoeck & Ruprecht, 2008.

Orelli, Conrad von. *Die Alttestamentliche Weissagung von der Vollendung des Gottesreiches in Ihrer geschichtlichen Entwicklung dargestellt*. Wien: Faesy, 1885.

———. *The Old Testament Prophecy of the Consummation of God's Kingdom*. Translated by John Banks. Clark's Foreign Theological Library New Series 22. Edinburgh: T. & T. Clark, 1885.

———. *The Twelve Minor Prophets*. Edinburgh: T. & T. Clark, 1888.

———. *The Prophecies of Jeremiah*. Translated by John Banks. Clark's Foreign Theological Library, New Series; 39. Edinburgh: T. & T. Clark, 1889.

———. *Die Propheten Jesaia und Jeremia*. München: C. H. Beck'sche Verlagsbuchhandlung (Oskar Beck), 1891.

Osswald, Eva. *Falsche Prophetie im Alten Testament*. Tübingen: Mohr Siebeck, 1962.

Osuji, Anthony Chinedu. *Where Is the Truth?: Narrative Exegesis and the Question of True and False Prophecy in Jer 26-29 (MT)*. BETL CCXIV. Leuven: Uitgeverij Peeters, 2010.

Oudenrijn, Marcus Van den. *De Prophetiae Charismate in Populo Israelitico*. Rome: Typographia Befani, 1926.

Overholt, Thomas W. *The Threat of Falsehood: A Study in the Theology of the Book of Jeremiah*. Studies in Biblical Theology; 16. London: SCM Press, 1970.

Parker, T. H. L. *Calvin's Old Testament Commentaries*. Edinburgh: T. & T. Clark, 1986. Reprint Louisville: Westminster John Knox Press, 1993.

Perdue, Leo G. *The Collapse of History: Reconstructing Old Testament Theology*. Minneapolis: Augsburg Fortress Press, 1994.

Persson, Per Erik. *Sacra Doctrina: Reason and Revelation in Aquinas*. Translated by Ross Mackenzie. Oxford: Blackwell, 1970.

Popkin, Richard H. "Spinoza and La Peyrère" in *Spinoza: New Perspectives*, ed. R. W. Shahan, and J. I. Biro, 177-198. Norman, OK: University of Oklahoma, 1978.

Preus, James S. "A Hidden Opponent in Spinoza's Tractatus" in *Harvard Theological Review* 88, (1995): 361-388.

_____. "Anthropomorphism and Spinoza's Innovations" in *Religion* 25, (1995): 1-8.
Puckett, David L. *John Calvin's Exegesis of the Old Testament*. Louisville: Westminster John Knox Press, 1995.
Qimron, E. "On the Interpretation of the List of False Prophets" in *Tarbiz* 62, (1992): 45-54.
Quasten, Johannes. "Theodoret of Cyrus" in *Patrology*, Vol. 3, 536-554. Westminster: Christian Classics, Inc., 1986.
Quell, Gottfried. *Wahre und falsche Propheten: Versuch einer Interpretation*. Gütersloh: C. Bertelsmann, 1952.
Maurus, Rabanus. *Expositionis Super Jeremiam Prophetam, Libri Viginti*. Patrologia Graeca, Vol. 111. Paris: n.d.
Rad, Gerhard von. *The Form-Critical Problem of the Hexateuch and Other Essays*. New York: McGraw-Hill, 1966.
_____. *Genesis*. Philadelphia: Westminster, 1961.
_____. *Das fünfte Buch Mose: Deuteronomium*. Das Alte Testament Deutsch 8, Göttingen: Vandenhoeck & Ruprecht, 1964.
_____. *Deuteronomy*. Chatham: SCM Press, 1966.
_____. *The Message of the Prophets*. New York: Harper & Row, 1972.
_____. *Old Testament Theology*. Translated by D.M.G. Stalker. 2 vols. The Old Testament Library. Louisville: Westminster John Knox Press, 2001.
_____. "Die Falschen Propheten" in *Zeitschrift für die Alttestamentliche Wissenschaft* 51, (1933): 109-120.
_____. "Grundprobleme einer Biblischen Theologie des Alten Testaments" in *Theologische Literaturzeitung* 68, (1943): 225-234.
_____. "Typologische Auslegung des Alten Testaments" in *Evangelische Theologie* 12, (1952): 17-33.
_____. *Gesammelte Studien zum Alten Testament*. München: Kaiser Verlag, 1958.
_____. "Typological Interpretation of the Old Testament" in *Interpretation* 15, (1961): 174-192.
_____. "Typological Intepretation of the Old Testament" in *Essays on Old Testament Hermeneutics*, ed. Claus Westermann, 17-39. Richmond, Va.: John Knox Press, 1966.
Rahmer, Moritz. *Die hebräischen Traditionen in den Werken des Hieronymus*, 2 vols. Breslau: Schletter, 1861-1902.
Ramlot, Francis Lèon. "Les Faux Prophètes" in *Dictionary de la Bible: Supplément* 8, (1971): cols. 1047-1048.
Rebenich, Stefan. "Jerome: The 'Vir Trilinguis' and the Hebraica Veritas" in *Vigiliae Christianae* 47 (1993): 50-77.
_____. *Jerome*. London: Routledge, 2002.
Rendtorff, Rolf. *Men of God*. Translated by Frank Clarke. London: SCM Press, 1968.

_____. "Erwägungen zur Frühgeschichte des Prophetentums in Israel" in *Zeitschrift für die Theologie und Kirche* 59, (1962): 145-167.
Renner, J. T. E. "False and True Prophecy" in *The Reformed Theological Review* 25, (1966): 95-104.
Reventlow, Henning. "Humanistic Exegesis: The Famous Hugo Grotius" in *Creative Biblical Exegesis: Christian and Jewish Hermeneutics Through the Centuries*, ed. B. Uffenheimer, and H. Reventlow, 175-191. Sheffield: Sheffield Academic Press, 1988.
Reventlow, Henning G. *The Authority of the Bible and the Rise of the Modern World*. Translated by John Bowden. London: SCM Press Ltd, 1984.
Robinson, Bernard P. "The Venerable Bede as Exegete" in *Downside Review* 112, (1994): 201-26.
Robinson, H. Wheeler. *Inspiration and Revelation in the Old Testament*. Oxford: Clarendon Press, 1953.
Rogerson, John W. *Old Testament Criticism in the Nineteenth Century: England and Germany*. Philadelphia: Fortress Press, 1985.
_____. "Ewald, Georg Heinrich August" in *Dictionary of Biblical Interpretation*, ed. J. H. Hayes, 363-364. Nashville: Abingdon, 1999.
_____. "Keil, Carl Friedrich (1807-1888), and Franz Delitzsch (1813-1890)." In *Dictionary of Major Biblical Interpreters*, ed. Donald K. McKim, 606-609. Grand Rapids: IVP, 2007.
Rowland, Christopher. "A Pragmatic Approach to Wirkungsgeschichte: Reflections on the Blackwell Bible Commentary Series and on the Writing of Its Commentary on the Apocalypse.". Online: bbibcomm.net/files/rowland2004.pdf. Last accessed: 28 November 2012.
Rowley, H.H. "The Prophet Jeremiah and the Book of Deuteronomy" in *Studies in Old Testament Prophecy; Studies Presented to Professor Theodore H. Robinson*, ed. H.H. Rowley, 157-174. Edinburgh: T. & T. Clark, 1950.
Sachsse, Eduard. *Die Propheten des A-T und ihre Gegner*. Berlin: Runge, 1919.
Sanders, James A. "Canonical Hermeneutics: True and False Prophecy" in *From Sacred Story to Sacred Text: Canon as Paradigm*, 87-105. Philadelphia: Fortress Press, 1987.
_____. "Jeremiah and the Future of Theological Scholarship" in *Andover Newton Quarterly* 13, (1972): 133-145.
_____. *Torah and Canon*. Philadelphia: Fortress Press, 1972.
_____. "Hermeneutics in True and False Prophecy" in *Canon and Authority: Essays in Old Testament Religion and Theology,* ed. George W. Coats, and Burke O. Long, 21-41. Philadelphia: Fortress Press, 1977.
Sandys-Wunsch, John. "Spinoza–the First Biblical Theologian" in *Zeitschrift für die Alttestamentliche Wissenschaft* 93, (1981): 327-341.
Schart, Aaron. Review of "Lange, Armin: *Vom prophetischen Wort zur prophetischen Tradition*" in *Theologische Literaturzeitung* 129, (2004): 159-162.

Schäublin, Christoph. *Untersuchungen zu Methode und Herkunft der antiochenischen Exegese.* Köln: P. Hanstein, 1974.
Schleiermacher, Friedrich. *The Christian Faith.* English trans. of 2nd German ed. ed. James S. Stewart, and Hugh R. Mackintosh. Edinburgh: T. & T. Clark, 1928.
Schulz-Flügel, Eva. "The Latin Old Testament Tradition" in *Hebrew Bible / Old Testament. The History of its Interpretation. I: From the Beginning to the Middle Ages (Until 1300).* Part 1: Antiquity, ed. Magne Sæbø, 55-62. Göttingen: Vandenhoeck & Ruprecht, 1996.
Seebass, H. "Jeremias Konflikt mit Chananja: Bemerkungen zu Jer 27 und 28" in *Zeitschrift für die Alttestamentliche Wissenschaft* 82, (1970): 449-452.
Sekine, Seiko. "The Emergence of the Text in the Redaction History of the Book of Jeremiah: On the Question of Authenticity" in *Schriftprophetie: Festschrift für Jörg Jeremias zum 65. Geburtstag,* ed. Friedhelm Hartenstein, Jutta Krispenz, and Aaron Schart. Neukirchen-Vluyn: Neukirchener, 2004.
Seiler, Georg Friedrich. *Biblische Hermeneutik; oder Grundsätze und Regeln zur Erläuterung der heiligen Schrift des A. und N. T.* 8 vols. Erlangen: Bibelanstalt, 1800.
_____. *Biblical Hermeneutics, or, the Art of Scripture Interpretation.* Translated by William Wright. 8 Vols. F. Westley and A. H. Davis, 1835.
Seitz, Christopher R. *Figured Out: Typology and Providence in Christian Scripture.* 1st ed. Louisville, Ky: Westminster John Knox Press, 2001.
_____. *Word Without End.* Waco: Baylor University Press, 2004.
_____. "Prophecy and Discernment" in *Theology* 111, (2006): 33-34.
_____. *Prophecy and Hermeneutics: Toward a New Introduction to the Prophets.* Grand Rapids: Baker Academic, 2007.
_____. "The Prophet Moses and the Canonical Shape of Jeremiah" in *Zeitschrift für die Alttestamentliche Wissenschaft* 101, (1989): 3-27.
Sheppard, Gerald T. "True and False Prophecy Within Scripture" in *Canon, Theology, and Old Testament Interpretation,* ed. Gene M. Tucker, David L. Petersen, and Robert R. Wilson, 262-282. Philadelphia: Fortress Press, 1988.
Sherlock, Thomas. *Discourses on the Use and Interpretation of Prophecy.* London: J. Pemberton, 1744.
Simonetti, Manlio. *Biblical Interpretation in the Early Church: An Historical Introduction to Patristic Exegesis.* Translated by John A. Hughes. ed. Anders Bergquist, and Markus Bockmuehl. Edinburgh: T. & T. Clark, 1994.
Siquans, Agnethe. *Der Deuteronomiumkommentar des Theodoret von Kyros.* Österreichische Biblische Studien 19. Frankfurt/Main: Peter Lang, 2002.

Skinner, John. *Prophecy and Religion: Studies in the Life of Jeremiah*. Cunningham Lectures 1920. Cambridge: Cambridge University Press, 1948.
Smalley, Beryl. *The Study of the Bible in the Middle Ages*. 3rd rev. ed. Oxford: Basil Blackwell, 1983.
Smend, Rudolf. "Gerhard Von Rad" in *Das Alte Testament und die Kultur der Moderne*, ed. Manfred Oeming, Konrad Schmid, and Michael Welker, Bd. 8, 13-24. Berlin: LIT Verlag, 2004.
⎯⎯⎯⎯. *From Astruc to Zimmerli: Old Testament Scholarship in Three Centuries*. Translated by Margaret Kohl. Tübingen: Mohr Siebeck, 2007.
Smith, George Adam. *The Book of the Twelve Prophets* vol. I. New York: AC Armstrong and Son, 1896.
⎯⎯⎯⎯. *The Book of Deuteronomy*. Cambridge: Cambridge University Press, 1918.
⎯⎯⎯⎯. *Jeremiah: Being the Baird Lecture for 1922*. 4th ed. New York: Harper, 1929.
Smolak, Kurt. "Theodoret von Cyrus" in *Alte Kirche II*, ed. Martin Greschat, 239-250. Stuttgart: Verlag W. Kohlhammer, 1984.
Stade, B. "Deuterosacharja. Eine Kritische Studie. 1 Theil" in *Zeitschrift für die Alttestamentliche Wissenschaft* 1, (1881): 1-96.
Staerk, Willy. "Das Wahrheitskriterium Der Atlichen Prophetie" in *Zeitschrift für systematische Theologie* 5, (1928): 76-101.
Stauffer, Richard. *Creator et Rector Mundi. Dieu, La Creation et La Providence Dans L'œuvre Homilétique de Calvin*. Lille: Atelier de reproduction des theses, 1978.
Steinmetz, David C. *Calvin in Context*. New York: Oxford University Press, 1995.
⎯⎯⎯⎯. "Calvin as an Interpreter of Genesis" in *Calvinus Sincerioris Religionis Vindex*, ed. Wilhelm H. Neuser, and Brian G. Armstrong, 53-66. Kirksville, MO: Sixteenth Century Journal Publishers, 1997.
Stevenson, D.E. *The False Prophet*. New York/Nashville: 1965.
Stummer, F. "Spuren jüdischer und christlicher Einflüsse auf die Übersetzung der grossen Propheten durch Hieronymus" in *Journal of the American Oriental Society* 8, (1928): 35-48.
Stump, Eleonore. "Biblical Commentary and Philosophy" in *The Cambridge Companion to Aquinas*, ed. Norman Kretzmann, and Eleonore Stump, 252-268. Cambridge: Cambridge University Press, 1993.
Swanson, Jenny. "The Glossa Ordinaria" in The Medieval Theologians, ed. G.R. Evans, 156-167. Oxford: Blackwell Publishers Ltd, 2001.
Sweeney, Marvin A. "The Truth in True and False Prophecy" in *Truth: Interdisciplinary Dialogues in a Pluralist Age*, ed. Christine Helmer, and Kristin De Troyer, 9-26. Leuven: Peeters, 2003.
Swete, H. B. "Theodorus of Mopsuestia" in *A Dictionary of Christian Biography, Literature, Sects and Doctrines*, vol. 4, ed. William Smith, and Henry Wace, 934-48. London: J. Murray, 1887.

Synave, Paul, and Pierre Benoit. *Prophecy and Inspiration: A Commentary on the Summa Theologica II-II, Questions 171-178.* New York: Desclee Co, 1961.

Thiel, Winfried. *Die deuteronomistische Redaktion von Jeremia 1-25.* WMANT; 41. Neukirchen-Vluyn: Neukirchener, 1973.

_____. *Jeremia 26-45.* WMANT; 52. Neukirchen-Vluyn: Neukirchener, 1981.

Thompson, John L. "Calvin as a Biblical Interpreter" in *The Cambridge Companion to John Calvin*, ed. Donald K. McKim. Cambridge: Cambridge University Press, 2004.

Thompson, R. J. *Moses and the Law in a Century of Criticism Since Graf.* Leiden: Brill, 1970.

Torjesen, Karen Jo. *Hermeneutical Procedure and Theological Method in Origen's Exegesis.* Patristische Texte und Studien, vol. 28. Berlin: De Gruyter, 1986.

Torrance, T.F. *The Hermeneutics of John Calvin.* Edinburgh: Scottish Academic Press, 1988.

Torrell, J-P. "Le Traité de la Prophétie de S. Thomas d' Aquin et la Théologie de la Révélation" in *La Doctrine de la Révélation Divine de Saint Thomas D' Aquin.* Actes du Symposium sur la Pensée de Saint Thomas D' Aquin Tenu À Rolduc, Les 4 et 5 Novembre 1989, ed. Leo Elders, 171-95. Città del Vaticano: Libreria Editrice Vaticana, 1990.

Tucker Jr., W. D. "George Adam Smith (1856-1942)" in *Dictionary of Major Biblical Interpreters*, ed. Donald K. McKim, 918-922. Downers Grove: IVP Academic, 2007.

Tucker, Gene M. "Prophecy and the Prophetic Literature" in *The Hebrew Bible and Its Modern Interpreters*, ed. Douglas A. Knight, and Gene M. Tucker, 325-368. Chico, Calif: Scholars Press, 1985.

Tugwell, Simon. *Albert and Thomas: Selected Writings.* New York: Paulist Press, 1988.

Turchetti, Mario. *Concordia O Tolleranza? F. Bauduin e I "Moyenneurs".* Milan: F. Angeli, 1984.

_____. "Religious Concord and Political Tolerance in Sixteenth— and Seventeenth—Century France" in *Sixteenth Century Journal* 22, (1991): 15-25.

Vaccari, Alberto. "La 'Theōria' Nella Scuola Exegetica de Antiochus" in *Biblica* 1, (1920): 3-36.

Valeton, J.J.P. "Prophet gegen Prophet" in *Alttestamentliche Abhandlungen Gott und Mensch im Lichte der prophetischen Offenbarung*, 41-68. Gütersloh: C. Bertelsmann, 1911.

van der Wall, Ernestine. "Between Grotius and Cocceius: The 'Theologica Prophetica' of Campegius Vitringa (1659-1722)" in *Hugo Grotius, Theologian: Essays in Honour of Ghm Posthumus Meyjes,* ed. H. J. M. Nellen, and E. Rabbie, 195-215. Leiden: E.J. Brill, 1994.

Venables, E. "Theodoretus" in *Dictionary of Christian Biography: Literature, Sects, and Doctrines,* vol. 4, ed. W. Smith, and H. Wace, 904-919. London: J. Murray, 1887.

Vessey, Mark. "Jerome's Origen: The Making of a Christian Literary Persona" in *Studia Patristica* 28, (1993): 135-145.

Vischer, Wilhelm. "Calvin, Exégète de L'ancien Testament" in *Études Théologiques et Religieuses* 40, (1965): 213-231.

Vriezen, Theodorus Christiaan. *An Outline of Old Testament Theology.* (3rd Dutch) 2nd Eng,. revised and enlarged ed. Oxford: Blackwell, 1970.

Wallace-Hadrill, D. S. *Christian Antioch: A Study of Early Christian Thought in the East.* Cambridge: Cambridge University Press, 1982.

Wanke, Gunther. *Untersuchungen zur sogenannten Baruchschrift.* BZAW; 122. Berlin: de Gruyter, 1971.

Ward, Benedicta S. L. G. *The Venerable Bede.* Outstanding Christian Thinkers. Wilton: Morehouse Publishing, 1990.

Watson, Francis. *Text and Truth: Redefining Biblical Theology.* Grand Rapids: Eerdmans, 1997.

Weippert, Helga. *Die Prosareden des Jeremiabuches.* BZAW; 132. Berlin: de Gruyter, 1973.

Weisheipl, James A. *Friar Thomas D'aquino.* Washington, D.C.: Catholic University of America Press, 1983.

Wellhausen, Julius. *Prolegomena zur Geschichte Israels.* 4. ausg. Berlin: Druck und verlag von G. Reimer, 1895.

Wenthe, Dean O. *Jeremiah, Lamentations.* Ancient Christian Commentary on Scripture, Old Testament XII, ed. Thomas C. Oden. Downers Grove: InterVarsity Press, 2009.

Whipple, John. "Hobbes on Miracles" in *Pacific Philosophical Quarterly* 89, (2008): 117-142.

Whitman, Jon. *Allegory: The Dynamics of an Ancient and Medieval Technique.* Oxford: Clarendon Press, 1987.

Wilcox, Peter. "The Lectures of John Calvin and the Nature of His Audience, 1555-1564" in *Archiv für Reformationsgeschichte* 87, (1996): 136-148.

_____. "Calvin as Commentator on the Prophets" in *Calvin and the Bible*, ed. Donald K. McKim, 107-130. Cambridge: Cambridge University Press, 2006.

Williams, Megan Hale. *The Monk and the Book: Jerome and the Making of Christian Scholarship.* Chicago: University of Chicago Press, 2006.

Wilson, Robert R. *Prophecy and Society in Ancient Israel.* Philadelphia: Fortress Press, 1980.

Wolff, Hans Walter. *Prophetische Alternative: Entdeckungen des Neuen im Alten Testament.* München: Chr. Kaiser-Verlag, 1982.

_____. *Confrontations with Prophets.* Philadelphia: Fortress, 1983.

Wolff, Hans Walter, Rolf Rendtorff, and Wolfhart Pannenberg. *Gerhard Von Rad: Seine Bedeutung für die Theologie; drei Reden von H.W. Wolff, R. Rendtorff, W. Pannenberg.* München: Chr. Kaiser Verlag, 1973.

Woude, Adam S. van der. "Micah in Dispute With the Pseudo-Prophets" in *Vetus Testamentum* 19, (1969): 244-260.

_____. "Micah IV 1-5: An Instance of the Pseudo-Prophets Quoting Isaiah" in *Symbolae Biblicae et Mesopotamicae Francisco Mario Theodoro de Liagre Böhl Dedicatae*, ed. M. A. Beek et al., 396-402. Leiden: Brill, 1973.

Young, Frances M. *From Nicaea to Chalcedon: A Guide to Literature and Its Background*. 1st Fortress Press ed. Philadelphia: Fortress Press, 1983.

_____. *Biblical Exegesis and the Formation of Christian Culture*. Cambridge: Cambridge University Press, 1997.

_____. "Alexandrian and Antiochene Exegesis" in *A History of Biblical Interpretation: Volume I: The Ancient Period*, ed. Alan J. Hauser, and Duane F. Watson, 334-354. Grand Rapids: Eerdmans, 2003.

Zachman, Randall C. "Gathering Meaning From the Context: Calvin's Exegetical Method" in *Journal of Religion* 82, (2002): 1-26.

_____. *John Calvin as Teacher, Pastor, and Theologian: The Shape of His Writings and Thought*. Grand Rapids: Baker Academic, 2006.

Zimmerli, Walter. *The Law and the Prophets*. Oxford: Basil Blackwell, 1965.

_____. *Old Testament Theology in Outline*. 2nd ed. Atlanta: John Knox Press, 1978.

_____. "Verheissung und Erfüllung" in *Evangelische Theologie* 12, (1952): 6ff.

_____. "Prophecy and Fulfillment" in *Essays on Old Testament Hermeneutics*, ed. Claus Westermann, 89-122. Richmond: John Knox Press, 1963.

_____. "Prophetic Proclamation and Reinterpretation" in *Tradition and Theology in the Old Testament*, ed. Douglas A. Knight, 69-100. London: SPCK, 1977.

Primary texts and translations

Andrée, A. *Gilbertus Universalis: Glossa Ordinaria in Lamentationes Ieremie Prophete. Prothemata et Liber I. A Critical Edition With an Introduction and a Translation*. Vol. LII. Studia Latina Stockholmiensia. Stockholm: Almquist & Wiksell International, 2005.

Aquinas, Thomas. *In Jeremiam prophetam expositio*. Opera Omnia, vol. 14; Parma: n.p.,,1863.

_____. *Summa Theologiae*. 5 vols. Ottawa: Studii Generalis, 1949.

_____. *Truth*. Translated by Robert W. Mulligan, James V. McGlynn, and Robert W. Schmidt. 3 vols. Library of Living Catholic Thought, Chicago: Regnery, 1952.

_____. *Quaestiones de Veritate*. 5 vols. Sancti Thomae De Aquino Opera Omnia Iussu Leonis. Edita. Rome: Romae ad Sanctae Sabinae, 1970.

The Venerable Bede. *In Primam Partem Samuhelis Libri IIII*. ed. D. Hurst CCSL 119. Turnholt: Brepols, 1969.

———. *De Tabernaculo et Vasis eius ac Vestibus Sacerdotum*. ed. D. Hurst CCSL 119A. Turnholt: Brepols, 1969.

Broshi, Magen, and Ada Yardene. "339. 4q List of False Prophets Ar (Plate Xi)." In *Qumran Cave 4; Xiv: Parabiblical Texts, Part 2*, ed. Magen Broshi, Esther Eshel, Joseph Fitzmeyer, Erik Larson, Carol Newsom, Lawrence Schiffman, Mark Smith, Michael Stone, John Strugnell, and Ada Yardeni, 77-79. Oxford: Clarendon Press, 1995.

Calvin, John. *Mosis Libri V, Cum Iohannis Caluini Commentariis. Genesis Seorsum: Reliqui Quatuor in Formam Harmoniae Digesti*. Geneva: Henr. Stephanus, 1563.

———. *Ioannis Calvini Opera Quae Supersunt Omnia*, vols. 29-87. Corpus Reformatorum, ed. Wilhelm Baum, Edward Cunitz, and Edward Reuss. Brunsvigae: Schwetschke [Bruhn], 1863.

———. *Commentaries on the Four Last Books of Moses, Arranged in the Form of a Harmony*. Translated by Charles W. Bingham. 4 vols. Calvin Theological Society, Grand Rapids: Eerdmans, 1950.

———. *Institutes of the Christian Religion*. 2 vols. Library of Christian Classics, ed. John T. McNeill. Philadelphia: Westminster Press, 1960.

———. *Sermons Sur Les Livres de Jérémie et des Lamentations*. Vol. VI. Supplementa Calvinia; Sermons Inédits, ed. Rudulphe Peter. Neukirchen-Vluyn: Neukirchener Verlag des Erziehungsvereins, 1971.

———. *Commentaries on the Book of the Prophet Jeremiah and the Lamentations*. Translated by John Owen. 5 vols. Grand Rapids: Baker, 1979.

Grotius, Hugo. *De Veritate Religionis Christianae*, vol.3., 1st ed. Opera Omnia, 1622.

———. *The Truth of the Christian Religion*. Translated by John Clarke. London: William Baynes, 1829.

Hazlett, Ian P. "Calvin's Latin Preface to His Proposed French Edition of Chrysostom's Homilies" in *Humanism and Reform: The Church in Europe, England, and Scotland*, ed. James Kirk, 129-150. Oxford: Blackwell, 1991.

Hobbes, Thomas. *Leviathan*, ed. J. C. A. Gaskin. Oxford World's Classics, Oxford: Oxford University Press, 1998.

Glossa Ordinaria: Prophetia Jeremiae, vol. 114. Patrologia Latina, ed. J-P. Migne. Paris, 1879.

Jerome. *Opera*, Patrologia Latina, vols. 22-30, ed. J-P. Migne. Paris,1844.

———. *In Hieremiam Prophetam libri VI*. Corpus Christianorum series Latina, vol. 74. ed. Sigofredus Reiter. Turnhout: Brepol, 1960.

———. *Commentarii in Prophetas Minores*. Corpus Christianorum series Latina, vol. 76-76A, ed. Marcus Adriaen, and Domenico Vallarsi. Turnhout: Brepols, 1969.

———. "Letter XVIII" in *Jerome: Letters and Select Works*, Nicene and Post-Nicene Fathers, Second Series, vol. 6, ed. Phillip Schaff, and Henry Wace, 22. Peabody, Mass.: Hendrickson, 2004.

Maimonides, Moses. *The Guide of the Perplexed*. Translated by Shlomo Pines. Chicago: University of Chicago, 1963.
Oecolampadius, Johann. *In Jeremiam Prophetam commentariorum*. ed. Jean Crespin. Genevae: E Typographie Crispiniana, 1558.
Origen. *Commentary on the Gospel According to John*. Translated by Ronald E. Heine. Washington D.C.: Catholic University of America Press, 1986.
Rufinus. *Opera*. Corpus Christianorum Series Latina, vol. 20, ed. Manlio Simonetti. Turnhout: Brepols, 1961.
Spinoza, Benedictus de. *Theological-Political Treatise*. Translated by Samuel Shirley. 2nd ed. Indianapolis: Hackett Publishing Co, 2001.
Theodoret of Cyrus. *Eranistes*, ed. G. H. Ettlinger. Oxford: Oxford University Press, 1975.
———. *Interpretatio in Ieremiam*. Patrologia Graeca, Vol. 81, ed. J-P. Migne and Schulze. Paris,1864.
———. *Interpretatio in Psalmos*. Patrologia Graeca, Vol. 80, ed. J-P. Migne and Schulze. Paris,1864.
———. *Commentaire sur Isaïe; Tome III (Sections 14-20)*. Sources Chrétiennes, vol. 315, ed. Jean-Noël Guinot. Paris: Les Éditions du Cerf, 1984.
———. *Commentary on the Psalms*. Translated by Robert C. Hill. Washington, D.C.: Catholic University of America Press, 2001.
———. *Commentary on the Prophet Jeremiah*. Translated by Robert C. Hill. Commentary on the Prophets, vol. 1. Brookline, Mass: Holy Cross Orthodox Press, 2006.
Vitringa, Campegius. *Typus Dotrinae Propheticae, in Quo de Prophetis et Prophetiis Agitur, Hujusque Scientiae Praecepta Tradantur*. Leeuwarden: n.p.,1716.
Whiston, William. *The Accomplishment of Scripture Prophecies: Being Eight Sermons Preach'd At the Catherdral Church of St. Paul, in the Year MDCCVII, At the Lecture Founded By the Honourable Robert Boyle Esq.: With an Appendix, to Which is Subjoin'd a Dissertation, to Prove That Our Savior Ascended Into Heaven...* London: B. Tooke, 1708.

Index: Author and Subject

Ada, Yardene, 2n6
Albert the Great, 40
Augustine, St., 36, 56
Aquinas, St. Thomas, 4, 36, 40-47, 66, 78, 177, 178

Bacon, Francis, 93
Baglow, Christopher T., 40, 41
Barr, James, 23
Barth, Karl, 138
Bede, The Venerable, 36
Benedict, St., 36
Benoit, Pierre, 41, 42
Beza, Theodore, 49
Bingen, Hildegard de, 37
Brenneman, James., 3, 4, 140, 158, 159-163, 164, 172, 178
Bultmann, Rudolf K., 18, 22, 27, 150
Broshi, Magen, 2n6,
Brueggeman, Walter, 3, 140, 162-163, 178
Buber, Martin, 138, 146, 153, 161, 177
Bullinger, Henry, 4, 55, 56, 61-63

Calmet, Antoine Augustin, 4, 70, 88-90, 91, 93
Calvin, John, 2, 4, 5, 18, 40, 48-68, 77, 78, 97, 150, 157, 171, 175-178
Capito, Wolfgang, 65
Carroll, Robert, 165, 168, 173, 178
Cassiodorus, 40n28
Childs, Brevard S., 2n4, 4, 22, 25, 28, 47, 88, 129, 130, 133, 149-156, 161, 172, 175, 178
Cocceius, Johannes, 84
Cornill, Carl H., 117
Crenshaw, James L., 140, 146, 149, 161, 163, 175, 177

Daniélou, Jean, 22-23, 28
Dawson, John David, 24
Delitzsch, Franz, 98, 101, 105-106, 108
Deutz, Rupert von, 37
Didymus, 10
Diodore of Tarsus, 19, 20, 27-28, 32-33
Dominic, 36
Duhm, Bernard, 4, 115-121, 129, 138, 140, 148, 160, 175, 177-178

Eichhorn, Johann Gottfried, 99, 110
Eichrodt, Walther, 22, 132, 150-151
Eusebius, 1
Eusebius of Cremona, 12
Ewald, Georg Heinrich, 4, 104, 110-115, 116, 123, 128, 160, 176

Frampton, Travis, 74
Frederick III, 48-50
Frei, Hans, 76, 176
Froelich, Karlfried, 25, 37

Gadamer, H. G., 2n4
Gese, Hartmut, 145
Gibson, Margaret, 37-38
Glossa Ordinaria, 4, 5, 36-40
Goppelt, Leonhard, 22
Graf, Karl Heinrich, 94, 99, 103, 126
Graves, Michael, 8n12
Grotius, Hugo, 69-70, 93
Groves, Joseph, 131-132
Grynaeus, Simon, 50
Guinot, Jean-Noël, 19-20, 25, 29

habilitas, 41
Harnack, Adalf von, 18, 108
Healy, Nicholas M., 42
Hengstenberg, Ernst Wilhelm, 4, 98-101, 128, 151, 177
Hidal, Sten, 25, 27
Hitzig, Ferdinand, 103-04
Hobbes, Thomas, 4, 70-73, 93, 177
Hoffman, J. C. K., 132, 151
Horbury, William, 27-28
Hvidt, Neils Christian, 1

Isidore of Seville, 41

Janowski, Bernd, 163
Jeremias, Jörg, 165
Jerome, 2, 5, 6-18, 20, 30, 36, 39, 43, 178
  Hebraica veritas, 8-9, 11, 13
  Use of Hebrew, 8
Jewish Exegesis, 2, 10

Kannengiesser, Charles, 5n1
Keil, Karl Friedrick, 4, 98, 101-105, 177
Kieffer, René, 7n8
Kihn, Heinrich, 21-22
King, Martin Luther, 1
Kittel, Rudolf, 135
Knierim, Rolf, 162
Koch, Klaus, 161
Köhler, Karl, 121-123, 126
Köhler, Ludwig, 132, 150
Kovacs, Judith, 2n5
Kraus, Hans Joachim, 22
Kuenen, Abraham, 4, 121-128, 129, 139, 140, 160, 166

Lampe, G. W. H., 23
Lange, Armin, 3, 4, 158, 163-167, 173, 175, 177-178
Leibniz, Gottfried Wilhelm, 70
Levenson, Jon D., 75-76
Louth, Andrew, 23
Lubac, Henri de, 22-23

Lucian of Samasota, 176
Luther, Martin, 5, 101-02, 141, 150, 175
Luz, Ulrich, 2n4

Maier, Christl, 178
Maimonides, 77, 81, 177
Marcion, 18
Martinich, Aloysius, 71, 73
Maurus, Rabanus, 43n45
McKane, William, 171, 175
Moberly, R. W. L., 3, 4, 158, 168-172, 174, 177
Montanism, 176
Mowinckel, Sigmund, 134, 160

Nellen, H. J., 69
Newton, Thomas, 4, 70, 90-92, 93, 177-178
Nietzsche, Friedrich, 173
Nicholls, Rachel, 2n4
Nisissen, Martti, 167, 178

O'Keefe, John, 20-21, 28
Oecolampadius, Johann, 4, 49, 65
Orelli, Hans Conrad von, 4, 105-107, 110, 128, 177
Origen, 1, 5n1, 7-8, 10, 16-17, 71, 175
Osswald, Eva, 146, 161
Osuji, Anthony Chinedu, 3n10, 168n70
Overholt, Thomas, 163

Pseudo-Chrysostom, 5n1

Quell, Gottfried, 139, 140-141, 146, 147, 157, 160, 164, 177
Qumran, 2

Rad, Gerhard von, 4, 22, 129, 130, 131-141, 144, 146, 147, 150, 152, 153, 161, 168, 177
Rendtorff, Rolf, 172
Robinson, H. W., 150

Rogerson, Jon, 115-116
Rowland, Christopher, 2n5
Rufus of Aquileia, 11
Rupert of Deutz, 1, 37

Sanders, James, 4, 129, 130, 133, 140, 141-149, 157, 159, 161-163, 177-178
Schäublin, Christoph, 24
Schleiermacher, Friedrich, 151
Seiler, Georg Frederick, 4, 95-97, 128, 177
Seitz, Christopher R., 131, 171
Sellin, Ernst, 132
Sheppard, Gerald, 161, 172
Sherlock, Thomas, 90
Simon, Richard, 94
Simonetti, Manlio, 27-28
Siquans, Agnethe, 19-20
Smith, George Adam, 4, 107-110, 129
Smolak, Kurt, 19
Spinoza, Benedict de, 4, 69, 73-83, 93, 94, 141, 175, 177
Staerk, W., 135
Stevenson, D. E., 164-165
Stump, Eleonore, 42
Subordinationism, 33
Synave, Paul, 41, 42

Tertullian, 176, 178
Theodore of Mopsuestia, 19, 20, 27-28
Theodore of Tarsus, 18

Theodoret of Cyrus, 4, 5, 18-34, 178
Thompson, John L., 50
Torjesen, Karen Jo, 23
Torrell, J–P., 40
Tugwell, Simon, 42
Typology, 23-28, 32

Vaccari, Alberto, 21-22
Valeton, J. J. P., 135
vaticania ex eventu, 29
Vergegenwärtigung, 132-133
Vischer, Wilhelm, 151
Vitringa, Campegius, 4, 70, 83-88, 91, 93, 151
Vriezen, T. C., 150, 156-157

Weisheipl, James A., 42
Wellhausen, Julius, 94, 106, 116, 126, 129
Wette, W. M. L. de, 94, 98, 110, 129
Whitman, Jon, 23-24
Whitson, William, 90
Williams, Megan H., 6, 8
Wirkungsgeschichte, 2
Wolff, Hans W., 168
Woolcombe, K. J., 23

Young, Abigail Ann, 1n2,
Young, Francis, 23-24, 28

Zimmerli, Walter, 115, 150, 153, 155

Index: Scripture Citations

Exodus
7:1, 96
7:8-13, 56n61
7:10, 56
7:12, 56n59
7:22, 56, 56n62-63
25:22, 78
25:25, 52n18

Numbers
11:24, 136
12:6-7, 78
12:6-8, 92
12:6, 55n52, 96
22:8, 58n74, 58n76, 67n137-39, 92
22:22-24, 173
23:4, 58n74, 59n77

Deuteronomy
13, 4, 13, 40, 43, 46, 80, 89, 91, 102, 127, 134
13:1-3, 56n57
13:1-5, 72, 101
13:1, 57n64-68, 58n70-72, 58n75, 60n90-91, 96, 152n160
13:2, 57n68-69
13:3, 56
13:17, 65
18, 4, 13, 15, 16, 34-35, 40, 46, 62, 96, 128, 134, 136, 152
18:15, 16, 34, 92
18:20-22, 97
18:20, 17
18:21-22, 72, 102
18:21, 55n46, 58n70, 104
18:22, 45, 80, 106, 146, 152, 152n160
31:9, 51, 52, 52n17, 52n19
34:9-11, 92
34:10, 64, 92-93

Joshua
1:17, 92

Judges
9:4, 152n157

Ruth
1:13, 152n157

1 Samuel
15:29, 81

2 Samuel
5:17-22, 143
10:5, 96

1 Kings
13, 71-72, 138, 173
18:4, 90
18:28, 107
19:6, 90
22, 71, 85, 125, 134, 170
22:23, 80

2 Kings
4:10, 90
4:38, 90
4:40, 90
19, 139
19:2, 124n182
24:9, 99

1 Chronicles
14:16

2 Chronicles
34, 81n72

Nehemiah
6:10-14, 173

Psalms
4:3, 152n157
19:7-9, 52n17, 58n76
37:15, 16
38:15, 43

Song of Songs
2:15, 100

Isaiah
1:1-3, 63n112
2:10, 159
6:1-2, 85
7:12, 124n182
20:2, 60
28:20-22, 143
29:1-8, 148
37:2, 124n182
40-66, 106
44:7, 58n73
45:27, 57
49:6, 34n176
51:1-3, 147
51:58, 152n157
55:9, 64n119
55:11, 45
58:9, 64n119
60:1, 26
65:23, 152n157

Jeremiah
1:1-10, 170
1:1-3, 54n41
1:5, 145
1:8, 35n178
1:13-14, 64n116
2:1-2, 64n117
2:3, 53n33
2:21, 96
2:25, 64n118
3:6-11, 170
3:13, 55n48
4:3-4, 170
5:4-5, 52n32
5:12-13, 119

5:12, 29
6:9, 53n34
6:11-15, 33
6:13-15, 170
6:16, 33, 34
6:17, 34
6:18-19, 34, 56n53, 63n111
6:27-30, 112
7:1-15, 170
7:21-24, 54, 54n39-40
7:22, 54
7:31, 53n35
7:32, 53n36
8:10b-12, 170
9:13-15, 55n48, 56n54
9:25-26, 64
10:3, 52n20
10:11, 33
10:12-13, 54n45
11:1-5, 53n23
11:6-8, 52n20, 52n21, 64n119
11:19, 112
12:16, 53n25
13:18-19, 17n69
14:12, 104n62
14:13-16, 167
14:14, 105
15:19, 112
16:10-13, 63n113
17:15-16, 30
17:19-21, 53n37
17:22, 51n22
18:1-11, 145n109
18:1-12, 170
18:7ff., 43n48
18:8, 81
18:10, 81
18:14-15, 53n26-28, 53n31
19:14-15, 56n53-54
20:7, 57n68
21:8-9, 53n29-30
21:9, 104n62
22:9, 56n54
22:12-13, 64n119
22:13-17, 10n28

22:13-19, 170
23, 30, 165
23-29, 4, 39, 43, 44n50, 56, 156
23:14, 40, 42
23:5-6, 32
23:9-22, 171
23:9-32, 167, 170
23:9-40, 112
23:9, 59, 112
23:10, 59
23:13, 39n19, 107, 156n186
23:14, 39, 87
23:15-16, 44
23:16-18, 166
23:16, 44
23:17, 103
23:18, 17, 156
23:19, 30, 45
23:19-20, 30
23:20, 39n20
23:21-24, 166
23:21, 110
23:22, 30, 35, 59, 156
23:22-40, 168
23:23, 145
23:27-29, 178
23:28, 59, 109
23:28-29, 30, 87
23:28b-31, 166
23:29, 103
23:30-32, 49, 103
23:32, 105
23:39-40, 32n166
24-29, 12
24:1-10, 17n68
24:9, 53n23, 55n48
24:10, 104n62
25, 114
25:3, 156
25:10, 64n119
26, 65, 124n182, 127
26-29, 112
26:1-19, 113
26:4-6, 55, 55n49-51, 56n54-55, 59n81

26:4, 156
26:5, 156
26:7-8, 59
26:112-15, 112
26:18-20, 45
26:20-23, 45, 66n126
26:20-24, 113
26:20, 45
27, 16, 60
27-29, 32n166, 44n50, 167
27:1-5, 61n94
27:5-7, 148
27:6-7, 112
27:8, 104n62
27:9-11, 17n68
27:13, 104n62
27:14, 39n21
27:15, 62n106, 65n121, 66n127, 167
27:16, 54n42
27:18-22, 112
27:18, 39n22, 40
28, 4, 31, 39, 117, 125, 134, 135, 136, 137, 152, 153, 166, 169
28:1-2, 60n84-88
28:2-4, 31
28:2, 104
28:3, 136
28:4, 14
28:5-6, 15, 54n41
28:5-9, 35, 44-46, 104, 109, 113, 118-9, 155-156
28:5-11, 118, 121
28:6-9, 112, 114
28:6, 31n165, 45
28:7-9, 15, 31, 40n24, 58n70, 61n100, 62n102-105
28:8-9, 104, 144
28:8, 104, 133
28:9, 81, 86, 146, 152n160
28:10, 60, 104
28:10-11, 43, 60n89, 61
28:11, 118
28:10-12, 16

28:10-12a, 14
28:12b-14, 16
28:14, 61n94, 148
28:15-16, 105
28:15, 13, 105
28:16, 46, 65n122-23, 105
28:17, 18, 99
29, 99, 114, 166
29:8c, 99
29:10, 112
29:11, 64n119
29:13, 64n119
29:17, 104n62, 167
29:23, 42, 99, 156n186
29:24-27, 54n44
30:24, 31n160
32, 67
32:16-18, 66
32:32, 54n43
34:8-17, 53n38
34:18-19, 52n20
36, 30n153, 33
36:9-10, 55n48
37, 124n182
37:1-2, 62
38, 124n182
44:20-23, 56n56
45, 32n166
50-51, 114
50:41, 55n48
50:42, 65n120

Lamentations
2:14, 107
4:13, 107

Ezekiel
1:1-2, 85
1:4, 99
13, 62, 100, 166
14, 100
14:9, 57n68, 80, 125
22:28, 168
29, 89
33, 148

33:23-29, 147

Daniel
3, 115

Hosea
11:3-4, 11n38
14:5-9, 11n34

Joel
2:13, 81
3:10, 159

Amos
4:4-6, 12n38
9:7, 148

Obadiah, 6

Jonah, 14-15

Micah
2:11-13, 107
2:11, 44, 87
4:6, 107

Habakkuk
1:6-11, 12n39

Zephaniah
1:2-3, 10n30

Zechariah
11:4f., 10n31
12-14, 107, 111, 177
13:2-6, 168
13:2, 107
14:16, 11n35

Malachi
1:11-13, 10n32

Sirach
46:1, 92

Matthew
7:15, 100
24:24, 56, 80

Luke
11:18, 91
13:31-32, 100

John
1:51, 15n60
14:6, 34

Acts
13:46-47, 34n176
20:29, 100

1 Corinthians
12:4-31, 1
14:33, 45

1 Thessalonians
5:3, 46

2 Thessalonians
2:11, 56

1 John
4:2-3

www.ingramcontent.com/pod-product-compliance
Lightning Source LLC
Chambersburg PA
CBHW030318080526

44584CB00012B/607